This is the most complete critical survey to date of women's literature in nineteenth-century France. Alison Finch's wide-ranging analysis of some sixty writers reflects the rich diversity of a century that begins with Mme de Staël's cosmopolitanism and ends with Rachilde's perverse eroticism. Finch's study brings out the contribution not only of major figures like George Sand but also of many other talented and important writers who have been unjustly neglected, including Flora Tristan, Claire de Duras and Delphine de Girardin. Her account opens new perspectives on the interchange between male and female authors and on women's literary traditions during the period. She discusses popular and serious writing: fiction, verse, drama, memoirs, journalism, feminist polemic, historiography, travelogues, children's tales, religious and political thought – often brave, innovative texts linked to women's social and legal status in an oppressive society. Extensive reference features include bibliographical guides to texts and writers.

ALISON FINCH is Reader in French at the University of Oxford and Fellow of Merton College, Oxford. She is the author of *Proust's Additions: The Making of 'A la recherche du temps perdu'* (1977), *Stendhal: La Chartreuse de Parme* (1984) and *Concordance de Stendhal* (1991). She also co-edited *Baudelaire, Mallarmé, Valéry* (1982).

CAMBRIDGE STUDIES IN FRENCH 65

WOMEN'S WRITING IN NINETEENTH-CENTURY FRANCE

Recent titles in the series include

A complete list of books in the series is given at the end of the volume.

*Auteur! répéterent en chœur le Bon Papa
et la Vieille Cousine.*

' "An author!" her grandpapa and old cousin chorused after her.' (From *Emilie ou la
jeune fille auteur*, by Sophie Ulliac-Trémadeure, 1837.)

WOMEN'S WRITING IN NINETEENTH-CENTURY FRANCE

ALISON FINCH

CAMBRIDGE
UNIVERSITY PRESS

PUBLISHED BY THE PRESS SYNDICATE OF THE UNIVERSITY OF CAMBRIDGE
The Pitt Building, Trumpington Street, Cambridge, United Kingdom

CAMBRIDGE UNIVERSITY PRESS
The Edinburgh Building, Cambridge CB2 2RU, UK   www.cup.cam.ac.uk
40 West 20th Street, New York, NY 10011–4211, USA   www.cup.org
10 Stamford Road, Oakleigh, Melbourne 3166, Australia
Ruiz de Alarcón 13, 28014 Madrid, Spain

First published 2000

Printed in the United Kingdom at the University Press, Cambridge

Typeface 11/12.5 pt Baskerville   [CE]

A catalogue record for this book is available from the British Library

Library of Congress Cataloguing in Publication data
Finch, Alison.
Women's writing in nineteenth-century France / Alison Finch.
p.   cm. – (Cambridge studies in French: 65)
Includes bibliographical references and index.
ISBN 0 521 63186 6 (hardback)
1. French literature – Women authors – History and criticism.
2. French literature – 19th century – History and criticism.
3. Women and literature – France.
I. Title: Women's writing in 19th century France.
II. Title.   III. Series.
PQ149.F66 2000
840.9′9287′09034–dc21   99–052348

ISBN 0 521 63186 6 hardback

For Sam and Jess

Contents

Illustrations

Every effort has been made to contact the copyright holders of all illustrations, and to make full acknowledgement for their use. If any errors or omissions have occurred, please contact the publishers, who will correct these in subsequent editions.

Note on the texts

Translations are mine unless otherwise indicated. Spelling in quotations has been modernized (e.g. 'talens' has been changed to 'talents'); italics and ellipses are mine unless otherwise indicated. Original dates of publication are given in my discussion and in the Appendices; dates in note-references and the Bibliography are those of the editions used.

Acknowledgements

I should like to thank Merton College and the Faculty of Modern Languages, Oxford, for generous grants towards the costs of my research; Nick Pollard of the Ashmolean Museum for help with illustrations; David Thomas of the Taylor Institution Library and Deborah Quare of St Hugh's College Library, Oxford, for kindness that went well beyond the call of duty; Margaret Topping and Peter Dylewski for their excellent practical assistance; and all those whom I consulted en route: Jennifer Birkett, Elizabeth Fallaize, Robert Gildea, Bill Howarth, Dorothy Knowles, Wendy Mercer, Naomi Schor and Clive Scott. I am particularly grateful to the readers enlisted by Cambridge University Press for their invaluable advice at key stages, and to my editors Linda Bree, Kate Brett and Micky Sheringham for their encouragement and patience. Finally, for his support during the whole project, I owe a quite special debt to my husband Malcolm Bowie – a committed feminist in word and deed.

CHAPTER I

Prejudice and reassessment

Since the early 1970s, with the growth of women's movements and university-based 'women's studies', publishers and critics have been looking again at women's writing in nineteenth-century France. Major figures such as Germaine de Staël, Marceline Desbordes-Valmore and George Sand had not entirely disappeared from view: some of their works remained in print, and were discussed by a few academics or more sporadically by biographers.[1] But they did not appear on university syllabuses, and almost all the others had been forgotten.[2] However, in the last thirty years the publishing houses 'des femmes' and Maspero have republished several hitherto 'buried' nineteenth-century texts by women; Madeleine Ambrière, in a recent literary history of the century, cites some thirty-five female authors; and scholars have written new studies of Staël, Desbordes-Valmore and Sand, incorporated other women writers into discussions of key nineteenth-century literary issues, and compiled women's biobibliographies.[3]

Important though these works have been, it has been difficult for them to give a sense of what women writers were doing in the century as a whole. Either they focus on one author; or the coverage is restricted to one theme, one genre or one part of the century; or the information about nineteenth-century France comes as part of a compendium in which writers of different periods and countries are briefly presented in alphabetical order.[4] A few essays assessing women's writing across the century do exist, but so far there has been no book-length survey.[5] Some such survey is, however, needed: the nineteenth century saw an explosion in women's writing.[6] They contributed to the culture at all levels, with not only novels, verse and drama, but also memoirs, political tracts, histories, literary criticism, advice-books, translations and opera libretti; many were hugely popular at the time. Julie de Krüdener's *Valérie*, first published

in 1803, continued to be re-issued right through the century, the last
edition appearing in 1898; Gyp's *Autour du mariage*, published in 1883,
reached its ninety-fourth edition in 1899.[7] This book, then, aims to
go some way towards filling the gap. My discussion and appendices
between them cover about ninety widely read writers; I have picked
out those who seemed most likely to give a sense of both general
currents and the variety of individual temperaments.[8]

The oblivion into which almost all these writers fell may be
provisionally attributed to two interconnected causes. Nineteenth-
century France was not uniformly sexist, and – as I shall show –
many of these women gained recognition from the male establishment during their lifetimes; but once individuals were dead their
works were usually rapidly demoted, either with condescension or
with an overt misogyny which 'gallantry' had kept in the background
while they were still alive.[9] Once-popular male writers have become
obscure too. But the women were subject not just to the natural ebb
and flow of literary taste, but to a dismissiveness or vindictiveness
that would alone give cause to reassess its objects. They might be
posthumously 'praised' in terms which deterred pursuit, as when
Théophile Gautier in the 1850s compliments a mother-and-daughter
pair of writers for their 'discretion' about their writing (nobody, he
says of one of them, ever saw an inkstain on her fingers), and for
having been personally 'so superior' to their works.[10] When a late-
century publisher reissued the best-selling *Valérie* in 1878, it would
seem to have been in his own commercial interests to promote the
work: nevertheless he could not refrain from including a preface
taken from a dictionary of national biography which claims that no
man would have written *Valérie*, a novel based on so little. According
to the editor himself, Krüdener's ability to create reverence for the
beauties of nature somehow reflects the passing of her own physical
beauty; and he notifies even corrigenda with a sneer, observing that
the noble lady, despite precautions, has come down to us with large
holes in her blue stockings.[11] Although *Valérie* is as representative a
Romantic work as Chateaubriand's *René* (1802), and no worse
written, such comments cumulatively killed off its reputation. The
outstanding case of such relegation is George Sand: internationally
acclaimed during her lifetime, her work started to be vilified almost
as soon as she died.[12]

The second reason for the belittling of these writers is that they
were often seen, both during and after their lives, not as individuals

but as a composite group marked off by their sex. They might be grouped thus to be admired, but since more often the sex was perceived as inferior, wholesale consignment to the shadows was easy. (All 'women-only' approaches, including this book, of course run the same – still necessary – risk.)[13] In the mid-1840s the most influential critic of the century, Sainte-Beuve, published a volume called *Portraits de femmes*, in the preface of which he observes that he thought it more convenient, indeed piquant ('même assez piquant'), to bring together all the sketches of literary women disseminated throughout five volumes of criticism and portraits. He starts with Mme de Sévigné because, he says, it is impossible to try to talk about women without first adjusting one's taste and putting oneself in, as it were, the right mood with this particular writer ('sans se mettre d'abord en goût et comme en humeur par Mme de Sévigné').[14] Baudelaire is even more inclined to denigrate women writers as a collectivity. In an 1852 essay on Poe, he claims that women write far too quickly and abundantly: their style trails and undulates like their clothing.[15] So it goes on: in his *Les Bas-bleus* of 1878 Barbey d'Aurevilly, with impeccable logic, asserts that women never write anything that lasts, and this is only fair, since they were not put into the world to do what we (men) do.[16] In 1929 Jean Larnac published his exceptionally wide-ranging and scholarly *Histoire de la littérature féminine en France*. This work is an odd mixture. Disarmingly, it expresses sympathy with women's struggles for emancipation and equal educational opportunities, and quotes with derision the view that their brains are too small for intellectual work. (The proponent of this view offered to have his own brain posthumously weighed: it turned out to be lighter than the average woman's . . .).[17] But Larnac's conclusions are unremittingly misogynistic. This now looks like mere inconsistency, but it doubtless conveyed to most of his 1930s readers a sense that here was the most balanced account to date of women's writing. If even Larnac was saying of Desbordes-Valmore that no woman writer ever showed less intelligence and that after her women had nothing more to say, or repeating the old chestnut that women writers know only how to depict themselves, their works in effect adding up to one work many times reshaped, then what was the point of pursuing the matter further?[18] Indeed, the standard mid-twentieth-century French literary history by Lagarde and Michard mentions only the famous three, and briefly at that, giving Staël seven pages, Desbordes-Valmore three and Sand eight (compared to male writers of equivalent or lesser importance such as Vigny, who has thirty, or the minor poet Heredia, who has five).[19]

Why, then, do the women writers of nineteenth-century France, almost all 'beneath the underdog' in Lagarde and Michard terms, deserve reassessment? Better knowledge of them helps both the literary historian and the historian of ideas, and the more popularizing ones can fill out our picture of the period's tastes and of the kind of works a newly literate public was turning to – among them, newly literate women.[20] If one's prime perspective on the century remains the canonical male authors, it is, to say the least, useful to know what the most intelligent, articulate and influential women of the period were thinking and imagining, since there was more mutual interchange between men and women writers on both intellectual and personal levels than has been supposed (many were friends or lovers).[21]

Where the women's writing forms a separate current, it offers an alternative perspective on familiar themes of the time, giving access to the 'other half' of a hitherto remorselessly male-dominated view of the century's literature. For example, the women writers do address – say – brother–sister relationships, or contrasts between town and country, or working-class slang; but they often treat them in quite distinctive ways. And nineteenth-century French feminism – which was itself, as one historian notes, 'very literary' – not only gave birth to women's discursive pieces and 'life-writing' but also inspired or infiltrated their fiction, verse and drama.[22]

A final reason for reading these writers is that they are enjoyable. There are exceptions: some of their works (like some by nineteenth-century male writers) are so out of tune with modern tastes that they now seem mere 'symptoms' of a defunct mind-set. Others have longueurs or awkwardness. But most of the women writers are shrewd, observant and intellectually curious; they describe pleasures, griefs and adventures with a sharpness of expression that still brings these alive. Their autobiographical works show their openness to new experiences and ideas (Suzanne Voilquin coolly narrates her experiment with hashish in Egypt – she ate it on sweets).[23] And the notion (sometimes conveyed, alas, by feminist critics) that nineteenth-century women writers are submerged in stereotype and sentiment is wrong. Even in those novels which are supposed to be the acme of sentimentality or 'Gothicness', they nevertheless engage with substantial and difficult issues. They evoke not just madness but its possible cures. Some of their heroines are swooning Madonnas, but others – or the same ones – hint at bisexuality. They may stage innocence versus villainy, but they also show the interplay between oppressive and rebellious character traits in the same individual.

Equally unsentimental is these writers' humour (the ignoring of which is the most singular omission to date in most critics' reassessments).[24] Almost without exception they are witty. Such is the early nineteenth-century novelist of whom Sainte-Beuve said that a book could be written called *L'Esprit de madame Sophie Gay*.[25] One of Gay's heroines, departing from the convent where she has been educated and about to begin her new social life, is suddenly overwhelmed at the thought of leaving her friends: 'je quittai ce triste couvent en versant autant de larmes que j'en eusse répandues si l'on était venu me dire qu'il y fallait passer un an de plus' ('I left that sad convent shedding as many tears as if I'd been given the news that I had to spend another year there').[26] They have a talent for banter and repartee: even in their most passionate works, there will usually be at least one character who habitually responds with flip and amusing comebacks, such as Staël's comte d'Erfeuil in *Corinne* (1807); while others pepper their writing with quickfire jokes like those in Delphine de Girardin's play *L'Ecole des journalistes* (1839). The editor of the newspaper *The Truth* (*La Vérité*) points out the foreign correspondent, who never stirs from the office:

> Ce petit, c'est Bertrand, voyageur du journal;
> Oui, sans que ça paraisse, il est au Sénégal.[27]

(That little man over there, that's Bertrand. He's our traveller. It doesn't show, but right now he's in Senegal.)

They are good at comedy of character: the children's writer Sophie de Ségur excels at depicting the naivety that reveals precisely the compromising facts that should remain hidden; and here is the mid-century Flora Tristan (Gauguin's grandmother) turning a slave-trader she meets on her travels into a greedy buffoon. At the sight of a huge leg of mutton and other meats,

Ses narines s'ouvraient; il passait sa langue sur ses lèvres minces et pâles; la sueur courait sur son front; il paraissait être dans un de ces moments où la jouissance, que nous ne pouvons contenir, sort par tous nos pores. Quand il se fut bien gorgé, ses traits reprirent peu à peu leur expression ordinaire, qui était de n'en avoir aucune, et il recommença à me parler sur le même ton qu'avant le dîner.[28]

(His nostrils opened; he passed his tongue over his thin, pale lips; sweat ran down his forehead; he was, apparently, caught up in one of those moments of transport when pleasure oozes from our every pore. When he was well and truly stuffed, his features gradually resumed their usual expression, which was to have none at all, and he began speaking to me again in the same tone as before dinner.)

The politically outspoken have at their command a sarcastic rhetoric with which to crush opponents: the late-century Maria Deraismes opens her attack on Dumas *fils*'s sexist *L'Homme-femme* (1872) as follows:

Et d'abord, il y a des hommes qui savent et des hommes qui ne savent pas.

M. Alexandre Dumas fils est l'homme *qui sait*. C'est pour cela qu'il a été chargé d'une mission providentielle afin de faire cesser les *malentendus* et de remettre *tout en place* ici-bas.

Donc, il nous déclare que si la société va tout de travers, c'est parce qu'on oublie de tenir compte des tendances et des fatalités originelles.

Or, comme M. Dumas a pour mandat de tout rétablir d'après le plan primordial, il commence par étudier la nature et nous dit avec la logique et la science qui lui font défaut, les choses qui suivent.[29]

(Right. First: there are men who know and men who don't.

M. Alexandre Dumas *fils* is the man *who knows*. That's why Providence has given him a mission to call a halt to *misunderstandings* and to put *everything back in its place* here below.

So: he declares that if society is going all wrong, it's because we've forgotten to take original tendencies – fate – into account.

Now, since M. Dumas has a mandate to put everything back to rights according to the primordial plan, he starts off with the study of nature and tells us, with the logic and science he doesn't have, the following.) (author's italics)

And they are capable of gallows humour: the twenty-three-year-old artist Marie Bashkirtseff, writing the preface to her diary when she knows she is dying of TB, remarks:

Là, supposez que je suis illustre. Nous commençons:

Je suis née le 11 novembre 1860. C'est épouvantable rien que de l'écrire. Mais je me console en pensant que je n'aurai certainement plus d'âge lorsque vous me lirez.[30]

(There now, imagine I'm famous. So let's start:

I was born on 11 November 1860. Just writing it down is awful. But it's a comfort to think I'll definitely be ageless by the time you read me.)

Finally, they know how to exploit an amusing theatricality. This is how the first Frenchwoman to explore Spitsbergen describes her most surprising encounter. Léonie d'Aunet (later one of Hugo's mistresses) has, in 1839, reached Havoysund in the Arctic, the northernmost dwelling on the globe. She and her otherwise all-male party have been asked to present to its inhabitants a bronze bust of the king, Louis-Philippe, who had briefly stayed there incognito in 1795. She comments that at 71 degrees of latitude both this bust and she herself, as the first Frenchwoman there, were fairly unusual; but they didn't walk off with the first prize for strangeness. ('Cependant nous n'eûmes pas les honneurs de l'étrangeté.') For there is something even more 'impossible':

Il y avait – je le donnerais à deviner en mille, on n'y arriverait pas! – il y avait *un perroquet!* Quoi! un perroquet à Havesund, au bout du monde, dans cette glace, dans ces ténèbres? Oui, un perroquet vivant; c'est-à-dire, cela avait bien été un perroquet, mais cela avait presque cessé d'en être un.

(There was – even if I gave you a thousand guesses, you'd never get it! – there was *a parrot!* What! a parrot at Havoysund, at the end of the world, in that ice and darkness? Yes, a live parrot; that is, it had certainly been a parrot, but it had almost stopped being one.) (author's italics)

She relates how she first saw the parrot, a 'volatile suspect' ('a suspect winged creature'), in a cage covered with wool, its overall colour so doubtful and improbable that she could not discover if it was green that had gone greyish or grey gone greenish ('le tout revêtu d'une couleur si douteuse et si improbable que je ne pus éclaircir si c'était du vert devenu grisâtre ou du gris devenu verdâtre'). She asks how its days pass. It is almost always asleep, waking completely only when the sun shines: 'Le soleil brille donc de temps en temps à Havesund? – Ah! madame, cinq ou six fois par an tout au plus! . . . ' ('So the sun does shine from time to time at Havoysund?' 'Oh, madam! five or six times a year at most! . . . ') (author's ellipsis).[31]

The sentimental is, then, only one of these writers' modes, and love is one among their many subjects. As well as a command of humour, they have other literary gifts: their stylistic abilities will be apparent in almost everything I quote, from the alliterations in Tristan's title *Pérégrinations d'une paria* to the technical mastery shown by the poets.

CHAPTER 2

Conditions for women writers

On the face of it, women writing in nineteenth-century France should have been starting from a promising point. By the end of the eighteenth century, even if the published woman writer still came under attack her right to existence was generally accepted in Europe.[1] Intelligent upper-class Frenchwomen before 1800 had, famously, had the additional advantage of the salons as focal points. In the seventeeth century, the *salonnières* had already affirmed that women were entitled to be learned and to arbitrate on matters of good taste, and they retained prestige throughout the eighteenth century as wits and intellectuals. But the Revolution dealt a body-blow to the salons. Some leading nineteenth-century women writers such as Girardin did still host them.[2] However, writers of humble origins – an increasing number – clearly could not, and others like George Sand preferred more informal gatherings.[3] If salons of a type did, then, continue throughout the century, it was in ever more diluted form, such that the playwright and novelist Virginie Ancelot could already in 1858 call one of her chronicles of salon life *Les Salons de Paris, foyers éteints* ('Paris Salons: Extinguished Hearths').[4] So this was one outlet no longer satisfactorily open to female intellectuals. Possibly, however, the fading of the salons was a benefit for creative women, in that it forced them both on to their own resources and into more public forums. (It has been suggested that running a salon may not always have been so 'liberating' as has been assumed, serving rather to channel and ultimately defuse women's creativity.)[5]

The wider social setting provided both stimuli and obstacles. Some improvements were made in the legal and social situation of Frenchwomen, but these were not consistent until after 1870, with the establishment of the Third Republic, and for most of the century the pre-existing and new restrictions on women were such that contemporary commentators could feel they were worse off than under the Ancien Régime.[6] Thus Napoleon's Civil Code, drawn up between 1800 and 1804, explicitly targeted women, enshrining their subordination to men in many areas, relegating them to the status of minors and excluding them from the definition of citizenship; and divorce was prohibited from 1816 to 1884.[7] The main causes for the new restrictions and for the continuation of old ones were the fears aroused in some quarters by women's activities during and immediately after the 1789 Revolution; and, subsequently, the association of feminism with the left wing, which meant that whenever leftist organizations were suppressed, so too was the political pressure for women's rights.[8]

French women writers were in an exceptional category, being by definition more self-determining and vocal than most of their female contemporaries, and being, many of them, financially independent, either because they were wealthy or because they earned a living from their writing.[9] At the biographical level, the picture is therefore mixed. Neither can we extrapolate simplistically from a general view of 'nineteenth-century French women' to any single imaginative work, since a woman may be writing to escape her own, or her sex's, conditions as much as to reflect them.[10] Yet the conditions are not without interest, often being a factor in the production, and sometimes visibly in the content, of the works. Even when the women were affected relatively little as individuals by legal inequalities, much of their writing shows they were aware of and infuriated by these. In many cases they did suffer personally from them. Ironically, Juliette Adam's royalties from her feminist work *Idées anti-proudhoniennes sur l'amour, la femme et le mariage* (1858) were confiscated by her estranged husband: the Civil Code gave him the right to do so.[11] Léonie d'Aunet was imprisoned and lost custody of her children when caught *in flagrante delicto* with Hugo – who got off scot-free because the law on adultery was indulgent to men but draconian to women. It was because she was impoverished by this that she took to writing; her views on double standards show in her play of the mid-1850s, *Jane Osborn.*

Memoirs, letters and the testimony of those who knew them give clues to the motives driving these women to put pen to paper, and the kinds of support or discouragement they received from family, professionals and fellow-writers. As children, many had excellent memories and were outstandingly quick mentally. The early-century poet Victoire Babois knew Racine's *Iphigénie* by heart at the age of seven, and without even realizing it acquired a kind of 'perfect pitch' for verse:

Ce qui est sûr, c'est que dès-lors et depuis, des vers mal lus me causaient de l'impatience et une sorte de malaise que j'avais peine à dissimuler; mais je ne voyais en cela que du goût pour la poésie, et non pas des dispositions poétiques.[12]

(What's certain is that from then on and ever since, badly read verse aroused in me impatience and a kind of unease that I found difficult to conceal; but I interpreted this only as a taste for poetry, not as poetic talent.)

Amable Tastu could write alexandrines from the age of eleven.[13] The child prodigy Elisa Mercœur could work out percentage interest rates in her head at the age of four; at the same age took only two days to learn all the capital and small letters of the alphabet; and knew Boileau by heart by the time she was seven.[14] (The cartoonist Honoré Daumier cruelly but wittily lampooned these prodigies: Illustration 1.)

Most of these women testify to their hunger for reading, acquired in their childhood and continuing throughout their adult lives. The working-class Suzanne Voilquin states simply that she passionately loved it; the aristocrat Henriette de La Tour du Pin gives more detail, describing her contrivances to get books during the difficult years of the emigration, and her joy when she retrieved her own library and was able to spend days putting the books back on the shelves.[15] Lest we take such pleasures for granted, we should remember that public figures were still declaring themselves against women's literacy, sometimes 'jokingly' but savagely none the less.[16] In addition, some important contemporary authors were not considered 'suitable'. The mid-century Gabrielle d'Altenheym, in a history of the French Academy, says that on no account should Musset's works, or Hugo's dramas or novels, be given to young readers; in many bourgeois families such strictures, coming from a respectable lady – the daughter of an Academician to boot – would be taken more seriously when it was a matter of girls' reading than boys'.[17] Despite these hindrances, and whatever their class, the women writers had considerable breadth of reading, and drew on it with critical acumen; they not only cite most of the major French writers from Montaigne to Voltaire, but move over European

LES BAS-BLEUS.

Ah! ma chère, quelle singulière éducation vous donnez à votre fille? mais à douze ans, moi, j'avais déja écrit un roman en deux volumes et même une fois terminé, ma mère m'avait défendu de le lire, tellement elle le trouvait avancé pour mon âge

1. 'Oh, my dear, what a peculiar education you're giving your daughter! Why, by the time I was twelve I'd already written a two-volume novel . . . and, you know, once I'd finished it, my mother wouldn't let me read it, she thought it was so advanced for my age.' (From *Les Bas-bleus*, by Honoré Daumier.)

literature from the Renaissance on, alluding to Petrarch, Klopstock, Shakespeare and Gray, amongst others.

Their education varied enormously, as might be expected. Women of noble birth were at a great advantage: if their families were willing, they could acquire almost the same kinds of knowledge as a man. La Tour du Pin had physics lessons three times a week and relates that a fifteen-year-old cousin read Tacitus while having her hair dressed (*Journal*, 1 51, 248). Sand too had some scientific and classical education.[18] But one of the noticeable restrictions in most women's range of reference, compared to that of their male contemporaries, was Greek and Latin literature. (There was still no Latin in girls' education in the late century.)[19] And even the well-to-do could bemoan their lack of education: in the mid-1870s, the sixteen-year-old Bashkirtseff, from a wealthy family, exclaims in her diary: 'Je m'enfonce dans les lectures sérieuses et je vois avec désespoir que je sais si peu! . . . J'ai la fièvre des études, et personne pour me guider' ('I'm plunging into serious reading, and I despair when I see how little I know! . . . I have a passion for study, and no one to guide me', *Journal*, 1 365). Later, at twenty-three, she complains of her lack of a 'reasonable' education, with which she could, she believes, have been 'remarkable'; she has read widely, 'Mais c'est un chaos' ('But it's chaotic', ibid., II 559–60). As for those of lower-class origin, they had to make do. The poet Marceline Desbordes-Valmore had no formal education, gaining her sense of verse from the plays in alexandrines which she learned as an actress, and from her working knowledge of eighteenth-century lyric opera, musical elegies and song.[20]

A good deal, then, depended on who could and would broaden the women's minds during their childhood. Many were educated by their own mothers; this might be a mixed blessing, for some talk of the sheer circumscription of these mothers' attitudes to learning. However, if there was a good relationship with the father (and statement after statement from these writers shows there often was), he might discuss politics or religion with the girl, opening up perspectives which the more intellectually timorous mother lacked. Such was the case of, among many, the late-century poet Louise Ackermann. Her father was a Voltairean of the old school ('de vieille roche'), but her mother wanted her to make her first communion; Louise's father, to counter this, gave her a copy of Voltaire. She then read everything, 'pell-mell' ('et pêle-mêle'), and began to 'rhyme'.

The mother, alarmed, took her books away, whereupon Louise fell ill and they had to be given back again.[21] Other relatives could help: Julie Daubié, a working-class girl, had little formal education, but was taught Latin and Greek by her brother, a priest. She sat for the Baccalauréat examination, despite opposition from the Ministry of Education, and in 1861 became the first woman in France to pass it. She subsequently obtained a degree from the Sorbonne.[22]

Equally important, no doubt, were family attitudes to women's creativity. A few were lucky enough to be encouraged by cultured and imaginative relatives of each sex, such as the Communarde Louise Michel, the illegitimate daughter of a local nobleman. She was close to her intelligent and affectionate grandparents on her father's side, and, following in the footsteps of both grandfather and grandmother, she not only read controversial literature (at twelve and thirteen cheekily citing risqué parts of Molière to repel un-wanted older suitors), but also composed verse, in her childhood writing mock-Virgilian pieces – collected by her as *La Grugéide* (*The Angreid*) – to avenge herself on people she disliked.[23] However, what emerges for a majority of those who did go on to publish is a pattern of one supportive family member and others at best indifferent. It is impossible to generalize about the gender of those most likely to do the encouraging or discouraging. Many women who wrote showed their own daughters the way forward, such as Léonie d'Aunet, whose daughter became a journalist; or they dedicated works to their daughters or other young female relatives such as nieces, thus indicating, or explicitly stating, that it was 'permissible' or praise-worthy for women to write.[24] In other cases, however, it seems to have been the men in the family who were sympathetic to, or actively supportive of, women's creativity as well as their education. Babois, who complained about her mother's attitude, sent her brother, from her sickbed, a copy of her verses, accompanied by an affectionate missive in a trembling hand (Illustration 2). He, at least, must have been receptive.[25] Alexandre Soumet, one of the foremost playwrights of the period, co-authored a play with his daughter (the Gabrielle d'Altenheym of stern views on Hugo and Musset): her name appears jointly with his on the title page.[26] Gautier, despite his condescension towards other women writers, encouraged his daugh-ter Judith, who went on to become a scholar and creative writer in a range of media.[27] Staël's father, on the other hand, notoriously forbade her mother to write in his presence and sardonically referred

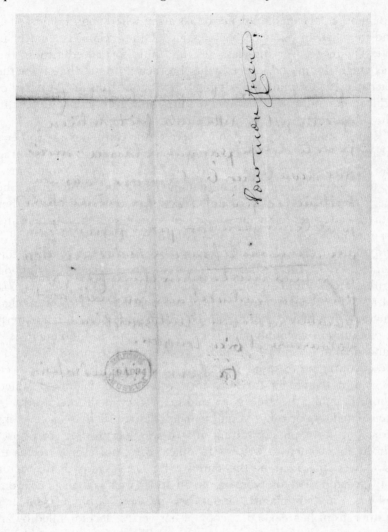

2. 'For my brother. O best and most cherished of brothers! your dear letter did me so much good. I will not tell you I love you; but that my Heart still beats in my Breast which is to say the same thing. I hardly write to you, for if I do not spend a quarter of an hour writing one line I write too badly. farewell dear brother, when will my Penance end? my days are tolerable but my Nights are very painful and very long. your sister, Victoire Babois.' (Letter from Victoire Babois to her brother, accompanying a copy of her verse.)

to Staël herself as Monsieur de Saint-Ecritoire, Sir Holy Writing-Desk, this nickname at a stroke labelling her unfeminine and sanctimonious.[28] Despite her adoration of her father, this did not stop the spirited Staël herself, but we cannot know how many talents withered irretrievably under similar onslaughts.

For some of these women, then, becoming fully fledged adult writers was a seamless process that began in their imaginative girlhood. For others, however, the catalyst was an emotional blow in their maturity. They might, for example, begin to compose as a way of exorcising grief felt over the death of a beloved child.[29] Elisa Mercœur's mother set out with the intention of publishing her dead daughter's work, jealously signing all copies to avoid counterfeit, offering copies of a portrait of Elisa for those who wanted them, and paying tribute to her in a preface; but the preface turns into an anguished and well-written 188-page letter to the world which, in its verve and indignation, is at least as compelling as Elisa's own verse (for she did not live long enough to fulfil her childhood promise). Some, apparently, wrote to purge sorrow or anger over failed love-affairs, such as Daniel Stern (Marie d'Agoult) and Louise Colet over, respectively, Liszt and Flaubert in *Nélida* and *Lui*; others wrote memoirs ostensibly for the information of younger members of the family; others were spurred on by outrage over the lot of the underprivileged.[30] Perhaps the greatest number wrote for money: such was the case of Sophie Cottin, whose husband had squandered her wealth and who wanted to help out an impoverished friend, and of many others, including George Sand herself.[31] But these motives, as and when put forward by the women themselves, may simply have been 'excuses', at a time when excuses were still sometimes needed, for women who had a burning wish to write anyway; and to read Stern's *Nélida* or Colet's *Lui* merely as purgative is to ignore all the other impressions and ideas expressed in these works.

Finally, these women's 'real lives' were a factor in the reception of their works. Open misogyny was, as I have suggested, normally kept under control during their lifetimes; even so, once they were launched on a writing career, the ambivalence of male contemporaries dogged them, working, seemingly arbitrarily, against or for them. Thus, the late-century periodical *La Renaissance littéraire et artistique* carried an article by one of its founders attacking Elizabeth Barrett Browning and en route declaring breezily that 'we' have little faith – a few brilliant exceptions notwithstanding – in the poetic genius of women: their temperament generally lacks the balance needed for the conception and execution of great works of poetry. The writer backs up his point with the claim that women can have no idea what passion is, since they cannot feel it (apparently Racine has had no impact on him?) ('elles ne peuvent soupçonner ce qu'est la passion, ne la pouvant éprouver').[32] Yet this same periodical published (alongside Rimbaud, Verlaine and Mallarmé) poetry by a number of women from Auguste Blanchecotte to Julia Daudet. And women writers did receive other kinds of support from men outside the family. Tutors and publishers sometimes encouraged them into print; such well-known authors as Chateaubriand, Lamartine and Hugo corresponded with them, dedicated works to them and met them for discussions. Occasionally there were ulterior motives: Elisa Mercœur's tutor eventually proposed to her despite an age difference of a generation; and the philandering Hugo may have had other reasons for being kind to young protégées. But we need not be unduly cynical: some of these women received State allowances for their writing, and a number won prizes from all-male Academies whose members cannot have had any hope of bedding them.[33] The novelist and polemicist Louise Gagneur was proposed to by her future husband before he had even met her, on the strength of a pamphlet she had written about pauperism: however rash, this action at least speaks for intellectual respect.[34]

Besides this, cultured or creative women supported each other. It would be unreal to pretend there was a universal sisterhood: Gay hated Genlis's moralizing and said so; Colet attacked Cottin and Céleste Mogador; Stern quarrelled with Sand, Sand quarrelled with the actress Judith who was supposed to be starring in one of her dramas (Judith promptly withdrew); Bashkirtseff, in turn, was unenthusiastic about Sand; while Juliette Adam, according to one commentator, 'heartily disliked' her censorious fellow-feminist Jenny d'Héricourt.[35] But they often praised, and even financially helped, each other, forming networks that complemented or replaced the salons.[36] Mme Récamier was a generous patron, giving material help to Desbordes-Valmore, among others.[37] The writers dedicated works not only to their female patrons and relatives but also to other major women writers; they confided details of composition to each other.[38] They paid written tribute to other female authors by publishing their own 'dependent' works (saluting the novelist Duras, for instance, in the form of their own poems about her heroine

Ourika).[39] The poet Amable Tastu wrote a composition to her 'Muse', Adélaïde Dufrénoy, lamenting her death.[40] And there was more than this professional and personal solidarity. At times of national crisis, women were apostrophized across the country, as when Anaïs Ségalas, in an epilogue to a collection that includes her patriotic poems *Les Algériennes*, exhorts Frenchwomen's hearts to beat with hers: for these 'songs' are a secret bond.[41] To be included in this image of national 'networks' are all the feminists' appeals to women as a sex, through newspaper articles, pamphlets or pre-faces.[42]

So writing women did bolster each others' morale; family and friends might be constricting but could also, apparently, proceed on the assumption that intelligent girls should be 'brought on'; many professional men were alive enough to talent not to care which sex its owner was – or not to care very much; and in some cases, warring tendencies in powerful individuals produced responses to female authors which *can* be construed as sexist, but may also constitute a regret that their potential was not quite being fulfilled. Although Sainte-Beuve, as we have seen, presented women writers as a perhaps 'odd' group, and shrank from full-blown praise, he did try to be, and often was, fair-minded and appreciative. Flaubert resorted to misogynistic imagery about women writers; yet his advice to Louise Colet to try to forget that she was a woman when writing may not have been entirely malicious or ill-founded.[43] In short, the culture which produced and reacted to literary women in nine-teenth-century France was – to put the matter strongly, as does Holmes – 'schizoid'; or, to put it more favourably, it was, at least, not monolithic.[44]

PART I

*The early nineteenth century: the age of Napoleon
and the aftermath of revolution (1800–1829)*

CHAPTER 3

Overview, 1800–1829

By 1800, most women were writing under their own names – already at the very end of the eighteenth century a Frenchwoman had, for the first time, signed an erotic novel: *Illyrine, ou l'Ecueil de l'expérience,* by Barbe-Suzanne-Aimable Giraux de Morency.[1] But others still felt the need to hide their identity (for instance, Marie Gacon-Dufour, who in 1801 published without attribution *Les Dangers d'un mariage forcé,* an unusually outspoken novel about pre-marital pregnancy that urged resistance to tyrannical parents' wishes).[2] And those who did identify themselves often sheltered behind the respectability of a 'Mme' followed by the husband's forename and surname.

During this first third of the century, contemporaries thought women's influence on literature was increasing in strength, whatever the realities of their situation and the fragmentation of traditional support structures like the salons. To some degree, this perception was a hangover from the eighteenth century, when women writers were still admitted into anthologies in significant numbers and also had anthologies devoted exclusively to them.[3] Genlis continued down this path with her 1811 *De l'influence des femmes sur la littérature française.* But it was felt that something new was happening too. Cohen cites three men in the public eye – a dramatist, an Academician and a publisher – who all, between 1816 and 1830, claimed that female authors were surpassing male ones in both quality and quantity; and Waller points out that Constant and Stendhal invoked the success of women writers as a way of ensuring their own.[4]

Fiction was the genre to which the women most readily turned – indeed, those writers cited as outstripping men were mainly novelists. The principal ones of the period (whether because of influence or volume) were Genlis, Souza, Staël, Duras, Krüdener, Gay and Cottin: their grip on the novel is attested to by such stories as the (possibly apocryphal) one of Napoleon choosing Gay's newly published *Anatole* (1815) to while away the night before his second abdication in the wake of Waterloo.[5] Some promising younger writers were making their débuts in verse (Desbordes-Valmore, Tastu and Gay's daughter Delphine), but had not quite found their voices; in the theatre, women were making a contribution, particularly in the newly popular melodrama. They also published housekeeping and child-rearing manuals; a few ventured more widely, with some political writing and a little literature and music criticism; and, despite the difficulties of open comment under the Empire, they were publicising their ideas quietly, either in characters' asides in fiction, or through the memoirs which had long been a more respectable form of writing than others for women, and which greatly increased in number in the wake of women's experiences of the Revolution and the emigration.[6]

In their techniques, the poets, at least, were resolutely traditional. But in the novel, different modes clashed more than at any time later in the century, often conveying a dizzying sense of any approach being acceptable whatever the novelty or, conversely, the time-lag. Thus Genlis's *Mademoiselle de Clermont* (1802), with its bare vocabulary and structure, might almost be a pastiche of the seventeenth-century *La Princesse de Clèves* (1678). Others still relied on the epistolary form, the 'frame narrator', or both, and were wedded to an exclamatory style that nevertheless shrank away from anything resembling colloquialism and that normally avoided sensuous description of landscape. However, the more innovative, even if they chose a familiar structure, at the same time took care to foreground heroines' voices – by way of their letters, for example.[7] Or they might seize on what they rightly sensed was a shift in literary 'requirements'. The outstanding example of this is Krüdener's *Valérie* (1803). With impressive speed – only one year after Chateaubriand's *René* – Krüdener, still using the epistolary form, captured what was to become the prevailing (though not universal) literary sensibility of this first part of the century: melancholia; a taste for lavish depictions of 'nature'; hopeless and unconsummated love; an even keener interest in Italy than in the previous century; and a new fascination with the mists of Northern Europe. (The hero, Gustave, is a Swede who expatiates on the beauties of his native land but spends much of the novel in Venice, thus killing two birds with one stone.)

The women also influenced the men. Even Larnac allows a degree of innovation to Krüdener, remarking that after the 'dried-out' ('desséché') style of the eighteenth century, readers liked her abundance of metaphors; while Waller, in *The Male Malady*, attributes the *mal du siècle* to male writers' conscious or unconscious desire to imitate novels by women and, further, their desire to appropriate characteristics of the 'real' women themselves.[8] Even if we do not go this far, there are other debts which it would be just to acknowledge. For example, Guilbert de Pixerécourt's theatre hit *La Fille de l'exilé* (1819) was based on the earlier and equally successful novel *Elisabeth, ou les exilés de Sibérie* (1806) by Cottin – who was braver to write it, since the story can be read as a challenge or appeal to Napoleon.[9] Most notable is the influence of women's writing on Stendhal's pre- and post-1829 works. First, on his *Armance* (1827): there is an impotent Octave who attempts suicide in Félicie de Choiseul-Meuse's porno-graphic *Julie, ou j'ai sauvé ma rose* (1807), and (this at least is well known) the central situation of *Armance* derives from Duras's *Olivier* (1821–2). Stendhal also took elements of *Le Rouge et le noir* (1830) from Duras's *Edouard* (1825), in which a lower-class hero becomes the (intermittent) secretary to a nobleman and falls in love with his daughter. And the pseudonym Stendhal is (as too few critics point out) close to 'Staël': for, in this first third of the century, Staël dominated.

CHAPTER 4

'Foremothers' and Germaine de Staël

Women writers of the nineteenth century looked to models, both to assess what it was acceptable to write about and to embolden themselves when they might be overstepping boundaries. They did cast back to some male writers, for example to those who created memorable or unusually finely drawn female characters. Molière's witty coquette Célimène lives on in a number of their novels and plays, and Marivaux is discernible in those plots of theirs which, with sophistication and humour, tell the story of 'the heart that does not yet know itself', and, through quid pro quos, manipulations and disguise, hint at the subjectivity of love. (Gay's novels and Alexandrine de Bawr's plays are among the main examples.) Rousseau's *La Nouvelle Héloïse* (1761) licensed subsequent women writers to talk about noble women falling in love with lower-status men and about extra-marital affairs and pregnancies. Richardson's Europe-wide success *Pamela: Virtue Rewarded* (1740) was also pivotal, showing how a woman novelist could compose without jeopardising her reputation: viz. by offering a paean to virtue; 'if the writing did not slip,' says Hufton, 'then logic surely insisted that the author was blameless?' (443–5). Indeed, many nineteenth-century French women writers refer to Richardson or his works by name.[1]

But the need to cast back to notable women – notable in literary and other ways – was even stronger.[2] Memorable females from history and myth recur frequently. In the middle of the century the feminist Eugénie Niboyet wrote a historical novel about Catherine the Great, stressing in a preface that Catherine conceived the legal code of her country and wielded the power that enabled her to set it in stone: she was an ardent, passionate woman, a legislator and a warrior armed to the teeth ('un guerrier armé de pied-en-cap') who achieved all that Russia needed to make it strong both internally and externally. The message 'women can do it' could hardly be plainer.[3]

3. Portrait of Madame de Staël, by François Gérard.

Mme Roland is cited by Colet and others, and is the heroine of an 1843 play by Virginie Ancelot in which she emerges as a pillar of strength and an exemplar of level-headedness; calm before insults, always intelligent, she observes at one point: 'Les hommes pardonnent plutôt à une femme beaucoup de folie qu'un peu de raison' ('Men are readier to forgive a woman a good deal of folly than a little reason').[4] Joan of Arc was one of the commonest figureheads.[5] (Marina Warner's well-known study discusses Joan's continuing appropriation in modern times by not only politicians but also feminists.)[6] Towards the end of the century, Pallas Athene became the *nec plus ultra* of 'role-models'. Not only a warrior and Zeus's favourite daughter, she is also the patron of all aspects of intelligence and creativity, as Maria Deraismes does not hesitate to point out:

Ce n'est plus la divinité tellurique aux multiples mamelles, spécifiant la réceptivité; ce n'est plus la passive Vesta et l'insignifiante Demeter, mais Athéné, la personnification de la pensée . . . C'est la première fois que dans les théogonies l'élément spiritualiste est représenté, et c'est sous la forme d'une femme qu'il apparaît![7]

(No longer do we have the many-breasted earth-goddess, signalling receptivity; no longer the passive Vesta or the insignificant Demeter, but Athene, the personification of thought . . . This is the first time theogonies have represented the spiritual element, and it is in the form of a woman that this appears!)

Women also recognized earlier female authors and intellectuals, paying often handsome tribute to literary 'foremothers': Genlis in a work specifically about their influence, as we have seen; and Gay, who in the first third of the century wrote a play about Mme de Sévigné, *Le Marquis de Pomenars*, in which Sévigné emerges as the wise artist vis-à-vis the skilled but (sexually and intellectually) promiscuous draughtsman Pomenars. The play ends with Sévigné affirming the link between her raconteur's ability and the daughter who will receive its fruits: 'suivez-moi tous, venez réjouir mon bon oncle de cette heureuse aventure; pendant que vous lui en ferez le récit, j'irai l'écrire à ma fille' ('follow me, everybody: let my kind uncle enjoy the story of this happy adventure; while you're telling him, I'll be writing it to my daughter').[8] Ancelot wrote a play about the famous *salonnière* the marquise de Rambouillet, revealing – as she explains to her own daughter in a preface – a distinguished mind, acting upon the literature of her century ('un esprit distingué, agissant sur la littérature de son siècle').[9] However, there are gaps.

The two foremost women novelists writing in French in the previous century, Marie-Jeanne Riccoboni and Isabelle de Charrière, are not mentioned in any of the post-1815 works I have surveyed; still more surprisingly, neither is the seventeenth-century Mme de Lafayette, who had already, well before Richardson and far more subtly than he, provided a 'prototype' for the woman novelist.[10] (The heroine of *La Princesse de Clèves* [1678] not only resists an extra-marital affair with the man she loves but, from a sense of both duty and self-preservation, refuses marriage to him even once she is widowed.) Stendhal pays tribute to Lafayette, but his female contemporaries and successors are strangely silent about this work. Either women writers experience more 'anxiety of influence' than is sometimes recognized – and three outstanding previous novelists would be more likely to arouse such anxiety than previous letter-writers or *salonnières*; or, in the nineteenth century, they felt the pressures to be such that a more recent model, one who very obviously shared their dilemmas and social concerns, was not only desirable but essential. She had not simply to be part of the nineteenth-century 'network' but to rise above it. This model – acknowledged as such, and looked up to for her personal bravery as well as for her writing – was Germaine de Staël (1766–1817).

Throughout her life Staël outspokenly espoused the cause of the oppressed, from slaves to women. During the Terror, she courageously tried to rescue friends; she later became the leading intellectual opponent of Napoleon's military dictatorship. In her defence of liberal values, she was 'the great "dissident" voice of the era, heard by all'.[11] Napoleon was annoyed by and fearful of her works, which promoted rival cultures; Protestantism rather than the Catholicism he was trying to re-establish; and freedom over despotism. After the publication of her novel *Delphine* in 1802, he forbade her to stay in or near Paris; when in 1807 she tried to publish *De l'Allemagne*, he had all copies seized and pulped, and ordered her to leave the country. Such was her fame as the true 'enemy' of Napoleon that when he was defeated, many leading European statesmen saw his downfall as her victory.

Her influence on French intellectual thought was profound. At the least she can be seen as the inventor of comparative literary criticism, but this would be so minimalist an assessment of her contribution as to be inaccurate. She gave a nineteenth-century 'stamp' to the ideas of Montesquieu, who had, some fifty years earlier, stressed the relativism of beliefs and laws, and the singularity of each culture's practices, attributable to a diversity of physical and moral factors. Montesquieu's influence marked male writers from beginning to end of the following century, for example Stendhal in the first half and Zola in the second. But this influence was mediated through Staël as both a powerful propagandist and herself an original thinker. In her theoretical works *De la littérature* (1800) and *De l'Allemagne* she pushed into so many further areas of comparative study, and launched so many debates, that 'the birth of European Romanticism' has been attributed to her; not only these two works, but 'every choice Staël makes helps shape the nineteenth century'.[12] At the beginning of the new era, Staël propelled it into modes of thought which were to enable first Hugo, then almost all the significant writers of the period, to reject French classicism and neo-classicism. She is sometimes repetitive, over-insistent or maddeningly wrong.[13] But in her ability to make her reader think, and in the désinvolture with which she tackles a breathtaking range of issues – from the importance of enthusiasm to the benefits the Madonna conferred on women's social status – she was and remains compelling.

Her two novels *Delphine* and *Corinne* (1802, 1807) also had an exceptional impact.[14] Delphine and Corinne are unusual and gifted women who fall in love with, and are loved by, Léonce and Oswald respectively. Delphine bravely defends the cause of women's independence; Corinne, a poet, has fame and status in her native Italy, where she is regarded as a kind of sibyl. But their men, after inner struggles, retreat from the women's unconventionality and talent. The main theme of *Delphine* is the double standards applied to men and women in all areas, but especially in those of public reputation and physical attractiveness; the main question of *Corinne* is: can a woman of genius be loved?

Women writing during Staël's life or just after her death in 1817 did not doubt her importance. The novelist and essayist Hortense Allart (Chateaubriand's mistress, and correspondent of many famous men of the time) published a work about her as early as the 1820s (*Lettres sur les ouvrages de Mme de Staël*, 1824), and in the memoirs she began in 1820, Henriette de La Tour du Pin devotes more space to her than to any other woman apart from Marie-Antoinette and those with whom she herself had close personal ties. La Tour du Pin can be dry about her: relating how Talleyrand had manipulated

Staël into obtaining the Foreign Ministry for him by claiming to be penniless and threatening to blow his brains out, she adds that while none of this was true, it was dramatic and Mme de Staël loved drama. But she comments approvingly on Staël's political and intellectual tolerance, and evidently regards Staël as one of the key political actors figuring in her own life.[15] Gay paid Staël the eloquent compliment of naming her own daughter Delphine (she was born two years after the publication of the novel).[16] Even more telling is the tribute of the modest poet Babois. Introducing a relatively political section of verse, her *Elégies nationales*, she says in an edition published eleven years after Staël's death:

Il est probable que beaucoup de personnes trouveront que ces trois morceaux . . . sortent des limites qu'on prescrit tacitement aux femmes, en France peut-être plus qu'ailleurs. Pour oser les franchir, il fallait être madame de Staël; elle l'a fait avec la conscience d'elle-même et toute l'assurance de son génie. Je la regarde de si loin qu'il ne m'appartient pas de l'imiter. . . (III)

(It is likely that a number of people will feel these three pieces . . . go beyond the limits tacitly prescribed for women, perhaps more in France than elsewhere. To dare to breach them I should have had to be Mme de Staël; she did it in full self-awareness and with all the confidence of her genius. I look upon her from such a distance that it is not for me to imitate her. . .)

Interest in Staël continued acute in the middle third of the century. In a novel of 1837 destined for 'young persons', Sophie Ulliac-Trémadeure calls her 'la femme la plus admirable et la plus justement célèbre de notre temps' ('the most admirable and justly famous woman of our time').[17] In 1839 Colet wrote a long poem, 'Corinne à Oswald'; here Corinne revives the debate about Oswald's wish to have her 'gentle and tender', yet without snuffing out her 'poetic ardour', and about her own longing to accept the public's praise while, as it were, offering this up to him. It ends with Corinne's affirmation that her belief in herself depends on him: 'Je crois à ma beauté, je crois à mon génie, / Puisque tu sais m'aimer!' ('I believe in my beauty, I believe in my genius, / Since you can love me!').[18] Elsewhere too Colet deliberately reminds her reader of Staël, giving the name Léonce to the 'Flaubert figure' of her novel *Lui*, and in one of the narratives of *Poème de la femme* calling a dashing but dastardly young man Lionel de Vernon – his first name resembling 'Léonce', his second borrowing that of Delphine's perfidious friend Mme de

Vernon.[19] More generally, 'Corinne' was still, thirty years on, short-hand for 'the creative woman'. In 1841, Girardin, writing in the newspaper *La Presse* for a wide audience of both sexes, whose tastes and assumptions she was adept at gauging, re-created a young singer who begs her interlocutor not to reveal that she has written the song as well as sung it: if her sisters knew that she scribbled ('griffonne') music, 'elles m'appelleraient Corinne, elles se moqueraient de moi' ('they'd call me Corinne, they'd laugh at me').[20]

Women in the last third of the century cited Staël by name less frequently, but she was still there as a yardstick: Bashkirtseff envies her stylistic 'facility and grace' in a diary entry of 1876, and when Tinayre's 1899 heroine, the intelligent and well-educated Hellé, arrives in Paris, she remarks that people expected to see in her 'une nouvelle Staël . . . une savante au bagout de conférencière' ('a new Staël . . . a learned woman with a lecturer's gift of the gab').[21]

The main ideas of *Delphine* and *Corinne* were also adopted in subsequent women's novels, plays and poetry throughout the century, sometimes with only the smallest adaptation to the new context or differing literary form. The links *Delphine* makes between women's subordination and a more general attachment to aristo-cratic rank, its identification between women and all other victims of oppression: these mark writers as diverse as Cottin, Duras and Desbordes-Valmore.[22] Delphine even tells her friend Elise that 'those of us who have suffered' are different from others and that in every relationship life can offer, in every country in the world, one should live with the oppressed; for those who are happy and powerful are missing half of all feelings and half of all ideas.[23] The insistence in this novel that 'opinion' is the enemy of women's independence also proved remarkably long-lived. In *Delphine*, 'opinion' appears in the epigraph (a quotation from Staël's own mother): 'Un homme doit savoir braver l'opinion, une femme s'y soumettre' ('A man must know how to brave opinion, a woman how to submit to it'). 'Opinion' goes on to become almost a torturing and persecutory persona in the narrative itself. This representation was to recur in later writers from Krüdener to d'Aunet. (Thus a mid-century heroine of the comtesse Dash's says slightingly of her own elder sister that she would never have committed a fault because of 'the veneration she felt for other people's opinion, to her mind the foremost power of all': 'la vénération où elle tenait l'opinion des autres, la première de toutes les puisssances à ses yeux'.)[24]

Also formative was Staël's depiction in *Corinne* of the problems faced by a gifted woman in a patriarchal society, and of the tensions that may be aroused in a man if a woman is more obviously talented than he. Thus the creativity of Girardin's 1833 verse heroine Napoline is smothered by her uncle, through any means from scolding to accusations of perversity; while Colet, in *Lui*, is outspoken on the theme of men's envy of talented women, as well as reiterating the more generous view (also put forward by Staël) that intelligent men do, after all, need and want intelligent women as companions.[25] This latter idea was stressed at the very end of the century by Tinayre, who in her *Hellé* not only names Staël, as we have seen, but revisits many central Staëlian problems: the educated or intelligent woman may be 'unmarriageable', and if she *is* to be loved, what kind of man will it be who loves her?

As with Staël's discursive works, some of the ideas structuring *Delphine* and *Corinne* resemble those of male Enlightenment thinkers and contemporary liberals, and as such could be expected to be shared by other thoughtful women writing at about the same time. But because Staël unflinchingly and multifariously extended the principles of liberalism to the cause of women, and maintained that women could be geniuses, she opened up new subjects for women writers. Her diversity also had its effect. Again she had predecessors in the *salonnières* and in the catholic Mme de Charrière; however, the forays of Staël's successors into a range of intellectual enterprises, and the willingness of even the more timid to engage in print with controversial issues, would appear from the testimonies to have owed something to her bravura. Like her, many individual women went on to write not only imaginative works in different genres but also discursive ones: political propaganda, literary criticism and history (Allart, Stern and Deraismes, for instance).[26] Later writers like Sand fused art or music criticism with fictional works, as Staël had done in *Corinne*.[27] If there is a single 'foremother' of women's writing in nineteenth-century France it is Staël.

CHAPTER 5

Writing about history: Henriette de La Tour du Pin

The memoir-writer Henriette de La Tour du Pin (1770–1853) cannot be thought of as any kind of 'foremother', since her memoirs, although started in 1820, were published only in 1906 (by her great-grandson: they then ran to many editions, reaching their twenty-first in 1920).[1] But part of the interest of reading her lies in her value as an example. La Tour du Pin displays the increasingly sophisticated attitude of many French women writers towards history in the nineteenth century. The other interest in reading her is for her own literary worth: not only was she at the centre of major European events, she is also an exceptionally skilful raconteur. Her book is 'one long suspense story and there is not a dull page in it . . . Nobody ever dropped so many international names without being guilty of name-dropping.'[2]

Of course, not all female authors of the period were complex in their approach to history. Like many best-selling male authors of the time, the most popularizing drew on relatively recent historical events merely to produce convenient *deus ex machina* endings to rather weakly structured imaginative works: for instance Mme Belfort at the beginning of the century, who in an 1801 play uses a recently ended Napoleonic campaign to create quid pro quos around the theme of 'the returning warrior not dead as feared'.[3] Or else they staged 'history' to regale their public with glamorized tales of barbarity, power, or exotic amours in long-gone settings: for example, near the end of the century, Jane Dieulafoy, who in her *Parysatis* (1890) 're-creates' the world of Cyrus and Artaxerxes with only a slapdash sense of the psychological differences between eras.[4]

However, many others wrote with insight about historical crises or processes. Thus, novels and drama returned throughout the century to the 1789 Revolution. This was partly because disguises, narrow escapes and other adventures under the Terror were a good source of gripping plots (again Dieulafoy seizes opportunities with her *Volontaire: 1792–93* of 1892).[5] But the Revolution and Terror also served as a reference to a collective memory and, for the more sophisticated writers, as events which in their specificity retained the power to raise still-awkward questions. Such questions (about, for instance, individuals' courage under an oppressive regime) are asked in two mid-century plays written from rather different political angles: the liberal-minded Ancelot's *Madame Roland* (1843), and *Une femme qui déteste son mari* (1856) by the more conservative Girardin. In these and other works, past events shade off into current political anxieties and *vice versa*. I discuss mid-century women writers' involvement with contemporary political debates in a later chapter. For the moment, let us look at the first third of the century, a period in which female authors are often supposed to have been too busy writing love-stories to have been other than ahistorical in their concerns.

This is not even true of the fiction of the time. Those novelists apparently most silent about historical processes nevertheless still indicated changes in social psychology, often with surprising radicalism: for example Krüdener, who, as part of the depiction of her mournful young nobleman Gustave, suggested as early as 1803 that aristocratic militarism was now a thing of the past.[6] Others were overt. *Delphine* is set in the period of the Revolution, and the history of those years plays its part as the novel goes on: the new (and short-lived) divorce legislation of 1792 has an important narrative function; Léonce eventually takes up arms against the Republican armies and, in the second finale, is executed by them.[7] Duras's *Ourika* (1824) has a still stronger sense of historical specificity; indeed, her commentator Lescure remarks in the 1878 edition that it is the 'tableau of an epoch' at a given moment.[8] Duras assumes that historical detail matters. Thus, if *Ourika* opens with the convent backdrop favoured by many contemporary authors, male and female alike, this is no generalized setting but is accompanied by a precise reference to Napoleon's permission for the re-establishment of some convents (1). Soon, the novella narrates the stages of the Revolution; dates are given, Robespierre's death figures; and Duras describes the varying psychological effects these stages have on both the heroine and the society surrounding her (26–32). *Ourika* has a less panoramic historical sweep than some later novels by men and women of the mid-century, but then it is a short work (some sixty pages). What is remarkable is the relation Duras establishes between history and the tenor of characters' thoughts and moods – a relation more concretely conveyed in *Ourika* than in the famous men's novellas of the early nineteenth century, *René* and *Adolphe*. Erich Auerbach, in *Mimesis*, hails Stendhal as the pioneer here, saying that with his *Le Rouge et le noir* (1830) he becomes the first 'modern' novelist of history; it may be that we should look a little further back.[9]

The memoir-writers of these decades, too, display a subtle understanding of the intertwining of personal and historical destinies, as well as awareness of the nature of their own enterprise. In part, this was because the recent turbulence of their own lives had precipitated them into a different perception of autobiography. Hufton observes that in earlier periods, memoir-writing as a literary genre was essentially confined to the great and famous or those who had been associated with them, but that wars, and above all the French Revolution, caused a 'truly amazing burgeoning' of this genre as highly literate aristocratic ladies thought their special experience, whether of suffering or adventures, worthy of recounting. Most important, 'The times in which the events were lived took over from the narrator's social standing as the point of interest for the reader' (*The Prospect Before Her*, 451–2). At the hinge of the century, then, came an important change: these memoir-writers started to see the self as history.[10] Not being novelists, they cannot quite earn the accolade of 'modern tragic realism based on the contemporary' (Auerbach's phrase); but they are keen-eyed chroniclers and racy story-tellers whose literary talents are not always easy to separate from those of the serious 'novelists of history'. Henriette de La Tour du Pin is the prime example of a writer who, even if she did not become a Stendhal, had the gifts to do so.

La Tour du Pin, a descendant of Irish and English Jacobites, wrote her memoirs for her sole surviving son. She started them at the age of fifty, and continued writing and revising them until her death in her eighties, in 1853. The memoirs cover her childhood, her life at the court of Louis XVI (her mother was lady-in-waiting to Marie-Antoinette), the 1789 Revolution, her years of exile in North America and England, and the first year of the Restoration. She took part in all the Court rituals, being close enough to the Royal Family to observe their habits and reactions. In the palace of Versailles when the people of Paris marched on and entered it in 1789, she was an eye-witness to key moments. The family emigrated to the United States (taking their piano with them), and once there she turned herself into a dairy farmer whose butter was the best for miles around. Finally, they returned to France and found favour with Napoleon. Her life, despite its pampered start, was hard: she was brought up from the age of twelve by an unremittingly hostile grandmother, lost five of her six children over the years, and ended her life in poverty. Her narrative, while acknowledging the pain of difficult events, is nevertheless written with irony, vigour and a good-humoured tolerance.

La Tour du Pin does not forget that she is an aristocrat. When it is a question of her marriage, 'name' and 'illustrious family' are important to her (I 77). And she relates with pride the following tale: when Napoleon was trying to win the allegiance of the nobility and was counting on Josephine to establish social relations with still young and fashionable former members of the royal household (and, says La Tour du Pin, this would have been quite a victory in her case), she kept Josephine waiting to increase the value of her condescension, and was the only one who refused to become a lady-in-waiting to her (II 212–15). But she is (and apparently was, even as a very young woman) humane and unusually free of prejudice, sometimes showing this through direct comment, as when she says that the peasant woman who looked after her in her childhood had better judgement than the great of the earth (I 6); sometimes through inference, when she lets stories or reported conversation make the point for her. In America she takes a French visitor for a ride through a wood. They meet an almost naked native American whom La Tour du Pin knows. He politely offers her, as riding crop, a stick which he has stripped with his tomahawk. 'And if you had been alone, Madame?' exclaims the visitor afterwards. 'I should have been just as little alarmed,' replies La Tour du Pin, 'and, you know, if I had had to defend myself from you and had told him to throw his tomahawk at you, he would have done so without hesitation' ('J'aurais été tout aussi rassurée, répondis-je. Sachez même que si, pour me défendre de vous, je lui avais dit de vous lancer son casse-tête, il l'aurait fait sans hésiter') (II 61–2). La Tour du Pin does not *say*, 'So you see, those of other races should be treated as human beings, and a white man is just as likely to rape as a "native".' As a good narrator, she knows when to pass on without comment. And her tales of her dealings with American slaves and slave-owners show, with the same lack of trumpeting, an active courage on the slaves' behalf.

La Tour du Pin also describes with a novelist's techniques the absurdity of the Court's behaviour just before the Revolution. While highlighting the charm and gaiety of her youthful social life, she chooses her moment to stab home the idea that the nobility deserved what was coming to it: the 1789 Revolution was, she says, almost the just punishment of the vices of the upper classes ('la juste punition des vices des hautes classes', 1 31). She shrewdly selects telling examples of that caste-bound behaviour which, for instance, demanded that even military victors coming hotfoot from their battles had to change into civilian clothes before they could appear before the King, so as not to upset Court etiquette – the inference being that this etiquette was more important than the national interest (1 72–3). Her impatience with such rituals gives rise to some of her most drily comical passages, in which (again like any novelist) she re-creates the incongruous or ridiculous. So, in 'curtsey lessons', the fat male teacher with his white-powdered hair wore a billowing underskirt, both to show his female pupils how to manage, and in order to switch roles himself between Queen and presenter ('M. Huart, gros homme, coiffé admirablement et poudré à blanc, avec un jupon bouffant, représentait la reine et se tenait debout au fond du salon', 1 109). And she is droll even about dangers: although, as she herself says, her name, rank and the position of her father-in-law would inevitably have meant imprisonment and death for her after the Revolution, she indicates that for some, at least, the panic emigration was another and perhaps unnecessary trend: 'France is a country much given to fashions and just then emigration became all the vogue' ('Tout est de mode en France; celle de l'émigration commença alors', 1 318–19, 199).

As well as understatement or suggestion, La Tour du Pin deploys the rhetorical tricks of first-person narrative. She is ironic about her own former assumptions, remarking that when the Revolution came, she thought she had made her greatest sacrifice in agreeing to do without her elegant maid and footman-hairdresser; she realized she might no longer go to balls but was resolved to bear these reverses with courage and determination ('J'entrevoyais, il est vrai, qu'il se pourrait que . . . je n'allasse plus au bal . . . Je me promettais de supporter ces revers avec courage et fermeté', 1 290). She comments at intervals that as she is *not* writing a history of the Revolution, she will not speak of all the discussions then taking place in society – which besides (she adds), as an eighteen- or nineteen-year-old she found very tedious (1 153, 181–2). Through this disarming sleight of hand she gives the double perspective of an older, wiser self commenting on a giddy younger one, while simultaneously reminding the reader of what those discussions were and keeping a balance between large-scale events and amusing or intimate details.

There is also a 'Balzacian' side to La Tour du Pin's narrative, as to those of many other women autobiographers. They have a distinctive sense of the material, not merely as a way of re-creating the uniqueness of place and moment but also, in the manner of the better-known nineteenth-century realists, as a means to show historical or cultural significance. When La Tour du Pin tells us that under the Ancien Régime the men used to have to wear swords to dinner, or that the King's sword was a continual hindrance to him ('Toujours embarrassé de son épée'), her picture of physical awkwardness and token military symbolism tells us about a society as well as about a custom (1 93, 114). Memoirs allowed these women to seize on details of clothing, food and furniture not for their own sake but to inform about mores or psychology; and again, many of them were doing so before Balzac.[11]

La Tour du Pin has thought not only about the nature of life-writing and the chronicle, but also about historiography. She moves readily from the anecdotal to the analytical, and likes explaining systems, as we see when she sets out to explain the selling of sections of American land to poor Irish, Scottish or French settlers sent by New York agents: 'Let us follow one such group of colonists, people I knew, so that you can see how the system worked' ('Suivons un de ces groupes de colons, que j'ai connu, pour faire comprendre cette sorte d'établissement', II 53). She opens the work with observations on the curious relationship between public and private events, talking of the different weightings of each and raising the question of what kind of structure to use for them (1 1–2). She brings out the bewildering differences four decades or so can effect in an observer's perspective on the same events, commenting on the blindness at the time to what seems so obvious now and the way individual aspects can become a 'purely historical generalization' with the passage of time ('une généralité purement historique', 1 160–1, 31). And she knows she is not giving – cannot give – a comprehensive account, remarking both at the beginning and at intervals throughout on the inevitable selectiveness of her narrative.[12]

This reflectiveness about what it is to be a historian recurs in

many other women writers of the century. It is not simply that they
see the self as history; or comment on shifts in social psychology; or
write actual histories. It is also that they increasingly think of
themselves as representatives of a historically significant class (take,
for instance, Suzanne Voilquin's title, *Souvenirs d'une fille du peuple*). Or
they remark on the *wrong* way to look at history. Here is Sand on
Albert, the young hero of *Consuelo*:

L'étude de l'histoire le passionnait sans l'éclairer. Il était toujours, en
apprenant les crimes et les injustices des hommes, agité d'émotions par trop
naïves, comme ce roi barbare qui, en écoutant la lecture de la passion de
Notre-Seigneur, s'écriait en brandissant sa lance: 'Ah! si j'avais été là avec
mes hommes d'armes, de telles choses ne seraient pas arrivées! j'aurais
haché ces méchants Juifs en mille pièces!'[13]

(The study of history thrilled him without enlightening him. When he
learned of men's crimes and injustices, he would become agitated and react
far too naively, like that barbarian king who, when Our Lord's Passion was
read out to him, brandished his lance and cried: 'Oh, if I'd been there with
my soldiers, nothing like that would ever have happened! I'd have hacked
those evil Jews into a thousand bits!')

Or they comment on the relationship between 'official' history and
other kinds. Girardin, in her function as journalist, constructs a
symbiotic dependence between journalism and the writing of history,
while at the same time allowing the latter its greater dignity. In an
article of 1844, she (rather waspishly) writes:

On nous a donc métamorphosé, malgré nous, en une espèce non pas
d'historien, mais de *mémorien*, un de ces écrivains sans valeur que les grands
écrivains consultent . . . nous sommes à l'historien ce que l'élève bar-
bouilleur est au peintre.[14]

(So we've been metamorphosed, whether we like it or not, into a species
not of historian, but of *memorian*, one of those writers of no value whom the
great writers consult . . . we are to the historian what the daubing pupil is
to the painter.) (author's neologism and italics)

A few weeks later, more seriously if still wittily, she conjures up the
difficulty of taking a historian's-eye view of contemporary events,
saying that historians are lucky: writing the history of the past is
nothing; what's tricky is the history of the present. It is awkward, she
continues, to see and understand at one and the same time; besides,
the present doesn't like being recounted; it always contrives to
thwart its narrators, it piles up events all at once so as to mix the

truth up, just as theatre managers all give their first performances on the same day so as to nonplus the literary critics:

le présent n'aime pas à être raconté; il s'arrange toujours de manière à déjouer les narrateurs, il entasse tous les événements à la fois pour embrouiller la vérité, comme les directeurs de théâtre donnent tous leurs premières représentations le même jour pour dérouter la critique (342–3).

These women even adumbrate the writing of 'history from below' or 'women's history' to complement 'high history'. In 1846, Ancelot reinvests women's 'banal' accounts with value, in an argument that bears on chronicling of all kinds:

le même objet observé de deux places différentes change tellement d'aspect, qu'un sujet présenterait certainement à une femme d'autres idées que celles qu'il éveillerait dans l'esprit d'un homme.

(the same object observed from two different positions looks so changed that a given subject would certainly present a woman with different ideas from those it would awaken in the mind of a man.)

She continues with a 'fable' about two travellers setting off from the same point. If one of them, the free and strong one, races along, choosing any route, taking risks and throwing himself into dangers, while the other wends his way apprehensively and quietly ('craintif et paisible'), confining his meticulous observations to a modest, slowly followed path, won't he, perhaps, discover what the bold traveller might miss in his fiery impatience ('ardente impatience')? And, once they have both reached the same stopping-point, won't the tale that each tells need help from the other to be complete?[15]

Others comment on women's almost complete absence from history, arguing that this is in part because of the forced inability of women to contribute to world events. Adam, in her attack of 1858 on the anti-feminist socialist Proudhon, writes:

L'histoire de l'humanité existe-t-elle? C'est l'histoire des mâles dans l'humanité qu'il faudrait dire . . . En effet, la femme, nous dit-on, existe à peine dans l'histoire; et l'on se sert de cet argument contre elle. Son absence de l'histoire équivaut à un brevet d'incapacité.

(Does the history of humanity exist? We should call it the history of the males of humanity. . . Indeed, woman, we are told, barely exists in history; and this argument is used against her. Her absence from history is the equivalent of a certificate of unfitness.)

Adam suggests that famous women of the past distract from a true perception of women's history (here is an alternative view of 'role-models'): she says that we should not use a few great female individuals who are like markers planted on the path of progress to show that men were not alone when humanity passed that way; for, she repeats – more ironically this time – 'J'avoue que la femme existe à peine dans l'histoire' ('I admit that woman barely exists in history').[16] Adam plays here on the double meaning of 'history' (one, that which happened; two, the writing of that which happened). Like many women in the century, she has a well-developed understanding of the circular relationship between prejudice, world events and subsequent accounts of those events. None, however, exemplifies the understanding more grippingly and entertainingly than La Tour du Pin.

Finally, there is another, and sadder, reason for being interested in La Tour du Pin's writing. As important a question as why women start to write is why they stop: why, having produced obviously talented work, they leave it unpublished or incomplete. (Emily Dickinson is one case in point.) The first page of La Tour du Pin's memoirs is dated 'Le 1er janvier 1820'. A new decade, a new enterprise? But this is also four years to the month after the death of her adored eldest son Humbert in January 1816. She had thirty-three years to write the memoirs, but never got beyond an account of 1815. Humbert had died in his mid-twenties in especially tragic circumstances. Offended by a military colleague, he asked his father what *a friend* who had been insulted thus should do. The father replied unhesitatingly that this was a matter for a duel. Humbert promptly challenged his insulter (by then very ready to retract) and was killed.[17] Possibly, then, it was to commemorate her son that La Tour du Pin started to write; equally possibly, she stopped her story at 1815 because to relive that particular grief was unbearable for a woman whose most passionate attachments were – it is clear from the memoirs – to this son and to her husband.

CHAPTER 6

Mad matriarchs and other family members: Sophie Cottin

When Henriette de La Tour du Pin's mother tried to claim money that was rightfully hers from her own mother, the elder woman flew into a passion. (This was the same grandmother who was to treat Henriette herself harshly.) Maternal affection, continues La Tour du Pin, 'gave way to one of those incredible hatreds so beloved of writers of romances and tragedies' ('une haine inconcevable, telle que les romans ou les tragédies en ont décrites, prit en elle la place de la tendresse maternelle', 1 4). 'Incredible', 'romances', 'tragedies': seemingly, she wants to disbelieve in the hatred, but for all that, and despite her humour, she goes on to provide chilling illustrations of her grandmother's psychological bullying.[1] Here, cited as both a reality and a creature of fancy, is one of those 'mad matriarchs' whom Gilbert and Gubar find in Jane Austen's novels (*Madwoman in the Attic*, 174). She is prevalent in French imaginative writing too. If we are looking for 'images of women', here is one of them – redolent of the witch, springing from the pages not only of male misogynists but of women. And other images of parents, siblings, uncles and aunts show us what 'family romances' haunted these writers.[2]

Sophie Cottin (1770–1807) brings a special passion to the representation of the imaginary family, and to that of girls' filial conflicts and filial submissiveness. Hugo tells us in the chapter 'L'année 1817' of *Les Misérables* that 'Mme Cottin was declared the foremost writer of the time' – possibly with some admixture of irony in the 'declared'.[3] None the less, long after her death her five novels were still very popular not only in France but abroad; as well as into English, they had been translated into Danish, German, Italian, Portuguese and Spanish.[4] Her *Elisabeth ou les exilés de Sibérie* (1806) was especially popular in Britain and the US.[5] Elisabeth is a plucky daughter who surmounts divers perils to gain the Tsar's pardon for her parents, exiled to Siberia for political reasons; the novel ends with her happy homecoming and almost simultaneous betrothal to her beloved (Illustration 4). Amélie, the heroine of *Amélie Mansfield* (1803), has an unhappier fate.[6] She is destined, by order of her grandfather, to marry her cousin Ernest, a bully. But in defiance she has a brief and unsuccessful marriage with an artist. This ruins her standing in the eyes of Ernest's mother (her aunt), the haughty, strong-willed Mme de Woldemar. Amélie is widowed; she later falls in love with Ernest without at first recognizing him, not having seen him for years. Ernest loves her in return, but the furious opposition of his proud mother literally kills off the relationship: the lovers die within a few hours of each other.

Elisabeth exemplifies both the mawkish and the more interesting depictions of loyal child–parent relationships in early nineteenth-century French women's writing. Numerous works (both discursive and imaginative) advocating filial duty, and enjoining daughters in particular to obedience, were still appearing.[7] Even those which showed a daughter's momentary rebellion or disaffection could still end on a 'mother/father knows best' note, as does Gay's 1813 *Léonie de Montbreuse*, of which the last words – uttered by the father – are: 'de tous les moyens d'arriver au bonheur, le plus sûr est celui que choisit la prévoyante tendresse d'un père' ('of all the paths to happiness, the surest is that chosen by a father's far-sighted tenderness', 296). In Cottin's *Elisabeth*, this promotion of filial duty reaches almost incestuous proportions. At a moment when Elisabeth and her admirer Smoloff are strongly attracted to each other (and Cottin provides a surprisingly erotic description of Smoloff's gaze upon Elisabeth), we are immediately reassured that Elisabeth's heart had no feeling which did not relate to her parents and was not entirely for them ('qui ne se rapportât à ses parents, et qui ne fût entièrement pour eux', 39). Indeed, to remove any lingering suspicion that Smoloff might come between Elisabeth and her parents Cottin indicates that he will be the perfect son-in-law. He sees Elisabeth's mother Phédora combing her daughter's hair and is 'deeply moved' by these simple and tender attentions – which daily touch Elisabeth herself ever more; Smoloff feels it is impossible to love Elisabeth without loving her mother too, and that to the happiness of marrying this girl is attached 'a happiness almost as great, that of being Phédora's son' ('un bonheur presqu'aussi grand, celui d'être le fils de Phédora', 58–9). Indeed, Elisabeth's final acceptance of him is couched as a plea to him never to leave her parents (161). Such

Elle se précipita tout en larmes devant la porte où dormaient ses parens :

4. 'She flung herself in tears before her sleeping parents' door': Elisabeth returns home. (From *Elisabeth ou les exilés de Sibérie*, by Sophie Cottin, 1820.)

strands of the plot point to underlying guilt about female eroticism, and fear at the prospect of breaking the filial tie; indeed, the epigraph of the work has already weighted the scales: 'La mère en prescrira la lecture à sa fille' ('The mother will direct her daughter to read this'). It was not uncommon, either at the time or previously, to see novels as a 'meeting-point' for mothers and daughters; the inhibiting effects of this on writers may be imagined.[8]

Nevertheless, even these dutiful works can put forward more challenging ideas: for instance, that characteristics from both parents can influence daughters. Thus, although Cottin may resort to stereotypes for Elisabeth's parents – the father having 'extraordinary energy' while the mother has 'angelic gentleness' – she also, more subtly, shows the fusion in the daughter of 'masculine' and 'feminine' qualities; for, it is said, Elisabeth received different types of education from her father and mother, and her character combined these (22–3). So daughters can – and in this novel spectacularly do – emulate their fathers' 'male' qualities. Another early novel, Duras's *Edouard* (1825), suggests that the mother forms some sort of half-way point between father and son: the father's determined character and the son's tendency to reverie meet in her, for she is like the harmonious nuance that unites two vivid and overly distinct colours ('comme la nuance harmonieuse qui unit deux couleurs vives et trop tranchées', 42). Through these fictional parents and their offspring, Cottin and Duras are apparently questioning the notion that certain characteristics are inherently male or female; and such questions about parent–child influence are put with greater force by mid- and late-century discursive writers. Deraismes points out that physical characteristics are inherited equally from mother and father, deducing from this that moral ones are too; while even the conservative Pauline Craven remarks that mothers should give their qualities to their sons, fathers to their daughters.[9]

However, the imaginative writers more usually create sharp differentiations between the parents or parent-substitutes – after all, these make for more exciting plots – and there is a degree of consistency in the differentiations. Mothers are normally self-sacrificing and idolized in pre-1830 fiction and verse, and remain so well on into the century: the feminist Niboyet is still claiming in 1847 that Russian women are 'sublime in their maternal devotion'; as late as 1880, the heroine of Thérèse Bentzon's *Yette* – now a fully qualified teacher – wants a flat, not in order to gain independence for its own sake, but as a repository for the 'dear relics' of her now dead mother.[10]

Even so, some tentatively query the 'naturalness' of maternal love. Once again, and despite *Elisabeth*, Cottin provides the template: Amélie, in order to be with Ernest, leaves the young son she has had by her husband. The child's bewilderment and pain are described in some detail; nevertheless, this is not enough to make Amélie return (III 68). Later writers are a little more vocal on the theme. George Sand sometimes undermines the idea that women are 'naturally' maternal:

Toutes les femmes peuvent avoir des enfants, toutes les femmes ne sont pas curieuses d'enfants pour cela . . . A dire vrai, un petit enfant est un rude maître, injuste comme un mari qui serait fol, obstiné comme une bête affamée.[11]

(All women can have children – that doesn't mean all women are interested in children . . . Truth to tell, a small child is a harsh task-master, as unjust as a crazy husband, as stubborn as a starving animal.)

And the poet Blanchecotte even wrote a sonnet 'To my mother', reproaching this mother for her lack of love: memories of my childhood torture me, says the narrator; my life was as isolated as if in a desert; 'I think of the days I spent in your indifference, of the painful disdain with which you greeted my love' ('Je pense aux jours passés dans votre indifférence, / Au douloureux dédain à mon amour offert', *Rêves et réalités*, 133).

There was, then, room for doubt about 'real' mothers: more than one might expect in a century when maternity was more than ever flagged as *the* role for a woman – from the left as well as from the right.[12] Furthermore, in the pre-1830 fiction the loving mothers may be conveniently dead; this leaves writers free to focus on (rare) disagreeable mothers or (more frequent) mother-figures such as adoptive mothers, older female relatives, family 'friends', potential mothers-in-law. These are deranged, destructive or both, and they clash head-on with sons' or daughters' sexual self-determination. All these early novelists – still more angrily than their eighteenth-century female forebears – depict the evils of arranged marriage, and it is almost always the mothers or mother-figures who do the forcing, as for instance in Krüdener's *Valérie*: the hero's friend has had to give up the woman he loves because his mother – not 'parents' or 'father', but mother – did not approve (178–9).[13]

The most militant and most theatrical depictions of this inter-generational struggle are in, respectively, Staël's two novels and

Amélie Mansfield. In *Delphine*, Léonce's mother is resolute that he shall
not betray his class and reputation, and she, together with the
mother of Léonce's intended bride, successfully constructs elaborate
mechanisms to ensure he does not marry Delphine.[14] In *Amélie
Mansfield*, the matriarch Mme de Woldemar first insists that Amélie
must marry Ernest, dismissing reports of his youthful violence against
her with the comment that it is 'unsuitable for women to harbour
such resentment' ('il ne convenait pas aux femmes d'avoir tant de
rancune'). Once Amélie has disgraced the family, she insists that
Ernest must *not* stay with Amélie. Mme de Woldemar's determination all but drives her mad: from the beginning, there are comments
on her 'lunatic' ('forcené') pride, and near the end one character
observes that she has become divided against herself; she does not
survive her niece and son for long. Throughout, the ferocity of her
hatred of Amélie is dramatically highlighted. She curses her,
removes her allotted place from the family pew, burns her portrait
and erases her name from the family tree; her physical revulsion
shows in her very movements ('il y avait dans son geste tant
d'aversion pour Amélie'); and she unhesitatingly humiliates her son
once he has fallen in love with Amélie: 'the noble Count de
Woldemar wants the hand of the woman who preferred a vile artist
to him!' ('le noble comte de Woldemar désire la main de celle qui lui
préféra un vil artiste!')[15]

The hyperbolically haughty or oppressive matriarch occurs less
often after the first third of the century, but she never quite goes
away. Her presence is felt mid-century in, for example, a satirical
poem by Anaïs Ségalas about the arrogant dreams of an old noble-
woman whose eyes 'couldn't possibly droop into a commoner's
sleep' ('Ne sauraient s'assoupir d'un sommeil roturier'), and who is
proud to possess 'parchments still more ancient than herself'.[16] She
resurfaces in Stern's *Nélida*, in the shape of the heroine's aunt, who
scarcely allows the girl out; will not let her go to balls; and has
prearranged her marriage at age eighteen, being completely under
the yoke of high society's conventions ('complètement sous le joug
des idées reçues dans le monde': 4, 7, 8). And the matriarch puts in a
full-blown reappearance in the popular end-of-century novelist
Henry (Alice) Gréville – at a safe distance in Russia, but strangely
recognizable. In *Les Koumiassine* (1877) Gréville describes a class-
ridden society in which the absurdly hidebound countess Koumiassine rules her husband and family with a rod of iron; generally an

object of humour, she becomes sinister when exerting this power over her adoptive daughter Vassilissa, a poor relation.[17] She has firm ideas as to Vassilissa's future husband, ideas Vassilissa does not share. She shakes Vassilissa, who still refuses:

La comtesse eut un moment l'idée de broyer sur le parquet, sous ses bottines, la frêle enfant qui lui résistait ainsi. C'était la première fois de sa vie qu'elle avait affaire à la résistance ouverte, avouée, sans concessions. (1 190)

(For a moment, the countess had the idea of crushing – with her boots, on the floor – the frail child who was resisting her. It was the first time she had ever encountered open and unreserved resistance.)

Vassilissa is threatened with the convent; all but imprisoned; shaken again and thrown to her knees (II 53–5). The countess is likened by other characters, including her own young son, to a wolf or ogre; she plays with Vassilissa like a cat with a mouse 'before coldly butchering it', and is said to be at that point of aberration where all events become subordinate to the idea one is pursuing (II 87–8, 98–9, 115, 209).

It would hardly be possible for male family members to be worse, and they are not. Once more, the pattern was laid down in the first third of the century. A few cold or harsh fathers appeared.[18] But even Oswald's father in *Corinne*, for all his patriarchal ordering of his son's marital future, is more moderate and reasoned than the pathologically repressive Lady Edgermond, the stepmother with whom Corinne spends the latter part of her adolescence. Older men sometimes argue in favour of love-matches, as does one relative in *Amélie Mansfield*; and fathers can rejoice in daughters' achievements: when Elisabeth returns from her trip, the father feels a 'tender pride'.[19] In an 1821 novel by Pauline Guizot, two siblings, Raoul and Adrienne, whose mother has died, are brought up by their father and grandmother. Adrienne is accustomed to 'quite striking injustices' from the grandmother, for 'the rule was that everything went her brother's way' ('il était de règle que tout cédât à son frère'); it seems natural to her not to ask for or expect anything for herself. However, her father notices the inequality 'forced upon her' ('à laquelle elle était soumise'), and shows her more marked tenderness in order to make amends for this ('l'en dédommager').[20] Thus fathers or father-figures come to the rescue and will do so throughout the century. Joy at finding long-lost fathers; grandfathers who encourage learning; daughters refusing to marry until fathers are taken off the list of émigrés; fathers less prejudiced than mothers, prouder of their daughters, more tolerant of tomboyishness: these pepper the backgrounds of nineteenth-century heroines created by women.[21] As we have seen, many fathers do seem to have been supportive in reality, but even if they were not, in imagination they are 'good'. An intelligent autobiographer sums it up – the Flora Tristan whose uncle is refusing to acknowledge her share in her father's inheritance because of her (disputed) illegitimacy:

Cet oncle qui m'avait fait tant de mal . . . eh bien! je l'aimais; je l'aimais *malgré ma volonté*, tant les premières impressions de l'enfance sont durables et puissantes! . . . Ah! qui peut expliquer les bizarreries du cœur humain? Nous aimons, nous haïssons, ainsi que Dieu le veut, sans pouvoir, le plus souvent, en assigner le motif.[22]

(This uncle who'd done me so much harm . . . well! I loved him; I loved him *against my will*, so durable and powerful are the earliest impressions of childhood! . . . Ah! who can explain the quirks of the human heart? We love and hate as God wishes, and more often than not we can't assign a cause.) (author's italics)

Fathers and father-figures are also sometimes identified with God, and later in the century some poets were to play on the cross-over between 'père' and 'Père', notably Desbordes-Valmore in her 'La couronne effeuillée'. The narrator will take her leafless crown to her father's garden, the garden where flowers can bloom once more; there, for a long time, her soul will kneel, will flood forth; her father has secrets that can conquer sadness:

> J'irai, j'irai porter ma couronne effeuillée
> Au jardin de mon père où revit toute fleur;
> J'y répandrai longtemps mon âme agenouillée:
> Mon père a des secrets pour vaincre la douleur.

The fact that this father is God becomes explicit only half-way through the five-stanza poem ('Chère âme,' he says, 'je suis Dieu': my house is yours, 232).[23] In Tastu, the father again has God-like power: he is the Zephyr who can create or destroy the humble veronica (speedwell) flower:

> Souvent, Véronique éphémère,
> Un souffle léger de ton père
> Suffit pour emporter ta fleur
>
> . . .
>
> Un jeu du Zéphir t'a fait naître,
> Un jeu du Zéphir te détruit!   (23–6)

(Often, fleeting Veronica, a light breath of your father's is enough to blow away your blossom . . . Zephyr's game gave birth to you, Zephyr's game destroys you!)

Even the late-century atheist poet Ackermann, for whom neither 'God' nor Nature is trustworthy, still figures God as a relatively benign father whereas Nature is a 'marâtre', harsh mother (French has a special word for this woman) (*Œuvres*, 152).[24]

Finally, male siblings have a generally good press from these women writers, again particularly from the early ones. Brothers or brother-figures (in the form of, say, cousins) often figure. Sometimes they conjure up titillating images of incest, à la *René*: this contemporary topos appears in *Valérie, Amélie Mansfield, Ourika* and *Olivier*.[25] But they hold back. (In Choiseul-Meuse's *Julie* of 1807, a brother and sister may be suspected of incest, but – in a novel where almost everything else happens – this suspicion is the only one that proves false: I 220–40; II 1–25.) By the end of the century, however, not only is brother–sister incest committed but the sister becomes pregnant as a result (in Camille Pert's *Le Frère* of 1896).[26]

However, brother-figures have other functions. They also support erring sisters, as does Amélie Mansfield's devoted brother Albert.[27] Still more interestingly, the brother–sister relationship may raise the issue of equality between the sexes. The heroine of Genlis's 1802 novel *Mademoiselle de Clermont* remarks that as she is twenty-two and her father is no longer alive, her brother's superior age and rank give him a purely formal authority over her; Nature has made her his equal, and she can decide her own future ('la nature m'a faite son égale . . . je puis disposer de moi-même . . .').[28] Similarly, where there is a bond such that brothers – or male cousins – are heroines' soul-mates, as in *Amélie Mansfield* or *Olivier*, this takes back to its origins Beauvoir's famous dictum that 'you are not born a woman, you become one'. To show sibling-figures so close that nothing differentiates them but the accident of gender suggests the arbitrariness of the conventions imposed on the growing child. If, then, early women writers 'take over' this popular contemporary subject, they mould it to their own ends.

Thus these authors were, in the first third of the century, setting up models of the family which were to influence their successors' writing. Good mothers are often out of the way, being replaced by bad or mad substitutes; fathers are loving and forward-looking, brothers generally friendly – or more. We can look at this configuration purely as the 'acting-out' of an Œdipal fantasy in which the mother is the hated rival (substitutes being necessary to avoid guilt), the father the adored and adoring parent. As such, the model looks like a displacement of the problem: these women 'should' have been blaming patriarchs, but the blame was focused on a supposed matriarchy. It may be, then, that they were expressing merely unconscious conflicts; or, in this first third of the century when melodrama was so popular, they may simply have been casting about for satisfactory villains. Yet parts of this picture, if not all, are recognizable from what we know of the women's lives, and doubtless it was through an upbringing by older females that usage was primarily transmitted. It may be supposed that these writers are locating one source of personal repression – the mothers who, apparently even more than the fathers, forced them to 'become women'; and they re-create them with horror.

CHAPTER 7

Rank and race: Claire de Duras

'The forced marriage' is not only a favourite illustration of maternal
tyranny. Given that arranged marriage was largely a matter for the
upper classes, it incorporates another still more popular topos of
these early decades: rank. As daughters of the Enlightenment,
women writers find varied vehicles for a critique of all kinds of social
stratification. Whatever their class, they highlight the problematic
nature of 'privilege' – privilege of gender, race, physical attributes.
No moderately broad-minded aristocrat could be unaware of this
perspective, as we have seen with La Tour du Pin, while in a
bourgeois writer like Cottin we find one character exclaiming:
'quand j'ai passé ma journée à faire du bien, je trouverais fort
mauvais qu'un noble prétendît valoir mieux que moi, seulement
parce que ses aïeux auraient été aux croisades' ('when I've spent my
day doing good, I'd take a poor view of any nobleman claiming he
was worth more than me just because his ancestors had been at the
Crusades – so he says').[1] Among other 1800–1815 writers questioning rank are Gay, who depicts a lower-class girl nearly raped by
the fickle young nobleman the heroine thinks she loves – her
sympathy for the girl is part of her awakening; and Genlis, whose
Mlle de Clermont (of a higher status than the man she loves)
exclaims, 'Que je le hais, ce rang funeste où le sort m'a placée'
('How I hate this fatal rank in which destiny has placed me'). She
can be still more vehement: 'Ce rang envié n'est qu'un rôle fatigant
ou barbare qui nous impose jusqu'au tombeau les plus douloureux
sacrifices et la loi honteuse d'une constante dissimulation!' ('This
envied rank is only a role – a tiring or barbaric one which forces on
us till the day of our death the most painful sacrifices and a shameful
law of constant dissimulation!')[2]

A number of writers extend this consideration of 'status'. Staël's
Lord Oswald Nelvil rescues social marginals and outcasts: he saves

from a fire lunatics trapped in their asylum and Jews in their ghetto, the locals being happy to leave them to their fate. This is one of his first acts: its generosity indicates that he is to some extent a fitting partner for Corinne. Staël and other writers also depict deformed or physically disadvantaged heroes and heroines: Sainte-Beuve comments on the literary trend, during this period, for infirmities or what he calls 'bizarreries' of nature.[3] When the women seize on these, it is sometimes with voyeurism, sometimes with an obvious wish to make a polemical point. So, in *Delphine*, a female character suggests that her husband's blindness makes him her 'equal', in that he becomes as dependent on her as she would normally be on him – and, she says, he will not be able to note her fading looks as time passes, which is always an ordeal for a woman (I 439–40). Here, then, a man's physical handicap 'levels out' sexual inequality. Staël's commentary is not without callousness. But the more feeling authors explore this area with compassion, and turn the 'dis-advantage' into a powerful symbol while preserving a sense of the suffering it brings to its owner. Such is Claire de Duras, a writer who since the early 1990s has started to achieve the recognition she deserves.[4]

Claire de Duras (1777–1838) had an often unhappy life.[5] Her parents separated in 1792, and the next year her father was guillotined (she heard of this from a newspaper crier on the dock at Bordeaux as she and her mother were setting sail for America). Her mother suffered from mental illness; the husband she married in 1797 treated her coldly and they quarrelled constantly. Nevertheless, she had the qualities of personality and intellect to take successful charge of the family finances during her and her mother's emigra-tion and later to run a famous salon under Louis XVIII. At the age of thirty-one she became, and remained, Chateaubriand's close friend and protector; in 1824, aged forty-seven, she began to publish the fiction she had previously circulated privately to friends.

Duras was personally unconfident, believing herself to be ugly; and she was sensitive to ridicule and parody. Parody was highly popular in France throughout the nineteenth century.[6] For example, in 1805 one of many parodies of melodrama was advertised as:

Roderic [sic] *et Cunégonde, ou l'Hermite de Montmartre, ou la Forteresse de Moulinos, ou le Revenant de la galerie de l'Ouest*, galimathias [sic] burlesco-mélo-patho-dramatique en 4 actes sans entr'actes . . . enjolivé de cavernes et de voleurs, égayé par un fantôme et réchauffé par un incendie.

(*Roderick and Cunégonde, or the Hermit of Montmartre, or the Fortress of Moulinos, or the Ghost of the West gallery*, a load of burlesco-melo-patho-dramatic rubbish in 4 acts with no intervals . . . embellished with caves and thieves, enlivened by a ghost and warmed up with a fire.)

Parasitic works, written under such pseudonyms as Larmaloeil (Tearineye), would appear very soon after the publication or performance of the 'host': thus, in the late century, *L'Assommoir pour rire* was put on less than one month after the stage version of the Zola novel. These parodies could be considered a tribute to the original or such good publicity that authors might even pen parodies of themselves, as did Alexandre Dumas in 1829. But Dumas was a man. Although some women (such as Krüdener) bore parody with panache, it was probably more difficult for most to endure, and would appear to have been so for Duras.[7] After the circulation of *Ourika* in unpublished form, she was dubbed Ourika, her two daughters Bourika and Bourgeonika, and absurd versions of *Ourika* appeared: it was to combat these that she went into print. Matters became worse after the circulation of *Olivier*: in 1826 Latouche published a licentious parody of this which, confused with the original, created such a scandal that Duras never published anything again.[8]

The only works, then, for which we know her are *Ourika* (1824), *Edouard* (1825) and *Olivier ou le secret* (written 1821–2, it had to wait until 1971 before publication).[9] Ourika is a young black girl rescued from the slave trade at the age of two and brought up by a French aristocrat, Mme de B. Perfectly happy until the age of fifteen, she suddenly realizes the true nature of her situation when, from behind a screen, she overhears a conversation between her benefactress and the marquise de *** (Illustration 5).

Qui voudra jamais [asks this marquise] épouser une négresse? Et si, à force d'argent, vous trouvez quelqu'un qui consente à avoir des enfants nègres, ce sera un homme d'une condition inférieure, et avec qui elle se trouvera malheureuse. (17)

(Who will ever want to marry a negress? And if, by throwing money at him, you find someone who'll agree to have negro children, it will be a man of inferior condition, with whom she'll be unhappy.)

Ourika becomes profoundly depressed and views her own face and body with loathing. She eventually realises (again with the 'help' of the marquise de ***) that she is in love with Mme de B.'s son Charles (hopelessly, since he is engaged to a beautiful French girl). She enters

5. Ourika behind the screen. (From *Ourika*, by Claire de Duras, 1824.)

a convent and dies from her depression. As Léon-François Hoffmann says, this is the first time in French literature that colour prejudice is exposed in all its absurdity; for nothing but her race distinguishes Ourika from the most accomplished girls.[10]

Duras's Edouard is from the bourgeoisie, the son of a well-known lawyer; this connection gains him entry into the circle of the aristocrat with whose daughter Natalie he falls in love. But from the beginning his feeling for her is bound up with his consciousness of his social inferiority: my destiny, he thinks, has separated me from her, I am not her equal, she would lower herself if she gave herself to me (48). This matters more to him than to her, but revealing incidents demonstrate the difficulty: thus the duc de L. . ., with 'deliberate malice', encourages a rumour that Natalie is already Edouard's mistress but then, with cool insolence, refuses to fight a duel with Edouard because of his inferior rank (119–25). Edouard leaves to fight with the French troops in America, allowing himself to be killed, while Natalie goes into a decline and dies.

The outline of *Olivier* is familiar as the source of Stendhal's *Armance* (1827). Two cousins, Louise and Olivier, love each other, but Olivier will neither commit himself to marriage nor directly explain his hesitation. Under pressure from Louise, who tells him she fears she is going mad, he speaks more plainly, but is still torn between his wish to disclose and not disclose:

Jamais, jamais je ne te serrerai dans mes bras, jamais nous ne serons unis. Ah! Louise, tu me demandes ce funeste secret, mais je ne puis te le dire, tout mon sang se révolte à cette pensée de dévoiler mon malheur. (186)

(Never, never will I hold you in my arms, never will we be as one. Ah! Louise, you ask me for my dreadful secret, but I can't tell you; every drop of blood in my body rises up in revolt at the thought of revealing my misfortune.)

Until the end Louise is still offering to sacrifice her reputation and become his mistress, but we cannot be sure what she has or has not guessed (194). Olivier shoots himself, and Louise goes mad.

These three novels of Duras's are economically narrated (the longest, *Edouard*, is less than 100 pages). Where they resort to the rhetorical devices of the period, such as exclamatory repetition, these are well motivated by the unusual and poignant contexts and are without bombast. The novels are also fine in their use of figurative language and submerged echoes of other authors. Olivier, for example, expresses his anguish through first a subdued, then a fuller metaphor: 'Mon âme, formée de traits à peine esquissés, comprend tout et ne maîtrise rien . . . Plus misérable que le roseau, je plie et ne me relève pas' ('My heart, made from barely sketched-out lines [or 'features'], understands everything, masters nothing . . . More wretched than the reed, I bend, I don't rise up again'). This metaphor, while indicating Olivier's physical state, invokes La Fontaine's fable *Le Chêne et le roseau*, in which the flexible reed survives the rigid oak toppled by the wind; here, however, Olivier is both reed and fallen oak ('ne me relève pas'). The wording of the image, with its 'misérable', also alludes to Pascal, for whom humanity is merely a 'thinking reed' possessed by 'misery' without God. Duras's metaphor makes her hero represent the equal helplessness of the mighty and the weak (with both class and bodily overtones), and, more generally, mankind.

This symbolism – what we might call a 'symbolism of disadvantage' – also shapes *Ourika* and *Edouard*. Can we go so far as to say that impotence, blackness and low rank all 'equal' womanhood?[11] Ourika herself would appear to envisage such connections: when the French Revolution comes she has a moment of hope, thinking that in this 'great disorder' she may find a place in society: 'toutes les formes renversées, tous les rangs confondus, tous les préjugés évanouis' ('all social forms overturned, all ranks intermingling, all prejudices vanished') would bring about a state of affairs where she would be 'moins étrangère' ('less foreign', 25). The triple repetition of 'tout' in this statement associates all victims of fixed classification. This then gives way to a more nuanced view, since Ourika soon sees that 'il resterait encore assez de mépris pour moi au milieu de tant d'adversité' ('there'd still be enough contempt left over for me in the midst of such adversity', 26). Nevertheless, the putative link between blackness and other disadvantaged states has been voiced, and the connection with womanhood is suggested also by the fact that Ourika understands her destiny only at the age of puberty. There is some confusion in the novel as to whether she is twelve or fifteen at this moment – but the point is that childhood is past and she is on the threshold of adulthood: she herself says that the overheard conversation 'opened my eyes and ended my youth' (15). Like most adolescent girls, Ourika now definitively realizes that her appearance is to be all-defining.

Ourika's lamentations over her blackness may also be read as a lament over being born a creature with a physical mark that is, or seems to be, as crippling as a deformity. She removes mirrors from her room and always wears gloves, clothes that cover her neck and arms, and a hat with a veil which she often keeps on even in the house. Little, in his sharp and scholarly reading of this work in the light of Frantz Fanon's *Peau noire masques blancs* (1952), argues that we must not over-allegorize Ourika's blackness.[12] But it would be equally limiting to ignore the tight nexus formed by Duras, not only between gender and status, but also between these and physical 'infirmity'.

A similar interplay of rank and gender takes place in *Edouard*.[13] Edouard's 'low' social status almost makes of him the woman and his beloved the man; besides, he displays a certain femaleness or androgyny. For example, the frame-narrator, when wounded, says that Edouard gives him a woman's care, with its charm and delicacy (30). Growing up, Edouard begins to enjoy both learning and his mother's affection; to describe this double process, he combines the imagery of both female virginity and the phallic: it was like the tearing of inner veils, the sudden growth of a young tree (37). When Natalie speaks to him in a newly tender tone, he likens himself to a woman, saying he preserved this tone like a mother clasping her child in her arms (71). And he himself points out the mixing of gender roles and social status in a statement that reflects the twin tensions of the novel:

Mais est-ce d'une femme . . . qu'on devrait recevoir protection et appui? Dans ce monde factice tout est interverti, ou plutôt c'est ma passion pour elle qui change ainsi les rapports naturels. (77)

(But is it a woman who should be protecting and supporting one? Everything's transposed in this artificial world, or rather it's my passion for her that's changing natural relations like this.)

Olivier ou le secret is even richer in implication than *Edouard*, partly because, as a 'secretive' narrative, it has a large number of metaphors. (Others besides that of the reed subtly suggest a combined physical, social and metaphysical condition.) The plot-presentation also entails ambiguities and hesitation: key scenes combine urgency with uncertainty. For instance, Olivier overhears two male characters say – something; he has a duel with one of them. Here is 'adventure', suspense, but we do not know exactly what comment has occasioned the duel; nor can we, even at this stage, be quite sure that Olivier is impotent. Excitement, hesitation, or both? In this tale almost everything is 'overheard' or guessed, little is real. Similarly with the enigma of the ending: Louise, in her madness, reveals nothing, simply walking daily, whatever the weather, to the place of her last rendez-vous with Olivier, then returning after sunset. As the modern editor of the work remarks, this repeated walk is an image of the ever-escaping secret (Virieux: *Olivier*, 55).

Duras has affinities here with contemporary male Romantic authors, many of whom foreground 'the indefinable' and, in Chateaubriand's famous phrase, 'le vague des passions' ('the vagueness of the passions'). But Duras suggests more profound hermeneutic questions than they do; *Olivier* introduces a modern preoccupation with 'interpretation', reticence and the sexuality (or not) of narratives.[14] (The epistolary form serves this purpose well, since all the communications are themselves written texts.) Had Duras not been a woman and cowed into silence, she would have published *Olivier* and would now be recognized as a pioneer.

The young Desbordes-Valmore also, in these early decades, sees the possibility of weaving together rank, gender and – even – women's writing, in a poem of 1819, 'Le Ver luisant'.[15] A conceited glow-worm, who talks of himself as a noble lord, is gobbled up by a female nightingale. (Desbordes-Valmore calls the bird not the masculine 'rossignol', but 'Philomèle', which enables her to refer to it in the feminine.) Philomela uses the 'nourishment' provided by the supposedly lordly worm to create her song, her art: 'S'en nourrit, pour chanter plus longtemps sa douleur' ('Feeds off it, the longer to sing her sorrow'). This contemptuous glow-worm had referred to his social inferiors as 'ces vers roturiers' ('commoner-worms'): is Desbordes-Valmore punning? As a working-class poet, she could be thought to be writing 'vers roturiers', 'a commoner's poetry', herself.[16] At the least, her representation of gender and rank acquires a threatening fluidity, as does that of other post-Revolutionary women writers.

Successors took the cue and copied or extended similar images of 'ranking'. Much popular literature of the whole century, by both men and women, caters to class feeling of various kinds, bringing into play villainous nobles, upright workers and virtuous lower-class women; or, it may be, a more snobbish audience is targeted with exquisitely refined aristocrats in 'society novels'.[17] However, mid- and late-century women writers often operate, like the early-century ones, on a more complex level. They continue, for instance, to explore the difficulties created by loves between upper-class women and lower-class men; or they highlight the double exploitation of working-class women by more socially powerful men – double because the men have both higher status and 'higher' gender.[18]

One cue they were slower to seize, however, was that of racism, whether anti-black or anti-semitic. The figure of Ourika herself remained popular, perhaps less as a black than as an outcast. But other depictions of blacks are equivocal, throughout the century.[19] Possibly this was in part owing to the Algerian campaign (1830 to about 1850), which meant that everything 'African' was for a while perceived as anti-French.[20] To be sure, impeccably liberal writers like Tristan, Colet or Voilquin express horror at slavery – but also, at times, an offensive aversion to blacks, or an unexamined assumption that white is beautiful, black is not; at the end of the century Bentzon, while attacking some prejudices, and remarking that blacks' 'habits of lying' in her fictional Martinique are a result of slavery, nevertheless reproduces with shameless condescension stereotypes of gambolling piccaninnies and feckless black men with rolling eyes.[21]

Women's picture of Jews is rather more favourable, although many harbour anti-Semitic feeling, whether overt or covert. Despite the fact that Michel and Calmann Lévy published a number of female authors, they glibly rehearse the usual calumnies at intervals throughout the century, from the young Girardin on deicide and the blood-curse in her 1820s poem 'Magdeleine' to others who tirelessly reproduce the image of the greedy Jew as money-maker (this appears in both Sand's correspondence and her travel writing).[22] In the last third of the century particularly, where anti-Semitism exists it becomes more pronounced: no doubt the rise of the nationalist right wing, and the Dreyfus Affair, played their part. Gyp, a self-declared anti-Semite, describes a 'repellent' Jewish section of the opera audience in her 1886 *Autour du divorce* (one of the works published by Calmann Lévy).[23] Krysinska, herself probably of Jewish origin, nevertheless stages a heartless Jewish usurer in a poem of the 1880s.[24] And in her *Réminiscences* of 1879, Pauline Craven relates with amused approval how, every time the child of an Italian friend saw a crucifix, she would exclaim 'Oh! brutti Giudei!' ('Bad Jews!', 259). However, in this last part of the century Louise Michel, as might be expected, gives a not only unprejudiced but affectionate view of an elderly Jewish woman and her customs; and earlier, in the mid-century, there are clear signs that the more thoughtful writers have not forgotten the lessons of the Enlightenment and are struggling against their own prejudices.[25] As well as pandering to anti-Semitic stereotype, Sand also details the horrors to which the Inquisition subjected Jews, and says of her talented and kind-hearted singer Consuelo that, although of Spanish origin, she could just as easily have been Jewish; Ségalas and Voilquin see Jews not as exploiters but as victims; and other writers prefer analysis to the knee-jerk response, including Tristan, who in *Pérégrinations d'une paria* discusses the economic roots of anti-Semitism and in *Union ouvrière* holds up Jews as an example to the working class: that of unity in the face of persecution.[26] Symptomatic is the case of Louise Colet, who in a youthful poem ('Le Chant d'Ahasvérus', written when she was twenty-six), bids her Jew, blasphemer of Christ, to wander to the end of the world, be forever proscribed, etc., but who by the time she wrote *Lui* at the age of fifty was repudiating these prejudices. Her narrator enters the Jewish cemetery of Venice, which an intolerant city had exiled beyond the city walls; he thinks of the contempt and proscription which for so long afflicted, even in death, the great Jewish race ('cette grande race juive'). He continues:

Belle, tenace, intelligente, à travers tant de siècles de persécutions, elle s'est maintenue distincte et forte; sa patience héréditaire a triomphé des obstacles et des humiliations; aujourd'hui ses fils règnent à l'égal des chrétiens: plusieurs par le génie des lettres et des arts, un plus grand nombre par l'industrie, cette puissance nouvelle des temps modernes . . . qui donc oserait se détourner d'eux! (206–7)[27]

(Fine-looking, tenacious, intelligent, this race has kept its distinctness and strength throughout centuries of persecution; its hereditary patience has triumphed over obstacles and humiliations; today its sons reign on the same footing as Christians: several through their literary and artistic genius, more through industry, the new power of modern times . . . who would dare to turn away from them!)

Some fear, however, still shows through in the 'Jew as industrialist' and the 'who would dare' near the end.

Almost none of these post-1830 women was, then, so humanely free of racism as those of the first third of the century, and none was so far-reaching or imaginative on the question of 'birth-disadvantages' as Duras. She and her contemporaries also probably played a quiet part in the development of French aesthetic theory. The undermining of 'ranking' of all kinds, and the focus on the 'physically unacceptable', helped forward that weakening of aesthetic hierarchies which Hugo and others were to promulgate from the late 1820s onwards.[28] Workers or weak and mediocre characters as central figures; hunchbacks as heroes; deformed old women as pitiful yet paradoxically dignified subjects (Baudelaire's 'Les Petites Vieilles'); humble objects as fitting matter for literature and painting: this shift in sensibility had precedents in pre-1800 painters or novelists, but was to attain its most radical form only in the middle and late nineteenth century. It owed something to the early nineteenth-century women writers. They extended the egalitarianism of 1789, and they understood better than most of their male contemporaries the symbolism of revaluing the 'low'.

CHAPTER 8

The invisible women of French theatre

At first sight it seems paradoxical to speak of 'invisible women' in this period of French theatre. There had been a few successful, and certainly visible, female theatre managers in the late eighteenth century, the most notable being Mlles Raucourt and Montansier.[1] We still know the names of outstanding nineteenth-century actresses: Mlle Mars (1779–1847), Marie Dorval (1798–1849), and the most illustrious, Sarah Bernhardt (1845–1923); some have left us their reflections or memoirs – Bernhardt herself, and Judith (1827–1912) – albeit ghosted in some cases.[2] As for playwrights, under the Ancien Régime there had been a handful of famous ones (for example, Marie-Anne Barbier, 1670–1745), and in the nineteenth century, some women already well launched in other genres wrote for the stage: Sand, Girardin, Rachilde.[3] But who were the other women playwrights? We know they existed: Charles Beaumont Wicks, in his monumental compilation of nineteenth-century French plays and playwrights, lists about 200 female authors (out of a total seven or eight thousand), and there may be more hiding under male pseudonyms or anonymous initials.[4] But even the *Bloomsbury Guide* excludes the vast majority of these. They fare still worse in a recent wide-ranging work on the French theatre (edited by a French woman) which includes only Sand and Rachilde, and then principally for their relations with actors and male playwrights rather than in their own right as authors.[5] Although F. W. J. Hemmings's fascinating books on nineteenth-century French theatre allow us to make informed guesses about conditions for women dramatists, he too says almost nothing specific about them.[6] Thus, if most nineteenth-century French women writers are half-forgotten, it is not an exaggeration to say that the 200 playwrights are still invisible. The early century is a good place to start exploring the reasons, and my two paradigmatic playwrights – the successful Bawr and the 'failure'

Elisa Mercœur – are taken from this period. But the chapter also encompasses the century as a whole, mainly because female dramatists' situation changed relatively little, or even worsened, as the century went on.

Women's theatrical activities in the first part of the century were not only subject to prejudices inherited from earlier periods, but also encountered new limitations. For example, female spectators were still banned from the 'parterre', the pit, which thus stayed rowdy and potentially aggressive to authors as well as performers; actresses remained in a minority on the prestigious Comédie Française reading committee (which decided what plays should be produced), and they had never been allowed to train novice actors, male or female.[7] But in addition, in 1824 women were explicitly forbidden to manage theatres.[8] And actresses were officially excluded from the Comédie Française reading committee in 1853.[9]

Despite the vast numbers of plays staged, nineteenth-century French drama was struggling against specific difficulties as a genre. Tight censorship; the need to play to the pit; and a pervasive uncertainty as to where drama was going – verse or prose? neoclassical, Shakespearean or 'modern'? – all inclined the 'canonical' writers to prefer, sooner or later, novels or poetry. The drama of the period is now generally perceived as impoverished.[10] Even the best plays by men are relatively little performed these days, or read outside the context of university syllabuses. If Hugo's *Le Roi s'amuse* (1832) and Dumas *fils*'s *La Dame aux camélias* (1852) have achieved lasting success, it is in their transpositions into opera by Verdi (*Rigoletto* and *La Traviata*); apart from these, the only still-popular play is Rostand's *Cyrano de Bergerac* (1897). It is all the more unlikely, then, that plays by women could have survived the general submerging. But there were special factors militating against them, not only in theatre administration but also as playwrights.

Although 200 female playwrights sounds a large number, their proportionate contribution was rather smaller than the men's. Of the 32,000 or so plays listed by Wicks, only about 700 in total had a woman as either sole author or co-author.[11] Well over a quarter of these were co-authored, and even though the *number* of plays written or contributed to by women rose steeply as the century went on, the *proportion* written in collaboration remained remarkably constant throughout the century.[12] Furthermore, during the century the proportion of joint efforts with more than one collaborator rose noticeably, and, in the last third of the century especially, the position of the woman's name among the list of contributors was often demoted.[13] Here, then, was one difficulty, for, as Hemmings says, plays written in collaboration were generally doomed to oblivion.[14]

Where women dramatists were writing as single authors, they had, it would seem, the chance to make a name for themselves. Indeed, Hemmings's analysis of Wicks suggests that even higher proportions of plays by men were co-authored.[15] But the majority of single-author plays by women were only one act long – and it became a bigger majority: in the first third of the century, just over half of all single-author plays by women were one-acters; by the end of the century three-quarters were.[16] To be considered a substantial dramatist, one had to write a four- or five-act play; one-acters were used as curtain-raisers or fillers-in, and might well not be attended by critics or literati.[17]

In addition, the most prolific single-author female dramatists of each period, and those who did write plays of more than one act, tended to conform to prevailing popular or light tastes. Thus in the first third of the century, Mme Barthélemy-Hadot and Mme Bawr, who between them wrote nearly half of the single-author women's plays of the period, concentrated exclusively on melodrama, comedy and vaudeville. Even after 1830, comedy and vaudeville still reigned supreme for women dramatists: Ancelot, who composed the largest number of single-author plays of the middle four decades (out-stripping even Sand), wrote all but two of her twenty-three plays in one or other of these two genres.[18] In the last third of the century, of Mme Chabrillan's twenty single-author plays, sixteen were one-acters or comedies; and Mme Bellier-Klecker, who wrote fourteen single-author pieces, concentrated almost exclusively on children's productions or ephemera: for example, she staged seven comedies or operettas within one month between 2 December 1896 and 2 January 1897, with such titles as *Les Surprises de Noël* ('Christmas Surprises'), *Papa Maman!*, *Monsieur l'Hiver* ('Mr Winter').[19] This is not to say that comedies and one-acters cannot be great plays or raise serious issues – some did, as I shall show; and, at the turn of the eighteenth to nineteenth century, children's theatre had in itself been an innovation (one credited to Mme de Genlis).[20] But it is obvious that a very large number of these single-author plays by women were designed to bloom only long enough to make a profit.[21]

However, women as co-authors would seem to have *contributed* marginally more to the substantial 'drames' as the century went on.[22] And their aptitude must have been taken seriously by their male co-authors, even if these became increasingly parsimonious in their acknowledgement of it. Hemmings tells a revealing tale: the mid-century playwright Legouvé sketched out a synopsis with his friend Goubaux, and the two sat down and worked together in silence until all the acts were completed. They then read the two versions out to Mme Legouvé, 'and,' says Hemmings, 'with her help the two were fused into one, the discarded scenes being consigned to the flames'.[23] Needless to say, Mme Legouvé was not named as a collaborator (she is not in Wicks's compendium). It is tempting to wonder how many other clever women – wives, daughters, actresses travelling with troupes – made inspired suggestions for the structuring of dramas, or thought up the witticisms and one-liners without which popular plays sink – then not even to appear as a set of initials on the billing. Of course, some young male playwrights or junior members of the troupe were also sidelined or plagiarized, but they would be more likely to push to make their names in spite of that.[24] The dry information in Wicks's five volumes suggests that there was a fluctuating reservoir of women with a good 'feel' for scripts, whose talent was exploited by male colleagues but who were hardly thought worthy of recognition – or who did not press for it themselves.

For the theatre remained tainted with an aura of 'the not-quite-respectable'. It is true that, as Hemmings points out, acting, the 'pariah profession', gradually lost its stigma: by the end of the century the sons and even the daughters of the bourgeoisie could contemplate taking up acting as 'just' another career and often did so.[25] But anecdotes show that for most of the century, conditions in the theatre were such that women writers who had anything to do with it needed to be less modest, or doughtier, than in more genteel and acceptable literary callings. (This is also the implication – negative, of course – behind Daumier's cartoon of an 'unfeminine' and arrogant woman playwright: Illustration 6.) It was bad enough for women in theatre administration or actresses. We do have a tale of one Mme Lobreau making a brave effort to control a drunken actor (she was the female manager of a Lyon theatre, before women were barred from these posts); but he ended up getting the better of her.[26] Even star actresses could feel that the theatre was disadvantaging them as women, or could be exposed to sexual blackmail. Sarah

LES BAS-BLEUS.

17.

Chez Aubert, Pl de la Bourse, 23.

Imp d'Aubert &c.

(*Le parterre de l'Odéon.*) — L'auteur ! . . l'auteur ! . . l'auteur ! . . .
— Messieurs, votre impatience va être satisfaite. . . vous désirez connaître l'auteur de l'ouvrage remar-
quable qui vient d'obtenir un si grand, et je dois le dire, si légitime succès. . . . cet auteur. . . . c'est môa !. .

6. '*The Odéon pit.* "Author! . . . author! . . . author! . . ." "Gentlemen, you're so
impatient, calm down . . . you want to know the author of the remarkable work that
has just scored such a great and, it must be said, well-deserved success . . . the
author concerned . . . is MMMEE!"' (From *Les Bas-bleus*, by Honoré Daumier.)

Bernhardt complained that the best theatrical parts were written for male characters (this is why she took on breeches roles); while Judith, no shrinking violet, relates how she was deprived of the prized role of *Phèdre* because she would not sleep with the friend of a powerful politician who was smitten with her stage presence.[27] For the writers themselves, there was the ordeal of reading their plays aloud for acceptance or rejection, one which made even men quiver with nerves or hand the job over to a friend; there was the heckling (or worse) from the pit, which could cause acknowledged male authors to flee the theatre if their play was being hissed or whistled at on the first night.[28] Negotiations had to be conducted with the cast if it wanted to make changes to the script, male managers had to be won over, rowdy hangers-on needed to be dealt with on the spot. In short, all the entertaining stories Hemmings collates take on a somewhat different dimension if one imagines how a woman dramatist anxious to avoid tarnishing her reputation would have responded. It is scarcely surprising that a number of them felt impelled to shelter behind male collaborators, and, where they are named as sole author, to rely still on a male relative as 'protection'. Thus, at the end of Mme Belfort's 1801 play *L'Artémise française* one of the male characters informs the audience that the author of such a weak work trembles for its success; should this author be afraid when celebrating the good-hearted French (who have just shown their prowess in war)? He begs the spectators not to declare war on the play themselves when this play is celebrating peace.[29] The audience then (on cue, presumably) demands the author; the actor – who was Mme Belfort's son – sings a few lines informing everybody (twice) that this author is his mother: all her wishes have been fulfilled, for to please the audience and to praise the Fatherland is to be doubly happy. This is belt-and-braces: son, brave French soldiers, France itself . . . all will shield the dramatist.

Few female playwrights claimed to be this timorous; but that the theatre was not always a congenial place for them is evident. The very successful early-century playwright Alexandrine de Bawr (the former wife of Saint-Simon, who, divorcing her abruptly, had left her penniless and obliged to earn her living) advises women not to write for the stage. She says in her memoirs that in the theatre especially, success depends on numerous circumstances that have nothing to do with the merits of a work; quite apart from the misfortunes that can arise from some caprice of the audience's, the playwright has to worry all the time about the dozens of mishaps that arise from the very nature of theatre. It is, she says, not just a matter of managing everyone's vanity, touchier there than elsewhere:

Si l'on veut être joué souvent, on a besoin de se procurer de puissants appuis, d'adresser des demandes fréquentes, ce qui ne peut se faire si l'on ne s'établit pas en quelque sorte dans les coulisses, où les hommes seuls peuvent se montrer fréquemment sans inconvenance. Je ne conseillerai donc jamais à une femme d'écrire pour le théâtre.

(If you want your plays to be staged with any frequency, you need to get powerful supporters and to keep pushing your demands, which you can't do unless you somehow establish yourself backstage, where only men can show themselves regularly without impropriety. That's why I'll never advise a woman to write for the theatre.)

To excuse herself from charges of hypocrisy, she claims that she herself had exceptional luck in launching her career, but that even once she was successful, some womanly delicacy ('Je ne sais quelle délicatesse féminine') made her feel it would be dreadful to be named on stage. And she ends by saying that she has, she believes, a better right than anyone to advise women against writing for the theatre. For if you are to look after your own interests, there – more than anywhere else – you need a sense of decorum ('tenue'), but also courage and perseverance; there you need to be able to bear a myriad hindrances and constant tiny annoyances without torturing yourself over them. In short, it is there that you must be – a man ('c'est là surtout . . . qu'il faut être homme').[30]

Girardin puts the matter still more viscerally when she contrasts the 'single-author' female dramatist with the mediocre male teams that were abundant by the mid-century:

Toute femme d'esprit qui a composé à elle seule d'importants ouvrages, vigoureusement écrits, savamment charpentés, dont le nom est une illustration, dont le talent est une fortune, a pour ennemis naturels tous les Molières de petits théâtres, travailleurs obstinés à la moustache noire, à la voix forte, aux bras nerveux, aux regards enflammés, nourris de mets succulents, abreuvés de vins capiteux, qui s'unissent par demi-douzaine et s'enferment avec importance pour écrire ensemble un petit vaudeville qui est sifflé. En vain cette femme voudrait traiter ces hommes-là comme des frères, en vain elle s'abaisserait jusqu'à fumer leurs cigares, jusqu'à boire du punch dans leurs verres, ces hommes forts ne pardonneront jamais à cette faible femme sa supériorité et son génie, parce que cette supériorité et ce génie sont la satire de leur impuissance et de leur misère.[31]

(Any intelligent woman who has composed, on her own, significant, strongly written, well-structured works, whose name is already famous, whose talent is worth a fortune, has as her natural enemies all the small-theatre Molières, those obstinate workers with their black moustaches, loud voices, sinewy arms, inflamed looks, full of succulent food, primed with heady wines, who get together by the half-dozen and self-importantly shut themselves away to write between them a little vaudeville that's hissed by the audience. The woman would like to treat the men as brothers, would stoop so low as to smoke their cigars, drink punch out of their glasses – it's no good, the strong men will never forgive the weak woman her superiority and genius, because these are a satire on their impotence and wretchedness.)

One woman, at least, did not overcome the obstacles that unexpectedly loomed up. Elisa Mercœur, from the moment she learned to read, had loved not only fiction but history and tragedy.[32] At the age of six she had an idea for the subject of a tragedy and wrote as follows to the Comédie Française: she and her mother were not very rich; she had written a tragedy; would they hear it? Her mother, and her male tutor, told her she needed to learn and read more before writing a tragedy – which advice only increased her eagerness; it was not until she saw *Phèdre* (at the age of seven) that she realized how much needed to be done and gave up the idea for the time being! She finally wrote her tragedy when she was nineteen or twenty (1829), and obtained a reading by the Comédie Française committee in 1831.

The tragedy survives in her collected works: *Boabdil, roi de Grenade* (I 315–424). It is neo-classical in both form and content: a five-act play in alexandrines that blends a tale of passionate love with politics – here, the politics of the warring tribes of Granada. In style, characterization and plotting, it is rather better than many others of the time. Elisa's scansion never falters (unlike that of other would-be teenage playwrights of the early century, such as the young Stendhal). The play charts with economy the inner conflicts of the weak ruler Boabdil (played on by his wicked henchman Aly and swinging between tyranny and remorse); it maintains suspense; and it builds up to a good *coup de théâtre* when, at the end, an unknown warrior steps forward to fight for Boabdil's fiancée, who has been falsely accused of infidelity and condemned to execution. The warrior, after his victory, turns out to be Boabdil himself. The political perspective is kept throughout via machinations of State and faction, playing off against each other. In addition (and this is a point Elisa herself was to make forcefully in the play's defence) the exotic décor alone would attract the public: the play is set largely in the Alhambra palace, and Elisa is careful to indicate in stage directions striking details of staging and costume.

The actors unanimously agreed to accept the play, but the manager M. Taylor, after some delaying tactics, refused it on the grounds that it had been read before an incomplete committee (this itself was his doing). Elisa confronted him, asking why she had been rejected. Taylor responded sarcastically: 'Mademoiselle, c'est au génie à le deviner' ('it's the privilege of genius to guess that one'). Elisa claimed she had had enough votes for an acceptance, but asked if she could try to get more. If she did get more, said Taylor, then she'd be accepted; so, asked Elisa, would he put her play on then? 'Non, mademoiselle. – Et pourquoi, s'il vous plaît? – Parce que je ne suis pas convaincu que vous puissiez attirer la foule' (' "No, mademoiselle." "Why not, please?" "Because I'm not convinced that you can pull in the crowds" '). Elisa objected that her name was already well known (this was true: she was by now a successfully published poet who had a State 'pension' and had attracted the interest of some powerful protectors). Taylor replied that this was immaterial. But, said Elisa, a woman's name had scored a brilliant success with 'The Beautiful Farmer's Wife' ('Cependant le nom d'une femme a valu un brillant succès à la *Belle Fermière*').[33] To this, Taylor rejoined that *that* play had great merit. Here Elisa's mother intervened, begging her to leave; the actor Monrose, a member of the reading committee, came in and contradicted Taylor's account of events, saying also that the tragedy was too significant to be heard only superficially ('la tragédie de mademoiselle est trop importante pour être entendue légèrement'). But after some further attempts, Elisa took the matter no further, sure that 'M. Taylor will stop at nothing if he wants to prevent a play appearing' ('aucun moyen ne doit répugner à M. Taylor lorsqu'il veut empêcher une pièce de paraître').

Elisa died about four years after this (1835); according to her mother, her last words were that there might be speculations as to the cause of her death: 'dis à ceux qui t'en parleront, que le refus de M. Taylor de faire jouer ma tragédie a seul fait mourir ta pauvre enfant!!! . . .' ('tell those who ask that M. Taylor's refusal to put on my tragedy was the sole cause of your poor child's death!!!. . .'; author's ellipsis).

Even allowing for exaggeration in both Elisa's and Mme

Mercœur's accounts, it seems unlikely that they would invent dialogue with such well-known actors as Joanny – another member of the reading committee whom they cite – and make entirely false claims that the play had the unanimous support of this committee; besides, Mme Mercœur reproduces letters about the affair, offering to show doubters the originals.[34] If Taylor did make Elisa read her play before an incomplete committee, he was stacking the cards against her from the outset. Perhaps what is important is that both Elisa and her mother believed that her play was being rejected because she was a woman ('But a woman's name scored a brilliant success. . .' objects Elisa to a voiced or unvoiced implication not transcribed in her text).

The play may have seemed rather old-fashioned to Taylor, but the battle of *Hernani* had only just been fought (1830), and was by no means yet won: quantities of verse plays in the mould of *Boabdil* would continue to be performed far on into the century. Elisa's hunch that her sex was a factor may therefore have been right; and her play may also have been rejected because – as Taylor's reply suggests – women were expected to produce only works which could, in his words, 'pull in the crowds'. Whether or not this refusal was really one cause of Elisa's death, again she or her mother or both thought it was. This story illustrates the barriers, both actual and psychological, facing women who longed to write great plays. Some twenty years later, indeed, Ancelot claimed to have given up any ambition to serious drama, asserting that it was not possible for the theatre to show the agonies of misery and vice, nor did she herself wish to ('il n'est ni dans mon goût ni dans les possibilités du théâtre de montrer les douleurs poignantes de la misère et du vice').[35] But after all, some did become well-known dramatists of their time; and those who did, both the popularizing and the more complex ones, once more help to undermine the assumption that what nineteenth-century women 'did best' was sentimental and formless fiction.

All the good women dramatists are witty and have a neat sense of structure: in the first third of the century notably Bawr, whose ingenious plots keep several balls in the air at once with remarkable lightness of touch; and in the middle third, Girardin and Ancelot. In Bawr's 1811 play *Le Double Stratagème*, Dormeuil, engaged to a much younger woman, has realized to his embarrassment that he prefers his fiancée's thirty-year-old aunt, who is nearer his age.[36] This – his servant remarks – is not surprising, for when the older woman arrived, he was struck by her freshness and beauty; he'd been expecting to see 'an aunt . . . well, you know, an aunt' ('Je m'attendais à voir une tante . . . une tante, enfin': author's ellipsis, 5). Now follow machinations to break the engagement. (Unknown to Dormeuil, his young fiancée herself loves another, one Melcour.) The machinations are orchestrated by the servant, who thinks a sure way to end the engagement will be to pretend that his master is suddenly impoverished because a rogue has run off with his money. But the servant gets into deeper and deeper waters as the ladies press him about the loss. He'll be very surprised, he assures them, if the rogue is caught: 'C'est un homme qui vivait fort retiré; on ne le voyait nulle part' ('He lived very quietly; nobody ever saw him anywhere', 14–15). But alas! Dormeuil's fiancée naturally feels she must now stick by him in his 'impoverishment'. Her real beloved, Melcour, realizes that to win her he will have to restore Dormeuil's fortunes, so sends a letter purporting to come from the imaginary rogue, saying he will return the lost money. The impact on Dormeuil and his servant of this letter, arriving from a man they thought existed only in their brains, is a perfectly timed comic moment. Dormeuil, however, soon realises the truth, and as a joke pretends to Melcour that he does not believe in the letter. Melcour replies that he's sure the letter is from the rogue. Dormeuil: 'Impossible. Je sais qu'il avait tout perdu au jeu.' Melcour: 'Il aura regagné.' ('Impossible. I know he'd gambled everything away.' 'He must have won it back', 30.) All ends happily if circuitously. Thus amusing and well-plotted plays are possible even in this period supposedly dominated by melodrama.

Later in the century, and despite Ancelot's self-proclaimed withdrawal from harrowing issues, some women did raise their heads above the parapet and used plays for social criticism, particularly from about 1850 to 1870. In *Lady Tartuffe* (1853) Girardin calques on Molière's play a picture of an unlovable female hypocrite who (it finally emerges) resorts to deceit because this is what an equally hypocritical society forces women to do. Léonie d'Aunet's *Jane Osborn* (1855) highlights the injustice of current attitudes to illegitimacy – although, as the modern editor Wendy Mercer shows, the play was completely misunderstood by some male reviewers, who took it as a condemnation rather than as a plea for tolerance. The feminist Deraismes, in her one-act *A bon chat bon rat* (1861), at first plays to the audience with an apparently conventional moneyed-boy-meets-moneyed-girl story, complete with good one-liners; but the play turns into a far from conventional critique of gender stereotypes, the young woman exposing these in areas ranging from dress and smoking to the assumption that women are 'there' to prepare food. To be at ease, suggests the young woman, 'considérez-moi comme un homme, moi, je vous considère entièrement comme une femme; vous comprenez?' 'Pas très bien,' replies her bemused interlocutor ('think of me as a man, and I'll think of you totally as a woman: understand?' 'Not really').[37] Another slightly later one-acter by Deraismes attacks double standards still more vigorously, this time the ones pertaining to adultery (*Retour à ma femme*, 1862).[38] Sand's popular dramatizations of her own novels also brought social questions to theatre audiences in the middle decades. These mid-century women who used theatre as a vehicle for their ideas were to some extent favoured by the prevailing taste, which allowed *pièces à thèse*, plays with an 'argument', and enjoyed *drame bourgeois*. (Similar works by men were, for example, Augier's *Le Gendre de M. Poirier*, 1854, and Dumas *fils*'s *Le Fils naturel*, 1858.) But – with a few exceptions, such as Louise Michel's five-act drama of 1888, *Le Coq rouge* – there would appear to have been a falling-off of will in the last third of the century, as the statistics indicate. It might be supposed that Bernhardt, for example, could write as unconventionally as she liked. She dominated the Paris stage from 1872 on, she was a highly charismatic and iconically androgynous figure, and from 1893 she was to run her own theatre company.[39] Yet her one play *L'Aveu* (1888), although it has concision and suspense and tries to raise controversial issues, ends up with a confusedly moralistic re-affirmation of 'norms'.[40] A young woman is married to a husband in his forties, the Général Comte de Roca. She has a baby son who – this is the 'confession' of the title – turns out to be not the son of the general but of his nephew Dr Robert, an atheistic scoundrel who raped the countess during her husband's absence. The general is furious when he hears the truth, and even the countess refers to the rape as 'your outrage' rather than her own (49). There is pathos – the nephew himself begs for understanding and pity. But the baby dies; it is as if the child of sin must perish to wipe out the 'crime' of both rapist and raped. (Illustration 7 shows the caricaturally stereotyped notions governing the play's plot, with the glaring stiff-backed military man, the mother cowering by the baby's cradle.)

Theatre did, then, offer an outlet for many women, and showed

7. The confession. (From *L'Aveu*, by Sarah Bernhardt, 1888.)

what they could do by way of repartee and taut plotting; but for most of the century, the material and creative constraints weighing on male dramatists affected them still more – and there are, no doubt, many whose words we can still read but whose names we have no chance of discovering.

PART II

Mid-century: George Sand and her contemporaries (1830–1869)

CHAPTER 9

Overview, 1830–1869

In these middle four decades, some older media or emphases survived in women's writing. Memoirs and the 'advice-work' remained popular. For example, Alida de Savignac's *La Jeune Propriétaire ou l'art de vivre* (1837) is a novel-cum-handbook advising on every aspect of running a country house: how to store eggs, how to dress wounds and keep accounts, your intonation when reading aloud (because winter evenings in the country can be boring) . . . Women writers' self-definition still owed a good deal to early Romanticism: their stress on female creativity and on feminist issues continued to draw on the twin ideas that it was permissible to laud the self as the well-spring of inspiration and that this self can and should stand out from society. However, they were discriminating, and sometimes commented ironically on outmoded forms such as melodrama and the concept of sensibility.[1] And other developments in style and subject are noticeable: for example, memoirs were now often more consciously crafted and better written than before, and increasingly adopted the form of the travelogue.

The novel, still a favourite with female authors, was diversifying in subject matter. Young lovers, adulterous involvements and money marriages remained in the foreground, to be sure, and there still existed an often absolute polarity in the fictional characterization of male characters, either 'bounders' or kind, melancholic types. But many of the women writers knew how to satisfy an insatiable public appetite with a blend of familiar parameters and new twists: the money marriages might now be to the 'nouveau riche' rather than to the aristocrat; men might have mixed traits or show they could change (Sand in particular helped to push women's fiction forward in this respect). And larger numbers of women were writing adventure stories. Gabrielle d'Altenheym's 1858 *Dieu pardonne, ou les deux frères* relates the hair-raising experiences of twin brothers: they swap identities when one is falsely convicted of murder and sentenced to death; settings range from the 'white shroud' of an Alpine valley to a prison galley on stormy seas.[2]

Although some, for ideological reasons, rejected the idea of literature as a 'well-wrought urn', being more anxious to urge it as morally or politically 'useful', nevertheless in their own fiction they were mostly becoming surer in their use of understatement, and showed greater care with structure and narrative technique: it is significant that a few, at least, were stressing in novels of this period that study, practice and revision help the artist.[3] Accompanying this new concern with fiction structure was the death of the epistolary novel, and more extended 'landscapes' to set the scene – on occasions, of course, bedevilled by excess epithets; but so were some of the men's. Here, for instance, is the opening of Henriette Reybaud's *Clémentine* (1861):

Onze heures sonnaient à l'horloge du château de la Roche-Farnoux, et la nuit sereine était faiblement éclairée par la lune. L'astre aux froids rayons promenait son disque pâle à travers de légers nuages et répandait un crépuscule transparent sur les plateaux arides qui séparent la haute Provence des fertiles rivages du littoral.[4]

(Eleven o'clock was striking on the clock of the Roche-Farnoux château, and the serene night was weakly lit by the moon. This heavenly body, with its cold rays, moved its pale disc through light clouds and spread a transparent twilight over the arid plains which separate upper Provence from the fertile shores of the coast.)

Although the ends of many women's novels (and, indeed, the tone of numerous poems) were still marked by loss and mourning, others, by contrast, were abandoning the languor and woeful exclamations of early-century productions – were indeed becoming racy, almost cheerful. For more and more women were writing for a mass market. (The densely adjectival novel just quoted became part of a series called 'Bibliothèque des Chemins de Fer', 'Railway Library'.)

These mid-century women writers also increasingly used 'Balzacian' techniques and focuses. Here it is almost impossible to talk of one-way influence. As La Tour du Pin's work shows, it is just as likely that the female memoir writers of the early century opened up 'realism' as that they were somehow retrospectively blessed in this enterprise by the mid-century men. From the 1830s to the late 1860s, so many women were describing food, clothes, furniture, money-making, manufacturing, and the role of all these in social stratification or mobility, that it is more accurate to speak of interchange with the male writers of these four decades than to 'pinpoint' who did what first. Balzac published the first part of *Illusions perdues* in 1837, with its long explanations of the mechanics of printing-presses; the year before, Sophie Ulliac-Trémadeure had given a detailed description of how porcelain kilns work, no less technical although rather more economical, and just as germane to the main subject of her novel as are the corresponding passages in Balzac.[5]

In other areas, however, it is easier to argue for the impact of pioneering men on women and vice versa. Chateaubriand's repeated assertion that some sights or emotions are simply too sublime or terrible to be susceptible of expression reappears in, for example, travel-writers' awestruck claims at key moments that they *cannot* describe a particular scene (they then often do so. . .).[6] Probably the most far-reaching, if at first subterranean, influence on women's writing was Flaubert, who in his *Madame Bovary* (1856) parodied that brand of literature so beloved by Emma, and dealt a slow-acting but none the less crushing death-blow to the exotic settings and well-dressed gentlemanly lovers still apparent in popularizing women's novels of the 1850s.

Conversely, women influenced men, both contemporary and later ones, in some areas. Desbordes-Valmore was to be acknowledged as a predecessor by Verlaine, whose main poetic works were published from the mid-1860s on; while Tristan's presentation of socialist 'voyants' (visionaries) in 1843 strikingly heralds aspects of Rimbaud's 'lettres du voyant' and some of his *Illuminations* (all written about three decades later in the early 1870s):

Dans le camp des *voyants* on entend avec émotion, avec amour, vibrer la grande voix humanitaire qui crie: – *Frères, place pour nous!* – Dans le camp des *voyants* on aperçoit distinctement le grand mouvement ascensionnel des classes inférieures qui s'élèvent graduellement, d'échelon en échelon, au bien-être et à la liberté.[7]

(In the camp of the *visionaries*, you can hear with emotion, with love, a great humanitarian voice vibrating, crying out: *'Brothers, make room for us!'* In the camp of the *visionaries* you can clearly see the great upward movement of the lower classes who are gradually rising, from rung to rung, towards well-being and freedom.) (author's italics)

Although Flaubert was satirizing aspects of women's writing in *Madame Bovary*, he also took a curious and ambivalent inspiration from it. That novel itself would not have been possible without women's reading of other women's writing (and 'Madame Bovary, c'est moi'). Flaubert's relationship with Colet shows the dual process of interest and revulsion at work. Alison Fairlie convincingly argues for the paradoxically formative role in 'Un Cœur simple' (1877) of Colet's 'La Paysanne' (a section of her mid-1850s *Poème de la femme*).[8] Another example is Colet's presentation of the woman as self-pitying victim and her own strong anti-clericalism, which worked their way at different levels into Emma's visit to Bournisien in *Madame Bovary*. In 1856 (the same year as the publication of *Madame Bovary*, but Flaubert had already, a few years previously, read Colet's verse in draft), one of the despairing heroines of *Poème de la femme* goes into a church; there,

> nasillant un psaume,
> Un prêtre savourait des prises de tabac,
> Et de sa grosse main secouait son rabat.
> Que lui dire à cet homme? Hélas! l'eût-il comprise?

(snuffling his way through a psalm, a priest was savouring pinches of snuff; his fat hand shook out his clerical bands. What could she say to this man? Alas! would he even have understood her?)

She leaves the church (79).

A similar mix of exploitation and rejection is apparent in Flaubert's approach to Sand. Quite apart from Colet's role, Flaubert, as is well known, claimed he wrote 'Un Cœur simple' in response to urgings by Sand to show a 'better side' to human nature. Albeit with profound ironies, he did in part fulfil the injunction with his Félicité.[9]

Sand was, in fact, the strongest female influence on male writers of this period and later. Amongst many direct and indirect debts were Musset's and Zola's. Sand conceived, researched and then ceded to Musset the plot of his most famous play *Lorenzaccio* (1834).[10] And it is unlikely that Zola's depiction of the working class would have been so humane and nuanced without hers. The lives of Zola's characters are harsher, and they are more painfully desperate, than in Sand, but many of them at least reach for the dignity already staged by her. She was a 'presiding genius' for men as well as for women.

CHAPTER 10

George Sand, presiding genius

George Sand (1804–76) was not quite to the mid-century what Staël
was to the first third. When Sand shocked, it was more for 'lifestyle'
decisions (open liaisons, men's clothes, smoking) than for head-on
clashes with the ruling elites of the time. If in her creative works she
took up the cause of the oppressed, she did so less defiantly and
more obliquely than Staël in *Delphine* and *Corinne*. Where Staël's
international reputation rested on her political views, Sand's rested
on her artistry (admired not only in France but also by Turgenev,
Dostoevsky, Heine, Thackeray, Thomas Hardy and others).[1] But her
presence was no less powerful and pervasive than Staël's. Sand's
output spanned the whole of this middle forty-year period, from the
work which made her famous – *Indiana*, published in 1832 – to the
staging of the dramatized *La Petite Fadette* in 1869; it went beyond,
into the Third Republic, with the publication of new works in 1871
and 1875, a year before her death.[2] Like Staël, Sand published in
numerous different forums: she wrote not only novels and drama but
journalism, memoirs, travelogues, and literary and art criticism. She
had Staël's versatility, writing penetratingly and subtly on topics
ranging from the main questions of the day, such as child-rearing or
the death penalty, to more specialized or recondite subjects such as
archaeology or the learning processes of animals. Like Staël, Sand
occupied a pivotal position in literary France, as is shown by her
surviving letters (some 18,000 all told).[3] As well as illustrious men of
the time, Sand knew numerous women writers from every background: the working-class Desbordes-Valmore, the aristocrat Marie
d'Agoult (Daniel Stern), the bourgeoise Girardin. And like Staël's,
Sand's life and works were an exemplar for contemporary and later
female authors – and not only in France: George Eliot took her
'George' from Sand. Girardin holds Sand up as a paradigm of
female intelligence; her fame and genius are cited by Voilquin; thinly

8. George Sand. (Photograph by Félix Nadar.)

disguised as 'Antonia Back', she is – much more than the 'Flaubert' figure – the 'star' of Colet's *Lui* (1860), one not without warts but as much admired as disparaged.[4] Bentzon, at the end of her 1872 *Un divorce*, writes a 'postscript' to Sand, claiming that she needed her as a patron, and her 'magic name' as a shield, before daring to tackle the doubly controversial question of divorce and what happens to the children of divorce.[5] Finally, just as certain characters and themes in Sand's work might not have been possible without Staël (for instance, 'the talented woman'), so too later writers were to reshape Sand's own most original creations. Descended from Lélia are the androgynous 'monster' Raoule of Rachilde's *Monsieur Vénus* (1884) and the controlling, non-desiring woman of Daniel Lesueur's 'La Légende de Satni-Khamoïs'.[6]

Recent works have put forward apologias for Sand from different angles. Schor argues that those aspects of Sand which we now find difficult to accept, such as her generous characters, stem from her debt to 'idealist' thought: it is impossible to judge these aspects with sympathy or even detachment nowadays, convinced as we are that Balzacian realism was the 'right' path for the novel to take in the nineteenth century. Dickenson, for her part, traces the fall of Sand's once glorious reputation, showing how permeated with misogyny are the condemnations of almost all later (and a few contemporary) male writers. Indeed, Baudelaire, Gautier, Nietzsche, Henry James, V. S. Pritchett and others litter their comments, seemingly uncontrollably, with anal and oral imagery. This is the imagery belonging to boys' infancy, the time when the mother seems at her most powerful. Thus Sand is: 'pisse-copie' ('text-pisser', Gautier), 'latrine' (Baudelaire), 'the Breton cow of French literature' (Renard), a 'thinking bosom' (Nietzsche). The metaphors go some way to explaining the almost hysterical rejection of Sand and, with her, other women writers who seemed in danger of becoming too successful.

Nevertheless, even well-primed readers may still feel a naive disappointment as they read more widely in Sand. Here is an obviously excellent story-teller and a stimulating thinker, the one for whom, of all nineteenth-century French women, it ought to be possible to claim canonical status. Yet in work after work she ends up resorting to stereotype for both male and female characters; despite a fine ear for rhythm, she can drop into purple prose; and for all her insight she can display a sweetness even more sugary than 'idealism'

would seem to require. Thus Dickenson, for example, concludes that
Sand is more 'feminist' in her discursive works than in the novels
themselves; while Schor, in an honest afterword, confesses that her
students still have difficulties with Sand and that she herself finds
some of Sand's works unpleasurable and one late one, at least,
'almost literally nauseating' (213–16).[7]

Sand is bound to disconcert if we look too hard at her compliance
with the norms of popular nineteenth-century fiction, or if we
expect her to be always a twentieth-century feminist. The female
Saint-Simonians themselves could 'falter' in their feminism (stressing, for example, the sanctity of motherhood as a way of promoting
the dignity of women). It is as well to remember the dangers that
could attach to out-and-out feminism in post-1789 France. Besides
the brutal repressions cited by Moses, the public prosecutor Chaum-
ette had famously threatened all non-conforming and 'non-dom-
estic' women with the guillotine the day after Olympe de Gouges's
execution in 1793.[8] In addition, like many mid-century authors,
Sand had to please a wide audience, since she was writing for
money (the wealthy Staël did not have to worry how many copies
her books sold).[9] But Sand's novels do in fact take up and push
forward all the main feminist positions of the previous thirty years
and of her own adult life, and they broach others with originality.
Gratifying the public in some parts of a given novel has the effect of
disarming this public vis-à-vis the radicalism of other parts. Sand's
compliance with patriarchy, where it existed, may or may not have
been 'treachery'; more important is the fact that it functions as a
rhetorical trick.[10]

Thus, Sand presents afresh the most disturbing strands of Staël's,
Cottin's and Duras's narratives. She reminds her public of the
intolerability of the loveless marriage (_Indiana_). In _Mauprat_ (1837), an
at first unthinking young nobleman eventually rejects the privileges
of his rank – a rank which had been, for him, identified with a
brutish masculine prerogative: this renunciation makes him a suitable partner for a morally superior woman who until then will not
have him. Cottin's articulate illegitimate character Adolphe in _Amélie
Mansfield_ had already argued that contempt for illegitimacy, and for
the woman thus 'dishonoured', is inseparable from the prizing of
rank; Sand explores in more detail society's aversion to both unwed
mother and illegitimate child in _François le champi_ and _Les Maîtres
Sonneurs_ (1850, 1853).

One of Sand's most far-reaching reinterpretations is that of the 'physical acceptability' of women. Duras and Staël had started to probe this: Duras through Ourika's self-hatred; Staël in *Delphine*. Delphine's sister-in-law believes herself too ill-favoured even to contemplate marriage; later in the novel there are comments on the aging that for a woman means the onset of a new timidity and the end of her social attractiveness. But other early-century writers, as well as contemporaries of Sand's, were equivocal here, evidently torn between some sense that it was unfair to overemphasize women's looks and an unquestioning acceptance of the right to be personally vain. The worst offenders are Colet and the Girardin who, as a young woman, wrote a coquettish poem called 'Le bonheur d'être belle', then, evidently guilt-stricken, added the equally unappealing pendant 'Le malheur d'être laide' ('The happiness of being beautiful' / 'The unhappiness of being ugly').[11] Léonie d'Aunet similarly did not know where she stood, one moment writing with an anthropologist's eye on the customs and costumes of Lapp women, but in the next breath adopting an almost giggling tone as she remarked on their sheer 'ugliness', presumably for the benefit of the Parisian *monde* whom she anticipated reading her.[12]

Sand, however, treats this question with unrivalled originality and compassion. Unlike Staël, whose Corinne is both talented and 'one of the most beautiful people in Rome', Sand makes Consuelo so plain that a would-be patron, the comte Zustiniani, is unwilling to grant that she may have the loveliest voice of her choir and exceptional musical understanding.[13] Others have to plead on Consuelo's behalf. However, Fadette, some six years later (1849), pleads on her own, and extends 'lookism' to 'speciesism'. If the world were just and reasonable, she says, it would pay more attention to her good heart than to her horrid face ('vilaine figure') and clothes:

Aussi, moi, je ne suis pas comme ceux qui disent: Voilà une chenille, une vilaine bête; ah! qu'elle est laide! il faut la tuer! . . . on dit que j'aime les mauvaises bêtes et que je suis sorcière, parce que je n'aime pas à faire souffrir une grenouille, à arracher les pattes à une guêpe et à clouer une chauve-souris vivante contre un arbre. Pauvre bête, que je lui dis, si on doit tuer tout ce qui est vilain, je n'aurais pas plus que toi le droit de vivre.[14]

(I'm not like those people who say: There's a caterpillar, horrid thing; ugh! isn't it ugly! let's kill it! . . . people say I like bad animals and I'm a witch, because I don't like hurting frogs, or pulling off a wasp's legs, or nailing a live bat up on a tree. Poor animal – that's what I say to it – if we've got to kill everything that looks horrid, I wouldn't have the right to live, any more than you.)

Certainly, both Consuelo and Fadette turn out in due course to acquire the 'feminine' attractiveness required of novel heroines. But by the time they do, they have broached troubling questions – Fadette going so far as to suggest that 'horrid looks' arouse murderous feelings.

Sand argues in other writings that an exclusive or undue focusing on 'beauty' may be undesirable for the writer. She rejected the 'art for art's sake' movement, saying in 1851, for example, that it was absurd to claim that literature could be constructed without *ideas*.[15] This was to caricature the new stress on form and suggestion, already strong and destined to gather momentum as the century went on. But Sand, with her sensitivity to cultural constructions of female 'ugliness', reads differently from male authors Gautier's dictum of 1835 'Tout ce qui est utile est laid' ('Everything that is useful is ugly'). Like other humanitarian thinkers of the time, she not only defends the idea that literature can be 'useful', but suggests through her novels a feminist perspective on the 'laid' and the 'beau', of which the tenor is: 'Beauty, whether woman's or art's, is not everything.'

The mid- to late-century writer Juliette Adam makes this connection specific, first signalling her affiliation with Sand (who had just died). Adam prefaces her 1878 novel *Laide* with a tribute to Sand, saying that despite Sand's encouragements, she had not hitherto dared to dedicate any of her books to her 'master' ('mon maître George Sand'); instead, she dedicates this one to Sand's memory – in gratitude, she says, for the greatest and tenderest of her female friendships. The heroine of *Laide* is Hélène, daughter to a widowed sculptor, the incurably superficial Martial. Hélène became 'ugly' at age eight after a bout of typhoid. Martial, finding her looks intolerable, keeps her isolated. A friend reproaches him, saying he should love his daughter even if she is ugly, for she's good. To this Martial responds that he'd prefer her if she *weren't* so virtuous: 'I'd like her to be bitter, implacable, with something hellish about her. That'd give her a *raison d'être*, she'd play her role, have her place, give back to destiny the face it gave her! . . . I seem a brute to you,' he goes on, 'because I'm more of an artist than a father. Is that my fault?' ('Je te parais féroce, parce que je suis plus artiste que père.

Est-ce ma faute?') And he concludes: 'I see an incompatibility on her face that's killed my fatherly love more surely than love between husband and wife is killed if they have incompatible characters.'[16] No supportive father here: Martial's aestheticism is synonymous with heartlessness and sexism. Hélène tries to come to terms with her looks, and works out how to behave both in society and towards her father. She concludes that the only option for a 'laide' is to behave like a 'good sort' ('se faire bon garçon'); and she reflects that artists 'break' their models just as curious children break their toys: 'Artistes, artistes!' (114–15). Like Consuelo and Fadette, Hélène eventually becomes attractive, and her story has a 'happy ending'; but the bulk of the novel, with its stark title, shows that Sand's lessons had not been wasted, and that a few women writers saw the association between female and artistic beauty as a damaging one, from the woman's viewpoint at least. This bequest of Sand's demonstrates that, here anyway, she *was* a 'realist'; for one character-istic of realism is to incorporate the 'ugly' into the work of art.

Sand's fiction may, then, be more cautious than that of some others, but she is no less profound; and the cautiousness is often part of her ability to imply rather than to state. For, despite her theoretical favouring of 'usefulness', and some inclination to be didactic, Sand is a suggestive writer. She often prefers to evoke central ideas rather than explain them; and these ideas perform not one but many narrative functions. Thus Sand follows previous nineteenth-century women's novels in contrasting a sexist 'society' with a primitive 'Nature' that offers a refuge for the beleaguered woman, as in *Indiana*. But in other works the town–country oppo-sition launches a humorously knowing exploration of folk-customs, local superstitions and regional linguistic habits whose only con-temporary rival is Nerval's *Sylvie* (1853), and which is original in its promotion of 'low culture'.[17] And Sand plays on the interactions of art, artisanship and history diversely as between one novel and the next (we might look at the difference in her treatment of music from *Consuelo* to *Les Maîtres Sonneurs*, as compared to the monothematic approach to the arts of some contemporaries).

Sometimes this 'multifunctionality' operates within individual works. In *La Petite Fadette*, the early-century interest in the sibling bond is reinterpreted in such a way that it no longer stands in symbolic or titillating isolation. The relationship between Landry and his twin brother Sylvain now creates a triangular situation that helps along the plot, at the same time smoothly demonstrating that masculinity need not accompany biological maleness; that sibling attraction can be homosexual as well as heterosexual; and that a kind of 'psychotherapy' can help cure the heartsick. Similarly, in *François le champi* Sand does not, in the manner of Staël, simply proclaim the injustice of discrimination against aging women, with their 'worsening' looks. Instead, the effects of aging are part of a gradual shift in which the difference in years between Madeleine and François at first matters, then does not; 'aging' is also interwoven with a subdued exploration of son–mother feelings and a meditation on the passage of time. Reading, in *François le champi*, not only has educational value (a theme dear to many women writers of the century); it is also a reflection in microcosm of the whole work, with Madeleine rearranging parts of texts to make them suitable for the still-young François.[18]

Sand, then, creates different perspectives on the same phenomenon with a rapid, darting intelligence sometimes lost to sight in the legends that have grown up around her. She is also unusual among women writers of the century for a related quality: her sanguine voice. She does see exploitation and tragedy where they exist. But this sanguine voice articulates her enjoyment of the 'other side' of the picture – in ideological terms, a weakness, perhaps looking contradictory or contrary; but in her writing, a strength.

For example, many women autobiographers of the century, both before and after Sand, lament the patchy quality of their education, using, as we have seen, words like 'chaos' to describe their unguided reading. Among the writers I have surveyed, Sand is the only one to propose that learning from a mother who has not herself been formally educated, absorbing knowledge like a magpie, abandoning programmatic training, may be a more interesting and creative upbringing for children than a structured plan. Of her father she says that, given his artist's temperament, his mother's lessons were the only thing that were any good to him; and talking of her mother's and grandmother's 'diametrically opposed' responses to children, she remarks insouciantly:

D'où l'on pourra conclure tout ce qu'on voudra. Quant à moi, je n'ai pas trouvé les théories applicables dans l'éducation des enfants. Ce sont des créatures si mobiles, que si on ne se fait pas mobile comme elles (quand on le peut), elles vous échappent à chaque heure de leur développement.[19]

(From which you can conclude whatever you like. As for me, I haven't found theories any good in children's education. They're such mobile creatures that if you don't make yourself as mobile as them (when you can), they escape you at each hour of their development.)

This calm appreciation of mobility goes, here, with a tone that also marks much of Sand's fiction and accounts for its success. Recent critics have shied away from the adjective 'charming' to characterize Sand: like 'elegant', it is one of those words that has been used to condescend to good women's writing. But critics also speak of 'charm' as part of the aesthetic effect of Montaigne's *Essais*, Stendhal's autobiography or Nerval's *Sylvie*: it contributes to a conscious casualness which makes argument or narrative fluid and opens them up to speculation, dream and experiment. 'Charm' also rests on the author's belief in her or his ability to 'cast spells', to enchant (as Valéry was to suggest when he called his collection of poems *Charmes*). Sand's charm is a narrative artifice, to be sure, but she was the first woman in the century to carry off the artifice with verve and during a very protracted period of production.

This 'charm' – in her case, a humorous, confiding tone – is particularly visible where it is most needed: at the beginning of her novels. Let us take only two examples: first the well-written opening paragraph of her earliest success, *Indiana*.

Par une soirée d'automne pluvieuse et fraîche, trois personnes rêveuses étaient gravement occupées, au fond d'un petit castel de la Brie, à regarder brûler les tisons du foyer et cheminer lentement l'aiguille de la pendule. Deux de ces hôtes silencieux semblaient s'abandonner en toute soumission au vague ennui qui pesait sur eux; mais le troisième donnait des marques de rébellion ouverte: il s'agitait sur son siège, étouffait à demi haut quelques bâillements mélancoliques, et frappait la pincette sur les bûches pétillantes, avec l'intention marquée de lutter contre l'ennemi commun.[20]

(One cool and rainy autumn evening, deep in a little manor house in Brie, three dreamy people were gravely occupied in watching the brands burn in the hearth and the hand of the clock progress slowly onwards. Two of these silent inhabitants seemed to be abandoning themselves submissively to the vague boredom which weighed down on them; but the third was showing signs of open rebellion: he fidgeted on his seat, stifled half-uttered melancholic yawns, and knocked the tongs against the crackling logs, obviously intending to fight the common enemy.)

The tension created by the dissidence of the third party; the slight wryness; the alliterations, rhythmic cadences and painterly effects; all carry that conviction of narrative control that readers want when they start a novel. The opening of *Consuelo*, quite different in its subject, has the same capacity to allure:

'Oui, oui, Mesdemoiselles, hochez la tête tant qu'il vous plaira; la plus sage et la meilleure d'entre vous, c'est. . . Mais je ne veux pas le dire; car c'est la seule de ma classe qui ait de la modestie, et je craindrais, en la nommant, de lui faire perdre à l'instant même cette rare vertu que je vous souhaite . . .'

'*In nomine Patris, et Filii, et Spiritus Sancti*,' chanta la Costanza d'un air effronté.

'*Amen*,' chantèrent en chœur toutes les autres petites filles.

'Vilain méchant!' dit la Clorinda en faisant une jolie moue, et en donnant un petit coup du manche de son éventail sur les doigts osseux et ridés que le maître de chant laissait dormir allongés sur le clavier muet de l'orgue.

'A d'autres!' dit le vieux professeur, de l'air profondément désabusé d'un homme qui, depuis quarante ans, affronte six heures par jour toutes les agaceries et toutes les mutineries de plusieurs générations d'enfants femelles. (i 41–2)

('Yes, yes, young ladies, toss your heads as much as you like; the best-behaved of you all and the most talented is. . . No, I'm not going to tell you; because she's the only modest one in the class, and I'm scared that if I say who it is, I'll make her lose – on the spot – that rare virtue. . . I wish you all had it. . .'

'*In nomine Patris, et Filii, et Spiritus Sancti*,' sang Costanza with a bold look.

'*Amen*,' sang the other little girls all together.

'You bad, horrid thing!' said Clorinda, pouting prettily and giving a little tap with her fan-handle on the singing-master's bony, wrinkled fingers, which were lying asleep on the silent keyboard of the organ.

'Don't tell me!' said the old teacher, with the profoundly disabused look of a man who, for forty years and for six hours a day, has had to tackle all the teasing and disobedience of several generations of female children.) (author's ellipses)

This keeps us guessing at the setting until the fourth paragraph; enlists us on the side of the wearily tolerant teacher and his judgement; and whets our appetite as to the identity of this exceptional heroine. Contributing to 'hook' the reader is the droll raconteur – underlining farcical moments and even commenting on his/her own writing; for when, in the next paragraph, the master is likened to a sea-shell left high and dry, the narrator adds: 'I maintain that no metaphor could be more appropriate.'

Sand, then, provided a model of female craftsmanship, showing how to set up the structure of a long work and escape from those sometimes clumsy expositions which were a matter of less concern

to early-century women novelists. Thanks not only to male contemporaries, but also to her, almost all women fiction-writers of
these four decades became better than the early ones at creating the
captivating starts and the ensuing suspense that are a crucial
component of novel-technique. Here, for instance, is the unasham-
edly 'reader-grabbing' opening of Dash's 1864 *La Duchesse de Lauzun*
(I have abbreviated very slightly, but the effect is plain):

> J'ai résolu d'écrire les aventures de ma vie, non pas tant à cause de moi
> que pour les gens dont je suis entourée. Je suis une pauvre femme, vouée à
> la douleur et à l'injustice, obligée de cacher soigneusesemnt ma pensée et
> mes émotions, car personne n'a pu les comprendre parmi ceux que je vois
> . . . dans la position que j'ai occupée, avec une existence telle que la
> mienne, les amis sont impossibles, on le verra bien.
>
> Cependant j'ai beaucoup vu, j'ai su quantité de choses. L'homme que
> j'ai épousé est un héros de roman; il a continué *sur* moi ses expériences
> romanesques, et n'a pas voulu que j'y échappasse. Je lui ai pardonné à son
> lit de mort, mais je ne puis oublier. (1–2)

> (I have resolved to write the adventures of my life, not so much for myself
> as for those around me. I am a poor woman, given over to grief and
> injustices, obliged to hide my thoughts and feelings carefully, for nobody,
> among those I now see, has been capable of understanding them . . . in the
> position I have occupied, with an existence like mine, friends are
> impossible, as you will see.
>
> And yet I have seen much, learned a great number of things. The man I
> married was a novel-hero who continued his fiction-like experiments *on* me,
> and did not want me ever to escape. I forgave him on his deathbed – but
> forget, I cannot.) (author's italics)

Facility of this kind was an important acquisition. But Sand's style
has more than facility; it is constructed so as to breathe assurance.

There were some writers in this middle period, however, who
created paradoxes on this very subject: whether or not they themselves 'breathed assurance', they took lack of assurance as a topic in
itself.

CHAPTER 11

Confidence and the woman writer: Amable Tastu and Sophie Ulliac-Trémadeure

At the beginning of the century, many women showed doubts as to whether they should be writing at all. That a number suppressed their own names speaks for itself. Cottin 'bitterly censured' women writers, including herself, in the preface to the first edition of *Amélie Mansfield*, and according to her biographer Michaud held it as axiomatic that women should not write.[1] Some worried about their own talents: Babois talks of the extreme and unconquerable shyness that 'fettered' all her abilities ('Une timidité extrême, invincible, enchaînait toutes mes facultés', *Œuvres*, 137). But in the early years, it was only Staël who tackled this question of artistic confidence head-on in an imaginative work: *Corinne*. Corinne's life with a parochial English family all but destroys her creativity, because their notion of womanhood stifles every expression of liveliness; and Staël also stresses that discouragement, or an unsupportive partner, inhibit women's imagination and performance. Thus, emulation, enthusiasm, everything that inspires genius, particularly need encouraging ('ont singulièrement besoin d'être encouragés'); Corinne needs a man of enough intelligence to set store by her own; finally, 'j'avais quelque orgueil de mon talent . . . mais à présent je ne me soucie de rien, et ce n'est pas le bonheur qui m'a détachée de ces vains plaisirs, c'est un profond découragement' ('I used to be rather proud of my talent . . . but now I don't care about anything, and it's not happiness that has detached me from these vain pleasures, it's a deep discouragement', II 89, 102, 120).

In life-writing of the mid-century, however, women became increasingly vocal on these themes, and in imaginative works they articulated the difficulties of the woman artist, creating a curious dialectic: they were becoming more confident in turning their unconfidence into the matter of literature. This is not an exclusively female procedure, of course: since Horace, poets have incorporated into their verse such sentiments as 'I send you, my book, out into the world, uncertain of your fate'; and in Vigny's 1835 play *Chatterton* the self-esteem of the male writer is vulnerable to incomprehension and ridicule. But the women writers create images of special problems beyond this.

The mid-century female author was no longer regarded as a 'pariah', according to an influential journal of the 1860s.[2] Nevertheless, as Slama and others point out, writing was still not the same for a woman as for a man: it led to a more radical change in her status and self-perception; besides, writing women continued to be specifically attacked.[3] That references to 'my poor woman's work' were more than just a trope, or a Romantic pose, for the mid-century Frenchwoman can be seen in Flora Tristan's plea for her political writing to be taken seriously in spite of the fact that she was a woman: 'Do not let my *woman's* status make my work seem repellent to you. Consider, I beg you, that love, intelligence, strength *have no sex*' (author's italics).[4] It is this sex-specific rejection that was also feared by Mme Mercœur when, in the same year (1843), she imagined critics asking her if she thought the 'title' of Elisa's mother gave her, an unknown, the right to write, or if she believed she had enough genius to be forgiven such boldness ('cette audace'):

Non, je n'ai point de génie, non, je le sais; je n'ai pas même ce que l'on rencontre si facilement dans toutes les classes, de *l'esprit* et du *savoir*, mais j'ai du jugement . . .

(No, I have no genius, no, I know I have not; I don't even have what is found so easily in all classes, *wit* and *knowledge*, but I have sound judgement . . .) (author's italics)

She claims the same rights to narrate as a man: people would not, she says, have tried to dissuade her from her biography of Elisa if they had considered that she was like a shipwrecked father who might tell how he and one of his sons miraculously escaped death. He would tell how they lived for years on the desert island where the waves had thrown them (she is referring to her single-parent upbringing of Elisa); he would tell, too, all he suffered when death took away this son who was so dear! 'People could not but be interested in the story of this unhappy father's misfortunes, so why should I be treated less favourably, since like him, and equally alone, I survived the shipwreck? Therefore, like him, equally alone, I must be able to tell my story' ('Alors, comme lui, seule aussi, je dois pouvoir conter', 1 ix–xii).

In verse and fiction, too, women gave their heroines or narrators these painful uncertainties. Girardin's 1833 poem 'Napoline' puts the problem in forceful doggerel. The budding poet Napoline has been brought up by a frivolous uncle who preaches double standards:

> Son oncle l'accablait de sermons superflus:
> Il nommait son brillant esprit de la folie,
> Il se moquait tout haut de sa mélancolie,
> Dénonçait ses talents comme autant de travers,
> L'accusait, devant moi! d'avoir rimé des vers,
> Lui vantait les vertus qu'il permettait aux femmes,
> Et noyait ses sermons dans des flots d'épigrammes.

(Her uncle overwhelmed her with superfluous sermons, called her brilliance madness, mocked her melancholy, denounced her talents as if they were just oddities, accused her, in front of me! [the female narrator] of having *rhymed*, vaunted those virtues he permitted women to have, and drowned his own sermons in floods of epigrams.)

Napoline eventually commits suicide.[5] Like Girardin's, Colet's poems of the 1830s also show keen interest in the idea that discouragement can crush talent, support make it bloom. She details the misunderstandings to which the young poetess may be subjected, and has a mother advise a gifted daughter to remain obscure. Here are the last lines of 'La Voix d'une mère' (1837):

> Laisse à l'homme la gloire,
> Les triomphes, le bruit
>   . . .
> Coule une vie obscure
> Que le devoir remplit:
> L'onde à l'ombre est plus pure,
> Rien ne trouble son lit.[6]

(Leave fame and noisy triumphs to men . . . Let life flow on obscurely, filled with duty: water overhung by shade is purer, nothing troubles its bed.)

Colet is elsewhere more affirmative, celebrating women's ability to write more successfully than men about certain subjects (the Magdalen, for instance), and claiming that writing – albeit a struggle – is the path to women's freedom.[7] But those last two lines of 'La Voix d'une mère', with their suggestions of a shadowy deathbed, hint at the link between 'buried women's talent' and 'buried and forgotten women'. Early-century women writers had already shown heroines fading into oblivion: Cottin's Amélie, Duras's Ourika and Louise, were said simply to disappear without trace (whereas male heroes often died 'with a bang' or left some memorial to posterity). But the connection had not yet been made with women's achievements or lack of them. Now, however, it became specific. The normally exuberant d'Aunet is eloquent about women's posthumous erasure from the slate. Towards the end of her journey back from the Polar regions, she looks round a Copenhagen museum exhibiting clothes of Swedish sovereigns. Having described those of the kings, she moves on to the queens. But the diadems, necklaces and gold-embroidered dresses leave, she says, a more melancholic impression. 'What woman was decked out in them? We barely know a few names; all this pomp recalls nothing. Poor women! yet they had youth, beauty, royalty – a triple crown; how can we not know them?' Only two names, she adds, surface from this forgetfulness, those of the great warrior Margaret and the great politician Christine; and she concludes: 'O femmes! aimez et soyez heureuses dans la vie, ou souffrez, travaillez, et faites-vous grandes pour la mort' ('Women, love and be happy in your lives, or else suffer, work, and make yourselves great in preparation for death', 233). So women, according to d'Aunet, have clear options. To live on after death, they must abjure love and happiness.

Here, then, is another area where the preoccupations of male and female authors ran in tandem without quite coinciding. Struggle and sacrifice for the sake of achievement and fame; decay, ruins, the passing of empires: these were not new themes, and they were being highlighted in this period by men too. But women presented their choices as even starker. For men, it was a matter of giving one's all to 'achievement' but still, perhaps, being unrecognized; for women, it was a matter of feeling the obligation to give up achievement entirely. And women depicted their compulsory humility in the face of death, their still more impossible afterlife, as an extra source of sorrow.

Two mid-century writers in particular – ironically, unknown nowadays – epitomize these choices and necessities. The poet Amable Tastu and the novelist Sophie Ulliac-Trémadeure express memorably the key questions: should I, as a woman, be writing at all? If so, have I the talent for it? Am I entitled to crave present fame and a name that will survive once I die?

Amable Tastu (1798–1885) wrote educational works and literary criticism, translated *Robinson Crusoe* into French, composed skilful

French imitations of the Irish poet Thomas Moore, and wrote continuations of other women's work or collaborated with them. However, it was for her own verse that she was mainly famous (it was praised by Sainte-Beuve).[8] She started to publish it in 1826 and went on into the 1830s and beyond with both reprints and new works; in many of these poems she evokes the woman writer's doubts.[9] In 'L'Etoile de la lyre', she stresses the modesty of her claims and her solidarity with other women writers, her sisters; none of them measures up to the male sun. Of all the constellations, says her narrator, I prefer the Lyre: 'under my absent-minded fingers, a few facile notes honour the beauty of this constellation'. When the king-sun, 'le roi du jour', appears, we forget the stars he effaces; we see only him. But you, Lyre, daughter of the night,

> Sans éclipser tes sœurs, tu répands auprès d'elles
>   Un feu tranquille et pur.
>
> Une gloire semblable est la seule où j'aspire;
> C'est d'un pareil destin que mon cœur est jaloux.
> Ah! dans la nuit des ans laisse briller ma lyre
>   De rayons aussi doux![10]

(Without eclipsing your sisters, you spread around them a calm, pure light. This fame is the only one to which I aspire; this is the destiny of which my heart is jealous. Ah! in the night of the years let my lyre shine with such gentle rays as these!)

Other poems similarly make self-deprecation the very motif. In 'A M. Victor Hugo', Tastu sings her own failure, her 'impotence': happy is he who 'does not feel his voice expire in his breast, nor his impotent lyre ['lyre impuissante'] slip from his hand'. She has never reached eagles' heights; 'my flight tended always to an earthly sojourn, and my gaze dropped before the brilliance of daylight' ('Toujours mon vol tendait au terrestre séjour, / Et mon œil s'est baissé devant l'éclat du jour', 139–40). In 'La Mort', she hopes that she will at least have a future female reader – who may herself thus perceive not a possible immortality, but rather her own mortality:

> Ces chants épars où j'ai laissé mon âme . . .
> Ils vivront peu; mais peut-être une femme,
> A leur douceur séduite par degré,
> Suivra de l'œil la page fugitive. . .
> Puis tout à coup s'arrêtera pensive,
> En répétant tout bas: Quoi, je mourrai!   (183–7)

(These scattered songs in which I've left my soul . . . won't live long; but perhaps a woman, charmed gradually by their gentleness, will glance over their fugitive pages . . . then suddenly pensively stop, repeating to herself: What? I too will die!) (second ellipsis Tastu's)

The most striking of Tastu's compositions is 'L'Ange gardien' – said by Sainte-Beuve to be the pearl of her whole poetic work (*Causeries du lundi*, xvi 4). If a single poem had to be picked out as voicing the nineteenth-century French woman writer's dilemmas, it would be this one. At every stage of the talented girl's life, the guardian angel watching over her beckons her away from the passion of her calling, advising her (like d'Aunet) that this is not the path to happiness. As a sleepless child, she thinks her imaginative thoughts, senses she is gifted; her friends call her in vain. But the angel tells her not to be solitary, and to play with them, as befits her age. Now the child grows into a girl-poet who would like to make her way freely by herself ('M'élancer seule, libre') among male rivals ('rivaux armés du luth sonore'). But the angel tells her that the only crown for her is the (bridal) orange-flower; she should not weep after dangerous honours, but follow a humbler, gentler path. 'Vierge, crois-moi, je conduis au bonheur' ('Maiden, believe me, I lead the way to happiness'). This – 'je conduis au bonheur' – is the last line of each of the angel's responses; the accompanying vocative varies according to the age of the woman.

The now grown woman says, 'Let me play this lute.' The angel: 'Have you, in your modest realm, seen to all the jobs, the meals, the pastimes?' ('As-tu réglé dans ton modeste empire / Tous les travaux, les repas, les loisirs?'). If so, *then* she may give her lyre a few snatched moments. She becomes a mother. She will, she says, play the lyre, force it to keep the promise it made her, so that she can show her son this way forward. No, says the angel: your child is asleep in the cradle; your bold songs will disturb his sleep, and if you go away, you won't be there when he wakes. Instead, train his young soul to vigour ('De sa jeune âme exerce la vigueur') – this is your goal.

Now the woman is old, and laments that she was unable to stop time passing: 'Alas! I didn't reach the palm offered me in its green-leaved youth, I've let it wither; and the fire that should have lit the waiting beacon on that shore – I let it die in an obscure hearth.' The angel tells her that the holy fire shut up in her soul burned far from profane eyes, like incense in holy places; she knew the gentleness of a

happy art, without going astray in the chase after fame: 'Enjoy this
memory in peace'. Finally, the woman is dying. She reflects that she
can leave this innocent life of hers without fear, and that her angel
has not abandoned her:

> Mais quoi! ne rien laisser après moi de moi-même!
> Briller, trembler, mourir comme un triste flambeau!
> Ne pas léguer du moins mes chants à ceux que j'aime,
> Un souvenir au monde, un nom à mon tombeau!

(Oh, but not to leave anything of myself after me! To shine, tremble, die
like a sad torch! Not to leave, at least, my songs to those I love – no
memory to the world, no name on my tomb!)

The angel tells her, in the last words of the poem:

> Il luit pour toi le jour de la promesse,
> Au port sacré je te dépose enfin,
> Et près des cieux ta coupable faiblesse
> Pleure un vain nom dans un monde plus vain.
> La tombe attend tes dépouilles mortelles,
> L'oubli tes chants; mais l'âme est au Seigneur.
> L'heure est venue, entends frémir mes ailes;
> Viens, suis mon vol, je conduis au bonheur!   (109–15)

(The promised day is glimmering for you; at last I lay you down at the
sacred harbour; so near to heaven, your guilty weakness weeps for a vain
renown in a yet vainer world. The tomb awaits your mortal remains,
forgetfulness awaits your songs; but your soul belongs to the Lord. The
time is come, hear my wings quiver; come, follow me as I fly, I lead the way
to happiness!)

Sainte-Beuve's comments on this poem are a mixture of the
perceptive and the blinkered – probably a good example of the limits
of comprehension of many sympathetic male readers at the time. At
first he misses the point, quoting with approval a journalist who
labelled the poem an example of 'the new type of domestic elegy';
but he then rightly remarks that 'the entire destiny of the woman-
poet, or she who would like to be one, is contained in this poem,
with her dreams, her enthusiasm, her desires'. However, he also
claims that the guardian angel blames nothing, forbids nothing
absolutely, but that the contrast between the two destinies shows by
itself ('se dessinait de lui-même'). Here, Sainte-Beuve seems not to
have seen how many imperatives the angel uses; and he concludes,
with one of those complacent biographical flourishes detested by
Proust, that

in this poem, Madame Tastu, at the very height of her verve and inspiration, gave the measure of her powers and set out limits for herself: at each stage of her life she will comply with the framework of her 'Ange gardien'; she will not go beyond it. (*Causeries du lundi*, xvi 4−6)

We may want to see more tension in the poem than this. It is both a recommendation to resignation and an expression of yearning. By spanning a lifetime, it encapsulates the frustration many women must have felt: the talented child ends as an unfulfilled dying woman who can look only to heaven for happiness now. The male angel keeps telling her where happiness lies; but the rhetoric of the poem speaks for itself: there is nothing in it about the pleasures of child-rearing and housework, only the angel's bland assurance that these lead to joy. It is the constant thwarting that comes alive, not the rewards of well-performed duty.

But in the poem that concludes the collection *Poésies*, the narrator not only repeats the by now familiar claim that she is content with 'ephemeral palms', has weaned her pride away from the idea of a longer future, and will be happy if her poems lull the joys or griefs of wives and mothers: she also expresses the hope that other French women will read her when she has gone, not now to remind them that they too are mortal, but to appeal to them in solidarity. Does it matter, she goes on, if when I die silence and forgetfulness reign? The nightingale's song leaves no trace,

> Et le doux bruit de l'onde expire sous la glace
> Où l'emprisonnent les hivers:
>
> Mais, dans la nuit muette, un regret qui s'éveille
> Est peut-être le prix des accents de l'oiseau;
> Peut-être on se souvient d'avoir prêté l'oreille
> Au frais murmure du ruisseau.   ('La Gloire', 299−303)

(And the gentle sound of the waves expires under the imprisoning ice of the winters; but, in the dumb night, an awakening regret is perhaps the prize brought by the bird's tones; perhaps people remember having lent an ear to the fresh murmur of the stream.)

Here, however tentatively, the stream is heard again after being frozen over: memory, women readers who come later, can dissolve the icy oblivion and bring a 'sister' back to life.[11]

Sophie Ulliac-Trémadeure (1794−1862) had devoted herself to literature from the age of twenty-two. She started with translations, and under the pseudonym Dudrezène went on to publish her own compositions with moderate success. She soon turned to writing exclusively for children, some of these works being awarded Academy prizes; she became the editor of the *Journal des jeunes personnes*. Her writing was a lifelong commitment: she carried on publishing up to a year before her death. Her two most interesting works are *Valérie, ou la jeune artiste* (1836) and *Emilie ou la jeune fille auteur: Ouvrage dédié aux jeunes personnes* (1837). Both were still being reprinted at the turn of the twentieth century (in 1901 and 1899 respectively), suggesting popularity with parents as well as their offspring. Indeed, *Emilie* stretches the definition of 'young persons': when Emilie undergoes conflicts between her wish to write and her marital duties, her exchanges with her husband can hardly have been deemed suitable in some families. (He tells her that since her love of literature can apparently win out over maternal and conjugal love, it is to be feared that one day it will also win out over her self-respect, meaningfully adding, 'There are examples'; or says that from a woman writer's impatience with daily tasks will come the abandonment of all her woman's duties – yes, *all* of them: 'oui, de *tous*, Emilie!').[12] This fiery and contentious work is essential reading for students of women's writing in nineteenth-century France.

Valérie, ou la jeune artiste had already broached the main questions. Valérie and her widowed father live in poverty, but he decides she should be a painter: uneducated himself, he wants to give her the opportunites he missed. The art-master tells him Valérie has remarkable talent: this fills him with joy, and he is henceforth kinder to her (in part, it is true, because he sees her skills will bring in money, 29). The art-master urges her and her fellow-pupils to put aside 'feminine' concerns: 'Young ladies . . . understand this: the woman who wants to be an artist while busying her mind with frills and furbelows will never be an artist in the noble sense of that word' (44–5). But Valérie for a time succumbs to the blandishments of her coquettish cousin Héloïse, 'and now the woman's character triumphed over that of the artist; Valérie was nothing but a vain girl, in love with clothes' (66–7). However, she does keep up her art, and is advised to try painting on porcelain. This is not 'real' art (as against, say, oil-painting), but the woman who employs her for porcelain decoration suggests she start with saleable work: 'resign yourself to turning out things that are often beneath your talent' – a lesson many women writers of the century learned (89–90).

Valérie's father and art-master regret that she is sacrificing that aspect of her studies which could have contributed to the development of 'a fine talent' (90–1). But she perseveres, earns money through hard work which leaves her no leisure (a sacrifice beyond the understanding of her wealthier cousin), and eventually comes back to painting, acquiring her own pupils. I won't marry: my father needs me, she tells Héloïse at the age of thirty:

J'ai d'ailleurs bien autre chose en tête qu'un mari!
– Bien autre chose! répéta Héloïse stupéfaite.
– C'est mon art, ma cousine! mon art, que j'aime par-dessus tout! qui est la passion de ma vie, une source de jouissances enivrantes, de bonheur pur . . . Une artiste, Héloïse, ne devient pas vieille fille; elle est artiste, voilà tout. (115–16)

('Besides, I have someting quite different in mind from a husband!' 'Quite different!' repeated Héloïse, stunned. 'It's my art, cousin! my art, which I love more than anything! which is the passion of my life – it gives me intoxicating pleasures, pure happiness . . . An artist, Héloïse, doesn't become an old maid; she's an artist, that's all.')

Valérie does indeed forget the rapid passage of time; she grows older without noticing it (117). After her father's death, she takes on only 'useful work' to increase her means of doing good. She teaches poor children, seeking them out in garrets 'where talent and even future genius suffer, stifling in the tight bonds of poverty' (126). When she dies, her simple grave, unlike that of her cousin Héloïse, is often visited; fresh flowers are always on it.

This work, although laying down radical precepts with a rather heavy hand, at the same time does not dare push them too far. Certainly the value and joy of creativity are stressed; an artistic vocation is seen as a 'solution' to the problems of aging and dependence on a husband. But Ulliac-Trémadeure is also anxious to prove that the woman artist can be morally good: Valérie's art has to be part of her filial duty. Indeed, at one point – with logical impossibility – she is said to love her art above all, but her old father even more; and when her father dies, again an excuse has to be found for Valérie's creativity: now her art helps the poor (119, 126).

Although *Emilie* is not without ambivalence, it bravely confronts some of the problems *Valérie* had sidestepped. Emilie Muller has no father to pre-empt a spouse (being brought up by her grandfather and old cousin Charlotte); she does marry and have a child; and she encounters more dilemmas than does Valérie: the name under which to produce work; her family's blend of pride, fear and mockery; the obstacles posed by housework and childcare.

The novel opens boldly with the words: 'Femme auteur! ces deux mots ne cessaient de retentir à l'oreille d'Emilie' ('Woman author! these two words kept ringing in Emilie's ears', 5). An older woman, Mme Matigny, has encouraged her, at the age of seventeen, to write; like Valérie, she wants to work for money (her grandfather having lost his income), and will start with translations; but she is also excited by the idea of writing itself. Her only hesitation is that her brother Théodore, currently in the army, 'va se récrier et se moquer de moi' ('will make a fuss, and laugh at me', 14). She announces her plan, whereupon the grandfather tells her that of all careers, that of literature is the most to be feared for a woman ('De toutes les carrières celle des lettres est pour une femme, la plus redoutable', 15; see *Frontispiece*). But Emilie replies that it is the finest and noblest of them all, and cites other women writers, among them Cottin (19; here once more the importance of female 'role-models' is plain).

Emilie achieves her ambitions, and gradually the streak of 'violence' and 'imperiousness' in her character is modified; however, says Ulliac-Trémadeure, in spite of herself her blood boils when she senses the dependence in which she will be continually kept by that title 'woman'; she despairs at the thought of all the obstacles facing her in her writing career, among them the 'servant's duties' to which woman seems to have been destined everywhere; and she weeps: 'Les hommes font ce qu'ils veulent, tandis que les femmes . . . Oh! quel supplice d'être femme!' ('Men do what they want, whereas women . . . Oh! what torture it is to be a woman!', 25–8).

Mme Matigny pleads on her behalf with the grandfather: Emilie may, she says, be among those women writers who honour France! 'But, madame,' inquires the grandfather, 'will she be among the number of happy women?' 'Le lot des femmes est l'obscurité' ('Women's lot is obscurity'). 'No doubt,' replies Mme Matigny; 'but between ourselves, M. Muller, you wouldn't be displeased if your granddaughter brought fame to the name honoured by both your excellent ancestors and yourself.' This cunning flattery wins round the grandfather; and a helpful abbé points out that heaven gave this child Emilie her intellectual faculties, while urging her, perhaps less helpfully, to pass on moral lessons through fiction – then these 'deceits' of the imagination cannot be thought of as 'lies' (39–41, 49, 71).

Emilie's work is accepted for publication; she is thrilled to be paid, and her grandfather himself urges her to sign her full name, rather than just 'Mlle Emilie M...', while pointing out that her brother has a 'right' to oppose her use of the full name (87–93). A letter from this brother tells her she can't even write: she's not inspired, it's not fitting for a woman – especially not if she wants to talk about love (107–10).

Pauvre enfant! [writes Ulliac-Trémadeure], oui, pauvre enfant! Elle était à-la-fois [*sic*] tourmentée de cette défiance de soi-même, qui est encore l'un des apanages du vrai talent, et de l'effroi que lui inspirait l'opinion publique.

(Poor child! yes, poor child! She was simultaneously tormented by that self-doubt which is, however, an attribute of true talent, and by her fear of public opinion.)

She is on the point of tearing up everything she has written, but then, re-reading and correcting it, forgets her woes – 'dominated by that higher power which snatches authors away from earth, removes them from everything round about' (113).

Emilie goes through a sequence of uplifting or disheartening experiences, among the latter the constant stops she has to make for housework at the very moment ('à l'instant même') when the fever of composition is 'intoxicating her with its magical delirium!' ('l'enivrait de son magique délire!', 142). Her brother becomes accustomed to the idea of having 'une sœur auteur' ('a sister-author'), though still begrudging in his praises and urging her to use initials rather than her full name: '*Montre tes écrits et cache ta personne*' ('*Show your writing, hide your person*', 157).

Emilie feels she can never marry: she already finds filial duties so irksome that she could not take on other kinds. 'If I marry,' she thinks, 'that means I will give up writing'; and she adds to herself: 'I love and hate my fate as God has made it' (186). But she does marry, in part to escape the hostility she has already attracted: she tells her brother that, thank God, she will no longer hear people repeating all around her: '*That's an authoress!*' ('*C'est une femme auteur!*'), nor see astonished looks glued to her face and searching her whole person for something extraordinary ('je ne verrai plus de regards étonnés s'attacher sur ma figure et chercher dans toute ma personne quelque chose d'extraordinaire!', 212–14).

In any case, she feels her inspiration has gone. But once married and with a daughter, she finds she can't stop writing; she does so in secret, asking a maid to look after the baby and deluding herself that she is writing for this baby (231–7). The old inspiration rises up in her: 'Et il faut être nourrice. . . berceuse. . . esclave!' ('And I have to be a wet-nurse. . . a cradle-rocker. . . a slave!', 257). Tensions increase between herself and her husband – who is not a tyrant, indeed offers her a degree of freedom and independence, but is still unable to understand or respond warmly to a passion he can see excludes both him and their child; he even proposes that he himself should bring up this daughter, so that she will never be more than 'an ordinary woman' (273, 280–1). He eventually dies; Emilie feels ashamed that she cannot silence the voice which murmurs deep inside her: '*You are free!*' For she shudders at the thought that if she stops writing, she will soon be forgotten ('et à la pensée de tomber dans l'oubli, elle frissonnait', 326–7).

Her niece has an aptitude for literature, but Emilie, telling her it is better to be loved than admired, persuades her to give up her ambitions: 'Sois femme avant tout!' ('Be a woman above all else!'). If one day you're alone – without a family – then dare to be a poet; but be it for yourself. Literature and inspiration give joys that the applause of the crowd can never match. The arts are a gift from heaven, but love of fame is a nightmare (358–9).

Emilie should perhaps be read principally as a work of propaganda which aims to arouse indignation. It comes close to satire at times, and in its clear-sighted statement of problems – still clearer than in *Corinne* – probably gave courage to those girls who were allowed to read it. The mere fact that this sombrely single-minded book, and 'L'Ange gardien', were composed at all speaks for women's longing to have men's confidence and freedom to write, and to be given an equal chance to let their own names survive as artists.

CHAPTER 12

Shame, embarrassment and Sophie's misfortunes: the comtesse de Ségur

On numerous occasions in *Emilie ou la jeune fille auteur*, Emilie blushes: when the abbé tells her not to write anything for which her conscience might reproach her; when she reads her brother's discouraging letter; when considering tearing up the verse and fiction that talk of love because '"people who read them could think ... what's not the case." And a burning blush immediately spread over Emilie's whole face' ('"ceux qui les liraient pourraient croire ... ce qui n'est pas." Et une brûlante rougeur couvrit aussitôt jusqu'au front de la jeune fille'). She has painful experiences of ostracism in salons, to which she is invited only to be marginalized or ridiculed by both women and men (who, for example, speak about women authors in front of her without mincing words – 'en termes peu ménagés').[1] This fear of embarrassment, mockery and rejection by polite society is another of the central themes running through women's writing of the mid-century. Again, the fear is not confined to women, nor solely to post-1830 works. It appears in, for example, Rousseau, and is felt by Laclos's Valmont and Stendhal's Julien Sorel. But the women's and their heroines' struggles with 'politeness', and their reactions when they realize they have over-stepped boundaries, are necessarily different from the men's. They are bound up with the idea of 'the woman's reputation' – therefore implicitly or explicitly with her sexual virtue – and also with her concerns about authorship. Indeed, this had been an anxiety since the sixteenth century: thus Montaigne's adoptive daughter, the writer Marie de Gournay, and in the eighteenth century Mme Roland, expressed fear of ridicule specifically with regard to their writing.[2]

In the early decades of the nineteenth century, Staël attached a marked importance to the impact of 'opinion' on women, as we have seen. Some of the most convincing sequences in *Delphine* are those which show the heroine being ostracized when she breaches the rules governing women's conduct: Staël stages on the one hand theatre-of-cruelty scenes, with humiliation in front of a whole roomful of people, and on the other, the 'drip-drip' effect of a more insidious ignoring of the unconventional woman. Duras too saw salon behaviour as an instrument of oppression through the agonies of embarrassment it imposed. Ourika describes how the 'falsity' of her position, the whispers, the surprise mixed with disdain, make her suffer a martyrdom: the company of savages is less to be feared than 'cette société cruelle qui me rendait responsable du mal qu'elle seule avait fait' ('a cruel society which made me responsible for the evil it, and it alone, had created', 37). Central here are both the concept of the 'inconvenable' and the word itself: Edouard, suffering a snub, looks back wistfully to the time in his youth when, surrounded by his equals, 'j'étais bien sûr de ne pas être *inconvenable*, ce mot créé pour désigner des torts qui n'en sont pas' ('I was sure of not being *unsuitable*, that word created to designate wrongs which are not wrong': 67, author's italics).[3] So pre-1830 female authors did depict the conflict between individualism and socialization, and occasionally highlighted external pressures on heroines to conform to 'womanliness'. The portrayal of these conflicts, however, reached fever pitch in the middle decades of the century.

True, one or two of these mid-century women writers iconoclastically proclaim their taste for the *inconvenable* or the *inconvenant* (which has the even stronger meaning of 'improper', 'unseemly'). Girardin uses the words at first to express pseudo-shock, but soon slips into a subtler approval of the 'unsuitable'. En route, she provides a good definition of what the mid-century deemed 'unladylike' – being noisy, untidy, enjoying or creating scandal, dressing 'wrong', being always on the move . . . Certain 'grandes dames' seem – claims Girardin – to have been born with a courtesan's soul:

Elles aiment le bruit, l'agitation, le désordre, et même un peu le scandale. Elles s'habillent d'une manière *inconvenante*, elles font événement partout. Elles ont horreur du repos . . . Dans le salon de ces femmes, rien ne se passe d'une façon *convenable*. On n'y parle point comme ailleurs. Là on ne se sent plus dans le monde. *On n'y éprouve plus le besoin de s'observer, de se contraindre et de se fuir*; les préférences s'y révèlent avec la plus aimable candeur, l'on se cherche, l'on se trouve; et quand on s'est trouvé, on ne se quitte plus. La société n'y est pas une réunion générale, c'est une collection de tête-à-tête attachants.[4]

(They like noise, agitation, disorder, they even rather like scandal. They dress in an *unseemly* way, they cause a stir everywhere. They hate repose . . . In their salons, nothing happens *suitably*. People don't speak there as they do elsewhere. It's as if you're not in society when you're there. *You don't feel as if you have to observe each other, constrain each other, avoid each other;* your preferences show through with the most agreeable frankness, you seek each other out, you find each other; then you stay together. Company in their salons isn't a general meeting, it's a collection of engaging tête-à-têtes.) (my italics)

But few are as relaxed as Girardin. Most present the clash between the *convenable* and the *inconvenable* as fraught with difficulty. Ancelot, even though personally nostalgic for the bygone glories of the great salons, returns often to the control exerted by 'le monde', and to the value of solitude for women: solitude – she observes to her own daughter – fortifies one against the petty vanities and spite of the salons.[5] And her play *Un divorce* shows in its physicality the recoiling away from the 'shamed' woman. Emeline is staying in a French hotel with her husband Edouard. She pretends to fellow-guests that a first marriage had ended in widowhood; in fact, married to an Englishman she did not love, she had divorced him, this being permitted in England. She has already been ostracized and shamed in Paris salons; hence the pretence. But the truth comes out, and in front of Emeline a fellow-guest exclaims to his fiancée, 'Nous la croyions veuve!' ('We thought she was a widow!') The fiancée, Hortense, replies: 'Et c'était un divorce! . . . ' ('And it was a divorce! . . . '). Now comes this stage direction: 'Hortense, par un mouvement marqué, s'éloigne d'Emeline' ('Hortense, with an obvious movement, draws away from Emeline'). This provokes Edouard to exclaim: 'Unhappy is he who braves opinion!' Emeline reproaches him: 'You used not to talk like that.' Edouard: 'Used not! . . . Good God! fearing one may have to blush with shame at any moment! . . . This situation is dreadful' ('Grand Dieu! craindre à chaque instant d'être contraint à rougir! . . . Cette situation est affreuse': IV 356, 366–8, author's ellipses). Thus, 'having to blush' is the worst fate.

Such images recur in numerous other mid-century women writers: they are evidently crucial for those seeking to put a shape on feelings of repression and to express a challenge to that repression. In *Nélida*, Stern frequently returns to the salons' cramping of creativity, their power to exclude.[6] Others highlight the potency of insult and ridicule. Even while claiming these can be defied, Sand compares them to physical torture, and distinguishes between the treatments meted out to men and women. Progressive thinkers, she says, used to be strangled or burned in the past; now they are exiled or imprisoned if they are men – insulted and scurrilously attacked if women. But – from the strappado of former times to the abusive irony of our own ('l'ironie injurieuse') – all of that is easy to bear if one has faith in the future.[7] In Colet's poetry, ridicule greets illegitimate pregnancy, women's old age, women's poverty; while mothers warn writing daughters that they should expect ridicule, will blush for their own work.[8]

As these last examples suggest, it was not merely upper-class women who were apprehensive about ridicule and the judgement of 'society'. Working-class writers were sensitive to them too, although sometimes turning the tables with their own irony, like the Blanche-cotte who remarks caustically: 'Il ne faut pas que l'air de vos salons joyeux / Soit un instant troublé par ma voix inquiète' ('Don't let the atmosphere of your joyous salons be disturbed for an instant by my anxious voice').[9] But it is without irony that 'rougir', 'l'opinion du monde' occur even in the intrepid Voilquin, whose own volte-faces reveal the main contradictions. She believes in free relationships and in divorce. But should she tell her fiancé about a previous relation-ship? He might let out the secret, and then she would be embar-rassed in front of her sister and brother-in-law ('et c'était dans ce cas m'exposer à rougir devant ma sœur et mon beau-frère'). Her eight years as an active Saint-Simonian enabled her, she says, to hold cheap the opinions of society – she, so timid and fearful about what people say. But to claim rights for women 'out loud' ('tout haut') would expose one to mockery ('aux railleries du monde'); in fact, it would take strong men to claim these rights. Here, Voilquin does add that the working-class woman is better able than the bourgeoise to be 'ardent and frank' because any change will better her position; nor do working-class women, unlike the bourgeoises, have to 'break a thousand social shackles' ('briser les mille entraves de la société'). Indeed, when two middle-class women – a doctor's nieces – assure her that 'distinguished' women must reject the doctrine of Uto-pianism if they do not want to be ridiculed ('sous peine de ridicule!'), Voilquin objects to them that nevertheless one must work for the realization of one's visions. But this supposedly greater indepen-dence of the working-class woman is belied by later comments. Voilquin meets a wildly unconventional woman who believes in free

love and openly protects Saint-Simonians; but Voilquin is oddly torn, remarking first that 'All true convictions, even rash ones, have their respectable side', then adding: 'I think doing violence to public feeling like this is not really part of woman's role' ('cette manière de faire violence au sentiment public me semble peu dans le rôle de la femme').[10] If Voilquin – who had the support of an affectionate and politically radical father, who was publicly known as a Saint-Simonian, and who, without wealth, children or husband, had nothing to lose – if Voilquin, seemingly unawares, could swing so rapidly between divergent views of 'the unconventional woman', how much more hesitant must others have been?

The pressure started in childhood, with the training of the little girl for womanliness. Even in books for adults, the heroine's development can sometimes suggest a coercion away from her 'naturally' rather wild state; but in their children's tales, women often lay out with unabashed plainness the girl's particular need to control her will and become docile. (The heroine of Mme Guizot's short story 'Le Chapeau' is the twelve-year-old Rosine, who has 'bouts of bad temper' but by the end has, naturally, learned to conquer them, and this within only twenty-four pages.)[11]

The comtesse de Ségur, in her character Sophie, depicts this process of girls' socialization more amusingly and sympathetically than any other woman writer in nineteenth-century France. Sophie de Ségur (1799–1874) was the daughter of that Count Rostopchine who was governor of Moscow when Napoleon and the Grande Armée arrived. (He is thought to have given the order to set Moscow on fire, thus forcing the retreat of the French.) The family settled in Paris when Sophie was sixteen; she married at twenty, and gave birth to eight children. From 1856 she published a long series of children's stories, of which the most famous is *Les Malheurs de Sophie* (1859). Critical interest in her has been increasing recently: Lloyd remarks that although the golden age for children's books in France began in the 1820s, the 'real birth' was the contract between Hachette and Mme de Ségur in 1855; while one critic claims Ségur may be on her way to inclusion in the canon.[12]

Sophie is an upper-class four-year-old who lives with her mother and father in a château. Her main playmate is her slightly older cousin Paul. Sophie is meant to be identified in part with her author: they share a first name, and in her dedication to her granddaughter, Mme de Ségur writes:

Chère enfant, tu me dis souvent: *Oh! grand'mère, que je vous aime! vous êtes si bonne!* Grand'mère n'a pas toujours été bonne . . . Voici des histoires vraies d'une petite fille que grand'mère a beaucoup connue dans son enfance; elle était colère, elle est devenue douce; elle était gourmande, elle est devenue sobre; elle était menteuse, elle est devenue sincère; elle était voleuse, elle est devenue honnête; enfin, elle était méchante, elle est devenue bonne. Grand'mère a tâché de faire de même.[13]

(Dear child, you often say to me: *Oh, grandmother, I do love you! you're so good!* Grandmother wasn't always good . . . Here are some true stories of a little girl grandmother knew very well in her childhood; she used to be bad-tempered, she became gentle; she was greedy, she learned not to be; she was a liar, she became truthful; she used to steal, she became honest; in a word, she used to be naughty, she became good. Grandmother has tried to do the same.) (author's italics)

This is preaching, but it is turned so delightfully that we might almost gloss it as: I was characterful but now no longer am; however, the old self peeks through, and I can at least re-create in imagination the Sophie that I once was!

Sophie has a string of little adventures which always end in tears. In the first, she mistreats a pretty wax doll. Enforced sunbathing makes its eyes disappear into its face; after an excessively vigorous wash, its cheeks and lips turn deathly pale; it goes bald because Sophie curls and burns its hair; its feet melt after a boiling foot-bath administered with the best of intentions. 'Depuis tous ces malheurs, Sophie n'aimait plus sa poupée, qui était devenue affreuse' ('After all these misfortunes, Sophie didn't love her doll any more – it looked awful'); and she and her friends bury it (11–20). There is something emblematic in this opening tale of the pretty doll that little girls are supposed to 'mother' and aspire to resemble. Sophie's piecemeal destruction of the doll at first pains her, but her conclusion that the doll can be discarded may be interpreted in two ways. First, as reinforcing an ideal of attractiveness? She no longer likes the doll because it is mutilated and ugly? Or as proposing insouciance – she doesn't care because pretty dolls are silly things anyway?

This tugging between convention and a sometimes hyperbolic unconventionality runs though all the stories. Many show Sophie 'playing' with animals to murderous effect: fish in a bowl, a cockerel, a bee, a squirrel, a cat and bird, a tortoise meet sticky ends. As her mother says in the penultimate chapter, 'You and Paul kill them all or let them die' (175). (However, Paul, the older and usually wiser child, does not normally initiate these 'games', but either follows

Sophie's lead or tries to remonstrate with her.) Sophie's other initiatives include failed efforts at coquettishness: she cuts off her eyebrows (Illustration 9), or comes in with hair she has deliberately made sopping wet with water from the roof-gutter because she thinks it will curl as a result. She is rough and highly disobedient, administering furious fisticuffs to Paul, making herself ill on food she is not supposed to eat and stealing from her mother.

The virtue of this work is that it demonstrates that 'femininity' is not innate. Little girls do not know by instinct how to make themselves physically appealing; the episode of the doll shows that their maternal feeling, such as it is, is imperfect and impermanent; they do not protect the vulnerable, being cruel to animals; they fight . . . They are demanding, they have desires, they are ingenious in their greed. Most of this is put down to a comical heedlessness in Sophie, not malice; but clearly it must be cured. Who better to cure it than the mother?

Sophie's mother, Mme de Réan, does allow Sophie to enjoy an uninhibited childhood in certain respects. Her hair is cut short like a boy's, she does not have to wear hat or gloves, and her mother thinks it a good idea for her to get used to being outside in all weathers (43–4). Nor is Mme de Réan especially unkind: the only time she administers corporal punishment is when Sophie steals the contents of her needlework-box (131). Otherwise, her approach is almost always: 'I ought to punish you, but you've been punished enough by your stomach-ache/the fright you got/your own remorse.' However, at these moments the comedy of the work vanishes. Mme de Réan speaks not just sternly but threateningly, often switching to the 'vous' form, invoking the anger of the Deity, and seeing to it that Sophie internalizes the guilt – much more efficacious as a means of lifelong control.

Mademoiselle, je devrais vous fouetter pour votre désobeissance; mais le bon Dieu vous a déjà punie par la frayeur que vous avez eue. (24)
. . . si j'avais appris par hasard, c'est-à-dire par la permission de Dieu, qui punit toujours les méchants, ce que tu viens de me raconter, je t'aurais punie sans pitié et avec sévérité. (32)

(Miss, I should whip you for your disobedience; but God has already punished you with the fright you got.
. . . if I'd learned by accident – that is, with God's permission; he always punishes the wicked – what you've just told me, I'd have punished you harshly, with no pity.)

9. Sophie cuts off her eyebrows, to general derision. (From *Les Malheurs de Sophie*, by the comtesse de Ségur, 1859.)

The father rarely appears, and no opposition to the mother seems possible: a maid who tells Sophie she thinks Mme de Réan too harsh, and contravenes her orders, is sacked (56–63).

Accompanying Sophie's repentance are blushes; and one response to her misadventures is a mockery that is not always affectionate. The occasions on which Sophie is ridiculed, or reddens, or is embarrassed, mount up over the work until they reach almost refrain-like proportions. 'Sophie devint rouge comme une cerise. "Que va dire maman?" se dit-elle'; 'Tout d'un coup Sophie tressaille, rougit; elle entend la voix de Mme de Réan' ('Sophie went cherry-red. "What will mama say?" she thought'; 'Suddenly Sophie trembled and blushed; she could hear Mme de Réan's voice', 27, 29). When Sophie drenches her hair, the mother ridicules her and exposes her to the further mockery of male family members. She finds the figure Sophie cuts so ridiculous, says Ségur, that she bursts out laughing and tells Sophie that if she could see how she looked, she'd laugh at herself too. As a punishment for going out when she was told not to, Sophie is to stay for dinner just as she is, hair sticking up and dress dripping wet, so that Papa and Paul can see her fine notions for themselves. At this very moment, in come Paul and M. de Réan:

tous deux s'arrêtèrent stupéfaits devant la pauvre Sophie, rouge, honteuse, désolée et ridicule; et tous deux éclatèrent de rire. Plus Sophie rougissait et baissait la tête, plus elle prenait un air embarrassé et malheureux, et plus ses cheveux ébouriffés et ses vêtements mouillés lui donnaient un air risible.[14]

(they both halted in amazement in front of poor Sophie – who was blushing, ashamed, sad and ridiculous; and they both burst out laughing. The more Sophie blushed and hung her head – the more sheepish and unhappy she looked – the more ludicrous her dishevelled hair and wet clothes made her seem.)

The father and Paul do at least plead on Sophie's behalf, and she is allowed to change into dry clothes, but not to dine with them (44–8). So it goes on:

A peine a-t-elle mis les pieds dans le salon, que tout le monde la regarde et éclate de rire . . . Sophie restait les bras pendants, la tête baissée, ne sachant où se cacher.
. . . très honteuse . . .
. . . rougissant . . .
La pauvre Sophie fut bientôt humiliée, car voici ce qui arriva deux jours après.

. . . confuse et mécontente . . .
Sophie rougit plus encore . . .
Elle était si honteuse qu'elle n'osait plus rentrer pour dîner. . .[15]

(Hardly had she stepped into the drawing-room ['salon'] than everyone looked at her and burst out laughing . . . Sophie stood there, arms drooping, head hanging, not knowing where to hide.
. . . very ashamed . . .
. . . blushing . . .
Poor Sophie was soon humiliated, because here is what happened two days later.
. . . abashed and cross . . .
Sophie went even redder . . .
She was so ashamed she didn't dare go to dinner . . .)

These, only a few examples among many, give a clue to the adult woman's fear of shame, exclusion, moral and even physical humiliation. Whether the fear arose from reality, fantasy or a mixture, the fact that the tales were so popular shows that the model spoke to something deep in both little girls and the grown women who read to them in nineteenth-century France.[16] They also echo the more remorseless picture found in adults' stories of the matriarch governed by convention and governing through it. Furthermore, this matriarch (with the help of Paul) condescends to Sophie's ways of thinking. For although Sophie has curiosity, it is meddling as often as it is disinterested, and her enterprising ideas never work (unlike those of, say, Richmal Crompton's William, often oddly successful). Sophie's 'ideas' are alluded to with growing scorn as the work continues:

Paul, *riant*
Oh! si tu as une idée, nous sommes sûrs de faire quelque sottise, car tes idées ne sont pas fameuses, en général. (135)

(Paul, *laughing*
Oh! if you've got an idea, we're sure to do something stupid, because your ideas aren't always that bright.)

After this, Ségur starts to italicize the word 'idée', as if by definition Sophie's can never merit the title: 'Un jour, Sophie eut une *idée*'; 'Madame de Réan: – Ah! c'est une de tes *idées*' ('One day, Sophie had an *idea*'; 'Mme de Réan: – Ah! it's one of your *ideas*', 170, 174).

'Les malheurs de Sophie', indeed. But this is a comic work, not a tragedy; it is less didactic than much children's writing of the time, and is never mawkish; and for all the humiliation, what survives is an endearing image of an energetic child who is never so cowed by the previous embarrassment that she cannot enjoy the next bit of rough-and-tumble.[17] Like Mme de Ségur, other women writers did not so easily give up the treasured image of the tomboy, and were not always prepared to renege on it in their own lives.

CHAPTER 13

Adventure and travel: Flora Tristan and Léonie d'Aunet

In the mid-century, women's images of themselves in fiction, verse and life-writing incorporated physical activity and bravery more explicitly than before. These had been in evidence before 1830: in particular, memoirs of émigrées necessarily included tales of narrow escapes and fortitude in adversity.[1] Desbordes-Valmore had celebrated energy in her 1826 'La Jeune Châtelaine': the young lady of the manor is forbidden by her lord and husband to run alone to the woods, or to sing a lively mocking song, or to look at his page-boy; but she disobeys. 'M'y voici, tout hors d'haleine, / Et pour la seconde fois' ('Here I am, quite out of breath, and for the second time'); she learns and does sing the song, she thinks constantly of the boy who, 'unawares' ('par mégarde'), also gets lost in the wood . . . Bodily and sexual liberty and the freedom to 'sing one's song' are bound up together; the physicality is emphasized in the 'tout hors d'haleine'.[2] Cottin also had active heroines: in the Biblical narrative *La Prise de Jéricho, ou la pécheresse convertie*, the adventurous Rahab is the saviour of the day; we see her running, albeit in a 'doe-like' manner.[3] Elisabeth in particular has an energetic childhood denied to most fictional females of this period. She climbs rocks to get birds' eggs, she fishes, she rows on the lake; she grows, says Cottin, with exercise (*Elisabeth*, 26–8). Having decided to make her heroic journey (800 leagues on foot), she exercises to prepare for it, and her suitor admires her for her courage (51, 65).

These images already begin, then, to chip away at the notion that nineteenth-century French women were browbeaten into a state of supine domesticity and confined indoors.[4] No doubt that is where some men wanted to see them, and a few public figures, both male and female, trumpeted the recommendation; but, as Hufton remarks, such pronouncements drew on

a misogynistic rhetoric as old as the classical world brought up to date by
an injection of Rousseau . . . This kind of rhetoric was dredged to the
surface whenever those in authority found women's protest inconvenient,
or when they wished to postulate the construction of an ideal society.
(*Prospect Before Her*, 479)

The rhetoric certainly did not correspond to the reality of working-
class women's lives; and in both imagination and fact, mid-century
writers of all social classes acknowledged the pressure but resisted it
– cautiously or flamboyantly, according to personality. Either they
showed heroines rushing and jumping, or – at the least – they
approvingly evoked energetic little girls or young peasant women.
Such were Blanchecotte's Scottish character Jobbie of 1854, whose
steps are 'Jamais ralentis, jamais las' ('Never slow, never tired'), and
Stern's Nélida, who as a child discovers the joys of physicality and
the countryside seemingly for the first time:

La timide enfant . . . séduite à la vue des horizons illimités qui s'ouvraient
devant elle, excitée par ce vent de liberté qui lui soufflait pour la première
fois à la face, se mit à courir de tout son cœur et de toutes ses jambes à
travers champs, non sans faire plus d'un faux pas dans les sillons raboteux,
non sans demeurer souvent accrochée aux branches par les rubans flottants
de sa robe de mousseline.[5]

(Shy little Nélida . . . charmed by the sight of the boundless horizons
opening up before her, excited by this wind of freedom blowing in her face
for the first time, began running across the fields with all her heart and as
fast as her legs would carry her, not without stumbling more than once in
the rough furrows, or being frequently hooked on the branches by the
flowing ribbons of her muslin dress.)

Nélida becomes more demure, but does not – Stern says – forget her
taste of freedom (31). Colet too writes memorably on this subject. In
her 1834 poem 'La Mer' – an as it were female precursor of
Rimbaud's 'Le Bateau ivre' – the narrator visualizes herself flying,
floating on the sea, overtaking its fast eddies, the universe opening
up to her:

> De ciel en ciel, de zone en zone,
> J'allais, intrépide amazone,
> Ayant la mer pour palefroi.[6]

(From sky to sky, from zone to zone, I went, an intrepid Amazon, the sea
my palfrey.)

Even in the grimmer *Poème de la femme* of 1853, a twelve-year-old
peasant girl has 'something in her whole manner reminding you of a

running doe'; while, in an androgynous image, an 'imprisoned' nun is likened to a harnessed stallion who can break free of this harness and flee to the wild country to rejoin his sister mares; he is, says the narrator, childhood with its indefatigable pace, whilst the horse that is always enchained and servile forgets even how to run (8, 133).

Sand too is fond of such pictures, saying of Consuelo that she goes down fifty treacherous underground steps with the skill and agility often lacking in girls brought up in salons, but which children of 'the people' acquire in their games, and which give them boldness and confidence for the rest of their lives (1 314). And it is Sand, more than any other writer of the mid-century, who focuses on the issues raised by girls' physical freedom in *La Petite Fadette*. Fadette is the nine-teenth-century tomboy par excellence (and resembles to some degree Sand's portrait of herself as a child in *Histoire de ma vie*). In her mid-teens, Fadette is still acting more like a boy than a girl. Her beloved Landry pleads with her to change, telling her that there's nothing girl-like about her, everything's boy-like ('tu n'as rien d'une fille et tout d'un garçon'), and this is why the local children call her 'le *mâlot*' ('the *boy-thing*'; author's italics). 'Do you think,' he asks, 'that it's right for you not to look like a girl yet, at the age of sixteen? You climb trees like a cat-squirrel, and when you jump bareback on to a mare you make her gallop as if she had the devil sitting on her.' He goes on:

C'est bon d'être forte et leste; c'est bon aussi de n'avoir peur de rien, et c'est un avantage de nature pour un homme. Mais pour une femme trop est trop, et tu as l'air de vouloir te faire remarquer. (136)

(It's good to be strong and nimble; it's also good not to be afraid of anything, and it's a natural advantage for a man. But for a woman, too much is too much, and you look as if you want to draw attention to yourself.)

The matter is put here with unique clarity. The girl can take pleasure in agility, speed, all kinds of movement, until she turns into a woman; then she must quieten down, and even bravery will be considered unfeminine. This transformation from young hoyden to decorous lady appears so frequently in writing by women that it could almost claim the status of an archetype. Susan Coolidge's Katy has to injure her spine to learn how to become, from a rough enterprising little girl, a passive woman who bears pain patiently.[7] But the transformation is not made without a longing for the previous state of freedom. (Doris Day said that of all the films she made, her favourite was *Calamity Jane*, in which, until her metamorphosis into a coy lover of housework, she plays a bareback-riding gun-toting male-clad girl.)

Despite Landry's veto on fearlessness, many women writers of the mid-century extol courage in danger – and not only by way of Joan of Arc. In 1831, Ségalas, in 'Les Françaises à Alger', describes the actions of two Frenchwomen who took up arms in a battle against Algerians and fought bravely, one having a limb amputated as a result. Ségalas outspokenly puts this in terms of 'a prejudice against women overcome'. The world of routine had closed off the path to these women warriors ('guerrières d'Alger'), building a bronze wall between them and fame; but their 'shut-in courage' breaks through its 'cold constraint' and 'leaps over the stupid confine of the prison of prejudice' ('Et franchit la stupide enceinte / De la prison des préjugés'). Don't doubt – she continues to the men – that women have just as much love of their country, and inner strength, as you – for after all, it is mothers' blood that runs in your soldiers' bodies. She appeals to all Frenchwomen: 'who,' she asks, 'can now doubt our daring ['notre audace']?' Heroines of Algiers, your brilliance and ardour must rebound on us; we are proud of your fine story, we proclaim your success; and, in order to live up to you, we want to turn your glory into a communal one. ('Nous voulons pour briller jusqu'à votre niveau, / Faire de votre gloire une gloire commune', 67–8). This verse could be better turned, and modern readers may well wish that the cause had been another. But the point is unmistakable: women can and should be as unflinching and pugnacious as men when circumstances demand. And some feminists of the period use the rhetoric of battle to urge women to resist (and to paint men as cowards . . .), for example Juliette Adam. 'Courage!' she tells her female reader in *Idées anti-proudhoniennes*: 'Ceignons nos reins et préparons-nous à la lutte, et qui pis est, à l'outrage' ('Let us gird up our loins and prepare for the fight, and, worse, for outrage'). Yes, she goes on, for outrage – because when men fight men they try only to kill each other; but when they fight women, their first impulse, whether because of offended pride or pure brutality, is to outrage her in her sex or in her person, knowing well that she is vanquished when they have dirtied her (21).

Given these desires for courage and vigour, women who in their own adult lives showed physical enterprise and publicized it were of special importance. We should not forget here the eloquent women speakers of the century, among them Voilquin, Colet and Deraismes, who often confronted extremely aggressive heckling and who travelled to other parts of France or Europe to promote their views or to witness major political events with their own eyes. Those who journeyed still further afield do more than anything to qualify the modern stereotype of the cowed nineteenth-century French housewife.

Like male travel-writers from the Renaissance on, they also seized on the travelogue to broach moral and social issues. Thus, at some moments, for polemical purposes women in highly repressive societies serve to allegorize the state of all women. But more often the travel-writers bring out the relativism of mores, especially those affecting women – some in an anecdotal manner, others more reflectively. Voilquin, for instance, distinguishes between degrees of oppression in different nations, and illustrates the subjectivity of concepts such as modesty (*Souvenirs*, 317). By implication, France does not always come off worst.[8] Mid-century women's travelogues, then, like the historical writing of others, demonstrate their awareness of the ideological specificity of a given culture.

Others used travel-writing to create a sense of the epic – this was to be especially noticeable in the post-1870 Louise Michel. But most mid-century women, too, exploit the structure of the quest, with goals sought for in distant lands and ordeals undergone; they envisage the clash of collectivities; and they stress the massiveness of national events or their aftermath. George Sand's *Un hiver à Majorque* is one example, only minimally 'about' Chopin's illness and more obviously concerned with, *inter alia*, the repercussions of the Inquisition, the large-scale movement of individuals, or the strange discoveries of the voyager. And for some, the reasons for the journey or its attendant dangers (more obvious for women than for men) lead them to stress feelings of banishment and social rejection – feelings which nevertheless bring a special strength. Voilquin concludes her memoirs with the comment that her final trip to Russia will mean accepting the life of a 'fortuneless exile' – but the financial independence she hopes to gain there will not only give her 'freedom of action' later, but also, far more extensively, 'my social and religious life' ('ma liberté d'action, c'est-à-dire ma vie sociale et religieuse', 397). Exile leads to renaissance.

Two of the most compelling travel-works of this middle period are

Tristan's *Pérégrinations d'une paria* (1838) and d'Aunet's *Voyage d'une femme au Spitzberg*, published sixteen years later (1854). The journeys they relate were undertaken respectively in 1833 and 1839. Between them they exemplify the main tendencies of women's travelogues of the time. They are also better written and more complex than imaginative works by the same writers: is it too fantastic to suppose that the physical boldness they felt able to describe in this context liberated their imaginations in other ways too?[9]

Flora Tristan (1803–44) was the illegitimate daughter of a French mother and a rich Peruvian father. She travelled to Peru to reclaim her paternal inheritance (unsuccessfully, as it turned out): this is the journey described in *Pérégrinations d'une paria*. After 1835, she became involved with socialist and feminist groups in Paris, and published political works, notably *Promenades dans Londres* (1840) and *Union ouvrière* (1843), her most famous work. She died in the middle of a promotional tour round France to advertise this book and promulgate its ideas.

Tristan was already a sharp political thinker by the time she wrote *Pérégrinations*. Its prevailing idea is that of a shared humanity that transcends national boundaries, but this rather loose catch-all combines with specific analyses of the social groupings she encountered. At the same time, the picaresque structure allows her to explore a range of feelings both amorous and familial; and her prose style lives up to the alliterative title, being generally polished and well cadenced. Here is her description of her anxious ride to the port on the day of her departure from France, the phonetic echoes reinforcing both the contradictions and connections between her dread and the sensory impressions she experiences. It is seven in the morning; Tristan keeps her head out of the window, noticing the gradually mounting noise in the streets and keen not to miss anything about this last dawning day:

Le souffle tiède de la brise arrivait sur mon *vi*sage; je sentais une surabondance de *vi*e, tandis que la *d*ouleur, le *d*ésespoir, étaient *d*ans mon âme: je ressemblais au patient qu'on *m*ène à la *m*ort; j'en*vi*ais le sort de ces femmes qui *v*enaient de la campagne *v*endre en *vi*lle leur lait, de ces ou*v*riers qui se rendaient au travail: té*m*o*i*n *m*oi-même de *m*on con*voi* funèbre, je *v*oyais *p*eut-être *p*our la dernière fois cette *p*opulation laborieuse. (7)

(The warm breath of the breeze reached my face; I felt a great abundance of life, while grief and despair were in my soul: I was like the condemned man being led to his death; I envied the lot of those women coming from

Im. de Lemercier, Benard et C.

Mᵐᵉ Flora TRISTAN .

10. Flora Tristan.

the country to sell their milk, those workers going to their labour: a witness to my own funeral procession, I was seeing for the last time, perhaps, this hard-working population.)

The episodic construction also allows Tristan to record quirky details in a more relaxed and humorous manner than her later discursive works permit. She alludes often casually to the risks of her travels and switches with engaging désinvolture from the political control exerted by her Peruvian uncle to Latin American fleas (106–8). She was the only woman on board the ship that took her to Peru in a five-month journey, and the captain fell in love with her – a love which she did not fully reciprocate but could not quite bring herself to discourage; she narrates the journey's claustrophia and discomforts, physical and psychological, in throwaway style, as when she has to shelter in a barrel, 'nouveau Diogène' ('a new Diogenes', 50). Soon after arrival, she journeyed to Arequipa across the Peruvian desert, once more the only woman in the group; again she relates this gripping tale without overdramatizing herself.

Tristan can, certainly, be vocal in her indignation about injustices, from sexism to the 'shame' heaped on illegitimate birth: until the age of fifteen, she says, 'I never knew about this absurd social distinction and its monstrous consequences' (92). But even in this she is able, like La Tour du Pin, to leave key conversations or documents to speak for themselves. Here is part of a nicely insolent letter from her uncle, which Tristan quotes without comment other than factual:

Convenons donc que vous n'êtes que la fille naturelle de mon frère, ce qui n'est pas une raison pour que vous soyez moins digne de ma considération et de ma tendre affection. (98)

(Let's agree, then, that you are only my brother's natural daughter, which is not a reason why you should be any the less worthy of my respect and tender affection.)

Tristan hits off this uncle's character with a novelist's eye – a political novelist's eye: she later observes that his letters were little masterpieces of diplomacy; he could have been Talleyrand, he could have been the prime minister of an absolute monarchy (136). With similar coolness, Tristan describes a political crisis in Peru that took place during her stay and in which she herself played an advisory role, indeed could have had a more leading one had she chosen: she was, she believes, the best-informed person in the country. 'I am in the middle of a society in revolution, I told myself; let us see by what means I could play a part, what instruments I might use'; she thinks of seizing power but cannot bring herself to do it because 'my woman's heart swelled within me' (215, 224–7). There may be some delusion here; what is important is the belief in herself – not wholly misplaced, as her political impact in France was to show.[10]

Pérégrinations d'une paria is a zestful work: monks' ribaldry, smoking women, extraordinary clothes and strange religious rituals all convey, as well as an acute intelligence and personal charisma, Tristan's thirst for new experiences. Towards the end she says she had wanted to ask her uncle for money to return via North America, 'so dominant is my taste for adventurous journeys' (356). And elsewhere, she says she wants women to travel to widen their intellectual horizons.[11]

Léonie d'Aunet's *Voyage d'une femme au Spitzberg* is a more deliberately popularizing work than Tristan's; she needed to make money, and she exploits the possibilities of the form with a consistent view to capturing a wide readership – no doubt having learned lessons from some of her predecessors in the genre. D'Aunet (1820–79) had already become famous for having taken part, at the age of only nineteen, in this expedition, initiated by the Commission du Nord. She was living at the time with the painter Biard, whom the organizing naval officer wanted to bring as the official painter of the crew. Léonie promised she would persuade Biard to come if she herself was allowed to accompany him. Her friends tried to dissuade her; in any case women were strictly forbidden on board French naval ships. But Léonie argued her way on to the boat that eventually left Hammerfest for the Polar journey.[12]

Truly adventurous female European explorers were still a rarity. That same year (before d'Aunet's return), Girardin had drawn attention to the qualities needed to be such a woman. She was writing about the first woman's ascent of Mont-Blanc. (This was by Mlle d'Angeville in 1838.) Girardin evokes the most dangerous moments: 'Oh! it's not possible, her will is failing, a woman can't expect herself to make such an effort . . . But suddenly the thought of her pride breathes new life into her.' She remembers, says Girardin, that a hundred pairs of field-glasses are trained on Mont-Blanc, watching for her arrival. Her strength returns and she courageously sets off again. On her descent she is greeted with 'transport': 'Ah! mademoiselle d'Angeville le dit elle-même, le succès change tous les noms; on me nommait folle au depart, on m'appelait héroïne au retour' ('Mlle d'Angeville says it herself, success changes names; they said I was a madwoman when I set out, a heroine when I returned'). And Girardin, characteristically teasing, asks if women now have the monopoly on brave enterprises, citing other adventurous ones.[13] But they were as yet relatively few. In the eighteenth century, Jeanne Barre, disguised as a man, had accompanied her lover Commerson to Tahiti.[14] Adélaïde-Edmée de la Briche undertook extensive travels in Europe from 1785 to 1832.[15] The *Bloomsbury Guide*, however, under its entry 'Travel writing', cites only British women; and those who were true explorers rather than just welltravelled tourists all came later than Léonie d'Aunet.[16]

D'Aunet knows how to exploit the singularity of her enterprise. The very title shows that she will capitalize on the fact that she is a woman, thus catching female readers; she casts the book as 'letters' to a brother, thereby suggesting to male readers that they can approve what she did – wouldn't they, too, like to have such a sister? Whereas Tristan can border on the nonchalant, d'Aunet plays to the gallery, almost 'hams it up'. We have seen this in the parrot incident; another example is the ship's arrival at the furthest navigable point of Spitsbergen, a bay. In November, the temperature drops so low at this latitude that mercury freezes and brandy has to be hacked out with a knife. But now it is July. (The passage is noticeably alliterated, as with Tristan's departure.)

On se représente, n'est-ce pas, ce lieu, où tout est froid et inerte, enveloppé d'un silence profond et lugubre? Eh bien! c'est tout le contraire qu'il faut se figurer; rien ne peut rendre le formidable tumulte d'un jour de dégel au Spitzberg.

La mer, hérissée de glaces aiguës, clapote bruyamment; les pics élevés de la côte glissent, se détachent et tombent dans le golfe avec un fracas épouvantable; les montagnes craquent et se fendent; les vagues se brisent, furieuses, contre les caps de granit; les îles de glace, en se désorganisant, produisent des pétillements semblables à des décharges de mousqueterie; le vent soulève des tourbillons de neige avec de rauques mugissements: c'est terrible et magnifique; on croit entendre le chœur des abîmes du vieux monde préludant à un nouveau chaos. (130)

(You picture this place, don't you, where everything is cold and inert, as enveloped in deep, lugubrious silence? Well! imagine the complete opposite; nothing can convey the formidable tumult of a day of thaw at Spitsbergen.

The sea, bristling with pointed ice, makes a loud lapping noise; the high peaks of the coast slide, come away and drop into the gulf with a frightful din; the mountains crack and split; the waves break furiously against the granite capes; the ice-islands, as they fall apart, sputter like muskets firing; the wind raises up whirlwinds of snow with a hoarse moaning: it is terrible and magnificent; you think you can hear the choir of the old world's abysses delivering the prelude to a new chaos.)

D'Aunet relates with the same gusto her experiences of the midnight sun and the aurora borealis; she rolls into marshes, she descends icy rapids with an adopted dog on board; and she wears men's clothes. In such exceptional conditions, she says, her costume had to undergo 'profound variations', becoming very convenient and perfectly uncouth ('très commode et parfaitement disgracieux'): she wore men's trousers and a cabin-boy's shirt in coarse blue cloth, a large neckerchief made of red wool, and a black leather belt. Felt-lined boots and a sailor's hat completed 'this outfit that is unlikely to set a trend' ('cet ensemble de toilette qui ne sera pas imité'); 'needless to say', underneath she was padded with flannel. Other additions, essential when she went up on deck, turned her into a 'shapeless package'; she had to cut her hair, which would otherwise get hopelessly tangled; all in all, 'additions and subtractions contributed, you can see, to making me peculiarly ugly: but, in a place like that, all you think about is suffering from the cold as little as possible, and any vanity is misguided' (136). A quasi-apologetic note is struck here; however, all those nineteenth-century women who broadcast their adoption of men's dress, or the freer female clothing of a few other countries, were performing a service of liberation for their more inhibited sisters – sowing the seeds, at least, of alternatives for the adult woman.[17]

D'Aunet draws attention to the complex mix of factors that made her enterprise almost, but not quite, impossible – to the blend of misogyny, begrudging tolerance and unwilling admiration that greeted it. One day, as winter approaches, she overhears a conversation among a small group of crew members to the effect that she should not have been allowed to come ('what an idea to have brought along a woman!') – particularly since she is (according to one of them) a rather feeble specimen. But the bosun tells them they have no common sense: so much the better if she is weak and delicate, even better if the rest think she would be the first to leave for safety in the event of the ship's being iced in. What is most to be feared on winter journeys is the crew's demoralization, but, with a woman on board, they need not worry. So long as they can keep her alive, they can say to the men who are weakening: 'Allons donc, n'avez-vous pas honte? Le froid n'est pas encore trop dur, vous voyez bien, puisqu'une femme le supporte' ('Go on, aren't you ashamed of yourselves? The cold isn't too awful yet, you can see that, if a woman can bear it'). So – d'Aunet concludes – she was assured of being well looked after (133–5).

Despite d'Aunet's humour, the journey was dangerous and harrowing at many moments, and here she has no need to be theatrical: she speaks unaffectedly of her illnesses and of the perpetual state of nervous agitation in which she was kept by the constant light, the cold, the bad food: 'il me semblait traverser un cauchemar' ('I felt I was living through a nightmare', 135–6). So these travellers, for all their sophistication in packaging and marketing their narratives, held up to nineteenth-century Frenchwomen a direct and honest model of female courage and of women who decidedly were not 'indoors'. This was not their only contribution. Like the other life-writers, the travellers took for granted that their writing might permissibly stray into all kinds of unusual physical circumstances: outlandish furniture, the structure of a copper-mine, stinks, food greedily enjoyed by both themselves and others, the feel of soggy clothing on the body – other material and sometimes burlesque details which would be enjoyed both for their significance and for their incongruity. They began to be the female Balzacs of the mid-century. But it is a journalist rather than a travel-writer who can lay claim to that title.

CHAPTER 14

The journalist: Delphine de Girardin

Like George Sand, Delphine de Girardin (1804–55) was a mid-century literary 'phenomenon'. She had a good start as the daughter of the witty novelist Sophie Gay, who encouraged her talents. She soon became famous equally for her looks, her personality and the works she published in different media, from the youthful poetry that won her a special mention in an 1822 Académie Française competition to her more mature fiction, plays and journalism. Lamartine, Vigny, Sand, Hugo, Gautier and Balzac admired her, and memoir-writers cite her as an obviously outstanding figure of the time. At age fifty-one, having recently produced some of her best work, she died of stomach cancer.[1]

Like Ségur, Girardin has attracted attention recently, principally for her journalism, of which two modern editions appeared in 1986.[2] This journalism consisted of deliberately fragmented commentaries on 'today's scene', semi-political sketches and short chronicles. Girardin published them between 1836 and 1848 under the pseudonym 'Vicomte de Launay' in *La Presse*, her husband's daily newspaper, which – like its rivals *Le Constitutionnel* and *Le Siècle* – had an average print-run of over 20,000.[3] This form suited Girardin's special gifts. It is striking to follow her development from the early poetry, bedevilled by bombast, sentimentality and loose wording, to the stylistic punch and taut structure of the *Lettres parisiennes* (the collective title of the journalism, published as a whole shortly after her death).[4] Even her drama, successful though it was, lacks the consistent bite and the attention to detail of the *Lettres parisiennes*. There is no equivalent in her verse or plays to this observant and satirical commentary of 1839 on the 'pets of the moment': are they monkeys? bear cubs? cute panthers ('de mignonnes panthères')? No: they are tortoises from Africa, for 'this animal which has no cry is, just the same, a language in itself, meaning: I have a friend, brother, uncle in Algeria; he has sent me cashmere scarves, Arab cloaks, flasks of jasmine perfume and gold-brocaded wallets, all things which usually come with tortoises.' This pet, continues Girardin, has the great advantage that you never have to think about it: you forget to feed it for a month – it bears no grudge; you walk on it – it doesn't feel a thing; it's in fact the model female companion, enduring all sorts of bad treatment without complaint (*Chroniques parisiennes*, 234–5).

Girardin was by no means the only woman journalist of the period. Magazines and newspapers were increasingly being seen as a domain into which women could venture as both consumers and contributors. In the previous century or even earlier, editors had begun to realize that women as well as men were reading their products, and to some extent tailored these accordingly; in nine-teenth-century France, a newspaper like *Le Petit Journal* – which in the 1860s reached a daily circulation of 200,000, exceptional for the time – had to appeal not only to men who might be hostile to women's education, but to educated women readers themselves.[5] Women had also been writing for and editing French journals since the eighteenth century. These might be fashion magazines or, later, literary periodicals.[6] Or women might use journalism for feminist or other propaganda. Two particularly powerful political journalists of the nineteenth century were Voilquin and Séverine (the pen-name of Caroline Rémy, 1855–1929). And already famous women (such as Sand, Tristan and later in the century Louise Michel) set up their own newspapers for specific causes.[7] But these publications were usually short-lived. Girardin wrote more sustainedly for the press than any other woman of the mid-century; and one of her twentieth-century editors claims that she invented the 'column', in which, ahead of her time, she was a historian of the *zeitgeist*. He even argues that it was because other women learned from her 'school' that they were able in these middle decades to move into politically committed journalism.[8] But, precisely because Girardin was not writing for a cause, she could give her fancy freer rein than could those more impassioned colleagues who were necessarily committed to stirring up readers' feelings on the issue in hand, and she could make the ephemerality of her format part of her subject-matter. She could also cheek readers, reproaching them for not having got a joke in a previous article and saying that from now on she will follow her pleasantries with detailed explanations: few nineteenth-century

women writers dared to tease like this (*Chroniques parisiennes*, 203).
Girardin was the most imaginative and self-reflexive woman journalist of the time, and in this particular mode, despite its obvious
superficiality, one of the most inventive nineteenth-century French
women writers.

Her taste for the bizarre and incongruous is one of the qualities
that marks her out. Like any fashion-writer or gossip columnist, she
describes this year's clothes and the trivia of life in Paris; but current
fashions become subsidiary to a sense of farce that seems to want to
take over or become surreal. The new handkerchiefs of 1836 are
irresistible, their rich borders in relief strewn with birds, peacocks,
marvellously embroidered parrots; but these are the hankies of
caprice, not for daily use: if you feel sad, for instance, however could
you resort to a parrot to wipe away your tears? (56). That same year,
the rage for moving house turns Paris into a 'shop of walking
furniture':

on ne peut traverser une rue sans rencontrer un secrétaire et un commode,
ou bien un canapé renversé, garni de toutes ses chaises, chaises menaçantes
suspendues merveilleusement dans les airs. Vous tournez une rue . . . et
vous vous trouvez nez à nez avec un buste de grand homme, qui marche à
reculons; à droite, s'avance un piano avec son tabouret, sa lyre et ses
pédales démontées; à gauche, paraît un guéridon qui semble demander
pourquoi son marbre ne l'a pas suivi. (51–2)

(you can't cross a road without meeting a desk and a chest-of-drawers, or
else an upside-down settee, garnished with all its chairs: threatening chairs,
marvellously hanging in the breezes. You turn into a street . . . and you
find you're rubbing noses with the bust of a great man, walking backwards;
to the right, a piano advances with its stool – rods and pedals dismantled;
to the left, a pedestal looms up, seeming to ask why its marble hasn't
followed it.) (author's ellipsis)

If Girardin reports on endless balls, the reporting itself becomes
wild:

Paris is dancing, jumping, enjoying itself on all sides . . . As for the centre
of Paris, it's not waltzing or dancing, not jumping or tumbling; it's turning,
rolling, falling, rushing, dashing headlong, it's engulfed, it whirls, it swoops
like an army, it envelops you like a waterspout, it drags you along like an
avalanche, it whisks you off like the simoon; it's hell breaking out, it's
demons on holiday. . . (72–3)

She relays rumours, as any columnist must, but a piece of 1837 turns
these into a hyperbolic rumination on hearsay: false news can always

barefacedly ('hardiment') count on a week of existence – not a general, universal existence, because it's already a little defunct in the place of its birth even as it starts up another life in the place where it will die. In vain will people supposed to be dead claim they're still alive, make unheard-of efforts to uproot the false news from boggy minds ('du sol embourbé des intelligences'). You will have to perform startling deeds to persuade your mourners that you're still among the living; and even that may not be enough: there will still be the stubborn ones who, on seeing you, would rather say you've been resuscitated than admit they were wrong when they provided all the details of your death (75–6).

This skewing of perspective leads to the combination or invention of unusual sense impressions, words and phrases. Ice-cream eaten in the presence of cigar-smokers is 'glace au tabac et à la vanille' ('tobacco-and-vanilla ice-cream'), the eater is – neologistically – bathed in 'vapeur cigarine' ('cigarine vapour', 203). Here are a few more of her neologisms (the last acknowledged in Littré's dictionary): 'encrophobe', 'reêtre', 'classiquissimes' ('inkophobe', 'to re-be', 'clas-sicissimo') (27, 167, 397). Alliteration, jokey rhymes, zeugma almost dictate meanings: when the future Napoleon III tries to raise the Strasbourg garrison in November 1836, Girardin sarcastically advises everyone to get ready, among them coach-drivers who are to prepare their whips, their phrases and their horse-feed: 'préparez vos fouets, vos phrases et votre avoine' (59–60).

Girardin's journalism is unusually 'literary' in other ways. More than a hundred years before Sarraute, she invented anonymized conversations (49, 398). Her articles are self-consciously structured, reworking given threads so as to turn them into refrains and leading to ironically explosive climaxes which tie pieces up with neat comments on their own production. An 1847 account of a fire at a ball (in which no one, apparently, died but which occasioned a little local mayhem) exemplifies this. Firemen appear, axes cut through walls, yet the genteel conversation continues through the smoke and coughing; suddenly a group of women rushes outside in a panic, but the 'Vicomte' herself stays calm, thinking: 'On that side, we can see three or four flames at most. On the other side, we can already count a hundred firemen. Let's see what happens, and so long as the firemen are in the majority, let's stay calm.' Others weep in fear while still mindful of the hierarchies: some women sob with the caretaker, others go to sob a few houses down the street, but undoubtedly what is preferable is to weep at the duchesse de P***'s house. 'De tous les effrois, c'était l'effroi du *meilleur genre*' ('Of all the fears, it was the one in the *best possible taste*'; author's italics). Meanwhile the comte de Nieuwerkerke (superintendent of the Beaux-Arts under Napoleon III) worries that a magnificent Murillo is shaking under the hacking of the firemen. He runs for a ladder and rescues the Murillo. The action is praiseworthy, says the Vicomte; but in this zeal, in the obvious anguish, there is something rather unflattering for the guests:

Cet empressement semblait leur dire: Grillez tous, ça m'est bien égal, on vous recommencera, vous autres, mais on ne recommencera jamais un Murillo.

(His haste seemed to be saying: Roast, the lot of you, I don't care, *you* can always be started again, but a Murillo never can be.)

While the firemen are demolishing the drawing-room, guests are still bravely dancing in the ballroom, and the orchestra is playing a waltz with obligato fireman accompaniment ('avec accompagnement du sapeur obligé'). The whole scene is somehow magical, taking one into an unknown, almost heavenly world, where people would see, recognize, love each other only through a cloud of incense; one thing, alas! destroys the illusion: the incense smells strongly of soot. In all this, there is time for the Vicomte to speculate about the different forms women's courage can take; for a young pedant to worry because a dozen people have used the masculine noun 'incendie' in the feminine; and for the guests to joke about Canova's Magdalen, also in the house: her tears would not save her from the fire; it would be a strange end for this famous penitent to perish at a social function. Hats get mixed up, there are comical alarms and excursions . . . But really, that evening, everyone does their duty: the firemen put out the fire, the architects knock the house down, the diplomats don't know a thing about it, and (these are the final words) 'nous-même enfin, vous nous rendrez cette justice, nous avons rempli consciencieusement nos devoirs d'observateur' ('as for ourself, you'll grant us this, we conscientiously carried out our duties as an observer', 398–412).

'Observer' of a special kind. No other woman writer of the century shared so many interests and techniques with Balzac. His influence on Girardin was strong, but she was a more intelligent reader of him than most of his male contemporaries, and exploited the influence not slavishly but creatively.[9] Like Balzac describing Mme Vauquer's boarding-house, Girardin makes material details so playful that the phonetic echoes and personifications start to govern the direction of the text; as the 'fireman's ball' shows, she likes the polyphonic. She is half-seduced by, half-scathing about, snobbery; like Balzac, she has an interest in the morally diverse and contra-dictory, distinguishing between the varying strands that make up 'courage', 'fear', 'protectiveness'; like him, she has fantasy and a metaphorical imagination, as when, in an 1844 piece, she imagines salons as gardens in which clumps of furniture resemble clumps of trees and bushes (365–6). And in a piece of 1841, she re-defines 'observation', construing the world as text and pointing out the difference between lived and remembered time. The career of observer, when conducted in good faith, she says, takes on a powerful charm. All objects are transformed; it's no longer Mme So-and-so you're going to see, it's a type you're going to study, a book-chapter you are going to leaf through, sometimes a novel whose finest page you are about to read. You almost always, she continues, make mistakes when you look deliberately; and you lose that which makes you guess well, that is, the freshness of the first impression. To collect good observations, you have to observe without making efforts, almost involuntarily; you must not seek for effects, you must entrust effects with the task of striking you ('il faut se fier à eux du soin de vous frapper eux-mêmes'); and it is only later, when you remember what you've seen, that you can undertake to explain it; for in the science of observation, the memory is more intelligent than the look ('dans la science observatrice, le souvenir est plus intelligent que le regard', 309–10).

Girardin is also the only female author of the mid-century apart from Sand to say, 'Let's take this common attitude and turn it inside out just for fun' – but she goes further, is more perverse, than Sand. Ridicule, as we have seen, was feared by most women writers of the early and mid-century, including, apparently, Girardin herself (as her 'Napoline' would suggest). But in 1839, she questions whether it really is so powerful and says 'Try it out on me!':

Autre banalité: on dit encore, et qui n'a dit cela au moins une fois dans sa vie: *En France, le ridicule tue tout*; et la foule de s'écrier: Ah! c'est bien vrai! Eh bien! nous, dût-on nous faire servir à prouver que cela est, nous vous dirons que cela n'est point. En France, le ridicule n'a jamais tué personne; il n'a jamais su ôter à un talent véritable une parcelle de sa valeur. En France, précisément, le ridicule n'a aucun empire.

(Another banal thing: people still say, and who hasn't at least once in his life: *In France, ridicule kills everything*; whereupon the crowd cries: Oh, how true! Well! even if you were to use us to prove it is so, we'll tell you that it is not so. In France, ridicule has never killed anyone; has never been able to take one jot of value away from real talent. In France, precisely, ridicule holds no sway.) (author's italics)

In support, she cites Chateaubriand, Lamartine and Hugo as figures who have been constantly ridiculed but still have great prestige (199–201). Girardin has the cussedness, in fact, to question many prevailing commonplaces. This does not mean she is right (we note that she cites no other woman than herself as self-evidently resistant to ridicule). But at the least she is refreshing, and at best open-endedly experiments with ideas.

How far were Girardin's wit and inventiveness helped on by her male pseudonym? As in the case of Sand, the pretence was soon penetrated (certainly by 1843, when the collected articles of the earlier years were published under her name as well as the Vicomte's). Besides, fewer and fewer women now found it necessary to adopt male pseudonyms: those who took them, like Marie d'Agoult or later in the century Jeanne Lapauze (Daniel Lesueur), may have been making a statement as much as choosing to 'hide'. For some, to use a man's name, even once the gaff was blown (or especially once it was), perhaps served as permission to flirt with androgyny. 'You know I'm a woman but you're letting me pretend to be a man.' Thus Sand's narrators, often initially male, soon – intermittently or constantly – inhabit a no-man's land where their sex becomes a matter of indifference or fluctuating perspective.

Because this is journalism, Girardin's pseudonym enables her to refer to herself in the masculine even more than does Sand, via semi-private, semi-public jokes: 'Quand je pense que je suis Français . . . !' ('When I think I'm a Frenchman . . . !', 58). She re-invents herself as having been a pretty boy who disliked uncomfortable clothes: 'Nous avions le malheur d'être un bel enfant' ('We had the misfortune to be a beautiful boy') who had to be dressed up for special occasions, complaining the while that these fancy garments pull, pinch, itch: 'he' is told one must suffer to be beautiful (170–1). Elsewhere, in a whimsical mingling of genders and ages, little girls at parties are said to criticize and denigrate with the aplomb of an old journalist – like the Vicomte? (293). And Girardin still more knowingly transfers supposedly gender-specific characteristics when, in that 1840 article about the 'unsuitable' salon, she launches into a discussion of the odd personas with which women are 'born'. Some are 'born' as nurses or courtesans. But there are others . . . Girardin pretends to hesitate: 'who are born . . . We dare not say it! – Come on, be brave: who are born as . . . a *police-constable!* a *city guard*, a *gendarme!*' These women – 'courageous', Girardin calls them – police salons zealously, hushing chatterboxes when the singing starts, telling men to give up their seats as women arrive, getting windows opened, doorways evacuated. Servants who don't know them obey them just as passers-by obey an unknown guard. And they have the voice to go with it: 'Plus d'un colonel voudrait trouver, pour dire *Portez arme*, l'accent qu'elles trouvent pour crier: *Chut! chut donc*' ('More than one colonel would like to find, for his *Shoulder arms*, the tone they find to shout *Quiet! quiet now*', 255–8).[10]

Girardin fell out of public view in part, perhaps, because of the inherently transient nature of this form in which she excelled; she may be difficult to revive because of her politics and her stance on women. She has no particularly fixed viewpoint in either area, sometimes showing sympathy for the underprivileged or espousing a feminist viewpoint; but, when expressing a more reactionary view, exhibiting a callousness that – for example – the right-wing Balzac does not descend to. She shrugs off, or parades tasteless jokes about, the misery of the silk workers of Lyon whose appalling conditions were brought to the public's attention by insurrections in the 1830s (179–86).[11] And, quisling-like, she extends an 1847 attack on Mme Roland to turn savagely on '*literary women*', who are 'made out of books' ('les *femmes littéraires*, c'est-à-dire des femmes faites avec des livres'); these women deserve to be book-bound, not dressed ('mériteraient d'être *reliées* plutot qu'habillées'); and writing women should mistrust their own reading, for 'to half-imitate authors you adore is not even parody, it's betrayal! . . . ' (421–3). Sand herself could be scornful of female intellectuals. But Girardin's dubious stands suggest not so much a rethinking as a lack of moral centre; the more hostile sallies seem often to be motivated by the desire to make a newspaper splash out of her own *chutzpah*. Whether this stems from complacency, or on the contrary betrays anxiety about her calling – exacerbated because she knows she is, after all, a woman – is a matter for speculation. But, whatever the motivation, Girardin does juggle with her medium in a quite new way. It is only in the female poets of the period that we find a comparably consistent exploration of the possibilities of form and language.

CHAPTER 15

Feeling and poetic technique: Marceline Desbordes-Valmore

Elegiac or lyric modes predominated in the verse written by nine-teenth-century French women. But they were adept at others, such as fable; longer rhymed narratives (which often recounted broken hearts and ruined lives); or the more flexible form of the song-lyric.[1] Some of this verse is awkward or contrived – as is some by male contemporaries. Girardin and others tend, for instance, to insert 'Oh!'s and repeat key words in order to fill out their alexandrines to the requisite twelve syllables. (In fact, many seem more comfortable with shorter lines, such as the octosyllable, which force them to be concise.) Colet, making a virtue of necessity, professes to despise close attention to technique, suggesting that it is arid by comparison with 'real' feeling, 'real' life.[2] She is promoting a Romantic view of creativity and perhaps even groping at a way forward to free verse. But in practice, this focus on what was said rather than how it was said could lead Colet, and some others, into doggerel held together mainly by the end-rhyme – again, it must be stressed, no worse than that of minor male poets of the period such as Pétrus Borel (1809–59).

Normally, however, the women poets were, or taught themselves to become, accomplished technicians. The rules governing French verse are more intricate than those governing English, and these women's mastery of it is all the more striking given that most of them had no formal training and no acquaintance with helpful concomi-tant exercises such as the intensive study or translation of Latin verse, which well-educated boys did as a matter of course.[3] Some were 'naturals', such as the eighteen-year-old Elisa Mercœur who filled in some 'rhymed endings' on the spot. This is a game ('bouts rimés') in which participants are provided with only the first letter and last word of each line of an otherwise blank poem. Mme Mercœur reproduces Elisa's correct and quite impressive effort.[4]

Others – Tastu, for example – improved steadily as from their very first attempts, obviously judging their own work with a critical eye, seeing where practice was needed, and acquiring an ever-suppler and finally flawless technical versatility. In Tastu's decasyllabic 'La Veille de Noël' ('Christmas Eve'), for instance, the mother sings a lullaby of which the chorus, with well-handled assonances, is:

> Pour mon enfant tourne, léger fuseau,
> Tourne sans bruit auprès de son berceau.

(Turn, light spindle, for my child, turn quietly by his cradle.)

It emerges that this spindle is making no privileged Christmas present: the exhausted mother has to work at night, even on Christmas Eve, to support her fatherless child, and finally the comforting chorus is (literally) split open at the end with the insertion of a line showing the child would otherwise die. The mother is addressing 'Hope':

> Entre mes doigts guide ce lin docile,
> Pour mon enfant tourne, léger fuseau;
> Seul tu soutiens sa vie encor débile;
> Tourne sans bruit auprès de son berceau.   (39–44)

(Guide this docile flax between my fingers, turn, light spindle, for my child; you alone support his still weakly life; turn quietly by his cradle.)

Also technically skilful was the humble seamstress Blanchecotte, who in her poem 'N'aimons jamais' ('Let us never love') uses the octosyllable to create a carnivalesque lilt that ironically contrasts with and highlights the bitterness of the speaker. Here are the opening lines:

> Arrachons de notre poitrine
> Ce cœur insensé qui bondit,
> Où la souffrance s'enracine
> Comme un germe amer et maudit!
> Le cœur étouffe la pensée,
> A son tour étouffons le cœur;
> Que l'âme soit débarrassée
> De ce maître dominateur.   (*Rêves*, 218)

(Let's tear from our breast this senseless, bounding heart, where suffering takes root like a bitter, accursed seed! The heart smothers thought, in turn let's smother the heart; let the soul be rid of this dominating master.)

Blanchecotte, like Tastu, uses phonetic networks well: here, the *er* and *m* in '*germe amer* et *m*audit' already give a sense of constriction (heightened by the brevity of the line); this is intensified in the next two lines, where the half-rhyme of 'cœur' and 'tour', and the repetition of *tou* in 'étouffe' and 'tour', reinforce the image of smothering and suffocating. The twin *d*s bringing together 'débarrassée' and 'dominateur' convey the clash of these opposed concepts, yet the determination of the narrator.[5]

So these women poets could achieve excellence of technique; however, a number found it difficult to use this in such a way as to suggest a wide range of feelings and physical sensations. The major male poets of the century combined psychological with metaphysical contradiction; re-created varying sense-impressions that blend with or jolt against each other; and expressed an often strong eroticism. Women, schooled to be modest about their ideas and their own sensuality, were starting to break down barriers; but up to about 1870, this modesty still gave the verse of many the air of being at best restricted in its aims, at worst a cottage industry. Let us take the case of sexual desire and see how women expressed it in all genres: this will give some idea of the problems faced by female writers of lyric poetry, the form *par excellence* in which it ought to be possible to evoke erotic feeling.

In the first three decades of the nineteenth century, most women were still struggling for ways in which to write about sexual desire. Exceptionally, in *Julie ou j'ai sauvé ma rose* (1807), Choiseul-Meuse did focus on it. She proclaims very early in the novel that all women have desires (1 8); the rose which Julie saves is – as might be supposed – her virginity, but (she often graphically explains) it is possible to have a physical relationship without the final act ever taking place, and this, cunningly, not only preserves one's virtue but avoids the master–slave bond which inevitably follows upon consummation. Thus the book is able to highlight the pleasures of foreplay and non-penetrative sex, with numerous barely euphemized references to the female erogenous zones. It is difficult to know how many other women wrote explicitly erotic works either during this early period or later: Louis Perceau, in his *Bibliographie du roman érotique au XIXe siècle*, names a few (including, with doubts, Sand), as does the *Bloomsbury Guide*; but Perceau implies that some male-authored pornographic works may have been deliberately attributed to women for titillation.[6]

It is likely that other early nineteenth-century women read the much-reprinted *Julie*.[7] But their own writing is far more discreet about female eroticism than about male. In this latter respect they seem relatively unabashed. Cottin, for example, has lascivious descriptions of men gazing at women clothed in such a way as to show all their curves.[8] The erotic feelings of female characters, however, are hinted at only through such occasional words as 'quiver', 'set aglow/aflame' ('frémir', 'embraser'), or – still more indirectly – through images of melancholy. Thus in *Amélie Mansfield* melancholy allows Amélie to feel desire for the Ernest she is trying to resist: the lapping of the waves of Lake Lugano, the noise of the oars and the boatmen's songs all form a 'melancholic concert which weakened, in spite of myself, the strength with which I was trying to arm myself' ('un concert mélancolique qui affaiblissait malgré moi les forces dont je cherchais à m'armer', II 61). Similarly, a mysterious Englishman in Gay's *Laure d'Estell* has a 'melancholic smile' which gives one's soul a 'soft, languorous feeling' ('un sentiment doux et langoureux', 143).[9] Critics have suggested that in this early period, melancholy – or the 'mal du siècle' that is one of the hallmarks of contemporary men's writing – is scarcely to be seen in female writers.[10] But this view needs to be modified: melancholy is there as a strong feeling and even an erotic stimulus; it is a way for these writers to talk about female sexuality.

After about 1830, a greater openness was becoming feasible. Contemporary and later female writers were indebted to Colet, who, more than any other, showed women frankly assessing men's bodies, and affirmed both their sexual pleasure and their right to be honest about it.[11] The heroine of *Lui* says that as her appointment with her lover Léonce approaches, something inflamed and giddying takes hold of her whole being. How, she asks, can one forget delights, and even – she will 'dare' to say it – intimate familiarities? Is the child immodest because it has a happy memory of having fallen asleep on its nurse's breast? And she claims that

l'image riante d'une caresse délectable ou du tressaillement de la volupté ranime [l'esprit] et l'égaye, et lui communique pour ainsi dire le contre-coup enivrant de ce que le corps seul semblait avoir ressenti! (392–3)[12]

(the joyful image of a delectable caress – of quivering with pleasure – brings the mind to life, cheers it, and communicates to it, so to speak, the other, intoxicating, side of what only the body seemed to have felt!)

Colet also writes of the liberating power of verse, saying that there is always, in its language, something exalted that goes beyond what the author meant; this, she believes, arises from rhyme, which can oblige the poet to use more tender words, and also from the use of the 'tu' form. Once more she is over-focused on content, but driving at something more generally interesting about the 'suggestiveness' of poetry.[13]

That inhibitions remained is nevertheless incontrovertible. To a degree, they existed for male authors too: Coward, in his survey of popular French literature of the middle period, observes that sex 'made a poor showing' at this time (77, 84). But many women clearly felt that even 'allowable' indications or suggestions were going too far for female characters at least.[14] Madeleine in Sand's *François le champi* is not allowed to understand her own desire until François reveals his; in *Mauprat*, we see Bernard's lust – particularly in a scene where he nearly rapes his beloved, Edmée – but Edmée is cool, virtually asexual. Melancholy as a convenient disguise for eroticism had not yet been entirely discarded by Sand or others.[15] And the male gaze retained its overriding importance well into the mid-century, again in all genres. When, in Ancelot's play *Un mariage raisonnable*, the heroine takes off her shapeless outdoor clothes one at a time, Ancelot's stage-directions are designed to appeal to the men in the audience: the actor playing the heroine's beloved is instructed to look on 'enchanted'.[16] The novelist Mme Reybaud, in *Clémentine* (1850), describes her young heroine as any male would: 'Ses formes, tout à la fois sveltes et fortes, annonçaient un complet développement' ('Her shape, both slim and firm, showed she was fully developed', 3). Tristan first describes the 'liberating' dress of Lima women from a distinctly erotic male perspective (*Pérégrinations*, 329–33). Even if some of this was a channel for writers' possible lesbianism, it was still an oblique one. And Colet herself says that successful women writers can expect an especially wounding form of sarcasm if they venture into any image of sexual union that is 'modestly bold' ('pudiquement hardie'): men's cynical wit will dirty and parody it, and once this wit has made us blush, further impure ideas will be thrown insultingly at us.[17] Indeed, the most acute embarrassment suffered by Ulliac-Trémadeure's Emilie is, as we have seen, occasioned by the fear that readers could think the amorous feelings she describes are her own – the very idea makes her want to destroy her work.

Desbordes-Valmore, so talented that even Baudelaire could bring himself to praise her,[18] was subject to the same inhibitions, perhaps still stronger ones. Her liking for elegy, and the recurrence of the word 'pleurs' ('tears'), suggest an underlying guilt about writing, or at least some reluctance to be celebratory or hedonistic. (The late nineteenth-century writer Lucien Descaves called her 'Notre-Dame-des-Pleurs'.)[19] Again we have melancholy, again 'Sophie's misfortunes'. . .[20] Yet she writes about enjoyment and rebellion too (including political rebellion), and, being a concise and subtle manipulator of language, she can appear to be adhering to 'acceptable' themes while evoking them in such a way as to encompass other perspectives, among them the erotic and the sexually ambiguous.

Marceline Desbordes (1785–1859) was born into an impoverished family and had a harsh childhood. When her mother died, she began to act for a living and travelled widely through France. After an unhappy love-affair and the birth and death of two illegitimate children, she married the actor Prosper Valmore. She continued to undergo poverty and suffering (the daughters she had by Valmore also died). But she achieved lasting recognition for her poetry; her use of rhythm influenced Verlaine, who viewed her as the only woman worthy of the title of 'poète maudit'.

Desbordes-Valmore can be radical and jolting. As Verlaine was to do, she makes extensive use of the *vers impair* (the line with an odd number of syllables): often the 5- or 7-syllable line, and even, on some occasions, the 11-syllable line – this would remain rare even in Verlaine's time.[21] The *vers impair* can be used to diverse ends – it may create a lilting or jokey or limping sensation – but it always conveys a sense of something being slightly off-balance or foreshortened, and Desbordes-Valmore exploits this to good effect. In her 1835 political poem 'Cantique des bannis' ('Canticle of the banished'), the 7-syllable line evokes unease from the outset, its irregular stresses emphasizing the idea that the world is out of joint (I have split the lines at the stress points, which give syllabic divisions of $3 + 4$, $2 + 5$, $1 + 6$, $3 + 4$):

> Notre-Dam/e des voyages,
> Du fond/ des moites nuages,
> Fait/es sur notre manteau,
> Scintiller/ votre flambeau . . .

(Our Lady of journeys, from the depths of clammy clouds sparkle your torch on our cloak . . .)

There follow poignant and biting pictures of the exiles; the narrator finally asks the Virgin to bend down to hear 'our savage, tender hymn' and to pity, here below, the sorrows no one else pities ('plaignez ici-bas, / Les douleurs qu'on n'y plaint pas!'). Political chasms remain irreconcilable (130–3).

In the 5-syllable 'Ma chambre' (1841), the short lines give voice to the pent-up sadness and suppressed anger of the narrator, abandoned by her lover. Here are the middle and last stanzas of this three-stanza poem:

> Aux autres cachée,
> Je brode mes fleurs;
> Sans être fâchée,
> Mon âme est en pleurs:
> Le ciel bleu sans voiles,
> Je le vois d'ici;
> Je vois les étoiles:
> Mais l'orage aussi!
>
> Vis-à-vis la mienne
> Une chaise attend:
> Elle fut la sienne,
> La nôtre un instant:
> D'un ruban signée,
> Cette chaise est là,
> Toute résignée,
> Comme me voilà! (152)

(Hidden from others, I embroider my flowers; without being angry, my soul is in tears: I see from here the blue sky without veils; I see the stars: but the storm also! Facing mine, a chair waits: it was his – ours, for an instant: signed with a ribbon, that chair is there, quite resigned, just as I am!)

We have to decide how 'resigned' the narrator really is. A good deal in the poem tugs in the opposite direction: the line 'Mais l'orage aussi!', forcing us to pause after only three syllables and give special emphasis to 'aussi'; the last exclamation 'Comme me voilà!', which can be read either as a simple statement or as defiance, paired with the 'storm' of the previous exclamation; and, perhaps especially, the abrupt lines with their irregular rhythm.

Desbordes-Valmore often uses the formal qualities of her poetry thus, to create not harmonies but tensions. Some of these tensions focus on gender – another link with Verlaine. Barbara Johnson, starting from Baudelaire's attempt to imprison Desbordes-Valmore in a quintessential 'femininity', argues that supposedly fixed gender attributes can be interchangeable in Baudelaire himself (males may be masochistic and hunted) and in Desbordes-Valmore (whose 'investment in poetry itself is in some sense homoerotic'). Johnson claims that Desbordes-Valmore 'offers her reader the chance to re-examine the relations between poetic convention and the construction of gender'.[22] The overt subject-matter of some poems supports this view, such as an invocation to the grave of her childhood friend Albertine: the narrator concludes with a plea to her 'more-than-sister' to come and see 'what I dare not write' trembling in her 'half-open heart'.[23] (Proust at any rate would appear to have seen lesbianism here, in his adoption of the name Albertine for his own Marcel[ine]–Albertine couple.) But, more evocatively, elsewhere Desbordes-Valmore uses the possibilities of gendering in French to create uncertainties. In two love-poems, she refers not to 'him' but to 'an image of him'; since 'image' is feminine in French, she is able to assert longing for a female presence throughout almost the whole poem.[24] In 'Dernière entrevue', a brief poem of fifteen two-line verses, the constant 'we' ('Wait, we're going to say farewell', etc.) means the reader must wait until the very last verse for definitive proof that the interlocutor is male: it is only then that the first masculine agreements appear, in 'Toi seul es sauvé devant Dieu!' ('You alone are saved in the eyes of God!'). We are also kept guessing for the first five verses as to whether the narrator is a man or a woman; at the precise moment when this becomes clear in the sixth verse, Desbordes-Valmore introduces the sudden notion that this could be a lesbian relationship. 'Voici celle qui m'a perdue . . . ' ('Here is the one [feminine] who/which ruined me . . .') (187–8). (Author's ellipsis: 'the one' is in fact a letter.)

Desbordes-Valmore's best-known poem is the brief 'Les Roses de Saadi' (probably 1848), praised by Baudelaire, described by Bonnefoy as one of her most beautiful, and included in a number of anthologies.[25] Saadi was a thirteenth-century Persian poet whose main work, in French *Le Gulistan* or *Le Jardin de roses*, was the most popular Oriental work in Europe after *The Arabian Nights* (La Fontaine, Voltaire and others imitated parts of it). It is a collection of precepts, anecdotes and epigrams. A new French translation by M. Semelet had appeared in 1834. In the introduction, Saadi (or his narrator) says how he came to compose the work and give it its title ('Gulistan' means 'land of roses'). He had gone to Mecca with a friend. Spring had returned, it was no longer so cold, the time of roses had come. He happened to spend a night in a garden with this friend. It was a magical place, full of charming trees. You could hear in the orchard a nightingale's song, as harmonious as sweet poetry. Next day, when the wish to go won out over the wish to stay, the narrator saw his friend who, having gathered in a fold of his robe roses, basil, bluebells and other fragrant herbs, wanted to return to the town. The narrator told him: 'The rose of gardens does not last long, the season of roses is soon past. I can compose a book called *The Rose Garden,* on the leaves of which the autumn wind will blow in vain. The rose lasts only five or six days, but this Rose Garden will be always beautiful.' No sooner had he said this than his friend, grasping the narrator's garment, told him that a generous man must acquit himself of his promise. The narrator started immediately; there were still roses in the garden when *The Rose Garden* was finished.

Desbordes-Valmore, then, composes her own poem from an exchange between two men; the incipit of a famous literary work of one culture, now absorbed into another; and a celebration of the power of art to represent and go beyond transitory beauty. All this would have been well known to her readers; she achieves the feat of playing on these multiple resonances while making her verses look like a love-poem written from a woman to a man:

> J'ai voulu ce matin te rapporter des roses;
> Mais j'en avais tant pris dans mes ceintures closes
> Que les nœuds trop serrés n'ont pu les contenir.
>
> Les nœuds ont éclaté. Les roses envolées
> Dans le vent, à la mer s'en sont toutes allées.
> Elles ont suivi l'eau pour ne plus revenir.
>
> La vague en a paru rouge et comme enflammée.
> Ce soir, ma robe encore en est toute embaumée . . .
> Respires-en sur moi l'odorant souvenir.[26]

(I wanted, this morning, to bring you roses; but I had taken so many into my closed girdles that the too-tight knots could not contain them. The knots burst. The roses, flying off down the wind, all went away to the sea. They followed the water, no more to come back. The wave seemed red from them, and as if inflamed. This evening, my robe is still full of their rich fragrance . . . Breathe on me their sweet-smelling memory.) (author's ellipsis)

Let us provisionally assume that this is a lover and more specifically a woman speaking; if we do, it is possible to interpret the poem in

the light of the tensions already explored between the expression
and repression of female sexuality. The 'pink' and 'rose' which are
the double meaning of the French 'rose', as well as the final 'red' and
'inflamed', suggest the flush and fire of eroticism ('roses' and 'flame'
having long been synonymous with love and desire in French
literature). More narrowly, one of the many readings the poem can
bear is that of an orgasm, perhaps particularly a woman's. The first
verse describes the offering up of flowers to the loved one, the
unexpected onset of an almost greedy yearning to offer more and
more, and the sudden collapse of constriction. The second verse, on
this reading, would describe the climax in the hemistich which is
given a sentence to itself: 'Les nœuds ont éclaté'. The pleasure
disperses, with, perhaps, a light, rippling effect: in the wind, to the
sea, following the water. The third verse might suggest afterglow;
then, in the calm of the evening, the memory of the bliss, perhaps
even the smell of the encounter. More narrowly still: something of
the particularity of female biology is implicit in the last verse; 'La
vague en a paru rouge et comme enflammée' could evoke the fluids
of menstruation and childbirth, here taking on the characteristics of
the elements. But the reds also encompass responses especially
highlighted by women of the mid-century: those not just of pleasure
but of embarrassment and shame. And the image of trying to take
everything one can, but losing even what has been gained because
one is hampered – by restrictive clothing with too-tight knots – could
stand as an allegory for a 'bound' woman's longings. (In Saadi, the
plants are gathered only into a fold of the robe.)

   That is to say, one thread of the poem is the female condition,
both erotic and social; into this, Desbordes-Valmore incorporates
the constriction and embarrassment surrounding the very evocation.
Yet, in fact, we should not begin to think until the penultimate line
that the narrator may be a woman (when s/he is said to wear a dress
– but 'robe' can, as we see from Saadi, also be a male robe), and we
never have proof that the addressee is a man. Furthermore, this
poem suggests so many different states of being that it cannot be
reduced to any single 'meaning'. It expresses yearning of any sort – a
reaching out to grasp the desired object, ideal or feeling, the 'roses'.
But in its ambition, this is an overreach which leads to a bursting of
the container and the escape of the reality or the dream that the
poor human had tried to capture. The reality – or dream – is lost
and will never return from the sea. The sea can be a vision of the

death into which the 'water' of life flows, or one of vastness and intangibility. But, even though these precious, beautiful and ephemeral things have gone, they leave the appearance of an aftermath (merely an appearance, because the waves only *seem* red, they are only *as if* inflamed); and they can be remembered. The memory is to be recaptured through smell, that smell leading to an invitation to closeness. The dream of the morning (youth?) has gone, but we still, in our evening (and the red on the waves also suggests sunset), have the pleasure of intimacy and mutual memory. 'Les Roses de Saadi', then, mingles 'female desire' with 'human desires' and ends on a suggestion of what the interlocutors may share through art (for this was the result in Saadi's work).

Even if we read the poem as evoking nothing but the tensions of 'woman's condition', it is still the most exquisite expression in the century of these tensions. Not all women writers cared to be this allusive, or indeed allusive at all. Scarcely surprisingly, many had plunged into the political issues of the time with an urgency which hardly left them inclined to search for the sublime.

CHAPTER 16

Women and politics

Intelligent women had from early in the century been interested in history and the special status of the historian. In the mid-century, a number tried to participate more actively in politics than at any time since the Revolution, and when, in their writings, they addressed current issues, they showed a new enthusiasm or passion. These four decades were, indeed, a high point for nineteenth-century women's political writing. The issues raised by the revolutions of 1830 and 1848 and the rebellions of the Lyonnais silk workers in 1831 and 1834 at the least caught their imaginations, more often inflamed them.[1] From about 1830, Saint-Simonism gave fresh impetus to arguments about social inequality; women responded, and sometimes contributed, to the increasing sophistication of theories of class.[2]

Saint-Simonism also launched provocative and unprecedented challenges to conventional gender-boundaries (for instance, it proposed a search for a 'female Messiah'); and it invited activism from women – though in practice this was an inconsistent invitation, as Moses shows. Saint-Simonism's repercussions were wide but its direct impact was limited.[3] However, French feminism underwent crucial developments in other respects in this middle period.[4] In addition, publications on 'woman' became very numerous during the mid-century, with men as well as women, misogynists as well as emancipators, contributing and (in both cases) making still more frequent connections than early in the century between 'woman' and 'the people'.[5]

Whatever their level of activity or quiescence, almost all female writers of both imaginative and discursive literature would appear to have been aware of current debates about politics and feminist issues. In the latter case, they might seize excuses to fight the women's corner at the most unexpected moments. Such was the Hortense Allart who, in 1837, prefaced her well-researched and extremely long *Histoire de la République de Florence* with a surprising dedication 'Aux femmes réformées' ('To reformed women') and proceeded to explain that precisely since she could not, in a 'civil history', uphold the cause of women, she was dedicating the work to those who wanted an improvement in their lot. Nor is this all: she expresses astonishment that women have so long been content with their limited existence, and adds:

Besides, the mind has no sex; science, justice, law have none. When once a woman has intelligence, she tackles everything that human intelligence tackles, and people have never inquired after the sex of truths ['jamais on ne s'est informé du sexe des vérités'].[6]

On other political questions, we should not expect all women writers to be on the 'correct' side: although a majority of those I surveyed were of liberal persuasions, some – as is already obvious – were callous or chauvinistic. What is important is that they took for granted their right to show their interest. Recent critics, as well as historians, have been correcting the idea that nineteenth-century French women were somehow divorced from politics. Kadish points out that in *Le Deuxième Sexe* Simone de Beauvoir underestimated her predecessors' concern with the political, and argues that recognition that they *were* 'political' should help restore them to the canon.[7] It was often a precisely targeted concern, too: it is rather disconcerting, for instance, to find imperialism and the economy structuring Ségur's children's book of 1867, *Le Mauvais Génie*.[8] The conquest of Algeria, where some of the action is set, is presented as unequivocally desirable; following upon victory, the kindly Anglo-Irish 'fairy godfather' (full of praise for the brave French soldiers) sets up factories near Algiers. The factories are a great success, and their owner returns two years later to oversee them for a while, residence in the colonized country clearly being unnecessary for the buoyant entrepreneur. He starts factories in France too, and the book closes with the young hero taking over the management and profits of one of these: what ending could be happier?

An execution takes place in *Le Mauvais Génie*, where it is conveniently accepted, even welcomed, by the unrepentant villain.[9] Capital punishment was another keenly debated subject of the period; if Ségur seems to exonerate it, it figures unfavourably in Colet and in Sand, who was a passionate abolitionist.[10] In her work as a whole, indeed, Sand comments on an unusually wide range of political and economic matters, from militarism to the formation of workers' guilds, from business affairs to manufacturing (these latter forming part of the plot of *Indiana*).[11]

Girardin, for her part, shows sound commercial sense when indicating the dubious relationship between a newspaper's editorial policy and its financial backing in *L'Ecole des journalistes* (14, 47–8). D'Aunet brings out the infiltration of fiscal and other governmental policies into characters' lives with references, in her drama *Jane Osborn*, to the anxious scanning of newspapers for information about consolidated debt and Robert Peel's speeches; and she shows herself no fool on the excuses one nation may use to annex another: of the Finns, she writes that the King of Sweden, Erik the Holy, came to conquer them, and, on the pretext of bringing them Christianity, seized their country ('sous prétexte de leur apporter le christianisme, s'empare de leur pays').[12] In 1843, when the international anti-slavery campaign was about to succeed in the French colonies, the play that Gabrielle d'Altenheym co-authored with her father, set in Roman times, had for heroine and hero an enslaved woman and her father. The father ends the play with the ringing cry: 'Plus d'escla-vage!!!' ('No more slavery!!!'; exclamation marks as in text).[13] Finally, Stern's *Nélida* has a much firmer political core than could be supposed from those critics who read it largely as a *cri de cœur* after the end of her relationship with Liszt. The despairing Nélida realizes that a worker who prevents her killing herself has as much reason for suicide as she, wretched as his conditions are; and the nun Mère Sainte-Elisabeth, a strong character who befriends and influences Nélida, turns out to be a committed socialist who leaves holy orders to become a working-class leader.[14] Some four years later Stern went on to write what has been considered her 'masterwork', *Histoire de la Révolution de 1848* (1850–3), in which a scholar's care for documentation and research is supported by political insight and a compelling narrative.[15]

Of course, there was sometimes a deliberate or semi-deliberate sidestepping of political issues; the most publicized case is that of Sand, who in the wake of 1848 declared such sidestepping to be intentional, thereby, however, drawing attention to the deplorable state of affairs she was 'avoiding'.[16] But others never pretended not to confront issues; the most illustrious example of political commit-ment is Flora Tristan.

It is not only in *Pérégrinations d'une paria* that this formid-able thinker, who understands *realpolitik* as well as the power of

Utopianism, tackles economics and major political questions (in *Pérégrinations*, as we have seen: war; diplomacy; slavery; women's oppression). In *Union ouvrière* (1843), one of the most important political works of the century, she promotes the right to work; peaceful revolution; social planning as against charity; education for both sexes; trade unionism; and the 'raising of consciousness' of the working class. *Union ouvrière* argues for a more professional type of workers' union than the trade guilds already existing. It proposes a form of social security for workers, paid for by small but regular levies; and a leader whom, crucially, the union would pay to be a full-time proponent of workers' claims: the precedent of O'Connell in Ireland is cited (267). This work predates the *Communist Manifesto* by five years and may well have been read by Marx, who was living in Paris and studying French socialist thought at the time of its publication.[17] It no doubt contributed to the 1848 revolution.

Tristan targets her appeal cleverly. She is (or claims she is) a reformist, not a revolutionary.[18] As well as the working class, she addresses sovereign, Church and bourgeoisie – in whose interests it would be to perceive the working class as 'useful' rather than 'always poor'; hence it would be in their interests to eradicate its misery.[19] She similarly pleads 'enlightened self-interest' to ask men to give women equal rights: the home in which the woman is respected will be happier for the man too (207). A whole section of *Union ouvrière* is, in fact, devoted to the position of women. But Tristan is careful to leave this until a relatively late stage (it is the third out of four chapters) and to give it a title that verges on the whimsical: 'Le *pourquoi* je mentionne les femmes' ('*Why and wherefore* I mention women': author's italics).

Tristan's narrative skills serve her well not just here but throughout *Union ouvrière*. She starts with a dramatic account of its publication (she had to get a list of subscribers – the names make interesting reading, including female and male writers, actresses, men and women both from high society and plying lowly trades). This already whets the reader's appetite. Then she plays on different registers and tones, sometimes using italics in bursts of indignation or entreaty, sometimes making her point through irony and humour. Digressions, such as they are, are normally anecdotes to illustrate the point in hand, but in any case she explains away any diffuseness as integral to her structure (183 nn.). When policy has to be stated and defined, she expertly 'crescendoes' from modest introductions to robust recommendations. Here is one example of a plain sentence structure progressing to a rhythmical one and then ending in a shocking absolute:

Dans la vie des ouvriers, la femme est tout. – Elle est leur unique providence. – Si elle leur manque, tout leur manque. Aussi disent-ils: 'C'est la femme qui fait ou défait la maison' et ceci est l'exacte vérité: c'est pourquoi on en a fait un proverbe. – Cependant quelle éducation, quelle instruction, quelle direction, quel développement moral ou physique reçoit la femme du peuple? – Aucun. (193)

(In the life of workers, the woman is everything. – She is their only providence. – If they do not have her, they have nothing. So they say: 'It's the woman who makes or mars the house' and this is the exact truth: that is why the phrase has become a proverb. – Yet, what education, what instruction, what guidance, what moral or physical development is given to the woman of the people? – None.)

Tristan alone would be enough to prove that it was possible for French women to have a visionary but pragmatic grasp of politics, and to convey this with all the rhetorical talent of contemporary male political thinkers, if not more. But (as is by now clear) she was not the only one. Niboyet in *Le Vrai Livre des femmes*, Sand on politics in her essays and articles, Adam in her discursive works, are also practical as well as idealistic; they are all deploying understatement and irony, alternating the bluntly prosaic with the cadenced, and using alliteration and assonance, as integral tools of advocacy.[20] Here is Allart attacking Catholicism on social as well as religious grounds: the unusual, almost experimental, lay-out is hers, as is the punctuation:

L'enseignement protestant, rendu plus large, serait profitable à tous. Comme le catholicisme arrive toujours avec:
    L'index.
    les couvents,
    les séminaires,
    le célibat,
    les miracles,
    les reliques,
    des mœurs dangereuses et fausses, il n'est plus de mise malgré les services payés si cher qu'il a rendus.
    Peut-on le réformer? Oui, mais on ne le fera jamais. Il restera comme une ruine.[21]

(Protestant teaching, if broadened, would benefit everybody. Since Catholicism always comes with:

The index.
convents,
seminaries,
celibacy,
miracles,
relics,
dangerous and false morals, it is no longer acceptable despite the services
– paid for so dearly – that it has given.
Can it be reformed? Yes, but that will never happen. It will remain like a
ruin.)

The rhetoric and ideas of the discursive works mark the others of
this period – or vice versa; it is, perhaps, artificial to set up a clear
distinction. For example, numerous women now press for better
education for both their sex and the working class, not only in
autobiographical works (as we saw earlier) but through verse and
novels.[22] One analogy common to all genres of women's writing is
that of the woman as not merely vaguely assimilable to 'the people',
but as proletarian or slave. This had been adumbrated in the late
eighteenth century, and, as we have seen, cast in a dignified and
symbolic form by Duras and a few others.[23] It was to gather force
and specificity. Woman, says Tristan, has always been judged
inferior: learned men have told her she has no intelligence or
understanding of higher questions, no logic in her ideas, no ability
for the so-called exact sciences; she is a being weak in body and
mind, pusillanimous and superstitious. But what can give us the
hope of appealing against this judgement is that equally, for 6,000
years, the wisest of the wise ('les sages des sages') passed a no less
terrible judgement on another human race: 'les PROLETAIRES'
(author's punctuation, here and in the following quotations). The
proletarian, she continues, was most surprised to learn in 1789 that
he had rights equal to his master's, and his surprise increased when
he was told he had 'a brain of absolutely the *same quality* as that of
the hereditary prince royal' ('un cerveau absolument de *même qualité*
que celui du prince royal héréditaire'). And if the Revolution showed
how false the old judgements were, and allowed men of merit and
valour to emerge from the working class, that is a good omen for
women 'when their 1789 chimes out' ('lorsque leur 89 aura sonné').
Elsewhere in *Union ouvrière*, Tristan asserts that if the working class
are slaves so too are women. They have always protested against
this. But the Declaration of the Rights of Man of 1789 was a solemn

act which proclaimed 'the *forgetfulness and scorn in which the new men held them*'. (Tristan does not mention here Olympe de Gouges's 'reply' to the 1789 Declaration of the Rights of Man – her *Déclaration des droits de la femme et de la citoyenne* of 1791 – but she must have known of it.) Since then, says Tristan, women's protest has taken on an energetic and violent character which proves that 'the exasperation of the slave is at its height' ('l'exaspération de l'esclave est au comble').[24] Moses and Rabine, throughout their book *Feminism, Socialism and French Romanticism*, show how common such connections between woman and worker/slave became in other feminists' writing just before the publication of *Union ouvrière*. Tristan's phrase about the slave's 'height of exasperation' rings true not only in the frequency of the comparisons, but also in the sometimes frenzied indignation with which they are made – different from the sober or mournful tones of the early-century writers.[25]

The upper-class woman seemed as debased as any lower-class one could be, for marriage turned her too into a slave – or indeed a prostitute.[26] And the politics of marriage remained a key issue for women writers. Money-marriages had not disappeared, as we saw from the 'overview' of this middle period (chap. 9); nor had those in which the groom was much older than the bride.[27] But whereas in the early century arranged marriage was the supreme preoccupation, in the mid-century the women writers were more concerned with the nature of the institution in itself, focusing increasingly on the pain of the loveless marriage; the simple undesirability of wedlock for the woman who wanted freedom; the double standards, both legal and psychological, attaching to adultery.[28] Deraismes pushes this latter analysis further than anyone, suggesting in her play *Retour à ma femme* that one-sided adultery entails sadism: 'Il vous était doux,' says the wronged wife, who has been pretending that she herself loves another:

Il vous était doux de penser qu'infidèle, je continuais de vous aimer comme par le passé. Votre triomphe se complétait par la douleur de la victime. Mais mon indifférence vous a jeté dans un dépit voisin de la fureur. (49)

(When you were unfaithful, you enjoyed thinking that I went on loving you just as I always had. Your triumph was sealed by the pain of the victim. But when I seemed indifferent, that made you resentful – furious, almost.)

Some women develop this into a consideration of the irrevocability of marriage and hence (by implication) the desirability of a

11. Maria Deraismes.

change in the divorce law – Sand in *Indiana* (1832), for example. (The Chambre des Députés passed divorce bills in 1831–34, but these were rejected by the Chambre des Pairs; there was also a pro-divorce petition in 1836, which was no more successful.)[29] The literary figure of the widow has a special function here. Carrying over from earlier periods, she was a popular character in early nineteenth-century fiction and drama. Staël's Delphine, Duras's Natalie, Bawr's heroines in *Le Double Stratagème* and *La Suite d'un bal masqué* are all widows, as is Mme d'Angerval in Gay's 1819 play *Le*

Marquis de Pomenars: this lady's elderly husband is said to have behaved very well by dying two months after the wedding (4). The widow, merry or not, already, then, enabled female writers to suggest that the happiest lot was to be a sexually experienced, financially independent woman, who had found a way out of marriage permitted by the law and could follow her amorous inclinations.

Ancelot continued to use the topos (the heroine of *Un mariage raisonnable* is a young widow), but drew attention to its implications. In the 1831 drama *Un divorce*, the very Hortense who disapproves of divorcees reveals herself in a Freudian slip: 'Et vous avez eu le bonheur . . . le malheur de devenir veuve?' ('So you were fortunately . . . unfortunately widowed?': author's ellipsis, 359). Some fifty years before divorce became legal again, this play aired the thorny question of the indissoluble union. How difficult it was to do so is suggested by the work's equivocal ending, veering between compassion and moralizing (the divorcee loses both her child and her second husband; a servant's silly wife, who had been considering divorce for purely frivolous reasons, no less arbitrarily decides against it). But at least Ancelot brought the subject forward, and voiced a matter-of-fact attitude to divorce through another character: Jenkinson, an English baronet who is (implausibly) a Saint-Simonian, and something of an idiot, but who, precisely because of that, is allowed radical views which (her prefatory material would indicate) were held by Ancelot herself. In England, says this eccentric, we have a remedy for 'these desperate cases': divorce. Divorce makes home comfortable – an English speciality! (340).

Tristan, Stern, Niboyet and Voilquin all also talked of the horrors of the unhappy 'marriage for life' and the need for divorce as a 'corrective' so that husbands shall not feel they can do as they like.[30] But in this directness they, and Sand and Ancelot, were in a minority. The very word 'divorce' appears to have been taboo for much of this period; quite apart from its possible unseemliness, divorce may have been associated with the excesses of the Revolution, since it was in the immediate post-revolutionary period that exceptionally liberal divorce laws had been drafted (1792). This association was made explicit, as late as 1856, by Girardin. In her play *Une femme qui déteste son mari*, set during the Terror, a bullying official insists a loyal wife must divorce her husband and leave her children, in order first to free herself of any aristocratic taint and secondly to marry him, the official (the play's title is ironic). No doubt this fear of the 'revolutionary' nature of divorce contributed to the general silence on the subject, or to the bad press some women felt obliged to give divorce when they did refer to it.

Even more taboo were mentions of rape, VD passed on to the woman without her knowledge, and paedophilia directed against girls. These appear very rarely outside polemical feminist writings: in the imaginative literature and life-writing I surveyed, it is only Colet and Voilquin who are brave enough to talk of these.[31] A few more do speak out about the plight of the prostitute or the woman who for whatever reason has no option but to sell her body.[32] At one point d'Aunet compares her Jane Osborn to Mary Magdalen (85): New Testament stories are one way for the more cautious to approach prostitution and the wider question of whether women should be blamed for past or present sexual 'faults'. They give sympathetic depictions of the Magdalen, popular enough in this period almost to have the status of another 'role-model'. She herself, or Magdalen-like figures, had already figured in the early decades to suggest that women who had strayed from virtue were redeemable.[33] In the mid-century, she or the 'woman taken in adultery' reappears in Blanchecotte's 'Madeleine'; in Caro's 1865 novel *Le Péché de Madeleine*; in, no doubt, the name of François le champi's adoptive mother Madeleine; and in Girardin's plea for understanding of an unfaithful wife – unfaithful only because her husband neglects her and 'the abyss has been prepared for her fall' ('on a préparé l'abîme pour sa chute').[34] Yet the words 'abyss', 'fall' – still resorted to in 1851 – show how fearful the mid-century female author could be: the political and feminist interest was there – at fever pitch, maybe; but where it was a question of challenging the grossly unfair laws on adultery, even so spirited a writer as Girardin had to shelter behind melodramatic cliché.

PART III

Naturalism and Symbolism: the beginnings of a new era (1870–1899)

CHAPTER 17

Overview, 1870–1899

From about 1840 on, women writers had been much less anxious about using their own names, but those who did usually still called themselves 'Madame', married or not. (Deraismes had defiantly called herself 'Mademoiselle' in the 1861–2 published version of her plays, but evidently felt the need for a title of some sort.) Shades of reluctance remained after 1870, with some women sheltering behind simple sexless initials (Louise Gagneur became M.-L. Gagneur for the controversial *Les Forçats du mariage*); a few, just as at the beginning of the century, used their husband's forenames as well as surnames (Mme Alphonse Daudet, Mme Augustus Craven).[1] But an ever larger number unapologetically used their own full names without a title; and if, after 1870, they took pseudonyms, these could be 'in-your-face': first names were dropped and the public was left with single words (Rachilde, Séverine) or even single syllables (Gyp).[2] Book-titles could be equally brisk – positively brusque by comparison with the winding ones of the first third of the century: *Névrosée* by Daniel Lesueur (1890), *Complice!...* by Pauline Caro (1893). Gyp specialized in these: *Pas jalouse!* (1893), *Sportmanomanie* (1898). Another straw in the wind was Dieulafoy's prefatory 'To the reader' in *Parysatis* (1890), which addressed this reader as 'tu'. All this speaks for a greater ease in these authors' sense of their public.

Among the genres, fiction continued to reign supreme. Children's stories were still popular with women writers. Judith Gautier, with her multiple scholarly and artistic interests, and the august connections that included Wagner, still felt it worth her while to contribute here; and the woman's best-seller of the century was a children's educational 'story' published by Augustine Fouillée in 1877: a wildfire hit, it was adopted as a school textbook and sold six million copies by 1900.[3] Although nothing could match the success of Zola in adult fiction, many of the most popular novels of the time were by women

– Henry Gréville (the pseudonym of Alice Durand-Gréville), Jane Dieulafoy, Pauline Caro.[4] The taste for exoticism and mechanically applied adjectives remained strong, and young lovers battled against obstacles still, to a degree, set up by an older generation (as in Caro's *Idylle nuptiale*, 1893, where the obstacles are overcome). But women's novels were becoming more consistently humorous, sometimes mischievous. And women also made substantial contributions to the poetry of the period, including prose poems and free verse. The 'tradition' of excellent polemical writing lived on: the mid-century feminists, older now, for the most part were no longer activists, but Deraismes, at least, was still writing as persuasively for the cause of women as she had ever done, and new talents were emerging, such as Louise Michel, and others in part influenced by the British suffrage movement but also dynamic in their own country. (Moses speaks of the 'dazzling' vitality of the feminist movement in these last three decades; international congresses were held in France, the 1878 one hosting representatives of eleven foreign countries and the 1889 one receiving favourable mention in more than six hundred newspapers round the world.)[5]

National upheavals at the beginning of this period were as profound as those of the mid-century, with the Franco-Prussian war and seige of Paris (1870–1), the Paris Commune (March–May 1871) and the difficult establishment of the Third Republic (1870–5). Although this was followed by a period of relative stability, the national trauma of the crushing defeat by Prussia, the aftermath of the Commune, and later the repercussions of the Dreyfus Affair in the 1890s, tended to polarize political opinion; so that it becomes easier to draw clear demarcations in this period between 'right-wing' and 'left-wing' women's writing. The long-overdue reforms for women introduced by the Third Republic also provided a new – or radically rejuvenated – agenda for all, including the apparently most conventional. Thus, the leap forward in educational provision meant that women became both consumers and teachers on an unprecedented scale, a development that figures in their imaginative works too.[6] And divorce, albeit on terms which favoured men, at last became legal once more in 1884, spawning dozens of works whose titles included the word, especially plays by both men and women. Thus, by male dramatists: *Les Surprises du divorce*, 1888 (parodying Marivaux's *La Surprise de l'amour*); *Pierrot divorcé*, 1895. (Female dramatists' titles were, in this respect at least, a little more staid: *Le Divorce de Sarah Moore,* 1885; *Le Divorce au village,* 1889.)[7] In Gyp's *Autour du divorce* (1886) the heroine, herself in search of a divorce, asks for a work on the subject: the bookseller recommends *Ohé! les divorcés!* ('Ahoy There! Had a Divorce?') by a certain Viensivoir ('Takea-peek'); in the law bookshop next visited by the heroine, a customer hides behind her veil when the assistant loudly announces the title he is giving her: *Le Formulaire du divorce* ('Divorce Formulae'). He stocks numerous others: *Code du divorce, Traité du divorce,* etc. ('Divorce Code', 'Treatise on Divorce', 41–2, 59–60).

Those women who were inclined to be experimental leaned in equal numbers towards Symbolism or Naturalism, although (as might be expected) the more genteel favoured the former; it was probably only Rachilde who successfully interwove both. Many acknowledged or displayed their debt to male predecessors and contemporaries. The diarist Bashkirtseff paid tribute to Flaubert, Zola and Balzac, whom she also wished to take as a model for her art (she would like to be a 'Balzac in painting', *Journal,* II 52, 413–14, 533–4, 546). Ackermann, taking up Leconte de Lisle's violent images of cosmic collapse (in, for example, his 'Solvet seclum' of 1861), pushed them into new areas in her 'end-of-a-world, end-of-the-world' tableaux of the 1870s.[8] The poetry of Daniel Lesueur also evoked the 'end of the world', now with a more Decadent aspect.[9]

Other women, innovative in their own right, prepared the ground for more famous late nineteenth- and early twentieth-century male writers. Judith Gautier wrote of rain and 'tears without cause' in a piece published in June 1872, shortly before Verlaine's composition of his renowned 'Il pleure dans mon cœur', presumed to be in October 1872:

Je ne sais pourquoi je voudrais pleurer dans cette île (pleurer sans cause, car je n'ai nul chagrin), au milieu de la pluie perpétuelle . . .[10]

(I don't know why I'd like to weep in this isle (weep without cause, for I have no sorrow), amidst the perpetual rain . . .)

Proust (1871–1922) knew Julia Daudet well: he frequented her house and had an affair with her son Lucien. He would almost certainly have read her prose poems and 'fragments', including one ex-pounding the impressions bound up with memories of childhood reading: poetry books, she says, seemed to her 'full of day and air', their short lines 'surrounded by white spaces like a musical atmo-sphere shaped by rhythm' ('entourées d'espaces blancs comme l'atmosphère musicale formée par le rythme'); she would read in summer, on a garden seat, 'surrounded by insects' buzzing and the light sounds of nature at rest' ('entourée d'un bourdonnement d'insectes, des bruits légers de la nature au repos').[11] Here can be heard not only the youthful author of *Les Plaisirs et les jours* (1896) but the mature one of *A la recherche du temps perdu*; and many women of the period penned sometimes anguished, but more often wistful or precious, short meditations that could well have been called 'Les Regrets, rêveries couleur du temps' ('Regrets, time-coloured reveries').[12]

Another 'precursor' of this period was Louise Ackermann. Besides her affinity with Leconte de Lisle, she has themes and lines that startlingly anticipate later ones of Valéry's (1871–1945). In her 'L'Homme à la Nature' (1871), Man tells Nature that *he* has counted her treasures, borne witness to her power, 'And my intelligence, eternal Nature! has held out to you your first mirror' (115–19). In 'L'Homme', man, thrown by chance on to this 'old globe', surfaces, the flotsam of the void ('Epave du néant'). A voice cries: 'Arrive! / Je t'attends pour penser' ('Come! I have been waiting for you so as to think'). Unconsciousness extended over nature; I – man – appeared, and so did Mind:

> Plongé dans le grand Tout, j'ai su m'y reconnaître;
> Je m'affirme et dis: 'Moi!'   (*Œuvres*, 167–9)

(Plunged into the great Whole, I was able to recognize myself in it; I affirm myself and say: 'Me!')

The mature Valéry expresses these ideas far more elegantly, but readers of, for instance, 'La Jeune Parque' and 'Le Cimetière marin' will recognize his affirmation of the 'Moi' and his stress on man as the only spark of consciousness in the universe. Equally proto-Valéryan is Ackermann's 'Satan. Fragment' (the very title has shades of both 'Fragments du Narcisse' and 'Ebauche d'un serpent') (*Œuvres*, 131–3). It starts: 'Nous voilà donc encore une fois en présence' ('So here we are again, face to face'), God and I. You counted without me – Satan tells God – when you made the first human couple: I had only to see man there, languid, stupid, wandering, vegetating like a mere animal, to conceive suddenly, intrepid as I am, the audacious scheme of vying with you for him. What! would I have left him, in the bosom of nature, for ever growing hopelessly more sluggish in that place ('s'engourdir en ce lieu')? I already loved him too much, the weak creature – I couldn't abandon him to God. Of Knowledge, Satan says it was no fall, but an ascent; you, God, closed Heaven – but man wouldn't have wanted to go back. 'That poor timid Adam is over and done with' ('C'en est fait pour toujours du pauvre Adam timide') – man is born. I, continues Satan, gave man his first glimmerings, his first light; and the poem ends: 'We both created our light, yes, but my *Fiat lux* triumphs over yours! . . . *You* have only your heaven to sow your stars; to launch my sun, *I* have the human mind!'

> Nous avons tous les deux créé notre lumière,
> Oui, mais mon *Fiat lux* l'emporte sur le tien!
>
> . . .
>
> Toi, tu n'as que ton ciel pour semer tes étoiles;
> Pour lancer mon soleil, moi, j'ai l'esprit humain!

Valéryans will see here not only themes and images of 'Ebauche', but also, in embryo at least, the Serpent's cheeky address to God and his bragging, often colloquial tone.

CHAPTER 18

A new boldness: Marcelle Tinayre, Louise Ackermann and Gyp

From the beginning of the century to the end, certain themes and characterizations remained constant in women's writing. By the 1870s these were starting to seem like stereotypes, if they had not already.

On the one hand, female authors were unwilling to abandon key idealizations: the woman as unswervingly chaste, or as the angel of the hearth. As one male character tells his young beloved in a popular novel of 1892, he believes in the seraphim, for otherwise to whom could he compare her? She herself is ignorant of love, purer than the edelweiss that grows on the highest mountains amidst the immaculate snow.[1] And for Julia Daudet in 1884, the only real life for a woman is a purely domestic one: she evokes those blank hours which girls spend in a 'limbo-like dream, most of them awaiting true existence: their wifely and motherly activities' ('rêve limbique où la plupart attendent la vraie existence, leur activité de femme et de mère'); she lovingly cites the late-night jobs of the mistress of the house, ensuring that her dwelling can set off into the night like a ship into an ocean of calm (*Fragments*, 58). The reluctance to jettison such images is not surprising. Just as some present-day feminists emphasize women's 'caring' qualities, so, too, many nineteenth-century writers saw 'virtue' and 'maternity' as one way of promoting woman to the dignity she deserved.[2]

On the other hand, female authors had also reinforced more undermining images of women since 1800 – often going beyond the call of duty. In 1813, one of Gay's heroines remarks without qualms that her friend has more 'strength of mind and true philosophy than is usual for women'; similarly, in 1867, in Ségur, a woman discovering an emergency becomes hysterical, while her male companion keeps his head: 'But Bonard was a man: he acted instead of screaming' ('Mais Bonard était homme: il agissait au lieu de crier').[3] These and other negative stereotypes were still very obvious in the late century: in Judith Gautier's 1888 play *La Marchande de sourires* ('Tradeswoman in Smiles'), the eponymous heroine, a self-seeking courtesan, ruins all around her; as 'the great criminal' she must finally die to atone for her crimes.[4] The only virtue that can in a small degree mitigate her evil is, predictably, maternal: her love for her daughter.

The more feminist writers, too, could reiterate almost the same images as their grandmothers and great-grandmothers. Excessively youthful brides, marriage as ball-and-chain (Gagneur); ridicule as the chief weapon against women – and a crushing one at that (Michel, Deraismes); a chafing against the posthumous oblivion that seems to be the female lot, and embarrassment or the 'convenances' as the great controllers, particularly for women writers (Bashkirtseff, Ackermann): we can occasionally wonder if by now these too were starting to take on the status of stereotype.[5] Were they perhaps also being picked up by canny popularizers to sell works? A dash of feminism would spread the appeal to a still wider market: this is one way of reading Gréville's 1877 novel *Les Koumiassine*, a mix of the liberal and the highly conventional.

But even where the women resort to obvious cliché-peddling (mothers always self-sacrificing, whores wicked), this may denote not opportunism, cowardice or intellectual laziness but distress and guilt. The stereotype is enlisted as a defence against further painful thought on the subject, or as an admission of helplessness. And in life-writing at least the old anguish is often expressed with a fresh poignancy. It would be cynical to believe we are seeing just a copy of pain rather than real pain in these outbursts from Daudet herself (1884) and from Bashkirtseff (1879):

Homme, j'aurais essayé de faire de la plus pure littérature en dehors de l'existence . . . J'aurais voulu faire triompher l'expression comprise dans sa plus fine, sa plus absolue vérité. Mais l'observation des femmes est restreinte, leur milieu d'art étroit, le temps manque, l'indépendance et le montant des conversations. On se contente d'un court aperçu très sensible parce qu'il est trop rapproché; et c'est de l'écriture appliquée aux émotions du foyer ou en résultant, qui émane de ces impressions trop vives et nerveuses.[6]

(As a man, I'd have tried to create the purest kind of literature: one that was outside existence . . . I should have liked to make expression triumph – understood in its finest, most absolute truth. But women's observation is restricted, their artistic milieu is narrow, they lack time, they don't have independent and tangy conversations. We rest content with a brief insight, very sensitive because it is too close up; and it's writing applied to, or arising from, household emotions, that issues forth from these over-vivid, nervy impressions.)

Ce que j'envie, c'est la liberté de se promener tout seul . . . voilà la liberté sans laquelle on ne peut pas devenir un vrai artiste. Vous croyez qu'on profite de ce qu'on voit, quand on est accompagné ou quand, pour aller au Louvre, il faut attendre sa voiture, sa demoiselle de compagnie ou sa famille?

 Ah! cré nom d'un chien, c'est alors que je rage d'être femme! . . . je me ferai si laide que je serai libre comme un homme . . . La pensée est enchaînée par suite de cette gêne stupide et énervante; même en me déguisant, en m'enlaidissant, je ne suis qu'à moitié libre et une femme qui rôde est une imprudence . . . C'est une des raisons pour lesquelles il n'y a pas d'artistes femmes. O crasse ignorance! ô sauvage routine! Ce n'est pas la peine d'en parler! . . . il faut crier et se rendre ridicule (je laisserai ce soin à d'autres) pour obtenir cette égalité dans cent ans. (*Journal*, II 105–6)

(What I envy is the freedom to take a walk alone . . . without *that* freedom, you can't become a great artist. Do you think you can get any benefit from what you see when someone's accompanying you or when, to go to the Louvre, you have to wait for your carriage, or your chaperone, or your family?

 Oh, damn it! that's when I feel furious I'm a woman! . . . I'll make myself so ugly that I'll be as free as a man . . . Your thinking is chained up by these stupid, annoying constraints; even if I disguise myself, uglify myself, I'll still only be half-free, and a woman roaming about – well, it's imprudent . . . That's one of the reasons why there are no women artists. Crass ignorance! Brutish routine! It's not worth talking about! . . . we must yell out and make ourselves ridiculous (I'll let others take care of that one) to get our equality in a hundred years' time.)

We might be back in the 1830s with Ulliac-Trémadeure's *Emilie*: in half a century, nothing seems to have changed. However we interpret the repetitions – whether as mechanical or as heartfelt – something in late nineteenth-century French culture still, clearly, made pre-existing models feel all too appropriate.

 Despite these survivals, there are nevertheless unmistakable shifts of emphasis in women's works after 1870, signalled by more than just the abrupt pseudonyms and novel-titles. One of these was the straightforward expression of the idea that things *are* changing and that what we have in these last years of the nineteenth century is the *modern woman*.[7] Gréville's *Les Koumiassine* ends with a stress on 'outgrowing the old-fashioned': when the matriarchal old countess visits

12. Marie Bashkirtseff.

her grown-up daughter and ward, they hide their children, for, charming though these children are, the countess cannot bear them for more than five minutes: 'That's not how I brought mine up . . . new times, new ways, but the old system was better' (II 328). This was in 1877; by the end of the 1890s, the idea was firmly established. Thus, one play of 1897 by the female dramatist Alquié de Rieu-peyroux was called *La Jeune Fille fin de siècle*. The novelist Marcelle Tinayre (1877–1948) is a key example here.[8] In her *Hellé* (1899), the heroine arrives in Paris to find that people are curious to know girls of her age because they represent the 'beginnings of the modern woman' ('ébauche de la femme moderne', 44). And when she criticises 'hyperbolic gallantry' – which she sees as merely a product of male egotism and female vanity – an older woman and mentor, Mme Marboy, tells her: 'You really are the new-era woman!' ('Ah! vous êtes bien la femme des temps nouveaux!', 230–1).

The word 'hardi' ('bold/daring/impudent') is increasingly used of female characters or of the writer's own self. Adam's *Laide* of 1878 makes the point forcefully: the heroine wonders if society doesn't prefer, to useless resignation, 'bold faults' ('défauts hardis') that bring the passions into play; she thinks it a kind of artistry to cope on one's own, out of a pleasure in boldness ('par plaisir de hardiesse'); when, finally, she does regain acceptance, her enjoyment of this shows in her 'rather bold' eyes ('ses yeux un peu hardis', 113–14, 239). In *Monsieur Vénus* (1884), Rachilde's heroine takes the sexual initiative with ironic boldness ('hardiesse ironique'), and on the day of her marriage she has a bold expression, 'physionomie hardie'.[9] Louise Michel too, at the beginning of her 1886 memoirs, says she will speak of herself boldly and frankly ('hardiment et franchement') (18). We have moved on from the decorum and downcast eyes of many pre-1870 heroines.

Women were also pushing forward the boundaries of what might permissibly be written about the physical realities of femaleness. Krysinska almost mentions menstruation: 'Comme des linges écla-boussés de sang, parmi des roses' ('Like linen splashed with blood, among roses').[10] Tinayre talks of the cracked nipples of a breast-feeding woman (perhaps emboldened by Tolstoy, whom she admires: Dolly in *Anna Karenina* suffers from painful nipples when nursing); and she refers matter-of-factly to girls' awakening sexual feeling and to the 'surprises of desire'.[11] In Pert's *Le Frère* (1896), the sister and later another woman assess the brother Robert's body with an erotic gaze normally reserved for male onlookers; while in *Monsieur Vénus*, Raoule is endowed with a 'mad sensuality' ('sensualité folle'), talks of the body hair of the man she desires (probably a first for mainstream French women writers), and seemingly has multiple orgasms in her carriage:

Et Raoule, bercée par le trot rapide de son attelage, mordait ses fourrures, la tête en arrière, le corsage gonflé, les bras crispés, avec de temps à autre un soupir de lassitude.[12]

(And Raoule, rocked by the rapid trot of her carriage and horses, bit her furs, head back, chest swelling, arms rigid, sighing from time to time with lassitude.)

In spite of the continuing anxiety about their work that we have seen in Daudet and Bashkirtseff, women were apparently surer of their right to authorship than earlier in the century. If Bentzon ends her 'Postscript' to *Un divorce* with a few modest words about her 'unskilled pen' ('plume mal habile'), it is clear that this is merely a flourish: she has just been explaining her novel in the same 'Postscript' with the utmost certainty, italicizing the phrase '*Il faut*':

It must happen – if not in reality, which involves half-measures and half-solutions, then at least in the novel, whose subject must be taken to extreme conclusions – it must come about that Elsbeth dies, since she has married Waldheim. (328–9)

And the creative drive could now more openly enlist a woman's eroticism. Daniel Lesueur's narrator does voice worry about her verse, apparently needing male approval to write; nevertheless, her beloved asks her to do so as a sign of her love, and their mutual desire joins in the very act of composition:

> Puisque tu n'es point las de mes cris de tendresse,
> Penche-toi sur ma lèvre, ils y vont éclater.
> Puisque pour toi mes chants offrent la même ivresse,
> Je veux, je veux chanter!

(Since you're not tired of my tender cries, bend close to my lips, there they will burst out. Since, for you too, my songs are heady, I *will* sing!)

I don't write of my love for you to calm any jealousy you may feel:

> Non, c'est que tu te plais à mes frivoles rimes,
> C'est que je pense et parle et vis pour ton plaisir,
> Et que j'ai, pour franchir toutes les hautes cimes,
> L'aile de ton désir.   ('Renouveau')[13]

(No, it's because you like my frivolous rhymes, it's because I think and speak and live for your pleasure, and because, to pass over every high peak, I have the wing of your desire.)

Although Bashkirtseff highlights restrictions, and is self-doubting at moments, the openness with which she expresses her sheer longing for fame – and for manhood – is difficult to imagine earlier in the century (even in Staël, the longing was more defensive); and she affirms her right to paint 'shocking' subjects, for example men in the nude: once, female pupils had to paint clothed models and be segregated from the males, but now differentiations have disappeared. Thus this girl of only sixteen wrote in 1877: 'the moment you have women artists taking life classes, naked men make no difference' ('du moment qu'elles font l'académie, l'homme nu, c'est la même chose', II 5).[14]

Women in the last third of the century were even more determined than their mid-century predecessors to focus on girls' robustness and need for physical freedom. In this, they received some support from the culture. A few works recommending exercise for women had appeared in the mid-century.[15] But the theories and practicalities took a leap forward after 1870. By the end of the century, medical myths about women's frailty and inherent 'illness' were almost completely dispelled; doctors were advising against corsets; and the introduction of tennis and cycling for women in the 1880s required suitable outfits.[16] Indeed, these innovations were plentifully publicized (Illustration 13).[17] Deraismes's 1872 attack on Dumas *fils* fits well with the changes. She scathingly points out the absurdity of his claim that 'masculine' equals 'movement', 'feminine' equals 'form'. It is evident – she says – that all beings, all individuals, are matter, form and movement; 'woman' does not specify 'form', any more than 'man' does; nor does man, any more than woman, characterize movement. Dumas had proposed a kind of struggle in which each sex tried to grasp in the other what it lacked in itself; Deraismes comments:

Dieu! que c'est ingénieux! Cet homme sans forme, cette femme sans mouvement, se livrant à un pugilat pour s'approprier les qualités qui leur manquent! C'est donc pour nous raconter de ces histoires-là que notre *grand* docteur monte sur son trépied?[18]

(Goodness! the ingenuity of it! This man with no form, this woman with no movement, going in for a brawl to grab the qualities they're missing! It's to tell us stories like that, is it, that our *great* scholar gets up on his tripod?)

13. 'No more corsets!' (Comic song.)

So when Gréville's fictional girls race breathlessly about the garden, the younger is compared to Atlanta; and if the elder is rebuked – on the grounds that she is a marriageable young lady who mustn't play the little girl any more – she articulates her regret not in terms of marriageability or otherwise, but as a simple matter of inconvenient clothing, saying that if she weren't afraid of tearing her dress, she thinks she'd climb to the top of a nearby poplar with no more difficulty than if she were running.[19] Bentzon's young heroine Yette is a 'garçon manqué' who enjoys clothes that do not 'gêner' ('trouble') her freedom of movement (*Yette*, 313, 345). Travelling to France from the West Indies, she is so adventurous (running about the ship's upper decks, climbing in the rigging) that the crew wish they could make her a cabin-boy: she is, they say, 'a brave little lion, she's got sea-legs, she's got a joke and a laugh – she has it all!' ('un petit lion pour le courage, le pied marin, le mot pour rire! toutes les qualités, quoi!', 324). As a child, Tinayre's broad-shouldered Hellé climbs, jumps ditches, runs for hours in the burning sun; although she is ignorant of the 'mannered ways' that well brought-up girls learn, adults look at her with the pleasure 'that the sight of a fresh, robust child gives' (*Hellé*, 14). Later in life, she encounters the older generation's prejudices against active adult women: Mme Marboy tells her that the best wives and mothers do not have the virile arms of 'our rational *sportswomen*' ('nos *sportswomen* raisonneuses'), while her uncle says he doesn't want to know these *sportswomen*: 'Walking through the streets, I met some strange creatures astride steel vehicles. They horrified me' ('J'ai rencontré par les rues des êtres bizarres qui chevauchaient des véhicules d'acier. Ils m'ont fait horreur': author's italics, 52). But Hellé is not put off and argues that walking, running and gymnastics make bodies beautiful (her admiration for Greek culture informing her feminism).

Although the 'proprieties' were still present as an irritation, women were wording attacks on them ever more strongly. 'Convenances' are branded as hypocritical by Tinayre, blushing as a taught affectation.[20] If, in *Monsieur Vénus*, Jacques reproaches Raoule with doing what, even between men, is not 'convenable', it is proof of his weakness; for this scandalous novel itself joyously routs the concept, and even the duel that finally kills Jacques is 'as unrespectable as it possibly could be' ('aussi incorrect que possible') (59, 244).

Female characters also adopt such unladylike customs as smoking, and drinking to the point of intoxication. None of Sand's female characters smoked, even though she famously did so herself. True, mid-century travel-writers had described women smoking, either relatively neutrally or with some approval for this sign of freedom – but then, these were foreigners.[21] In 1861, the young Deraismes's Antoinette was offered a cigar on stage with the words: 'Entre camarades?' ('As between comrades?'); but she refused, saying she was not Spanish.[22] The mid-century women were a little more relaxed about other intoxicants. Voilquin related her experience with hashish, and Girardin felt able to talk of writing as a delectably heady wine and ink as a cassis-like liqueur.[23] However, inebriation was, on the whole, again something to which other nations – or delinquents – succumbed.[24] These inhibitions, although still active in a majority of late-century women writers, were showing signs of being cast aside by some. As part of a game to fill soap bubbles with smoke, Gyp's heroine Paulette smokes an enormous cigar.[25] In Rachilde, women smoke both tobacco and hashish, specifically identifying these as masculine activities now being 'appropriated'; while Krysinska talks of women finding Dionysos and androgyny all at once, and celebrates drunkenness in a poem called 'Bacchanale'.[26]

As I indicated in the 'overview', new educational opportunities and salaried work for women were figuring in such writers as Tinayre and Bentzon – not without counterblasts: Gréville makes one of the villainesses of *Les Koumiassine* a young woman who is said to be very intelligent and well educated, but who along with her diplomas and ambitions has a 'dry' heart, is mocked by the other characters, and in due course gets her just deserts, ending up with a lower-class husband and no children (I 116, II 190, 239). On the other hand, when Bentzon's Yette is urged not to work by her protectress Mme Darcey (for a girl of her class should not act 'like a labourer' but find other means of support and protection), M. Darcey, in a voice 'trembling with a little contained emotion', tells Yette:

Oui, oui . . . vous gagnerez votre vie, n'en deplaise à ma femme, non pas comme un manœuvre, mais comme un homme, ni plus ni moins, et sans déroger pour cela. (373)

(Yes, yes . . . you'll earn your living, with due respect to my wife, not like a labourer but like a man, neither more nor less, and without cheapening yourself for all that.) (author's ellipsis)

Yette does eventually qualify as a teacher – even if, saved by marriage, she never actually takes up the job she is offered (409).[27]

Equally important were the new areas of religious and scientific inquiry into which women were penetrating from 1870 on. Of the pre-1870 writers I surveyed, only La Tour du Pin and Sand express an interest in science. Religion, on the other hand, figures in women's imaginative works throughout the century, but for the most part superficially, as a source of 'props' for the dramas enacted in their novels or verse: convents, ruined chapels, mothers watching from heaven can all enhance terror or mystery at tense moments. Abbés abound, as either spicy scoundrels or wise advisers.[28] Dedication of oneself to God, when all else has failed, may conveniently tie up the end of a work, a *deus ex machina* indeed. Typical is Dash's *La Marquise de Parabère* (1842), whose eponymous heroine is loved by a priest, René; after a series of high-society scenes and political intrigues, the marquise dies and René becomes a Trappist, sustained by the memory of his loved one, now waiting for him in heaven.[29] A few (such as Desbordes-Valmore) are more profound in their invocation of religious images; some, like their male contemporaries and predecessors, delve deeply. They may try to weigh up the differences between Protestantism and Catholicism (usually, when they do so, distancing themselves from Catholicism, or at least cautiously proposing that Protestantism deserves respect).[30] Voilquin and Sand argue against belief in hell (one of the grounds on which Baudelaire savages Sand in *Mon cœur mis à nu*).[31] Some (like male thinkers too, of course) see Christ as the guarantor or promoter of social equality.[32] And a handful before 1870, even if believers themselves, attack or satirize religious institutions; one or two express global doubts.[33]

But it is as if after about 1870 women felt better able to express views on religion and science. If non-believers, they more openly proclaimed atheism; they squarely tackled scientific theory and applications. Louise Ackermann (1813–90), the precocious daughter, as we saw, of a Catholic mother and a Voltairean father, is a case in point. Influenced by positivist thought, she was the first French-woman to foreground scientific ideas in imaginative works and to integrate an (often passionate) critique of religion into verse works. She had started to do so in poems written in the 1860s, but not published until 1871, when they appeared under the title *Poésies philosophiques*; these, at the junction of the middle and late century, indicate what women were now starting to dare to say in print – though no doubt only a few: Larnac is probably scarcely overstating when he writes that Ackermann's atheism was a stance not tenable for a woman ('Une telle position chez une femme n'était pas tenable': *Histoire de la littérature féminine*, 203). In poems with titles such as 'Le Positivisme', 'Le Nuage', 'La Nature à l'homme', 'Pascal', or 'Prométhée' (dedicated to Stern), Ackermann enlists life-cycles, evolutionary theory, even water-cycles, to stress the self-seekingness of a Nature which, concerned only to reproduce itself, can manage without Man; to evoke the bleak preciousness of life with no thought of a hereafter; but also to conjure up the splendour of Man's courage and self-awareness in a Godless universe. Her verse has an epic quality not to be found in other female poets of the century; it is uncompromising and can be haunting.

Thus in 'Le Positivisme' she writes of the void that opens up beyond all human knowledge – a void that Faith was quick to seize. It turned that obscure abyss into its domain. But the moment has come – we are expelling you, the dominatrix Faith, from your divine kingdoms: 'No longer will you know where to lodge your phantoms; we are closing up the Unknown' ('Tu ne vas plus savoir où loger tes fantômes; / Nous fermons l'Inconnu', 91–2). In 'Paroles d'un amant', Ackermann sternly refuses belief in an afterlife: when we die, we die – I don't want eternity, it's a threat! It is enough to have the grave rising up between us; I don't want a world (i.e. the afterlife) doing so too. As long as I feel a living breast tremble and beat fast under my least caress, 'I let reality ravish me' and have no useless regrets ('Par la réalité je me laisse ravir': 'ravir' has the same double meaning as the English 'ravish': delight or abduct/rape) (105–8).

Nor does Ackermann hesitate to reproach Pascal. You were irritated – she tells him – to think that one could sleep peacefully over the abyss; you wanted fear, hope, anxiety to dig a powerful goad into our souls. But you will lead us only to the feet of a jealous, disloyal, implacable God who hates and deliberately blinds his creature Man. We will find another path without you, Pascal, for our chosen goal is to conquer not an illusion, but reality. Science opens up a new road ('La Science nous ouvre une route nouvelle'); and, even if Christ were to show us, in his splendid sky, our thrones prepared for us from all eternity, we would never have enough 'No!s' for the 'sinister Cross' that has opposed progress ('Pascal', 139–58).

In the closing poem of the collection, Ackermann envisages her narrator as in a shipwreck, uttering a last cry. The ship – Ackermann perhaps unnecessarily tells us – is the ship of humanity ('la nef humaine'), and we are the passengers. I won't, says the female narrator, let the waters swallow me up dumb and resigned ('muette et résignée'). Since my pale companions stay silent, it is for my voice to bear aloft the anathemas amassing against the heavens: I have assembled all despairs in myself:

> Qu'ils vibrent donc si fort, mes accents intrépides,
> Que ces mêmes cieux sourds en tressaillent surpris;
> Les airs n'ont pas besoin, ni les vagues stupides,
>   Pour frissonner d'avoir compris.
>
>   . . .
>
> Eh bien: ce cri d'angoisse et d'horreur infinie,
> Je l'ai jeté; je puis sombrer!   ('Le Cri',179–82)

(Let my intrepid tones vibrate so loud that these same deaf heavens shudder in surprise; the air does not need, nor do the stupid waves, to understand in order to shiver . . . Well: that cry of anguish and infinite horror, I've uttered it; I can sink!)

There are piercing phrases in Ackermann; if her heavy-handedness is sometimes off-putting, it was nevertheless a feat for a woman to proclaim atheism this fiercely. And to take it upon herself to be the spokeswoman for humanity, issuing a last desperate cry which the cosmos will 'understand', is to show a defiance missing from those sadder proclamations of woman's complete demise that we have heard echoing through the century.

Others followed her. Of course committed Catholic writers such as Pauline Craven were still writing for equally committed readers; Krysinska's narrators affirm faith at moments.[34] But Lesueur says religion is an illusion, albeit one which gives grandeur to our efforts (*Poésies*, 3–4). Bashkirtseff enjoys, in this last third of the century, being irreverent about the Pope, his cardinals and his priests; on learning she has TB, she gives her own angry diagnosis: 'Dieu est méchant' ('God is wicked': *Journal*, I 93–4, 134, II 419). Tinayre allows her characters to be outspoken about their disbelief; while Rachilde is no less profane about religion than about everything else, with blasphemous parodies and tasteless religious similes. The publishing history of 'France's best-loved schoolbook', *Le Tour de la France par deux enfants*, is instructive. In its earlier print-runs (from 1877), the book promoted religious education and Catholic morality. But its author, Augustine Fouillée, was an atheist who had chosen her pseudonym, G. Bruno, in memory of Giordano Bruno, an Italian freethinker burned in Rome by order of the Inquisition in

1600; and in the mid-1890s, after a dozen or so years of free, lay and compulsory primary education (brought in by Jules Ferry's laws), Bruno 'cleared' the book of all religious references. Churches, bell-towers, even the phrase 'Mon Dieu' disappeared.

As for science, Lesueur, in the wake of Ackermann, evokes molecules, a universe in constant evolution, the burning-out of the sun.[35] Deraismes supports her feminist arguments with theories of heredity and physiology, and calls for the rigour of a scientific approach to gender.[36] Michel too talks of her confidence in science, from its usefulness for girls' sexual education to her belief in the theory of evolution and her conviction of the invaluable discoveries that lie ahead; she describes her own scientific observations and experiments.[37] New subjects appear, then – doubtless encouraged by Naturalism, but also indicative of a boldness that allowed the tenets of Naturalism to be not merely absorbed but paraded. It was boldness, too, that allowed Gyp to create in the early 1880s her Paulette, at first sight the quintessential 'new woman'.

'Gyp' was the pseudonym of the countess Gabrielle de Mirabeau (1850–1932). She published some 100 hugely popular novels. Paulette is only the most famous of her range of cheeky heroines (she has been said to be a precursor of Colette in this respect).[38] In *Autour du mariage* and its sequel novel *Autour du divorce* (1883, 1886), Paulette marries M. d'Alaly, divorces him, realizes she loves him after all and is reunited with him. M. d'Alaly is the conventional shockable husband – whom, however, Paulette wraps round her little finger; he can only stutter or gape when she drops one of her many outrageous remarks. Paulette's mother, similarly, has conventional and often naive ideas of what young women should think before marriage and after. She does at least try, haltingly, to tell Paulette in advance that sex can be enjoyable:

Dieu, qui veut que son peuple soit nombreux . . . et qui veut aussi le bonheur de ses créatures . . . n'a pas permis que . . . que l'acte. . . destiné à . . . donner la vie . . . fût douloureux à accomplir. . . . Ce que tu éprouveras sera plutôt . . . de l'étonnement que . . . autre chose . . . (*Autour du mariage*, 28–9)[39]

(God, who wants his people to be numerous . . . and who also wants his creatures to be happy. . . has not permitted . . . the act . . . meant to . . . create life . . . to be painful to perform . . . What you'll feel will be more . . . astonishment than . . . anything else . . .) (author's ellipses)

But it is a wasted effort: Paulette already knows. And all through the

two novels she asserts her rights: to be outspoken; to claim pleasure
in bed – she asks her husband to teach her different ways of love-
making from the usual 'boring' one; to disobey him (you've already
had your freedom before marriage, she tells him – now I want
some); to defend her right to read 'forbidden' texts on the grounds
that he does too; to dress as immodestly as she likes; and to thwart or
be rude to her fussy and hidebound mother-in-law. If her husband
objects to her swimming costume, she answers by way of reassurance
that whereas others can see, *he* can touch; she swims – going out to a
raft with young men, for which her husband also reproaches her, to
no avail; she appreciatively assesses the body of a male fellow-
performer in theatricals. When her husband says, 'les allures des
femmes d'aujourd'hui sont si étranges! Jamais, autrefois, une grande
dame ne se serait permis de . . . ', Paulette interrupts: 'Parlez donc
pas des grandes dames! Ça n'existe plus!' ('the ways of women today
are so strange! Once, never would a great lady have let herself . . . '
'Don't talk to me about great ladies! Dead as dodos!', 130). When he
timidly ventures that 'La réserve est une qualité si séduisante chez
une femme', she retorts: 'Turlututu! la réserve une qualité? Allons
donc! Ce sont les maris qui inventent ces préceptes et ces sentences
. . . ridicules . . . ' ('Reserve is such an attractive quality in a
woman.' 'Fiddlesticks! reserve, a quality? Come off it! It's only
husbands who invent these . . . ridiculous rules and maxims . . .')
(127). Now the repressive man is being ridiculed by the woman, not
vice versa – being turned into a Moliéresque Arnolphe.

The 'convenances' are named, only to be dismissed out of hand.
When M. d'Alaly reproaches his new wife with not being 'convenable', Paulette, irritated ('crispée'), merely exclaims 'Oh!' (151).
When her mother-in-law attacks her for having 'manners not
admissible in our society' and for 'the absolute scorn you profess for
the *convenances*', Paulette replies: 'so much the better', reminding her
mother-in-law that she herself had scandalous affairs in her youth.
It's better to seem a slut ('une fille') than to behave like one while
seeming virtuous (345–7). The older woman is embarrassed by the
younger: again a turn-around since the early and mid-century.
Paulette's machinations finally enable her to see off this matriarch.
The last words of *Autour du divorce* are Paulette's laughing ones to her
husband: 'Dis donc? . . . si ta mère nous voyait!!!' ('Hey? . . . what if
your mother could see us!!!', 411). That change to a bolder 'body-
language' we have seen in other women writers is also more radical

and emphatic in Gyp. A wedding guest criticizes the bride Paulette for having 'too much aplomb', but she promptly responds that girls who 'hide their blushes', who 'look crestfallen' ('baissent le nez'), are no longer fashionable; only those who've had an 'accident' do so (58).

In short, as one of Paulette's lawyers says in *Autour du divorce*, 'Drôle de petit produit moderne! . . .' ('Funny little modern product! . . . ', 165). Yet an uncomfortable strand runs through Gyp's depiction of this unquestionably 'new' woman. It is part of Paulette's unembarrassability to dress just as she wants – not only in the swimming costume that upsets her husband, but in trousers too. But it is hardly ever the freedom these garments bring that is at issue. It is far more a matter of tight, even clinging, outfits that show Paulette's figure to full advantage and encourage bevies of lustful men to stare at or follow her. As she herself explains to her mother only five pages into the tale, we're not in 1844, back with Ingres, any more! Fashions are now figure-hugging (8–9). This point is made so often, and Paulette's shape in these modern outfits is described so salaciously, that sooner or later we will wonder whether this new woman is really liberated, or whether she is 'liberated' so that Gyp can titillate her audience with passages bordering on pornography (as when Paulette wears a flesh-coloured undergarment and nothing else for a part in theatricals: 216–17). Is Paulette cheeky or, more knowingly, saucy? Is she assertive, or a coquette with merely pseudo-independent whims?

In short, for every occasion on which Paulette speaks her mind, there is another on which she is only a sex-object. Nor is she truly unconventional, never indulging in anything so disgraceful as pre- or extra-marital sex.[40] Yet this itself helps. Gyp, with a sure touch, seizes upon many of the repressions that had tortured female characters since the beginning of the century, and envisages a heroine who thumbs her nose at them without 'falling'. In this picture created by one overweening and fascistic woman, there is still complicity with sexism – even abject complicity – but at the same time an ostentatious 'progress'. Paradoxically, Gyp's best-selling books must have loosened many women's constrained images of their social and marital selves.[41]

CHAPTER 19

Experiment: Naturalism, Symbolism and Marie Krysinska

One of the faults for which Paulette's mother-in-law reproves her is her speech: 'you must', she tells her, 'make a total change in your tone, language and manners'; and a page later the point is put more strongly:

Votre langage aussi est déplorable. Vous parlez argot! De mon temps, jamais une femme ne se fût permis de dire de semblables choses . . . (344–5)

(Your language is deplorable too. You use slang! In my day, never would a woman have allowed herself to say such things . . .) (author's ellipsis)

Mme d'Alaly is right and wrong. Since the beginning of the century, comic or pastoral dramatists such as Mme de Montanclos had reproduced amusing tics of speech or 'country talk' as part of the expected entertainment – in the mouths of, say, ungrammatical servants and lower-class lovers of both sexes.[1] And a few other writers had been trying out the 'inconvenable' in the speech of their characters. In *Edouard* Duras not only draws attention to different registers of language, but is pioneering in her politicized interpretation of them.[2] She even writes a long note on the strong (and lively) expressions Edouard's uncle uses when he is – wrongly – congratulating Edouard on his supposed affair with Natalie. Expressions become forced in corrupt circles, says Duras, but such corruption need not matter if in the end honour saves all (*Edouard*, 116 n). This strikes an apologetic note, as if it is shocking (for a woman writer?) to use 'strong' language even in fiction. *Edouard* was written a few years before the *Préface de Cromwell* (1827), in which Hugo not only permits but promulgates the blend of formal with vulgar registers; if Duras had been writing ten years later, she might have been able to promote her own short-lived 'mixing' of styles more wholeheartedly.

In the mid-century, Sand, as we have seen, moved French narrative along with her stylized rendering of 'Berrichon' speech and her almost ethnographic assertions that this speech has an interest in its own right.[3] Girardin, as might be anticipated from her own style, enjoys the quirks of speech ('et *vice Versailles*', says one Mrs Malaprop); while throughout *Le Mauvais Génie*, Ségur gives a hyperbolic rendering of her Anglo-Irishman's language: this flamboyant character, who on the one hand is ignorant of the most basic rules of French pronunciation, on the other uses words and phrases unlikely to enter a normal beginner's vocabulary, such as 'fainéant' and 'mauvais garnement' ('lazybones', 'scapegrace').[4] But the point is that this woman felt able to cast restraint to the winds and use obviously 'abnormal' language. For the picture is different for most pre-1870 female authors. Staël, in her translation of Goethe's *Faust*, consistently and deliberately mistranslated to the point of distortion in order to suppress vulgarisms and colloquialisms, and alter or remove physical vocabulary (for instance, that which alluded to 'undignified' parts of the body): as Isbell says, where Goethe used a 'low style' Staël turned it into a 'high' one. She was adapting it to what she thought would be acceptable to the French public (that is, permitting nothing that would not have been allowed by the seventeenth-century 'bienséances', the literary proprieties), but her motivation was probably double: self-protective too.[5] Both Colet in *Lui* and Stern in *Nélida* allude to the vulgar language of their 'Sand' figure and her circle, but without reproducing it.[6] The only interest most of these women writers show in different registers is to record, with an occasional comment, switches between *vous* and *tu*.[7] (This concern with *tutoiement/vouvoiement*, which carries a high emotional charge, continued to be more marked in women's than in men's literature well into the last third of the century.)[8]

So Baudelaire's blend of dignified and 'ignoble' or grotesque vocabulary; the vulgarisms of Balzac's characters; the argot of *Les Misérables*; even the comedy of cliché and platitude that delights Stendhal and Flaubert; were clearly areas into which women almost all felt unable to stray. They would not have been ladylike if they had. Paulette's mother-in-law, then, is being largely accurate when she says that in her day, no woman (or 'lady', anyway) would have spoken like Paulette – and, we can add, no woman would have written like Gyp: both author and character share an extravagant enjoyment of slang. The mother and husband are worried by it too; but Paulette presses on regardless. A certain man is 'juteux', a flashy dresser, for, as she explains, 'No one says "stylish" any more, or "dressy", you say "flashy", everyone knows that!' ('On ne dit plus chic, ni gommeux, on dit "juteux", tout le monde sait ça!': *Autour du mariage*, 173). In *Autour du divorce*, M. d'Alaly comes to accept that slang is 'essential' to his wife, sighing: 'when she can't speak slang or be a bit peculiar, she doesn't enjoy herself much' ('quand elle ne peut ni parler argot ni se livrer à des excentricités, elle ne s'amuse pas fort', 118). Finally, it is a sign that he has come round to her way of thinking when, during their reconciliation, he uses the word 'mufle' ('coarse'):

Paulette, *saisie.* – Oh! . . . (*A part.*) Il a changé de langage aussi! . . . Chaque fois que je parlais comme ça, j'etais grondée! . . . (340–1)

(Paulette, *staggered.* – Oh! . . . (*Aside.*) He's changed language too! . . . Whenever I talked like that, I got ticked off! . . .) (author's ellipses)

Naturalism helped Gyp to incorporate racy colloquialisms into her narrative, but she does have originality. Zola's *L'Assommoir* (1877), with its slangy speech (both direct and reported), had appeared only five or six years before she began publishing; and in the material I surveyed she is not only the first woman writer to use slang, but is the first to present it as part of the battle of the sexes and the generations (something Zola does not do). This was her contribution to Naturalism; and from her, younger women writers learned how to write rudely, a more important acquisition than the newly 'scientific' emphases.[9]

This is not Gyp's only originality. As in the last quotation, long sections of her novels are set out as if in drama. The dialogue-narrative had already had a minor vogue in France between 1750 and 1800, appearing in works by Diderot and Crébillon *fils*, for example. Occasional mid-century writers, both male and female, used it sporadically (Ségur, for example). But it enjoyed a resurgence from the 1880s on. Gyp was its most prolific practitioner and was almost certainly the instigator of the late-century trend. This not only survived (in, for instance, Roger Martin du Gard's *Jean Barois*, 1913) but laid the ground for the collage effects of later twentieth-century novels, most notably Nathalie Sarraute's works (1939 on), with their swirl of conversations and thoughts breaking in on each other without the intervening 'she said', 'he thought'. Sarraute is also heralded in Gyp's extensive use of ellipses to suggest the confused or the unsayable.

Gyp does not, however, stray into those other experimental

movements characteristic of the late century which can be broadly labelled 'Symbolist' and 'stream of consciousness', and which, as I have suggested, some women found more acceptable than Naturalism, with its associations of violence and crudeness. They readily adapted to the modes and subjects of Symbolism, writing prose poems and (less often) verse ones resonant with half-voiced moods and staging a blurry Nature or single figures loaded with a dream-like significance. Such was Judith Gautier, who published pieces about the instability of objects in the fog or, say, the rootlessness of drifting with the sea.[10] Blanchecotte too, now in her forties, created 'pointilliste' word-pictures, as in her aptly titled 'Impression':

> Nuage, azur, lueurs, brusques magnificences,
> Matins brillants, soirs orageux, changeants tableaux;
> . . .
> Oh! quel rêve . . .
> De suivre dans la nuit les petites lumières
> Qui tachent de clartés la profondeur des soirs![11]

(Cloud, azure, glimmers, brusque magnificence, brilliant mornings, stormy evenings, changing tableaux; . . . Oh! what a dream . . . to follow in the night the little lights that gleam-stain the deep deep evenings!)

This was published in 1873, a year before the coining of the term 'Impressionism' in the wake of the 1874 exhibition that included Monet's *Impression, soleil levant*; it shows how alive many women writers were to changing aesthetic emphases.

Women's life-writing of the period may also have made its contribution to the development of the 'interior monologue' in this period. (Edouard Dujardin is generally held to have initiated this with *Les Lauriers sont coupés*, 1888.) Mid-century life-writing by women was, as I have suggested, more obviously 'crafted' than that of their predecessors. But two of the most interesting self-portraitists of the late century, Marie Bashkirtseff and Louise Michel, deliberately exploit the *décousu*, as opposed to the simply picaresque. They adopt an almost wave-like structure which allows them to proceed sometimes in gasping fragments, sometimes with elegiac refrains of a quasi-symphonic character impossible to imagine in d'Aunet, Tristan or Voilquin. Signs of excess emotion, carelessness, haste? Maybe. But both Bashkirtseff and Michel have a relatively sophisticated aesthetic which indicates that they identified aspects of their writing with new literary movements.

Bashkirtseff in her preface (1884) unapologetically highlights her own associative procedures in what is to follow (*Journal*, I 12). Already, as a thirteen-year-old, she had written a brief parody of the excessive clarity of didactic literature (1874); and she makes us reconsider her whole work when in 1882 she writes that 'imbeciles' think that to be ' "modern" or a realist' one must put down the first thing that comes along, without arranging it. She goes on: 'Ne l'arrangez pas, mais *choisissez* et *surprenez*, tout est là' ('Don't arrange it, but *choose* and *surprise*, that's the secret': author's italics, I 12, 59; II 383).

Michel, too, calmly underlines the exploratory construction of her *Mémoires* (1886); half-way through she suggests a new term for it: 'psycho-biologie' (156). These memoirs are 'fragments', 'flotsam' ('épaves'); they are full of poignant memories, which I'll often recount 'according as the impressions come', for I claim for my thought and pen 'the right to vagrancy' ('au hasard de l'impression', 'le droit de vagabondage': 17). A little later, she breaks off to exclaim, in paragraphs that are themselves so short as to be fragmentary:

Il faut me laisser écrire les choses comme elles me viennent!
On dirait des tableaux passant à perte de vue et s'en allant sans fin dans l'ombre, – je ne sais où. (32)

(I must be allowed to write things as they come to me!
It's as if there are pictures passing by as far as the eye can see and going away endlessly into shadow – where, I don't know.)

Indeed, the 'facts' of her life are woven into an atemporal narration nearly as often as into a strictly chronological one. But by the end, this half-jolting, half-associative form has come to seem the most appropriate one for Michel's switches from gaiety to heart-rending scenes, from passionate pleas for the victimized back to tenderness or cordiality. Disparities between, and within, her personal and political experiences are re-created in a discrete structure which can accommodate both digression and underlying harmonies. Thus, towards the end she even heads one chapter 'Encore une parenthèse' ('Yet another parenthesis', 235). But, exiled in New Caledonia, she meditates on the cyclical nature of memory, with a post-Baudelairean and pre-Proustian stress on the powers of smell:

Là-bas, de temps à autre, les yeux fixés sur la mer, la pensée libre dans l'espace, je revoyais les jours d'autrefois. Je sentais l'odeur des roses du fond du clos, du foin coupé au soleil d'été, l'âpre odeur du chanvre que j'aimais tant autrefois; maintenant je n'y songe plus.

Je revoyais tout; mille détails qui ne m'avaient point frappée jadis me revenaient dans les souvenirs fouillés . . . (241)

(Over there, from time to time, my eyes on the sea, my thoughts free in space, I saw again the days of old. I smelled the fragrance of the roses at the bottom of the close, of the hay cut under the summer sun, the acrid hemp-smell I once loved so much; now I don't think about it any more.

I saw everything again; hundreds of details that, long ago, hadn't struck me came back as I burrowed into my memories . . .)

Michel was also the only life-writer of the century to attempt a sustained metaphorical network – one which, we shall see, is as central to the meaning of her memoirs as are the events that provoke it.[12]

However, it is Marie Krysinska who has the strongest claim of the late century to be a technical innovator, and the less agreeable claim to be the woman writer most successfully air-brushed from the literary history of nineteenth-century France. Apart from very isolated mentions here and there in works of literary criticism, her name was virtually unknown in Western Europe and the US until Clive Scott's discussion of her poetry in his 1990 book on French free verse.[13] She is mentioned by neither Sartori and Zimmerman nor the *Bloomsbury Guide*, and it was not until 1993 that she put in an appearance in the French biographical archive; even then, the extracts about her were taken from works on French song, not French literature.[14] The only book-length account of her life and writings is in Polish.[15]

Marie Krysinska (1857–1908) was born in Poland and settled in Paris at the age of sixteen; she married an illustrator and lithographer, Georges Bellenger, but continued to use her maiden name.[16] She was an accepted member of the Bohemian circles of the time and was one of the rare women admitted to literary club meetings. She started as a song-writer/singer ('chansonnière') at the Chat Noir cabaret, setting poems by Verlaine and Cros to music, and was soon publishing her own poetry in leading literary journals. She wrote fiction too, but this is less powerful than her verse, which, like that of her contemporaries, suggests fugitive sensations and equivocal yearnings: sometimes through obviously 'symbolic' objects or creatures, but, more often and more originally, by means of ambiguous adjectives which recur with subtle modifications, conveying both circularity and dimly felt variation. Her intensive alliterations and assonances create an illusion that words are melting into each other in such a way as to confuse the reader's sense of a graspable 'content'; this phonetic echoing is often playful and humorous.

Krysinska was also one of the initiators, or the initiator, of a poetic technique that half-respects the traditional rules of French versification but also extends and defies them: the free verse that was to become the mode *par excellence* of twentieth-century French poets. Most commentators assume free verse proper to have been introduced in the early 1880s (rather than by, say, Rimbaud in his prose poems of the early 1870s). Krysinska and her contemporary supporters claimed that it was she who 'invented' it rather than the other contender: Gustave Kahn (1850–1936), the poet, editor and critic who played a major role in the Symbolist movement from the middle of the 1880s. Krysinska's claim rests on the fact that between October 1882 and December 1883, she published seven poems – five in *Le Chat noir*, one in *La Vie moderne*, and one in *La Libre Revue* – which looked like free verse or the beginnings of it.[17] Scott discusses the controversy with scrupulous fairness.[18] He remarks that these poems, with each frequently short sentence beginning a new line, but with overruns mostly conforming to a prose margin, had 'an ambiguous look to them' which worried Kahn when he came across one of them in 1883, while doing military service in Tunisia. Here is Kahn's account:

Je regardais la feuille et j'y vis un poème en vers libres, ou typographié tel, poème en prose ou en vers libres, selon le gré, très directement ressemblant à mes essais. Il était signé d'une personne qui me connaissait bien, et voulait bien, moi absent, se conformer étroitement à mon esthétique; je faisais école.

(Looking at the sheet of paper, I saw a poem in free verse, or laid out as such, a prose poem or a free verse poem – as you will – looking very straightforwardly like my efforts. It was signed by a person who knew me well, and who in my absence seemed to want to conform strictly to my aesthetics; I was founding a school.)

Scott comments:

Kahn's equivocation is designed, one sees, not to give Krysinska the benefit of the doubt, but to give himself that benefit; her priority in print merely confirms his priority in instigation. Be that as it may, when Krysinska republished these poems she tended to adopt a different, less ambiguous, typographical disposition . . .

Thus the first three lines of 'Symphonie en gris' appeared as follows when originally published in 1882, that is, resembling a prose poem:

Plus d'ardentes lueurs sur le ciel alourdi, qui semble tristement rêver.
Les arbres, sans mouvement, mettent dans le loin une dentelle grise.
Sur le ciel qui semble tristement rêver, plus d'ardentes lueurs.

(No more ardent glimmers against the heavy sky, which seems to dream sadly.
The trees, without movement, place far off a grey lace.
Against the sky which seems to dream sadly, no more ardent glimmers.)

But when she republished the poem in 1890 in *Rythmes pittoresques*, Krysinska laid it out in such a way as to show how the lines resemble, yet deviate from, 'normal' French verse:

> Plus d'ardentes lueurs sur le ciel alourdi,
> Qui semble tristement rêver.
> Les arbres, sans mouvement,
> Mettent dans le loin une dentelle grise.
> Sur le ciel qui semble tristement rêver,
> Plus d'ardentes lueurs.[19]

To many, says Scott, 'this looked like chicanery attempting to mask wisdom after the event; but others supported the claims to antecedence which she made, or which were made on her behalf', and she and J.-H. Rosny continued to press her case in the prefaces of *Rythmes pittoresques* and *Joies errantes* (1894).

Even if Krysinska was not *the* innovator, she was clearly *an* innovator, and one whose work was original enough to alarm her nearest male rival. No doubt the question will never be settled. (The two works on French song cited by the *Archives biographiques* say respectively that she 'created' free verse and that she 'used' – 'maniait' – it.) But Krysinska at the least has remarkable expertise in the new form. She enjoys playing with the reader's anticipation that a familiar form is being revived: she will, for example, use words or titles that evoke ballads or folk-song – which she then proceeds to undercut with highly irregular line-lengths whose positioning on the page demands as much attention as the content.[20] Similarly, in 'Les Danses' – a section which includes, for example, a 'Menuet' and a 'Valse' – she seems to represent, yet does not, different dance rhythms; for in French free verse one can choose whether or not to give mute 'e' its full syllabic count, and this means that far from echoing anything like short 'fixed' bars with firm stresses, as in the minuet, Krysinska's longer lines may be 10/11 syllables, even 9/10/11.[21] And if the words themselves have an 'olde-worlde' smoothness ('flowered silk of long bodices shivering with discreet, libertine love', etc.), this smoothness is belied and parodied by ostentatiously jerky enjambements and by an eccentric and unassimilable layout.

Also parodic is her 'Sérénade'.[22] This starts:

> La Nuit, gracieuse et farouche sirène,
> Flotte dans le calme bleu ethéréen,
> Ouvrant ses yeux purs – qui sont des astres –
> Et pleure de longues larmes tranquilles,
> Des larmes de lumière, tremblant un peu,
> Dans la paix dormante de l'eau
> Où les navires à l'amarre
> Sont des fantômes de navires,
> Si pâlement profilés sur le ciel . . .

(Night, a gracious, wild mermaid, floats in the ether-blue calm, opening her pure eyes – which are stars – and weeps long, tranquil tears, tears of light, trembling slightly, in the sleeping peace of the water where moored ships are ghosts of ships, so palely profiled against the sky. . .)

This apparently peaceful scene has a strand of unease, created by the oxymoron 'gracieuse et farouche' of the first line and the pun of 'des astres' in the third ('désastres'), but perhaps principally by the half-obeyed, half-flouted rules of French versification. Thus Krysinska makes 'sirène' part-rhyme with 'ethéréen': this pairing of feminine with masculine ending is not 'allowed', but it does at least lead us to expect, in the fourth line, a rhyme with 'des astres', an expectation which 'tranquilles' frustrates. At the end of lines 5 and 6, the monosyllables 'peu' and 'eau' are visually but not acoustically akin; while the 'navires', 'amarre' and (again) 'navires' of lines 7 and 8 once more create not full rhymes but now somewhat cacophonous half-rhymes. Meanwhile the picture itself keeps fading out of focus, then to return. The poem continues thus – now precious, now violent – and building up to a finale in which the dawn is no fresh promise but is a 'pink threat', 'la menace rose / Du jour', heralding only anxieties:

> Et voici retentir dans l'air assoupi
> Le clairon qui sonne le retour
> Des soucis – brutale cohorte.
> Le haïssable chant du coq
> Lance la narquoise sérénade:
> – Aux pires hôtes ouvrez vos portes,
> Voici le jour!

(Now hear resounding in the drowsy air the bugle that rings out the return of anxieties – a brutal cohort. The hateful cock's song launches the quizzical serenade: – Open your doors to the worst inmates, here is day!)

The 'narquoise sérénade', the sly, quizzical, deflated serenade, is the one Krysinska has just created.

Similarly ludic and disturbing are the line-lengths of 'Effet de soir', which irreverently adjust, then respect, then readjust, the sacred alexandrine. Here, for example, is the middle section, with long lines of respectively 13, 12, 12, 11 syllables.[23]

> Ce furent des Midis déments les démentes heures
> Et les espérantes Envolées des jours proches –
>   Si lointains! -
>
> Qui se levaient ainsi que des Ombres maudites
>   De leurs tombeaux;
> Et je crus entendre leurs connues antiennes, –
>   Menteuses antiennes. –
> Mais c'était seulement un crapaud
>   Qui radotait.   (*Rythmes pittoresques*, 24–5)

(What came was the demented hours of demented Middays, and the hopeful Flights of near days – so distant! – which arose like accursed Shades from their tombs; and I thought I heard their well-known antiphons, – lying antiphons. – But it was only a toad, rambling.)

The content, too, is deliberately off-centre. The narrator is evoking memories that return in an old forgotten garden – but these are not the memories of the morning of childhood, nor the 'evening' ones suggested by the title. All they re-create is madness, whirling time, deceit – then to be reduced to a toad's croak. At her best, then, Krysinska's techniques allow her to play games with the idea of intangibility, and to create moods that hover 'modernistically' between real agony and the suspicion that this is only a pretence of agony.

Szarama-Swolkieniowa, near the end of her generally sympathetic account, alleges that Krysinska's content is conventional or derivative, and that it is in her technical skills that we must look for her innovativeness (*Maria Krysińska*, 113–14). This, written in 1972, is a harsher judgement than would be made now, after three decades of 'women's studies'. Krysinska can be vapid and occasionally 'preachy', and her family resemblance to Baudelaire and Verlaine is sometimes obvious; but male writers share patterns of resemblance too ... Szarama-Swolkieniowa may not have noticed that Krysinska's 'conventionality' – such as it is – is often there to be undermined; and in as much as Krysinska has assimilated Verlaine, it is his unsettling sides that she echoes, reinventing them as she does so. Whether or not Krysinska is to be regarded as a pioneer, her most powerful poems show her role in late-century poetry to be as important as Gyp's is in Naturalism and the dialogue novel. The concepts of 'free verse' and 'Symbolism', in their inception at least, arose from group discussions as much as from strong individual talents. Krysinska was acknowledged and fêted as a contributor by other members of these groups, and much of her work predates that of the most famous nineteenth-century French free-verse writer, Laforgue. The least one can say is that it is unjust to write her out of the picture.

CHAPTER 20

Cruelty to humans and animals: Louise Michel

The early poem by Krysinska whose layout disconcerted Kahn was 'Le Hibou', a tableau, with strongly religious overtones, of an owl's crucifixion by a peasant. In its later publication in *Rythmes pittoresques*, it is part of a section called 'Symboles' (43–5). Here is its opening:

Il agonise, l'oiseau crucifié, l'oiseau crucifié sur la porte.

Ses ailes ouvertes sont clouées, et de ses blessures, de grandes perles de sang tombent lentement comme des larmes.

Il agonise, l'oiseau crucifié!

Un paysan à l'œil gai l'a pris ce matin, tout effaré de soleil cruel, et l'a cloué sur la porte.

(It is dying, the crucified bird, the bird crucified on the door. Its open wings are nailed, and from its wounds great pearls of blood fall slowly like tears. It is dying, the crucified bird! A merry-eyed peasant took it this morning, all flustered with cruel sun, and nailed it to the door.)

Now, the merry-eyed peasant is sitting at the same door and playing on a flute of wood. The sun sets, the flute sings of and celebrates this sunset in its melancholic majesty; it sobs with anguish towards the sky, which speaks to it of a better country that has no cruel suns. The crucified bird hears the song; forgetting its torture and widening its bleeding wounds, it leans forward to hear better.

'Le Hibou' effects an interchange between the helpless submission to pain; a cruel gaiety; and an art (the flute-playing) which both incorporates and rises above the insouciance of its practitioner. It has some of the 'aestheticized' sadism of *fin-de-siècle* Decadence. But for other writers, cruelty was not 'Decadent'; it was a political reality. One such was the activist Louise Michel, who has been attracting renewed attention since the 1976 republication of her memoirs.[1]

Women in the last third of the nineteenth century were no less politically aware than their mothers and grandmothers. A few might still feel it was not quite seemly for women to be too vocal on the subject. In 1879 Pauline Craven praised Lady Palmerston's political insight but in the same breath commended her 'womanly' discretion:

elle avait l'habitude et l'intelligence des grandes affaires, qui s'étaient si souvent traitées devant elle; mais elle possédait au suprême degré le tact qui, en pareille matière, marque la limite qu'une femme, lorsqu'elle en parle, ne doit jamais franchir. (*Réminiscences*, 11)

(she was accustomed to, and understood, the high politics that had so often been discussed in front of her; but she had to a supreme degree the tact that, in such matters, marks the boundary a woman must never cross when she is talking about them.)

But in the following pages Craven cannot help expressing her own interest in politics, and indicating her views on (for example) British Home Office policy.[2] And others lacked even her token restraint. Sharp divisions between left and right, between feminists and traditionalists, were all the more reason for joining the debate. Thus the creation of the Third Republic provoked Gyp to comment – albeit jokily – on the difference between Republic and monarchy (government by 900 idiots rather than just the one); Tinayre to explore the dichotomy between genuine reformers and career politicians; and Bashkirtseff to voice socialist, even 'Communard', sympathies.[3] Only a year after the Franco-Prussian war, Bentzon published *Un divorce* (1872), which is set in Germany; she had to negotiate her way round the difficulties of presenting this work to the French public, and her arguments in the 'Postscript' in favour of her novel exploit the differences between 'Prussia' and 'Germany' with some sophistication. Ackermann, in a prefatory poem of January 1874, 'Mon livre', asserts that she *will* write about current concerns in these 'days of fever', however harsh the resulting verse. She has, she says, felt all the 'frissons' of her epoch run down her spine:

> Et je ne prendrais pas parti dans ce grand drame?
> Quoi! ce cœur qui bat là, pour être un cœur de femme,
> En est-il moins un cœur humain? (69–71)

(So how would I not take part in this great drama? What! is this heart beating here, for all that it is a woman's, any less a human heart?)

And Lesueur, in '*Sursum corda!*', a long poem which won the 1885 Grand Prix de Poésie of the Académie Française, urges the still-demoralized, hence 'sleepy' and unambitious, French to conquer not towns but souls, to win over other nations not with cannons but through art and intellectual influence.[4]

At the same time, creeping into the writings of women in this post-1870 period was a depiction of physical cruelty that was both more detailed and more emphatic than before. It is impossible to differentiate clearly between the factors in the sounding of this new note. The horrors of the Franco-Prussian war and the aftermath of the Commune; Naturalism, and, as I have suggested, Decadence; the slow removal of inhibitions, encouraged by the Third Republic's increasing acknowledgement of women's rights: all no doubt played a part in helping women feel that, like their male predecessors, they too could talk about bodily suffering – sometimes to revel in it, sometimes to protest with repugnance. For some, liberal values now encompassed the treatment meted out to lower as well as higher species, and comparisons switch relatively freely between underprivileged humans on the one hand and animals on the other.

From an early stage in the century, it is true, such writers as Desbordes-Valmore enlisted animal 'characters' in fables that highlighted power relations, either between different social ranks as often in La Fontaine, or between men and women.[5] In others, animals became easily readable allegories for the unfortunate (Tastu's caged birds in 'Les Oiseaux du sacre' are political prisoners).[6] More specifically, they were allegories for women. The centuries-old misogynistic ploy of likening women not only to children but also to animals was not dead in the nineteenth century (Priollaud quotes Flaubert, Maurras and Proudhon on the theme); but the women writers provide the obverse side.[7] When Voilquin's mother tells her that women must put up with their lot, for 'where the goat is tethered, there must she graze', the young Suzanne retorts 'audaciously': 'No, no, the goat can break her tie and go somewhere else to graze' ('Non, non, la chèvre peut rompre son lien et aller brouter ailleurs'); and as an adult, urging herself on to further effort, she reflects that she, as a working-class woman, is like the ant whose tiny step may none the less affect the universe.[8]

Other pre-1870 women more directly considered the function of animals in human society – some of course simply at the level of entertainment, and quite indifferent to notions of cruelty. La Tour du Pin, as one might expect, sees nothing but splendour in bullfights, while later in the century Girardin is flippant to a degree in her narration of a hunt:

le cerf s'est conduit noblement; en véritable connaisseur, en *cicerone* de bon goût, il a parcouru les vallons les plus pittoresques, les pays les plus célèbres; il a traversé tout le parc d'Ermenonville, il a salué en passant, rapidement il est vrai, la tombe de Jean-Jacques, ce mortel qui, comme lui, se croyait toujours poursuivi . . . Après six heures de course, la victime ingénieuse est allée tomber dans le bel étang de Morfontaine; elle a choisi le site le plus poétique pour y mourir![9]

(the stag conducted itself nobly; as a veritable connoisseur, a cicerone of good taste, it ran through the most picturesque dales, the most celebrated regions; it crossed the entire park of Ermenonville, it greeted on the way, rapidly it's true, the tomb of Jean-Jacques [Rousseau], that mortal who, like it, thought he was always being pursued . . . After six hours' running, the ingenious victim went to the lovely pool of Morfontaine, there to fall in; it chose the most poetic site in which to die!)

But few were this pitiless. Sand, as we know, links cruelty to animals, and 'speciesism', with sexism and an undue valuing of good looks. Ségur, for her part, can hardly be thought of as a defender of animals' rights (in *Le Mauvais Génie* turkey after turkey is gaily strangled to satify M. Georgey's Gargantuan appetite); nevertheless, it is part of Sophie's moral education to learn that the animals she maltreats are not mere playthings.[10] Tristan calls animals the 'companions' of humans and says they too are creatures of God; she goes to a bullfight in Lima as a matter of cultural curiosity, but such is her horror, and that of the Englishman accompanying her, that they have to leave, affected equally by the bulls' and horses' suffering and by the exultation of the spectators: 'cet attrait qu'offre à tout un peuple le spectacle de la douleur me paraissait l'indice du dernier degré de corruption' ('this charm that a whole people finds in the spectacle of pain seemed to me to indicate the ultimate degree of corruption').[11]

Already visible, then, was an interest in animals both as symbols and as legitimate objects of sympathy in their own right, but such uses become more arresting in the last third of the century. Ackermann relates how as a lonely, wild child she identified with . . . woodlice. Her best moments were spent in a corner of the garden watching flies, insects and especially these 'cloportes':

Je me sentais une sympathie toute particulière pour cette petite bête laide et craintive. J'aurais voulu, comme elle, pouvoir me replier sur moi-même et me dissimuler.

(I felt a quite special sympathy for this ugly, apprehensive little creature. I'd have liked to be able to curl up and hide, just as it could.)

From all this, she still has, she says, a great tenderness for 'whatever has life' ('tout ce qui a vie').[12] Bentzon, in *Yette* (1880), has an entire chapter on cock-fighting: 'Combat de coqs'.[13] Yette, in the town of Saint-Pierre in Martinique, renews acquaintance with another Creole family whose son displays towards animals an 'inconceivable cruelty': like many of his young friends, he himself enjoys fighting and additionally getting animals to tear each other apart ('s'entre-déchirer'). Yette protests, for she hates any living creature being tormented, however uninteresting it is ('détestait que l'on tourmentât un être vivant, si peu intéressant qu'il fût'); she repeats to the boy, 'What if you were in their place!' But he laughs, almost cross at being compared to an animal. Significantly, women never go to the cock-pit – the boy draws himself up pompously as he tells Yette this; and, also significantly, Yette contrasts these cocks with their own fowl at home, saying theirs are happier because they can do what they like. Here the parallel becomes clear with Yette's own untrammelled girlhood, about to be lost.[14]

No writer of the late century, however, pays as much attention to animals as Louise Michel (1830–1905). Michel was illegitimate, 'ce qu'on appelle bâtarde' as she says ('what's called a bastard', *Mémoires*, 309.)[15] She became a schoolteacher and a revolutionary; she did not marry, and although she may have loved the Communard Théophile Ferré, she also expresses strong feelings for women in her writings.[16] She was allowed to play a leading role in the Commune, exceptional for a woman: not only as a field nurse, but as a vigilante, a strategist and a combatant (by all accounts an unusually humane one).[17] She was afterwards sentenced to exile in New Caledonia: she was so popular that the judiciary did not dare execute her, as it did others. She returned to France in 1880 but had to leave again because of her involvement with the anarchist movement; she then taught in London. She died in the middle of a lecture tour. Her funeral was attended by huge numbers of people: the author of the 'memorandum' at the end of Michel's *La Commune* says that the crowd was 'unheard of', outstripping those at Emile de Girardin's and Gambetta's funerals, and would have been still larger if not for police brutality; he adds that at theirs, the crowds came as a political demonstration, whereas at hers, most were there to show personal sympathy and gratitude for her altruism.[18] Michel wrote not only the autobiographical works *Mémoires* (1886) and *La Commune* (1898), but also novels, verse and the words to songs (for example, in May

14. *Louise Michel lecturing the Communards at the Satory camp.* (By Jules Girardet.)

1871, 'Chanson des prisons').[19] Her life-writing is remarkable as the story (backed up by witnesses) of a seemingly fearless woman, who despite arrests and imprisonments gives uncowed responses at her trials (where she asks for the death penalty, believing the regime will be discredited if it executes any more women); displays unshakable sang-froid and conviction as a speaker and political activist; and faces exile not with resignation, but with a determination to make the best of it for herself and those among whom she finds herself – fellow-deportees and natives alike. She faces it, too, with a naturalist's curiosity (Maclean says that 150 years later she would probably have been an outstanding zoologist or biologist).[20] Michel is one of those women we find throughout the century hungry for learning, reading voraciously; she attended biology lectures, and in exile observed and deduced what she could about wildlife. (Those who were teachers, or training to be so, were, she says, 'avid for the knowledge which women only snatch where they can': *Mémoires*, 99.)

Michel's life-writing is ardent and often harrowing. She describes in ghastly detail the summary executions that took place during the crushing of the Commune and the barbarity shown to ex-Communards, regardless of their level of participation, by their compatriots. She indignantly points out the injustice of French society, pleading again and again for some fruit to come from all the sacrifices. These pleas can become like an extended hymn, rolling on in apocalyptic visions, and with harsh variations on the regeneration image at the end of Zola's *Germinal* (1885): for Michel not only evokes the thousands of humble workers who have been 'absorbed' into the ground in their anonymously exploited lives, but also calls for the recently blood-soaked earth to give back new life in the coming Revolution. Women in particular have been 'milled down' and effaced, but they, and the men, will still live on – the 'bread' will remain (*Mémoires*, 122). If the battle starts up again, do you think – she asks her reader in *La Commune* – that memories are all buried underground and that spilled blood never bears flowers ('ne fleurisse jamais')? The vengeance of the disinherited is more powerful than the earth itself. And she evokes those who were buried in haste swelling up underground, and, like sprouting grain, raising and cracking the surface. When the earth of the Champ-de-Mars is next dug up for an exhibition, perhaps, in spite of the flames lit on the long rows in which the slaughtered were laid and blanketed with tar ('sous les lits de goudron') – perhaps we shall see the whitened, charred bones appear, lined up at the battle front, as they were during the May days (*Commune*, 314, 328–9).

Michel compares her own writing to an epic (*Commune*, 187). It can border on the mythical or the grand, yet she is not pompous: her writing is also humorous and even teasing at moments, and she finds time to describe the details of family life; then, later, loving scenes with her mother and friend; or unexpected distractions from the Commune's battles (such as reading Baudelaire at the height of the fighting, or playing an organ in an abandoned church, to the horror of her fellow-Communards: she is oblivious of the fact that she is giving away their position: *Commune*, 223, 252–3). Between the intimate and the epic or quasi-mythical, animals have a connecting role. Michel both describes them in their particularity and creates a series of images – half-fable, half-metaphor – in which they usually represent the exploited and the victimized. She is unsentimental about them, saying that dangerous animals (vipers, wolves) should be exterminated for the common good – like brutal rulers; she also sees animals' cruelty to each other (owls bite off mice's legs so that they cannot escape but will still provide fresh meat for the owlets: *Mémoires*, 97, 285). Nor does she place animals higher in the hierarchy than humans. Rather, her expressions of pity first prepare for, then reinforce, her pictures of human pain. She says herself that she has been accused of having more solicitude for animals than for humans, and has been asked why one should be moved by the plight of brutes when rational beings are so unhappy. It's because – she responds – everything goes together, from the bird whose clutch of eggs we crush to the human nests decimated by war (*Mémoires*, 97).

Thus, as only a child she notes with revulsion what humans – both adults and children – do to animals.

Au fond de ma révolte contre les forts, je trouve du plus loin qu'il me souvienne l'horreur des tortures infligées aux bêtes.

Depuis la grenouille que les paysans coupent en deux, laissant se traîner au soleil la moitié supérieure, les yeux horriblement sortis, les bras tremblants, cherchant à s'enfouir sous la terre, jusqu'à l'oie dont on cloue les pattes, jusqu'au cheval qu'on fait épuiser par les sangsues ou fouiller par les cornes des taureaux, la bête subit, lamentable, le supplice infligé par l'homme.

(At the base of my revolt against the strong, I find, as far back as I can remember, horror at the tortures inflicted on animals.

From the frog cut in two by peasants, who leave the upper half to drag along in the sun, its eyes sticking out horribly, its arms trembling, trying to hide under the earth, to the goose whose feet are nailed down, to the exhausted horse used to feed leeches or the one whose innards are dug through by bulls' horns, the animal undergoes, in its pitifulness, the agony inflicted by man.)

Peasants have the 'sad custom' of giving young animals to their children to play with; so you can see poor little birds opening their beaks to two- or three-year-old mites ('mioches') who innocently push earth in; they hang up the nestling by one foot to make it fly, watching its small featherless wings moving. At other times – she goes on – the child drags puppies and kittens, like carriages, over stones or along streams. When the animal bites the father crushes it under his clog. But this cruelty goes with a passive subservience to those in authority over the peasants themselves: 'the more ferocious man is towards animals, the more grovelling he is before the men who dominate him' ('plus l'homme est féroce envers la bête, plus il est rampant devant les hommes qui le dominent'). Michel explains that it was from her pity for animals that she began to understand the nature of power and its abuses – 'the crimes of force'. For those who have power over peoples behave the same towards them! 'Cette réflexion ne pouvait manquer de me venir' ('This reflection could not fail to occur to me'). She begs her 'dear country friends' to forgive her for dwelling on the sufferings animals endure with them: 'In that harsh labour which keeps you bent over an unkind earth, you suffer so much yourselves that you end up scorning all suffering.' And Michel asks, in a question which has a paragraph to itself: 'Cela finira-t-il jamais?' ('Will it ever end?', *Mémoires*, 91–2).

Cruelty is not confined to the country. Some of the lectures Michel attended as a young woman involved vivisection. Even in laboratory splints – she writes – the animal is sensitive to caresses or brutality. It more often has the brutality: when one side has been researched ('fouillé'), the animal is turned over so that the other side can be done; sometimes, in spite of the straps that keep it immobile, in its pain it disturbs the delicate tissue of the flesh being worked on; then a threat or blow teaches it that man is king of the animals. Sometimes, too,

pendant une démonstration éloquente, le professeur pique le scalpel dans la bête comme dans une pelote: on ne peut pas gesticuler avec cela à la main, n'est-ce pas? et puisque l'animal est sacrifié, cela ne fait plus rien.

(during an eloquent demonstration, the professor will stick the scalpel into the animal as if into a pellet: one can't gesticulate with that in one's hand, can one? and since the animal is already sacrificed, it doesn't matter any more.)

Michel calls for an end to these experiments – as useless, she says, as those which madmen conducted upon children in the infancy of chemistry; and she even envisages a future in which meat-eating will be unnecessary, since science will perfect a still more nutritious type of food (*Mémoires*, 97–8).

This base established, Michel continues to move from animals to humans and back again: decapitated geese make her reflect on the guillotine, prostitutes are sold or bartered animals (*Mémoires*, 157, 284–5). One especially memorable comparison is her metonymic link between the fate of the Lille textile workers (who worked in shockingly unhealthy conditions) and that of silkworms – silk being one of the fabrics produced. This is a central image since, as we know from historians, sewing and other kinds of textile work were the main occupations open to working-class girls who did not want to become prostitutes: they were paid at below-subsistence rates because it was assumed that all women were contributing only a secondary wage to a male-headed household.[21] The callousness shown to the women is by far the most important focus of Michel's account, but at the same time the gradually unfolding comparison uses phonetic play ('fil/fille', 'thread/girl'), and classical references to the 'thread' of life being cut, to create an allegory in which the girls become the silkworms. The 'fileuses' of Lille are on strike. Their work in the cellars kills them prematurely; all they want is two or three sous more. Surely, says Michel, this is not too much to give the women who work so hard for the rich, women like the silkworm that is boiled when it has spun its cocoon (so that the silk can be retrieved unharmed): 'Elles aussi, quand le labeur est achevé, il faut qu'elles meurent; il faut que la vie s'arrête avec le fil' ('They too, when their toil is over, must die; life must end with the thread'). For who would look after them in their old age? Not their own daughters:

Est-ce que leurs filles, à peine hors du berceau, ne se seront pas enchaînées à la même torture? Il faut bien que les riches usent et abusent de leurs troupeaux.

Les vers à soie, les filles du peuple, c'est fait pour filer. (*Mémoires*, 266)

(Won't their daughters, hardly out of the cradle, be chained to the same torture? After all, the rich must use and abuse their herds.

Silkworms, daughters of the people, they're there to spin.)

Needless to say, these animal allegories are not merely expressive of the status quo: Michel is trying to shake her addressees out of what she sees as the stupid passivity of the beast. So the masses who will not claim their liberty are like animals in the abattoir, and the peasant woman whose two children have starved to death, but who still believes not everyone can have bread, is sheep-like: 'Avez-vous vu les moutons tendre la gorge au couteau? Cette femme avait une tête de brébis' ('Have you seen sheep stretching out their throats to the knife? That woman had a ewe's head').[22] Indeed, she particularly calls upon women not to be like lambs to the slaughter, for although 'man suffers everwhere in this accursed society', no exploitation or suffering is comparable to woman's: but where would we be if lambs refused to have their throats cut? ('Où en serait-on si les agneaux ne voulaient plus être égorgés?'). The lambs can, indeed, become threatening female animals, changing into lionesses, tigresses, octopuses (feminine in French): 'Quelquefois les agneaux se changent en lionnes, en tigresses, en pieuvres' (*Mémoires*, 84–5).

It is difficult – and unnecessary – to separate Michel's arguments from the savage fables embodying them. Other women's 'fables' of this period also evoke horror. But now, as sometimes with Krysinska, we are back in a Huysmanian dream-world of morbid ornamentation – of jewelled tortoises dying because of their rich encrustations.[23] 'Ghastliness' becomes a self-conscious game. Whether such games are merely silly – the precious or masturbatory fantasies of female quislings – can be explored through Rachilde's writings.

CHAPTER 21

Rachilde and the horror of gender confusion

Rachilde was the pseudonym of Marguerite Eymery (1860–1953). She began her career in journalism and published her first novel, *Monsieur Vénus*, when she was twenty-four; it was greeted with shock by some, and banned in Belgium where it was first published. It remains her most commented-upon work, although some critics are starting to rank *La Tour d'amour* (1899) with it.[1] At the age of twenty-nine, she married Alfred Vallette, the editor of the *Mercure de France*, and was active in literary circles (it was she who persuaded the director of the Théâtre de l'Œuvre to stage Jarry's *Ubu Roi* in 1896). She went on publishing plays, novels and other works until the age of eighty-seven. Like *Monsieur Vénus*, many have provocative titles, such as *La Marquise de Sade* (1887) or *Madame Adonis* (1888). In 1928 she brought out an autobiographical pamphlet called *Pourquoi je ne suis pas féministe*, and her choices of subject and plot have sometimes been interpreted as misogynistic. (Biographers make connections with her father's longing for a son and her own sense of worthlessness as a child.)

After Sand, Rachilde is probably the nineteenth-century French woman writer in whom critics have shown the most interest in recent years. Her works have been seized upon as a striking example of Decadent writing, and discussed alongside those of Huysmans, Gourmont and Mirbeau as extending a *fin-de-siècle* syndrome of fetishism and deathliness.[2] Some of these critics are uncomplimentary, using such words as 'ludicrous' of Rachilde's plots or arguing that to gain acceptance she parroted Decadent stereotypes of monstrous females.[3] Of course it is correct to situate Rachilde with her immediate male contemporaries, as well as in other male traditions going from Sade and Laclos to Baudelaire, Rimbaud and Lautréamont: the perverse or the 'evil'; the anti-pastoral; the aesthetics of disgust. Her writing leads into works by (again) male

15. Rachilde. (Portrait by M. van Bever, 1898.)

writers of the early twentieth century such as Gide and Proust: the
often comic adventures of Proust's Charlus and other gay characters
are foreshadowed in Rachilde's delight at the 'mix-ups' generated by
polymorphous sexuality, and in the upper-class Raoule's 'playing at
"keeping low company"' ('encanaillement fictif': *Monsieur Vénus*, 36).

But it is equally correct to read Rachilde in the context of the
preceding eight or nine decades of women's writing; otherwise we
shall not appreciate the variations she wove on specifically 'women's
themes', nor see how violently she kicked over particular traces.
Rachilde's work does not merely 'buy into' sexual stereotypes but
hits out at them.[4] Whether or not we now judge *Monsieur Vénus*
'ludicrous', its banning, and the muddled and sexist reactions of
writers like Barrès, show how out-of-order it was at the time; and
much of Rachilde's other work has the same outrageousness.[5] Sand
had created her 'monstrous' Lélia in the 1830s; Girardin as the
Vicomte de Launay had dared to be preposterous in the 1840s; and
in the 1860s Ségur had indulged in a little lavatorial humour – in the
shape of a turkey which defecates over the trousers of its would-be
consumer.[6] But Lélia is languid, the Vicomte well-behaved and
Ségur mild by comparison with Rachilde. Just as they needed Gyp's
slang, French women writers needed a female author who could
make a virtue out of being grotesque, burlesque, 'grand guignol'.

In *Monsieur Vénus*, Raoule de Vénérande, who has been brought up
by her timid and religious aunt, discovers a beautiful young working-
class man named Jacques, who lives with his prostitute sister Marie.
Using some persuasion and more coercion, she engineers a relationship with him in which she behaves like the man and he like the
woman: cross-dressing is only the simplest manifestation. Her close
male friend the baron de Raittolbe veers between amusement at her
antics on the one hand, and, on the other, desire or contempt for
Jacques. Finally, these two men fight a duel in which Jacques dies.
Raoule has a wax model made of him which, however, has his own
hair, nails and teeth; at night, she embraces it and kisses its
mechanically animated mouth.

This bare summary gives no idea of the panache and black
humour with which the novel is written, nor all the levels on which
Rachilde's Raoule forces us to invert gender roles. The female's
'natural' obedience, modesty, masochism, passivity and low ranking
are, as it were, removed from her and transferred wholesale to the
man; and in other ways too Rachilde takes up the main feminist

themes of the century and twists them into a startling new life. Thus, when the narrator affirms a continuity between women of all classes, between marriage and prostitution, we might be hearing any Saint-Simonienne of fifty years previously:

The virtuous wife, at the moment she gives herself to her virtuous husband, is in the same situation as the prostitute at the moment she gives herself to her lover. Nature made them naked, these victims, and the only thing society has instituted for them is clothing. (131)

But, viewed through the lenses of this affirmation, Raoule's iconoclasm suddenly seems singularly brave. And Rachilde suggests on almost every page of the novel that 'you are not born a woman (or a man), you become one', for Raoule works on the assumption that gender characteristics can and will be changed, as if in some educational process. The more Jacques forgets his own sex, the more Raoule deliberately increases his opportunities to become womanly. Part of the lesson is not to frighten the male she wishes to 'stifle' in him ('ne pas trop effrayer le mâle qu'elle désirait étouffer en lui'); so she at first treats degrading ideas as jokes, only to make him take them seriously later. (Like this very novel?) Thus when she sends him a huge bouquet with the accompanying message 'Un fiancé ne peut faire mieux!' ('A fiancé can do no better!'), Jacques 'goes very red' but puts the flowers in vases, 'se jouant la comédie vis-à-vis de lui-même, se prenant à être une femme pour le plaisir de l'art' ('putting on an act for himself, starting to be a woman for the artistic pleasure of the thing', 117). All is culture, not nature. . . (Like this very novel?) By the end, Jacques is so feminized that even as he lies dying he rejects Raittolbe's offer to suck his wound clean on the grounds that the baron's moustaches would prick him (244).

Thus Rachilde's reversal of the usual gender roles is not a mechanical upside-downness; she makes us rethink them.[7] Why (it is implied) should we be shocked when Raoule makes it clear she values Jacques only for his body and he hears in his head his sister's mocking words?

Eh! va donc, imbécile, toi qui te figurais que tu étais un artiste. Va donc, joujou de contrebande, va donc, amusette d'alcôve, fais ton métier. (62)

(Get along with you, idiot who thought you were an artist. Get along, you contraband toy, you bedroom plaything, do what you're paid for.)

After all, this buying of women's bodies and this mockery of their creative ambitions is a regular occurrence. Or, as Raittolbe puts it still more bluntly:

– Oui! la chair! pensait-il, la chair fraîche, souveraine puissance du monde. Elle a raison, cette créature pervertie! Jacques aurait beau posséder toutes les noblesses, toutes les sciences, tous les talents, tous les courages, si son teint n'avait pas la pureté du teint des roses, nous ne le suivrions pas ainsi de nos yeux stupides! (187)

('Yes! flesh!' he thought, 'fresh flesh, *the* sovereign power. That perverted creature [Raoule] is right! It wouldn't matter if Jacques had all the nobility, learning, talent and courage that ever were in the world: if his complexion weren't as pure as a rose's, our stupid eyes wouldn't follow him like that!')

Why shouldn't Jacques – like any woman – perceive himself as an animal or slave?:

Je ne suis pas un homme! . . . riposta Jacques, frémissant d'une rage impuissante; je suis l'animal battu qui revient lécher tes mains! Je suis l'esclave qui aime pendant qu'il amuse! (185)

('I'm no man! . . .' retorted Jacques, quivering with impotent rage, 'I'm a beaten animal that comes back to lick your hands! I'm a slave, in love even as he entertains!')

If he suffers from feeling himself to be unacceptable in the salons, this can happen to women too . . . As he says, 'on n'épouse pas sa maîtresse, ça ne se fait pas dans tes salons! . . . ' ('one doesn't marry one's mistress, it's just not done in your salons! . . . ': author's ellipsis, 185). Why shouldn't he learn that to be forced into an entirely female role may annul sexual desire? For Jacques not only feels 'impotent rage' but discovers by the end that he *is* impotent: not one of his sister's prostitute 'colleagues', he tells Raoule in a halting voice, has been able to revive what she has sacrilegiously killed ('n'a pu faire revivre ce que tu as tué, sacrilège!', 228). Finally, Jacques's last transmogrification turns the tables on the 'woman as doll' image.[8] So, if we read *Monsieur Vénus* only as a Decadent work, we shall miss its satire on the peculiarly nineteenth-century brand of sexism that many women before Rachilde felt had spoiled their lives. It is a sardonic critique of this sexism – perhaps a revenge – complete with verbatim echoes of predecessors.

Rachilde also at last allows into the open images of homosexuality or bisexuality. These had been suggested by earlier women writers. Their own feminism, and men's 'masculinizing' of blue-stockings (a staple jibe in cartoons of the century), were almost bound to lead

women, perhaps sometimes unawares, towards the idea of androgyny at least. As writers like Allart say, 'the mind has no sex'; Colet
creates in *Lui* a woman who is told she 'could be a man', could wear
men's clothes, because she can compose satirical verse; Ulliac-
Trémadeure writes that the (female) creator of male characters feels
with them, and hints that relationships with men are to be rejected
in favour of women's self-fulfilment. All this already implied that
women could be more 'male' and less exclusively heterosexual than
conventional thinking admitted.[9] Choiseul-Meuse had included a
few lesbian scenes in her *Julie*; there are carefully veiled indications
in Blanchecotte of a love 'that dare not speak its name'; Stern – to
some extent following on from Diderot's *La Religieuse* – gives her
Mother Superior apparently lesbian feelings for Nélida; and Tastu
talks of 'la lyre lesbienne' when referring to her friend and patron
the older poet Adélaïde Dufrénoy.[10] Indeed, Tastu and others cite
Sappho herself – although it is often, seemingly, not her lesbianism
they have in mind but, less controversially, her fame as a woman
writer. (However, at unconscious levels the one idea may not exclude
the other.)[11] Sand, in the Sylvinet of *La Petite Fadette*, comes closer
than any others to a sympathetic portrayal of a male gay.[12] But on
the whole pre-1870 women were too timorous to talk openly about
gay inclinations of any kind: in this respect they were strikingly
unlike male contemporaries such as Balzac and Baudelaire.

In the late century, Deraismes does go a little further than
predecessors in proclaiming psychological 'androgyny' when she
talks of both men and women as being a mix of different qualities,
none of which is exclusively masculine or feminine.[13] And Bashkirtseff sounds a triumphalist note at overcoming her gender 'inside':

Je n'ai de la femme que l'enveloppe, et cette enveloppe est diablement
féminine; quant au reste, il est diablement autre chose. Ce n'est pas moi qui
le dis, puisque je m'imagine que toutes les femmes sont comme moi.[14]

(The only thing about me that's woman is the envelope, and that envelope
is devilishly feminine; as for the rest, it's devilishly something else. It's not
just me who says it – I imagine all women are like me.)

But Rachilde breaks all pre-existing limits, and paves the way for
many twentieth-century authors (most immediately, the group of
lesbian writers assembled round Natalie Barney's Paris salon).[15]
Raoule's very surname suggests her androgyny (Vénérande = Venus
+ andros). Not only is she unafraid to talk about lesbianism, she

indignantly rejects it as too 'common': 'être Sapho, ce serait être tout le monde!' ('Sappho – everyone is Sappho!', *Monsieur Vénus*, 90). Similarly, homosexuality for Jacques would be more 'natural' than what Raoule has taught him (240).

One of the most amusing ways in which Rachilde destroys sex conventions is in her switching of grammatical genders. Although the gendering of French nouns can be an obstacle for women in, say, the professional sphere (where lawyers, doctors, teachers, professors, etc., have to be masculine), it also offers greater potential for play than does English. A French writer has only to feminize incorrectly an adjective or past participle to create a startlingly jokey effect; a woman has only to refer to herself as 'on' to be able to use masculine adjectives. And other writers before Rachilde had availed themselves of this privilege – not only by adopting male personas for their own authorship, or tricking readers with oddly gendered pronouns like Desbordes-Valmore. Ignorant of the rules of French pronunciation, as we have seen, Ségur's Anglo-Irishman constantly makes funny and shocking gender slips: thus two male characters, Julien and M. Bonard, become 'lé pétite Juliène', 'lé pétite Bonarde'. Sand can say of Consuelo: 'She alone, in a word, was a [female] musician and a master' ('une musicienne et un maître'). And here again is Bashkirt-seff, longing to be divested of everything that is not her artistic personality and finally able to make herself '*un* individu' and an 'on' who is not 'contente' and 'fière' but 'content' and 'fier':

A l'atelier tout disparaît; on n'a ni nom ni famille; on n'est plus la fille de sa mère, on est soi-même, on est un individu et on a devant soi l'art, et rien d'autre. On se sent si content, si libre, si fier!

(In the studio everything disappears; you have no name, no family; you're no longer your mother's daughter, you are yourself, you are an individual [masculine] and you have before you art, and nothing else. You feel so pleased, so free, so proud! [all adjectives masculine].)[16]

But Rachilde not only flirts with the possibilities of these linguistic switches, she exploits them mercilessly in the characters' speech. The surrounding narrative does give the characters themselves agreements in the right gender, but this conformity serves as a foil for the strangeness of what is going on elsewhere. Even when beside herself with anger, Raoule remembers to use the 'right' (that is, the 'wrong') gender: 'Je suis *jaloux!* rugit-elle affolée' (' "I'm a *jealous fellow!*" she roared, out of her wits'): here the proximity of 'jaloux' and 'affolée' is quite dizzying.[17] Jacques coquettishly tells Raoule that 'j'ai résolu de te paraître agaçante!' ('I've decided to seem annoying [fem.] to you!') or, later, that he fears he is 'laide' ('ugly' [fem.]) (126, 187). These effects culminate in a climax parodying all novels in which love conquers the disapproval of society: but this is conquest with a difference, for it is Raoule speaking to Jacques:

Qu'importe le souvenir d'amour de tous les siècles et la réprobation de tous les mortels?. . . Tu es belle. . . Je suis homme, je t'adore et tu m'aimes! (215)

(What do they matter, the memory of love echoing down all the centuries and the censure of all mortals?. . . You are beautiful [fem.]. . . I am a man, I adore you and you love me!) (author's ellipses)

These reversals are often exuberant – almost the knockabout stuff of pantomime dame/principal boy or carnival travesty. But mingling with the exuberance are comments which show – if we could not have guessed – how difficult it was, after all, for a woman to write like this. The novel opens on an image of disgust: Raoule reacts with nausea to the smell of cooking apples that greets her as she enters Jacques's apartment, and only gradually grows used to it – then to find she rather likes it after all (25–31). This is the distaste that has to be overcome before she can think herself into, let alone start to enjoy, the transgressions she is herself about to initiate.[18] And at a later moment of crisis, Raoule says she needs to feel disgusted by Jacques in order not to feel vulnerable and 'womanly': gender confusion comes at a price (61).

In *La Tour d'amour* (1899), the price is more than disgust; it is dread.[19] The narrator, a young man called Jean Malheux ('mâle malheureux', 'unhappy male'?), takes up a job as assistant lighthouse keeper to the old man in charge, Mathurin Barnabas. (The previous assistant has died.) Barnabas is mad, the lighthouse is preternaturally claustrophobic, the sea is full of disagreeable creatures; eventually, it throws up drowned bodies or bits of them. Jean escapes for some 'shore leave' and meets a young woman, Marie; he almost believes himself saved from his ménage with Barnabas, but Marie turns out to be flighty. He returns to the lighthouse; Barnabas dies, and Jean takes his place as chief lighthouse keeper, declaring he will never go on land again.

This work foreshadows those of some outstanding twentieth-century authors: Beckett, in the inescapable interdependence of the two isolated men; Sartre, in the slimy nausea of the sea and its contents; Céline, in its style – for Rachilde has moved on from Gyp's *Autour du mariage*, and now incorporates colloquialism into the first-person narrative: 'que je lui répondis,' says Jean ('says I back to him'); or: 'Je ne comprenais rien de rien en ce temps-là, faut croire. Enfin, qu'est-ce que ça pouvait me fiche leurs manigances avec le vieux?' ('I didn't understand a damn thing then, you got to believe it. Anyway, why the hell should I care about their little schemes with the old bloke?', 6).

The novel is tautly constructed. Seen through the eyes of the (at first) innocent narrator, the suspense and abhorrence are intensified. For instance, we realize before Jean that the long tresses attached to a certain peculiar cap of Barnabas's have been cut from the head of a drowned woman; when the hair changes from blonde to brown, this is because a recent shipwreck has provided a fresh female corpse. We also have foreknowledge of the slow 'corruption' of the narrator. It starts when Jean loses patience with his pet canaries, which are fighting, and throws them out of the lighthouse 'with a mad gesture'; they spin a moment, then are swallowed by a wave: 'Bonsoir les oiseaux!' says Jean ('Night-night birdies!', 107–8). But, although we see better than he how his mind is being 'taken over', we still believe enough in his possible rescue (both physical and mental) to feel the poignancy of the subsequent highs and lows. He looks forward to his meeting with Marie, then feels disappointment and a reinforced loneliness when she is out: he could weep, he says; the sadness rises in his throat, 'like a tide of tears held in for a very long time' (186). After this he becomes more and more possessed. Eventually, on another shore visit, he stabs a prostitute who had, he says, grabbed him like an octopus and given him a long kiss – a sucking, abominable kiss, stinking of musk; he goes off proudly thinking 'Ben, quoi? J'ai tué la mer!' ('How's about that? I've killed the sea!', 237–8). Yet this is still not complete madness: he remains the saner of the two men – and the more capable, for Barnabas has had a stroke and can no longer speak. Barnabas had already, even before the stroke, spent time studying the alphabet, claiming he had forgotten how to read; and the book ends with Jean telling us that, as he too is now afraid of forgetting the alphabet, he has started to write his story – the story about the great book of the lighthouse ('mon histoire sur le grand livre du phare'). He will do his duty. But the 'idée fixe' of duty is the start of madness. And, he says, I am mad: I don't hope for anything more (260–2).

So the tale closes on a note of urgency – this is the last human testimony before the loss of language – but also on an uncertainty: if the Jean writing the book is already even madder than the earlier Jean who stabbed the prostitute, what is the status of the narrative we have just been reading? As well as Beckett, Sartre and Céline, *La Tour d'amour*, then, adumbrates those other twentieth-century works that have self-generating endings and unreliable narrators, and that foreground doubts about language. Some of these modernist narratives are celebratory. *La Tour d'amour* is, however, dismaying, not least because of the androgynously intertwined triple personas of light-house, sea and old man.

We can see the lighthouse as phallic.[20] Stretching up into the sky, it symbolizes a search for the absolute. 'Le phare semblait se tendre de plus en plus, exaspéré dans l'irradiation de l'impossible' ('The lighthouse seemed to strain up ever more, exasperated in its irradiation of the impossible', 198). But it also looks like the 'mast of a sinking ship' which makes you feel you're going in all directions at once (the architect, says Jean, must be proud of his creation!: 31). As well as its 210 stairs to the top, there are others – and you never find out where they go; when you climb those 210 stairs, you have to go up all at once or you become giddy. It is very hot and stuffy at the top; you're sucked up as if by a mouth of light; and the red walls give off moisture inside (26, 33–4). Both externally and internally, then, the lighthouse is vertiginous; inside, it is a red place of mysterious passages, dampness.[21] It is vaginal as well as phallic.

The inner dampness comes of course from the surrounding sea. The sea was a choice subject for other post-1870 women writers, suiting their 'impressionism'. In *La Tour d'amour*, more explicitly than in any of Rachilde's contemporaries, it is a 'mer/mère': a bad mother at that. It smells of rottenness, fish entrails, other things 'I dare not say' (81). It gives birth to drowned men: 'C'est le temps de ses relevailles à cette expulseuse d'hommes', Barnabas tells Jean ('That man-expeller – it's the time for her post-birth churching', 84). It does not provide nutritious food: the drowned men, if not cast up after nine days, finally lodge by the lighthouse, polluting the water and hence the sea-creatures – which at first Jean unwisely eats. They make him sick; but in any case he finds the things he sees in the water more and more repellent: crawling and zig-zagging crabs and lampreys; a floating finger, detached – so Barnabas explains – because the combined action of the sea and the ring it bore has eventually severed it, and then 'le doigt libre s'en va, droit comme flèche, indiquer la grande route du néant' ('the free finger goes off, straight as an arrow, pointing to the highway of nothingness', 86–7).

Barnabas himself resembles the sea. His eyes shine with a phosphorescence like that of the water with its decaying bodies; he knows all the secrets of the 'pays de macchabées' ('land of the corpses'); his grip is that of an octopus.[22] He colludes with the sea, causing shipwrecks by not working the light properly and failing to rescue the drowning (114–15). And he is 'female' in other ways. In a dream-like sequence, Jean hears him at night singing like a woman; the song is haunting enough to 'mener Satan au cimetière' ('conjure up Satan in the cemetery', 40–4). To sing, the bald old man puts on his hair – that strange cap with tresses. Jean eventually understands a few words of the refrain:

> C'était la tour, prends-garde,
> C'etait la tour. . . d'amour!
> D'amour. . . our. . . our. . . ur!　　　　　　(74)

(It was the tower, beware, it was the tower. . . of love! Of love . . . uv. . . uv . . . urve!) (author's ellipses)

The song and novel-title parody all romance; and Barnabas the troubadour becomes the outrageous androgyne incarnate. On examination the cap turns out to be an oddly blubbery affair; Barnabas is soon wearing it all day, keeping the hair shiny with sardine oil, and seeming both older and younger, like a drunken old woman and a coquette: he is 'like shame made man'.[23]

After his brief respite on land, Jean feels increasingly curious about six cupboards up the spiral stair, all shut mysteriously tight. Meanwhile his thoughts grow ever crazier, until he believes he is 'vertigo personified', the centre of catastrophes: 'Je porte en moi tous les malheurs' (207). Climbing down the outside of the lighthouse, he manages to look through a forbidden window. Another head looks back at him. It is a woman's, as if in an aquarium where a 'rare monster' swims: it has long whitened blonde hair round 'the oval of a horribly sad face, a young woman's face contemplating the sea with eyes full of tears' (223–4). The shock makes Jean fall into the sea; he is ill for a week, believes he has imagined it (226–7). Drunk, he thinks: '*How bored she must get behind the glass, the sea-head!*' ('*la tête de la mer!*': author's italics, 231). But when the old man is dying, he tells Jean to get him the woman, 'since you've seen her'. Jean opens the door and finds a head preserved in alcohol: Barnabas had cut more than just hair from corpses. We now learn for the first time how Jean's predecessor died. He had committed suicide on seeing the head: 'she made me kill someone', remarks Barnabas plaintively! Jean throws the head out; it sinks 'to the very bottom of the abysses' (253–7).

This hyperbolic tale thrusts symbols at us on every page, yet in its detail is as riveting as any well-told story of a lost soul – lost because it is in a world where the 'female' and the 'male', the viscous and the upright, are not only experienced at extremes but also fluctuate and become interchangeable – not delightfully or liberatingly, but hypnotically and horribly. It is a Godless, insane world. Godless: when Jean hears demonic voices yelling – actually those of shipwrecked humans who cannot be saved – he crosses himself, even though he is not religious: the old man, seeing this, swivels his eyes: 'Ben quoi, qu'il fit mécontent, puisque Dieu est mort!' ('"Oy, come off it," says he, displeased: "God's dead!"') With these words ends a chapter (104).[24] Insane: as we see. Some other women writers of the century had made their heroines or heroes mad, either because of abandonment or because they had visions not shared by others.[25] But the real madness of the century is staged in Rachilde's 'tower of love', leading to isolation, abandonment to the elements and a dance of death orchestrated by the fearsome sea-mother. It took this reckless, biting woman to bring up to consciousness, in the very last year of the century, the terror that had lain under its sense of 'maleness' and 'femaleness'.

CHAPTER 22

Postscript: England

Of the foreign countries appearing in nineteenth-century French women's writing, Britain was the most frequently mentioned, either as 'the land where things are different' or as fictional heroes' country of origin. (Few of these writers distinguished between England and Britain, except – in the wake of Sir Walter Scott – to give the Scots a little added glamour; since they usually simply said 'Angleterre', I follow suit in the first instance.)

Especially during or shortly after the Napoleonic wars, some reactions were hostile. Babois registered the boorishness of the English armies; Staël retained mixed feelings all her life; some fictional Englishmen were cold or excessively phlegmatic; and the young Tastu in 1824 proclaimed a spirit of industrial competition in rather unhappy verse:

> Et toi, fière Albion, sa constante ennemie,
> De la France mourante épiant l'agonie,
> D'un triomphe assuré l'orgueil enflait ton sein;
> Regarde, elle est debout, et le glaive à la main!
> . . .
> Rival de Birmingham, notre acier étincelle.[1]

(And you, proud Albion, France's constant enemy – on the watch for the last throes of our dying country – your breast was swelling with the pride of sure and certain triumph; but look, France stands upright, sword in hand! . . . Rivalling Birmingham, our steel sparkles.)

In the mid-century, d'Aunet's play *Jane Osborn* presented England as riddled with sexism; and, on the basis of both serious research and personal observation, Tristan drew up an indictment of working-class conditions there in her *Promenades dans Londres* (1840). (Many French socialists of the time were highly critical of England.)[2] But in most of these writers, most of the time, the picture was benign. England produces eccentrics (a commonplace of the period), but generous ones; and it is, apparently, a land that allows its women greater freedom than does France.[3]

So, in Duras's *Edouard* and Gay's *Laure d'Estell*, England is held up as a country where merit is rewarded over rank – already, then, a step in the direction of recognition of women's rights.[4] In Girardin's 1833 'Napoline', it is said that only Englishmen will agree to marry without a large dowry; England is a better place for women of genius than France, for there they encounter less ridicule.[5] Later, in her journalism, Girardin continues to claim superiority for the English over the 'gossipy' French, saying that the English, the real English at least ('les vrais Anglais du moins'), visit each other for the pleasure of being together and do not feel obliged to chatter ('babiller') for an hour just to let you know they're there. She hopes that French lords, 'nos grands seigneurs', who already copy the manners and customs of their English counterparts, may one day copy them in more serious matters: 'Have patience, they will soon get round to imitating them in their intelligent participation in national affairs.'[6] In Ancelot's *Un mariage raisonnable* (1835), Lady Nelmoor remarks: 'In that country, girls count for something; they talk, they're active, they allow men to like them, they can make choices' ('elles parlent, agissent, plaisent et choisissent'). Her friend Emma replies: 'You mean, it's like here with married women! Our neighbours have lots of good points! You don't waste any time there' ('Il paraît que c'est comme ici les femmes mariées! Nos voisins ont beaucoup de bon! chez eux point de temps perdu': 287–8). Beneath the joke a serious point is being made. In Ancelot's *Un divorce*, an English husband simply accepts the divorce his wife wants; and we have already met another Englishman from this play, the liberal if strange Jenkinson: without false modesty, he introduces himself as an 'English, or rather, cosmopolitan baronet' who enjoys life, is curious about it, and is obliging by nature . . . (346). Ségur's Georgey is an inflated version of Jenkinson: hugely odd, ever helpful, ready to share his wealth and rescue those less fortunate than himself: in fact, 'pas imbécile, mais trop bon' ('not an idiot – he's too kind', 57). Not unlike Sir Ralph Brown in Sand's *Indiana*, Georgey is in the end the saviour of the day, engineering happy endings in so thoroughgoing a manner that he might almost be the author herself. And in 1861 Deraismes returns to 'Lady Nelmoor's' perspective: in her *A bon chat bon rat*, the sexist Octave, believing the heroine Antoinette to be English, at first tells us that for a travelling Englishwoman to be pretty would contradict the laws of nature, but soon hints at a deeper reason for his prejudice: 'Ces Anglaises ont un sans-gêne incroyable' ('These Englishwomen are incredibly unceremonious', 7–8).

By the end of the century, the worst we are reading of the English is that they have bad taste.[7] Interest still runs high. The life-writer Pauline Craven flags her reminiscences of a visit to England as an attempt at a detached comparative 'sociology', saying she is writing not biography, nor a panegyric, but 'only precise, if incomplete, memories of a neighbouring society, different from our own – today more than ever' (*Réminiscences*, 135). For instance, Craven opposes English humour to French 'raillerie' ('malice', 'poking fun', 127). And she is a particularly interesting case of a staunchly conservative Catholic writer who proclaims all the traditional virtues (family must come first for women, etc.), and disapproves of Englishwomen who reject them, yet details their independence in a tone which also reveals a certain surprised admiration: Englishwomen are allowed to speak in religious assemblies; Englishwomen are careless of domestic duties because they have adopted 'a kind of apostleship women are rarely allowed in our society' ('chez nous'); one Lady Ellesmere – a social reformer who neglects sartorial niceties because 'time is too short' – does not even look in the mirror before going to see the Queen![8] As for Gyp, she picks up these and earlier threads when M. d'Alaly, about to marry Paulette, reassures himself as to her upbringing with this thought: 'they haven't brought her up the English way, letting her have her head' ('elle n'a pas été élevée à l'anglaise, la bride sur le cou', 10–11).

More seriously, it is clearly England that Gagneur has in mind when she claims that 'other countries' which allow divorce are less licentious and hypocritical than France.[9] Miss Junior, the English governess in Gréville's *Les Koumiassine*, is a figure of fun, but it is her nationality that is stressed when she pities Vassilissa for the marriage being forced on her – she becomes 'l'Anglaise': 'the sincere pity that the Englishwoman felt for the victim' (I 217). Bashkirtseff, at least, is convinced everything is better in England: France is preferable to Italy, but England is preferable to France, for there one is free and happy. There's so much misery in England! you'll say. But generally, the English people ('le peuple anglais') is the happiest (*Journal*, I 137–8). And Michel praises the England that has offered her a refuge – unsurprisingly, no doubt; however, it is with an admixture of sarcasm that lends the compliments a little force where they are made. Despite certain old-fashioned attitudes, and remaining abuses such as capital punishment, the English are, in her view, more liberal than French bourgeois 'so-called republicans'. She contrasts French newspapers' lies about her with the perfect courtesy shown by the English press (because, she remarks wryly, she was less badly bred and ridiculous than anticipated); she notes that England thinks it has a duty to look after the hungry and homeless, whilst adding that in order to make their superannuated ('surannées') institutions last longer, the English 'warm them up' with women's enthusiasm. Thus women direct workhouses. 'There will be women in Parliament,' says Michel; and at a lecture in Lyon, she goes so far as to tell her audience that whereas in France anarchists are in the dock, in England 'they are members of the House of Commons'.[10]

This last example shows that for Michel and, of course, for others, 'England' could be as much a symbol as a real place, figuring in a range of rhetorical or aesthetic effects: now presented blandly as an object of sober discussion, now an easy Fantasyland.[11] But that it remained prestigious for most of these women throughout the century is indisputable. Some of the reasons are obvious. England had been a constant source of comparison with France for Enlightenment thinkers, who had a generally favourable view of its political institutions and economy; this view continued to influence the nineteenth century. During the Terror, Britain had provided asylum for émigrés, among whom were a number of early-century aristocratic women writers – particularly memoir-writers, whose works would continue to appear throughout the century, published posthumously as they often were. The steady flow of translated British novels (a veritable flood in the early decades) no doubt gave readers strong, if unprovable, images of 'Englishwomen's' lives.[12] Britain's later sheltering of liberals such as Hugo (in the Channel Islands from 1855 to 1870) probably again nurtured, and to some extent inflated, the picture of a country more 'protective' than France. But, alongside elements of rose-tinting, it is likely that these writers had an intuition or a concrete understanding of the differences outlined by recent historians between the two societies' treatment of women. Nineteenth-century Britain, and its sister culture the United States, were patriarchal and oppressive. Nevertheless, France lagged well behind them in granting women's rights, from the passing of laws affecting the better-off (for example, married women's entitlement to control their own property) to the relaxation of conventions governing the most poverty-stricken (such as women workers' ability to strike without appealing to a men's trade union).[13] Provision for French women's education was poorer at most points of the social scale. Girls' gymnastics; young middle-class women's freedom to go out alone; older women's autonomy in the organization of charitable activities – all came later in France or were hedged about with greater difficulties than across the Channel or the Atlantic. Fraisse and Perrot attribute some of this disparity to the differences between Catholicism and Protestantism, going so far as to claim that 'Protestants showed much greater confidence in the judgement of women than did Catholics; thus women in countries where the Reformation dominated were more advanced than their counterparts elsewhere.'[14] The pattern continues into the twentieth century: all the other major nations involved in the First World War gave women the vote by 1920; in France they did not get it until 1944.[15]

If, then, French female authors allude to England more frequently and admiringly than do nineteenth-century French males, this is not merely an Emma Bovaryish belief that happiness is always to be found elsewhere; they feel, not without justification, that conditions there would be better for them as individuals. Conditions would also have been better for them as writers. Babois hints at this when she says that some pieces she has written go beyond the limits tacitly prescribed for women 'perhaps more in France than elsewhere'.[16] The salons notwithstanding, nineteenth-century British women writers had behind them a more supportive tradition than their French contemporaries. Slama remarks that middle-class women were writing a hundred years earlier in England than in France; while Hufton points out that the large gatherings of the 'bluestockings' in eighteenth-century London were designed to encourage women rather than to host brilliant men like those who, in eighteenth-century France, had 'views on womanhood which were in the main deeply conservative'. 'The bluestocking ladies transcended the *salonnières* in that they very actively promoted women's writing. They were mostly writers themselves and carefully nurtured networks promoting serious works by women.'[17]

It also hardly needs saying that women's writing emerging from nineteenth-century France has been less well regarded in its own country than women's writing from nineteenth-century Britain or North America. Leaving aside the larger number of authors who have fallen into complete obscurity, even the work of the three major ones (Staël, Sand, Desbordes-Valmore) has not been considered on a par with that of Jane Austen, Emily Brontë, George Eliot or Emily Dickinson. The same disparity is apparent in the case of the more popularized writers. No French woman's work of the nineteenth century has been allowed to grip the public imagination to the same degree as Mary Shelley's *Frankenstein, or the Modern Prometheus* (1818) or Charlotte Brontë's *Jane Eyre* (1847), both still read or avidly replayed in different media. Even children's books written by women in nineteenth-century France have had a harder time of it. Ségur's stories have survived and are now published in the popular Folio Junior series, but they come, these days, with an apology in the very blurb for their 'old-fashioned' moralizing ('la morale peut sembler aujourd'hui désuète', 'their moralizing may seem obsolete nowadays').[18] Louisa May Alcott and Susan Coolidge moralize in the *Little Women* and *Katy* series (both of the 1860s), but their modern editors do not feel the need to make excuses before the reader has even started the book.

These contrasts continue to be perceptible in the twentieth century. We have only to compare the national and international reputations of Colette (1873–1954) or Marguerite Yourcenar (1903–87) with that of Virginia Woolf (1882–1941) to see that the problem, whatever its causes, did not disappear overnight.[19] Elizabeth Fallaize cites some still-startling discrepancies between the two cultures. In 1988, for instance, 58% of newly published British fiction was by women, as opposed to 25% in France; there are also significant gender differences as between literary-prize juries, the shortlists they draw up, and the winners. Writing in 1993, Fallaize observed that in contrast to the Goncourt Prize competition, which frequently has not a single woman's name in its final shortlist and has been won by only two women in the period since 1968, the Booker Prize shortlist has only once not contained any women (in 1991); has sometimes indeed had a majority of women; and the prize itself has been won by women on a number of occasions.[20]

As Toril Moi says (not entirely uncritically), all feminist critics after Kate Millett, regardless of their otherwise differing interests, share the view that social and cultural contexts must be studied if literature is to be 'properly understood' (*Textual/Sexual Politics*, 24). To compare legal situations, literary themes and posthumous reputations is relatively easy. To compare the 'quality' of nineteenth-century female authors' work as between France on the one hand, and Britain or North America on the other, might form the subject of another book-length study, and one fraught with difficulties, given the suspicions that now surround such concepts as 'greatness' or even 'aesthetic success'. But any such study would have to start from the recognition that, in their inner self-imaging as well as in their social lives, these brilliant women of France were struggling against even greater odds than their Anglo-American counterparts.

CHAPTER 23

Legacies

Women's writing of this period does not always fit comfortably into what are now considered the main trends of nineteenth-century French literature. It is not only a matter of how far the female authors can be considered 'realists'. Male authors were defining themselves against Greek, Latin and French classical literature, mixing stylistic registers, promulgating suggestion not statement, and adopting narrative perspectives that made readers wince as well as weep or smile. But the women's only education in the French classics was snatched reading of whatever plays happened to be on the shelves at home, and still in the 1890s many were longing to discover Graeco-Roman civilization for themselves; they were unlikely, then, to run in tandem with the male writers in this respect. For a long time, they feared to adopt an improper register. Rather than rejecting 'statement' and didacticism, a number recommended these: their writing must seem 'moral', or else, for understandable reasons, they wanted it to be politically 'useful' (and here the enduring influence of Staël may have been a mixed blessing).[1] So they may in retrospect seem to have been on the 'wrong' side of key nineteenth-century aesthetic debates, recoiling from the idea of 'art for art's sake' which was to help shape modernist self-reflexiveness. As for the choice of narrative perspective, the evidence suggests that in the women writers' minds this was not so much a choice between sympathy and detachment, or between reliable or slippery narrators, as between whether to write permissibly, 'like a woman', or impermissibly like a man – a division more likely to lead to ambivalence than to a fruitful or mordant ambiguity. (As late as the mid-century, some were still wondering whether they should be writing at all.)

Irony is now regarded as one of the principal nineteenth-century literary modes; but, as we have seen, the women writers – who were very able to deploy irony themselves in discursive writings – were apparently rather frightened of it when they reconstructed the world in their imaginations. There, humorous though they can be, they often associate irony as such with ridicule of themselves, with female flightiness, or with male flippancy and irresponsibility, and they do not always exploit it fully. Similarly with satire: nineteenth-century men, from Stendhal on, write stingingly about excessive concern with 'public face'; for them, it is a matter of deflating the vanity or hypocrisy of bourgeois, entrepreneur, cleric, sycophant. But for most of the women, 'public face' is seen in terms of shame and female honour: they fight it, but almost none can conceive of it as something so patently absurd that it can be gaily mocked.

We expect from nineteenth-century literature a blossoming of sensory description, and to some extent we find this in the female poets, novelists and travel-writers, but it is rarely as hedonistic or luscious as in the male writers: guilt about sensuality can slip easily into guilt about sensuousness.[2] The somewhat later nineteeth-century French preoccupation with the dandy, or the city, seems to us now to anticipate the modern emphasis on the artifice of art. Both bear the stamp of human rearrangement; and the city, unlike 'raw' Nature, confronts the 'flâneur' with constant man-made incongruities. But it is perhaps more difficult for the woman to see clothes as metaphors when she is being pressed (with what penalties for disobedience) to be a 'dandy' herself; and more difficult for urban 'mooching' to become an analogy for the tortuous, contradictory windings of the mind if she believes she cannot indulge in it without danger or unaccompanied by a chaperone.

This lack of synchronicity with the men has been another factor in the sweeping aside of women's writing in nineteenth-century France. But in other areas the women either kept pace with the men or had preceded them. As I have gone along I have given a selection of cross-overs from their writing to men's. Some of these are bound to seem arbitrary in the detail; and the argument can always be put that it is immaterial if Valéry 'stole' certain half-lines from Ackermann, for after all, it is he who turned them into 'great' poetry whereas she did not. But another way to construe this process is to say that whatever the supposed faults of the women's works, they were promising enough to be used as, effectively, 'drafts'. Many are as good as, or better than, the early publications of the canonical male writers or the manuscript stages of their famous works: any number of scholarly studies tracing the genesis of these will demonstrate the case. Where the women lacked something, then, it was not potential, but the men's faith in themselves to press on with revision and improvement, and their sheer persistence.

Perhaps, however, the women's main impact on nineteenth-century men's writing was in a sense the most obvious one: that is, the feminist ideas that show in, or even structure, many of these men's works. Critics such as Waller, Kelly and Kadish discuss the 'feminization' of men's writing and the difficulty of finding firm and stable notions of gender identity in nineteenth-century French literature by men. They generally attribute this to semi-conscious or predatory impulses: confusion about father-figures in the wake of the Revolution, anxiety about 'degeneracy', envy of successful women writers. Others, such as Frank and Beizer, highlight the fore-grounding of androgyny in nineteenth-century men's works, but incline to see it as part of the 'Romantic agony' or as a return to – say – *commedia dell'arte* feminine Pierrots. These interpretations are valid, but they need not exclude more generous ones. Some male writers, such as Hugo, Stendhal and Rimbaud, were self-declared feminists. And the misogyny openly expressed by others should not make us suppose that all of their work was sexist. Many seem at some other level, albeit with resistance, to understand, and even acknowl-edge the justice of, the feminist case. Moses argues that although the political successes of nineteenth-century feminism date from the years of Republican dominance of the movement (that is, from after 1871), the earlier Utopian socialist feminists were able to create a reservoir of good feeling and sympathy for women that was trans-lated into an improved image of women in literature (*French Feminism*, 235). More specifically, Slama points out that the growth of women's writing and their self-portraits 'taught' men about the realities of women's lives ('Femmes écrivains', 226–7). Certainly, as part of their promotion of 'low-status subjects', the female writers had put low-class women on the agenda from an early stage in the century. Thus the same Dumas *fils* who was to write the sexist *L'Homme-femme* could also write *La Dame aux camélias*, whose heroine is a prostitute killed by bourgeois prejudice. Maupassant, whose letters give vent to an often profound misogyny, could write 'Le Papa de Simon', a compassion-ate story about the ostracism of an illegitimate child and the plight of his mother; and the famous 'Boule de suif', again about a prostitute more 'moral' than the bourgeois who exploit and condemn her. Zola's best-known heroine, the Gervaise of *L'Assommoir*, probably owes her existence to his female predecessors.

As for gender instability, this had been exploited by writers from Ovid to Shakespeare. But if it became a hallmark of nineteenth-century French literature, this was another contribution of the women's. The idea that biological sex does not automatically bring with it fixed mental attributes was put forward by the female imaginative writers, at first tentatively or symbolically, but then with gathering force as the century went on. It was a necessary tenet of the more politically active feminists too. It is true that when expediency demanded, these feminists stressed women's 'difference'; but cartoons of the time, portraying feminist women with rifles and men being left at home to 'suckle' babies or sew on buttons, show that it was the claims of equality or transferable characteristics that seized the public imagination.[3] At a finer level, the male writers play with this idea too. Gautier suggests in his poem 'Contralto' that the real aesthetic delight comes from a voice which is neither exclusively masculine nor feminine, but has elements of both, with now one side taking over, now the other.[4] Baudelaire can be seen as incorporating 'a disavowed woman', 'his own hysterical self', into his writing.[5] Balzac explores fluctuating sexuality in such works as *La Fille aux yeux d'or*, and through metaphor assigns female traits to male characters or vice versa: Rastignac, eager to make fresh conquests, is compared to a female date palm waiting to be fertilized; nature seems to have made a 'sex-mistake' in creating Bette a woman and her protégé Wenceslas a man. And in his foreword to the *Comédie humaine*, Balzac, writing that everything is more complex for humans than for animals, includes gender definition: the lioness is simply the female of the lion, whereas 'in Society woman is not always the female to the male' ('dans la Société la femme ne se trouve pas toujours être la femelle du mâle').[6] Flaubert writes of Emma Bovary and her lover Léon that it is if she were the man and he the woman; and his constant puncturing of hand-me-down ideas ('idées reçues') includes those held about 'masculinity' and 'femininity' by both men and women. Since we know that women writers were arguing or suggesting a persuasive case against gender stereotyping, and since we know the men read them, it is implausible to suppose that these men acquired their new stress on mutable gender only from the myth of the androgyne; or from post-Revolutionary confusion; or from male feminists like the eighteenth-century Condorcet; or – for all their own originality – from inner inspiration.

One further notable legacy to French writing has been, so far, scarcely acknowledged. Currently, the most famous and internationally influential work written by a Frenchwoman is Simone de Beauvoir's *Le Deuxième Sexe* (1949), the founding text of post-war feminism. Born in 1908, Beauvoir undoubtedly read in her childhood and teens many of these nineteenth-century women writers, still in print, still popular, the later ones still writing into the twentieth century; and in *Le Deuxième Sexe*, she cites by name Staël, Stern, Girardin, Michel, Niboyet, Auclert, Tristan, Deraismes, Sand, Ségur and Bashkirtseff – quoting extensively from this last. *Le Deuxième Sexe* owes its special character not only to existentialism: its presentation unmistakably resembles that of works by French female predecessors, in its mingling of fiction and life-writing as sources of evidence, and in its blend of argument with powerfully narrated vignettes of clashes between individual mothers and daughters, husbands and wives. The mix of sarcasm and compassion with which Beauvoir builds up her 'images of women', the lucid yet passionate style, even the particular metaphors chosen, often read as if straight from the pages of Maria Deraismes or any of the nineteenth-century women novelists who chafed at the situation of their sex:

cette réalité mystérieuse et menacée qu'est la féminité . . . Suffit-il d'un jupon à frou-frou pour la faire descendre sur terre?
le mariage en l'asservissant à un homme la fait maîtresse d'un foyer . . . on laisse encore la jeune fille incapable de gagner sa vie; elle ne peut que végéter en parasite au foyer paternel . . .[7]

(that mysterious, threatened reality that is femininity . . . Is a frilly petticoat enough to make it descend upon earth?
marriage, enslaving her to a man, makes her mistress of the hearth . . . the girl is still left incapable of earning her living; she can only vegetate, parasite-like, in the paternal home . . .)

We might be reading Niboyet, Ulliac-Trémadeure, even Tinayre; hovering are shades of Duras, Staël, Bentzon, perhaps Tastu. Beauvoir does not always want to admit her debt to her French 'foremothers'. But their writings, whether militant or elegiac, helped to shape her ideas of what it means to be female, and thence the ideas of twentieth-century women in many other countries.

All these debts once settled, it is to be hoped that the women writers of nineteenth-century France can be reinstated in accounts of mainstream French writing. They did establish a distinct female tradition, through which – sometimes by degrees, sometimes in sudden bounds – they pushed forward what it was permissible for women to write about; twentieth-century successors were able to continue the process. But they also need repositioning in other traditions: Tristan within French socialist theory; La Tour du Pin and Bashkirtseff in nineteenth-century life-writing; Tastu in the growth of literary self-reflexiveness in nineteenth-century France. Both ways of looking at them are equally important. And, although innovation in itself is not everything, the women did have 'firsts' too. Here are some reminders: Staël as the inventor of comparative literary criticism and the interpreter of Romanticism to France; Duras as the creator of the first black character with a European background and a modern black consciousness; Sand as an internationally inspiring female author, to the extent that George Eliot was proud to adopt her 'forename'; Girardin as the initiator of the newspaper column; Ségur's contract with Hachette as the birth of publishing for children in France; Gyp as the first novelist to show the sexual politics of vulgar language and as the instigator of the modern dialogue novel; Krysinska as a strong contender for the founding publication of the main twentieth-century verse-form; Rachilde as the only writer in nineteenth-century France to combine, long before any male successor, the interdependence of a mad male 'couple'; nausea as a condition of an uneasy consciousness; and a self-generating first-person colloquial narrative. What these women achieved was remarkable.

Appendices

Appendices A and B are inevitably selective, particularly for drama. Other authors and/or works may be found in the secondary works in my bibliography and in my main sources for the Appendices: the *Bloomsbury Guide to Women's Literature*; the Larousse *Grand Dictionnaire universel du XIXe siècle*; the *Dictionnaire de biographie française* (as yet incomplete); the *Archives biographiques françaises*; and the Bibliothèque Nationale *Catalogue des imprimés*.

Appendix A

GENRES: WOMEN'S CONTRIBUTION

PROSE FICTION

1800	Guizot	*La Chapelle d'Ayton*
	Cottin	*Malvina*
	Souza	*Emilie et Alphonse*
1801	Gacon-Dufour	*Les Dangers d'un mariage forcé*
	Gacon-Dufour	*La Femme-grenadier*
1802	Estournelles	*Alphonse et Mathilde*
	Gacon-Dufour	*Mélicrète et Zirphile*
	Gay	*Laure d'Estell*
	Genlis	*Mademoiselle de Clermont*
	Lagrave	*La Chaumière incendiée*
	Lagrave	*M. Ménard ou l'homme comme il y en a peu*
	Souza	*Charles et Marie*
	Staël	*Delphine*
1803	Cottin	*Amélie Mansfield*
	Guibert	*Fedaretta*

	Krüdener	*Valérie*
	Lagrave	*Hector de Romagny ou l'erreur d'une bonne mère*
	Lagrave	*Juliette Belfour ou les talents récompensés*
1804	Genlis	*La Duchesse de La Vallière*
	Lagrave	*Paulina*
1805	Cottin	*Mathilde ou mémoires tirés de l'histoire des Croisades*
	Lagrave	*La Méprise du coche ou à quelque chose malheur est bon*
	Merard de Saint-Just	*Six mois d'exil ou les orphelins par la Révolution*
1806	Cottin	*Elisabeth ou les exilés de Sibérie*
	Gacon-Dufour	*Les Dangers de la prévention*
	Genlis	*Alphonsine ou la tendresse maternelle*
	Genlis	*Mme de Maintenon*
	Renneville	*Lettres d'Octavie, une pensionnaire*
1807	Choiseul-Meuse	*Julie ou j'ai sauvé ma rose*
	Staël	*Corinne*
1808	Genlis	*Bélisaire*
	Robert	*Amélia et Caroline ou l'amour et l'amitié*
	Souza	*Eugène de Rothelin*
1809	Robert	*Alphonse et Mathilde ou la famille espagnole*
1810	Robert	*Rose et Albert ou le tombeau d'Emma*
1811	Beauharnais	*La Marmotte philosophe ou le philosophe en domino*
	Souza	*Eugénie et Mathilde*
	Renneville	*Contes à ma petite fille et à mon petit garçon*
	Renneville	*La Mère gouvernante*
1812	Guizot	*Les Enfants: contes à l'usage de la jeunesse*
1813	Gay	*Léonie de Montbreuse*
	Genlis	*Mlle de Lafayette ou le siècle de Louis XIII*

1815	Dufrénoy	*Etrennes à ma fille*
	Gay	*Anatole*
1816	Renneville	*Le Conteur moraliste*
	Renneville	*Les Secrets du cœur*
1817	Bawr	*Auguste et Frédéric*
1820	Lagrave	*La Méprise de diligence*
	Renneville	*Zélie*
1821	Estournelles	*Pascaline*
	Guizot	*L'Ecolier ou Raoul et Victor*
	Renneville	*Les Bons Petits Enfants*
1821–22	Duras	*Olivier ou le secret*
1823	Guizot	*Nouveaux contes*
	Savignac	*La Comtesse de Meley*
1824	Duras	*Ourika*
1825	Duras	*Edouard*
1826	Allart	*Settimie*
	Savignac	*Les Petits Proverbes dramatiques*
1828	Allart	*Gertrude*
	Gay	*Théobald*
	Savignac	*Les Vacances*
1829	Savignac	*Pauvre Cécile*
1832	Allart	*L'Indienne*
	Bawr	*Raoul ou l'Enéide*
	Gay	*Un mariage sous l'Empire*
	Girardin	*Contes d'une vieille fille à ses neveux*
	Sand	*Indiana*
1833	Allart	*La Vie rose*
	Ulliac-Trémadeure	*La Virago*
	Sand	*Lélia* (second version: 1839)
	Sand	*Valentine*
1834	Gay	*La Duchesse de Chateauroux*
	Sand	*Jacques*
1835	Bawr	*Histoires fausses et vraies*
1836	Altenheym	*Les Filiales*
	Gay	*La Comtesse d'Egmont*
	Girardin	*La Canne de M. de Balzac*
	Ulliac-Trémadeure	*Valérie ou la jeune artiste*
1837	Sand	*Mauprat*
	Savignac	*La Jeune Propriétaire ou l'art de vivre à la campagne*

	Ulliac-Trémadeure	*Emilie ou la jeune fille auteur*
1838	Arnaud	*La Comtesse de Sergy*
	Altenheym	*Nouvelles Filiales*
	Sand	*Spiridion*
	Tristan	*Méphis*
1839	Dash	*L'Ecran*
	Niboyet	*Les Deux Frères*
	Sand	*Les Sept Cordes de la lyre*
1840	Gay	*Marie de Mancini*
	Sand	*Le Compagnon du Tour de France*
1841	Arnaud	*Clémence*
	Niboyet	*Lucien*
	Niboyet	*Quinze jours de vacances*
1842–44	Sand	*Consuelo / La Comtesse de Rudolstadt*
1842	Dash	*La Marquise de Parabère*
	Dash	*Les Bals masqués*
1843	Altenheym	*Berthe Bertha*
1844	Sand	*Jeanne*
1845	Sand	*Le Meunier d'Angibault*
1846	Sand	*La Mare au Diable*
	Stern	*Nélida*
1847	Niboyet	*Catherine II et ses filles d'honneur*
1849	Sand	*La Petite Fadette*
1850	Dash	*La Marquise sanglante*
	Reybaud	*Clémentine*
	Sand	*François le champi*
1852	Bawr	*Cecilia ou mémoires d'une héritière*
1853	Sand	*Les Maîtres Sonneurs*
1855	Ancelot	*Georgine*
	Dash	*La Comtesse de Bossut*
1856	Aunet	*Un mariage en province*
	Colet	*Une histoire de soldat*
1857	Ancelot	*Une route sans issue*
	Aunet	*Une vengeance*
	Mogador	*Les Voleurs d'or*
	Ségur	*Nouveaux contes de fées*
1858	Ancelot	*Un nœud de ruban*
	Altenheym	*Dieu pardonne ou les deux frères*
	Dash	*La Duchesse de Lauzun*
	Mogador	*Sapho*

1859	Ségur	*Les Malheurs de Sophie*
	Ulliac-Trémadeure	*La Maîtresse de maison*
1860	Colet	*Lui*
1862	Dash	*Un amour à la Bastille*
	Léo	*Un mariage scandaleux*
1863	Audouard	*Un mari mystifié*
	Gagneur	*Le Calvaire des femmes*
1864	Caro	*Le Péché de Madeleine*
1866	Caro	*Flamien*
	Gagneur	*La Croisade noire*
	Léo	*Un divorce*
	Rattazzi	*Les Mariages de la Créole*
	Reybaud	*Les Deux Marguerites*
1867	Gagneur	*Les Réprouvées*
	Ségur	*Le Mauvais Génie*
1868	Caro	*Histoire du Souci*
	Craven	*Anne Séverin*
	Rattazzi	*Si j'étais reine!*
1869	Gautier	*Le Dragon impérial*
1870	Gagneur	*Les Forçats du mariage*
1871	Belloc	*Histoires et contes de la grand-mère*
	Craven	*Fleurange*
1872	Allart	*Les Enchantements de Prudence*
	Bentzon	*Un divorce*
	Dash	*L'Arbre de la Vierge*
1873	Belloc	*Le Fond du sac de la grand-mère*
1874	Arnaud	*Une tendre dévote*
	Craven	*Le Mot de l'énigme*
	Gagneur	*Les Crimes de l'amour*
1875	Gautier	*La Sœur du soleil*
1877	Bruno	*Le Tour de la France par deux enfants*
	Chartroule	*Les Vestales de l'Eglise*
	Descard	*Mlle de Kervallez*
	Gréville	*Les Koumiassine*
	Gréville	*Les Epreuves de Raïssa*
1878	Adam	*Laide*
	Bentzon	*Un remords*
	Descard	*En Poitou*
1879	Adam	*Grecque*

	Arnaud	*La Cousine Adèle*
	Chartroule	*Les Dévoyés*
	Chartroule	*Mme Ducroisy*
1880	Bentzon	*Yette: histoire d'une jeune Créole*
	Descard	*Anne du Valmoët*
	Mannoury d'Ectot	*Les Cousines de la colonelle*
early 1880s	Mannoury d'Ectot	*Le Roman de Violette*
1881	Gagneur	*Un chevalier de sacristie*
	Gagneur	*Le Roman d'un prêtre*
	Michel	*La Misère*
1882	Craven	*Eliane*
	Descard	*Les Chemins de la vie*
	Gagneur	*Le Crime de l'abbé Maufrac*
	Gautier	*Isoline et la fleur serpent*
	Gyp	*Petit Bob*
	Gyp	*La Vertu de la baronne*
	Michel	*Les Méprisées*
1883	Adam	*Païenne*
	Gyp	*Autour du mariage*
	Gyp	*Ce que femme veut...?*
	Michel	*La Fille du peuple*
	Stern	*Valentia* (posth.)
1884	Bentzon	*Tony*
	Gautier	*La Femme de Putiphar*
	Rachilde	*Monsieur Vénus*
1885	Gyp	*Elles et lui*
	Tinayre	*Vive les vacances*
1886	Audouard	*Singulière nuit de noces*
	Craven	*Le Valbriant*
	Gyp	*Autour du divorce*
1887	Marni	*La Femme de Silva*
	Rachilde	*La Marquise de Sade*
	Tinayre	*L'Enfant gaulois*
1888	Gyp	*Mlle Loulou*
	Gyp	*Pauvres p'tites femmes!!!*
	Rachilde	*Madame Adonis*
1889	Descard	*La Cousine Esther*
	Gréville	*Un violon russe*
	Marni	*L'Amour coupable*
1890	Descard	*Annie*

	Dieulafoy	*Parysatis*
	Gréville	*Louk Loukitch*
	Lesueur	*Névrosée*
1892	Caro	*Amour de jeune fille*
	Caro	*Fruits amers*
	Dieulafoy	*Volontaire, 1792–93*
1893	Caro	*Complice!...*
	Gyp	*Pas jalouse!*
	Lesueur	*Justice de femme*
1894	Lesueur	*Haine d'amour*
1895	Pert	*Amoureuses*
1896	Gyp	*Bijou*
	Pert	*Amante*
	Pert	*Le Frère*
1897	Dieulafoy	*Déchéance*
	Rachilde	*Les Hors Nature*
1898	Caro	*Idylle nuptiale*
	Gyp	*Sportmanomanie*
	Pert	*Les Florifères*
	Rachilde	*L'Heure sexuelle*
	Tinayre	*La Rançon*
1899	Rachilde	*La Tour d'amour*
	Tinayre	*Hellé*

VERSE AND PROSE POEMS

1801	Beauharnais	*L'Ile de la félicité*
1806	Beauharnais	*Vers à Madame Montison*
1807	Dufrénoy	*Elégies*
1810	Babois	*Elégies et poésies diverses*
1811	Beauharnais	*La Cyn-Achantide ou le voyage de Zizi et d'Azor*
1819	Desbordes-Valmore	*Elégies et romances*
1822	Girardin	*Le Dévouement des médecins français et des sœurs de Sainte Camille dans la peste de Barcelone*
1824	Girardin	*Essais poétiques*
1825	Desbordes-Valmore	*Elégies et poésies nouvelles*
	Girardin	*Nouveaux essais poétiques*
1825 on	Mercœur	*Œuvres complètes*

1826	Tastu	*Poésies*
1831	Ségalas	*Les Algériennes; Poésies diverses*
1833	Desbordes-Valmore	*Les Pleurs*
1835	Tastu	*Poésies nouvelles*
1836	Colet	*Les Fleurs du midi*
	Ségalas	*Oiseaux de passage*
1839	Desbordes-Valmore	*Pauvres fleurs*
1843	Desbordes-Valmore	*Bouquets et prières*
1846	Colet	*Les Chants des vaincus, poésies nouvelles*
1847	Ségalas	*La Femme*
1848	Altenheym	*Le Siècle*
1852	Colet	*Ce qui est dans le cœur des femmes*
1854	Colet	*Ce qu'on rêve en aimant*
1855	Blanchecotte	*Rêves et réalités*
1856	Colet	*Le Poème de la femme*
1867	Gautier	*Le Livre de jade* (translated fragments)
1871	Ackermann	*Poésies philosophiques*
1872–73	Gautier	Prose poems in *La Renaissance littéraire et artistique*
1875	Blanchecotte	*Les Militantes*
1884	Daudet	*Fragments d'un livre inédit*
1888	Gautier	*Les Noces de Fingal*
1890	Krysinska	*Rythmes pittoresques*
1894	Krysinska	*Joies errantes*
1896	Lesueur	*Poésies*

DRAMA

1801	Belfort	*L'Artémise française ou les heureux effets de la paix*
1803	Montanclos	*Alison et Silvain ou les habitants de Vaucluse*
	Montanclos	*La Bonne Maîtresse*
1811	Bawr	*Le Rival obligeant*
	Bawr	*Le Double Stratagème*
1820	Gay	*Le Marquis de Pomenars*
1831	Ancelot	*Un divorce*
1835	Ancelot	*Un mariage raisonnable*

	Bawr	*Charlotte Brown*
1836	Ancelot	*Marie ou les trois époques*
1839	Girardin	*L'Ecole des journalistes*
1840–72	Sand	Adaptations of own novels; original plays
1841	Altenheym (with Soumet)	*Le Gladiateur*
1843	Ancelot	*Madame Roland*
	Girardin	*Judith*
1844	Altenheym (with Soumet)	*Jane Grey*
1847	Girardin	*Cléopâtre*
1853	Girardin	*Lady Tartuffe*
1855	Aunet	*Jane Osborn*
1857	Stern	*Jeanne d'Arc*
1863	Deraismes	*Théâtre chez soi*
	Audouard	*Il n'y a pas d'amour sans jalousie et de jalousie sans amour*
1877	Gréville	*Denise*
1888	Bernhardt	*L'Aveu*
	Gautier	*La Marchande de sourires*
1891	Rachilde	*Théâtre*
1894	Gautier	*La Sonate du clair de lune* (libretto to one-act opera)
1899	Lapauze	*Théâtre féministe*

LIFE-WRITING

	Beauharnais	*A la mémoire de Mme du Bocage*
1802	Beauharnais	*A la mémoire de Mme du Bocage*
approx. 1810 on	Rémusat	*Mémoires de Madame de Rémusat, 1802–1808*
1810–18	Chastenay	*Mémoires sur l'Ancien Régime*
1820 on	La Tour du Pin	*Journal d'une femme de cinquante ans, 1778–1815*
1822	Campan	*Mémoires sur la vie privée de Marie-Antoinette*
1825	Genlis	*Mémoires inédits*
1831–34	Abrantès	*Mémoires sur Napoléon, la Révolution, le Directoire et la Restauration*

1832	Briche	*Les Voyages en Suisse de Mme de la Briche, 1785–1832*
1833	Desbordes-Valmore	*L'Atelier d'un peintre*
1834	Gay	*Souvenirs d'une vieille femme*
1835 on	Boigne	*Récits d'une tante*
1838	Tristan	*Pérégrinations d'une paria*
1841	Niboyet	*Souvenirs d'enfance*
1843	Mercœur (Mme)	See Mercœur, *Œuvres complètes* (under 'Verse and prose poems')
1851	Blaze de Bury	*Voyage en Autriche, en Hongrie et en Allemagne pendant les événements de 1848 et de 1849*
1853	Bawr	*Mes souvenirs*
1853–54	Mogador	*Adieux au monde*
1854	Aunet	*Voyage d'une femme au Spitzberg*
1855	Sand	*Histoire de ma vie*
1858	Ancelot	*Les Salons de Paris, foyers éteints*
1866	Ancelot	*Un salon de Paris 1824–64*
	Craven	*Récit d'une sœur, souvenirs de famille*
	Voilquin	*Souvenirs d'une fille du peuple*
1868	Blanchecotte	*Impressions d'une femme, pensées, sentiments et portraits*
1872	Blanchecotte	*Tablettes d'une femme pendant la Commune*
1874	Ackermann	'Ma vie', in *Œuvres*
1877	Craven	*Le Travail d'une âme, étude d'une conversion*
	Stern	*Mes souvenirs* (posth.)
1879	Craven	*Réminiscences: souvenirs d'Angleterre et d'Italie*
1880	Witt	*M. Guizot dans sa famille et avec ses amis, 1787–1874*
1881	Craven	*Une année de méditations*
1883	Daudet	*L'Enfance d'une Parisienne*
1886	Dieulafoy	*La Perse, la Chaldée et la Susiane*
	Michel	*Mémoires*
1887	Guibert	*Lettres inédites* (posth.)
	Bashkirtseff	*Journal* (posth.)
1898	Michel	*La Commune, histoire et souvenirs*

IDEAS

1800	Bourdic-Viot	*Eloge de Montaigne*
	Staël	*De la littérature*
1801	Gacon-Dufour	*Contre le projet de loi de S*** M**** [Sylvain Maréchal]
1802	Guizot	*Essais de littérature et de morale*
1805	Gacon-Dufour	*De la nécessité de l'instruction pour les femmes*
1806	Guibert	*Leçons sur la nature*
1809	Guibert (ed.)	*Lettres de Mlle de Lespinasse au comte de Guibert*
1810	Staël	*De l'Allemagne*
1811	Genlis	*De l'influence des femmes sur la littérature française comme protectrices des lettres et comme auteurs*
1818	Staël	*Considérations sur les principaux événements de la Révolution française* (posth.)
1821	Bawr	*Cours de littérature*
1823	Bawr	*Histoire de la musique*
	Dufrénoy and Tastu	*Le Livre des femmes*
1824	Allart	*Lettres sur les ouvrages de Mme de Staël*
	Rémusat	*Essai sur l'éducation des femmes*
1826	Guizot	*Lettres de famille sur l'éducation domestique*
1828–32	Necker de Saussure	*L'Education progressive*
1830	Robert	*Les Crimes des reines de France* (posth.)
1833	Démar	*Appel d'une femme au peuple sur l'affranchissement de la femme*
	Gay	*Physiologie du ridicule*
1834	Démar	*Ma loi d'avenir*
1836	Allart	*La Femme et la démocratie de notre temps*
	Tastu	*Education maternelle*
1837	Allart	*Histoire de la République de Florence*
1840	Tristan	*Promenades dans Londres*

1842	Niboyet	*Dieu manifesté par les œuvres de la création*
1843	Tastu	*Tableau de la littérature italienne*
	Tristan	*Union ouvrière*
1844	Tastu	*Tableau de la littérature allemande*
1847	Stern	*Essai sur la liberté*
1849	Stern	*Esquisses morales et politiques*
1850–53	Stern	*Histoire de la Révolution de 1848*
1857	Allart	*Essai sur l'histoire politique, depuis l'invasion des barbares jusqu'en 1848*
1858	Adam	*Idées antiproudhoniennes sur l'amour, la femme et le mariage*
	Altenheym	*Les Marguerites de France*
1859	Daubié	*La Femme pauvre au XIXe siècle* (publ. 1866)
1860	Altenheym	*Les Fauteuils illustres*
	Dash	*Le Livre des femmes*
	Héricourt	*La Femme affranchie*
1863	Niboyet	*Le Vrai Livre des femmes*
1864	Allart	*Essai sur la religion intérieure*
1868	Deraismes	*Nos principes et nos mœurs*
1869	Léo	*Les Femmes et les mœurs*
1872	Deraismes	*Eve contre Dumas fils*
	Gagneur	*Le Divorce*
1873	Deraismes	*France et progrès*
1879	Daudet	*Impressions de nature et d'art*
	Sand	*Questions d'art et de littérature* (posth.)
	Sand	*Questions politiques et sociales* (posth.)
1881	Gréville	*Instruction morale et civique des jeunes filles*
1881–84	Sand	*Correspondance* (posth.)
1882	Witt	*Les Chroniqueurs de l'histoire de France*
1887	Barine	*Portraits de femmes*
1890	Barine	*Princesses et grandes dames*
1891	Deraismes	*Eve dans l'humanité*
1893	Barine	*Alfred de Musset*

	Séverine	*Pages rouges*
1894	Séverine	*Notes d'une Frondeuse*
1895	Deraismes	*Œuvres complètes* (posth.)
1896	Bentzon	*Les Américaines chez elles*
	Séverine	*En marche*
1898	Barine	*Poètes et névrosés*

JOURNALISM

Main journals with dates of foundation / duration

1808	*Athénée des Dames*
1832	*Journal des Femmes* (became *Journal de Modes* 1835–8)
1832–34	*Tribune des Femmes*
1836–38	*Gazette des Femmes*
1848 (March-June)	*Voix des Femmes*
1869–91	*Le Droit des Femmes*
1881	*La Citoyenne*
1890s	*La Fronde*

Main individual contributors

1808–	Renneville (largely in charge of *Athénée des Dames*)
1830–	Arnaud (articles, political pamphlets)
1832–34	Voilquin (ed. *Tribune des Femmes*)
1836–	Tristan (*Gazette des Femmes*)
1836–48	Girardin (column, 'Lettres parisiennes', in *La Presse*; pseud. Vicomte de Launay)
1844–	Niboyet (founded *La Paix des deux mondes*, 1844, and *Voix des Femmes*, 1848)
mid-century	Aubert (edited and contributed to fashion journals)
1866	Audouard (pamphlet *Guerre aux hommes*; founded literary review *Le Papillon*)
late 1860s–	Léo (contributions to *La Sociale* and *Le Droit des Femmes*)
1869–91	Deraismes (co-editor with Léon Richer of *Le Droit des Femmes*)

1877–	Adam (founded *La Nouvelle Revue*)
1881–91	Auclert (set up *La Citoyenne*)
1881–	Séverine (contributed to, then managed, *Le Cri du Peuple*)

Appendix B

BIOBIBLIOGRAPHIES

Abrantès, Laure d' (1785–1838). Aristocratic novelist and memoir-writer. Main work: *Mémoires sur Napoléon, la Révolution, le Directoire et la Restauration* (18 vols., 1831–34).

Ackermann, Louise (1813–90). Atheist poet. Collected work: *Œuvres* (1885), containing *Ma vie, Premières poésies, Poésies philosophiques*.

Adam [Lamber], Juliette (1836–1936). Republican and feminist novelist, polemicist, *salonnière*. Main works: *Idées antiproudhoniennes sur l'amour, la femme et le mariage* (1858); *Laide* (1878); *Grecque* (1879); *Païenne* (1883).

Allart, Hortense (1801–79). Novelist and essayist. She had a number of romantic liaisons, including one with Chateaubriand. Influenced by feminism, she was involved with the *Gazette des Femmes*, and argued in favour of free love and improved status for women. Best-known work: *Les Enchantements de Prudence* (1872), whose heroine leads a relatively independent life. Also: *Lettres sur les ouvrages de Mme de Staël* (1824); *Settimie* (1826); *Gertrude* (1828); *Histoire de la République de Florence* (1837); *Essai sur l'histoire politique depuis l'invasion des barbares jusqu'en 1848* (1857).

Alquié de Rieupeyroux [or Alq], Louise d' (1840–?1901). Writer of practical and pedagogical works, journalism, drama.

Altenheym, Gabrielle d' [or Beuvain d'Altenheim; Daltenheym; d'Alteinhem] (1814–86). Poet, novelist, literary critic. Daughter of writer Alexandre Soumet, with whom she collaborated on two plays. Main works: *Nouvelles Filiales* (1838); *Le Gladiateur* (with Soumet, 1841); *Dieu pardonne, ou Les Deux Frères*; *Les Marguerites de France* (1858); *Les Fauteuils illustres* (1860).

Ancelot, Virginie (1792–1875). Dramatist; also memoir-writer, novelist. Collected plays: *Théâtre complet* (4 vols., 1848). Memoirs: *Les Salons de Paris, foyers éteints* (1858); *Un salon de Paris 1824–64* (1866). Main novels: *Georgine* (1855); *Une route sans issue* (1857); *Un nœud de ruban* (1858).

Arnaud, Angélique (1799–1884). Novelist and feminist. Her novels are: *La Comtesse de Sergy* (1838); *Clémence* (1841); *Une tendre dévote* (1874); *La Cousine Adèle* (1879).

Aubert, Constance (1803–?). Daughter of d'Abrantès; collaborated with her on novels; wrote and edited fashion journalism. Main work: *Manuel d'économie élégante* (1859).

Auclert, Hubertine (1848–1914). Feminist polemical writer. Founded the group *Le Droit des Femmes* in 1876; set up weekly newspaper *La Citoyenne* (1881–91).

Audouard, Olympe (1830–90). Novelist, travel-writer, journalist. Founded literary review *Le Papillon*. Pamphlet: *Guerre aux hommes* (1866). Drama: *Il n'y a pas d'amour sans jalousie et de jalousie sans amour* (1863). Novels: *Un mari mystifié* (1863); *Singulière nuit de noces* (1886).

Aunet, Léonie d' (1820–79). Travel-writer, dramatist, fiction writer. Famous at the age of nineteen for taking part in the celebrated voyage of discovery to Spitsbergen with the Commission du Nord; the first Frenchwoman to set foot on Spitsbergen and to cross Lapland. In 1845 she was caught committing adultery with Hugo, imprisoned, and impoverished as a result. She published her lively and readable *Voyage d'une femme au Spitzberg* in 1854 and had some plays staged, for example *Jane Osborn* (1855). Fiction includes *Un mariage en province* (1856); *Une vengeance* (1857).

Babois, Marguerite-Victoire (1760–1839). Poet. Daughter of a shop-keeper; friend of the verse-writers and dramatists Jean-François Ducis and Marie-Joseph Chénier. Inspired to write by grief over the death of her daughter in 1792. Collected work: *Œuvres* (1828).

Barine, Arvède [pseud. of Louise-Cécile Vincens] (1840–1908). Critic, historian, biographer; her speciality was pen-portraits of famous women. Main works: *Portraits de femmes* (1887); *Princesses et grandes dames* (1890); *Alfred de Musset* (1893); *Poètes et névrosés* (1898).

Barthélemy-Hadot, Marie-Adélaïde Richard (1763–1821). Novelist and dramatist. Her main output for the theatre was about 1803–16.

Bashkirtseff, Marie (1860–84). Russian aristocrat and painter who came to France as a child. She left a diary in French, begun when she was twelve and continuing until just before her death from TB at age twenty-three: *Journal de Marie Bashkirtseff* (1887, posth.). Her diary figures prominently in Simone de Beauvoir's *Le Deuxième Sexe.*

Bawr, Alexandrine de (1773–1860). Dramatist; also novelist. Daughter of an actress and an aristocratic father; married and was divorced from Saint-Simon. She had a state allowance from Louis XVIII. Among her plays are: *Le Double Stratagème* (1811); *La Suite d'un bal masqué* (1813). Fiction: *Raoule ou l'Enéide* (1832); *Cecilia ou mémoires d'une héritière* (1852). Memoirs: *Mes souvenirs* (1853).

Beauharnais, Marie-Anne-Françoise de (1738–1813). Aunt of Josephine Bonaparte. Fiction-writer, poet, *salonnière.* Had feminist views; wrote mainly fantastical, philosophical and humorous tales. Main nineteenth-century works: *L'Ile de la félicité* (1801); *La Cyn-Achantide* and *La Marmotte philosophe* (1811).

Belloc, Louise (1796–1881). Translator, educational writer, children's writer. Books include: *Histoire et contes de la grand-mère* (1871); *Le Fond du sac de la grand-mère* (1873).

Bentzon [Blanc], Thérèse (1840–1907). Translator, novelist, critic. Introduced Mark Twain, Henry James and Walt Whitman to French readers. Among her novels are: *Un divorce* (1872); *Yette: Histoire d'une jeune Créole* (1880).

Blanchecotte, Auguste (1830–95). Working-class poet. A seamstress whose first collection of poetry, *Rêves et réalités* (1855), was awarded a prize by the Académie Française. Her other works include *Impressions d'une femme, pensées, sentiments et portraits* (1868); *Tablettes d'une femme pendant la Commune* (1872); *Les Militantes* (1875).

Blaze de Bury, Rose (?-1894). Journalist, travel-writer, novelist. Believed to be the illegitimate daughter of an English aristocrat. Involved in financial and political negotiations between England and Austria in the 1860s; wrote in both French and English (for English journals). Best-known work: *Voyage en Autriche, en Hongrie et en Allemagne pendant les événements de 1848 et de 1849* (1851).

Boigne, Louise de (1781–1866). Memoir-writer. An émigrée, and *salonnière* under the Empire. Her memoirs are a valuable record of the history of her time. Begun in 1835, they were published in 1907 under the title *Récits d'une tante.*

Bourdic-Viot, Marie-Henriette de [also: Mme d'Antremont] (1746–1802). Poet and essayist. Mainly known for late eighteenth-century works; her inaugural speech on her reception as a member of the Academy of Nîmes (1782) was published in 1800: *Eloge de Montaigne*.

Briche, Adélaïde-Edmée de la (1755–1844). Memoir- and travel-writer, *salonnière*. Her travel memoirs were published in 1935 (ed. P. de Zurich): *Les Voyages en Suisse de Mme de Briche 1785–1832*.

Bruno, G. [pseud. of Augustine Fouillée] (1833–1923). Author of the 'best-loved schoolbook' of late nineteenth-century France: *Le Tour de la France par deux enfants* (1877). Published shortly before primary education was made compulsory, it sold 6 million copies by 1900, was used in Church and state schools alike, and was known to French children well into the twentieth century. It gives an illustrated tour of France and is humanist in outlook.

Campan, Jeanne-Louise-Henriette (1752–1822). Memoir-writer and educational writer. First lady's maid and companion to Marie-Antoinette. Her memoirs focus on the private life of Marie-Antoinette: *Mémoires* (1822).

Caro, Pauline (1835–1901). Novelist; wife of philosopher Elme-Marie Caro. First novel published anonymously: *Le Péché de Madeleine* (1864). Other works include *Flamien* (1866); *Histoire du souci* (1868); *Amour de jeune fille* and *Fruits amers* (1892); *Complice!...* (1893); *Idylle nuptiale* (1898).

Chartroule, Marie-Amélie [pseud. Marc de Montifaud] (1850–?). Erotic novelist. Main works: *Les Vestales de l'Eglise* (1877); *Les Dévoyés* and *Mme Ducroisy* (1879) (condemned to four months' imprisonment after the publication of these two works).

Chastenay, Louise-Marie de (1770–?1838). Memoir-writer, essayist, translator. An accomplished musician, botanist and historian. One of the few nineteenth-century French women writers who never married. Main work: *Mémoires* (written 1810–18, published 1896–97).

Choiseul-Meuse, Félicie de (nineteenth century). Erotic novelist about whose life nothing is known. Best-known novel: *Julie ou j'ai sauvé ma rose* (1807).

Colet, Louise (1810–76). Poet and novelist. Daughter of a wine merchant. Had affairs with Musset and notably Flaubert, who wrote famous letters to her outlining his aesthetic theories; their liaison ended in 1854. Main works: *Poésies complètes* (1844); a tripartite feminist work, *Poème de la femme* (1853–56); a novel, *Lui* (1860).

Cottin, Sophie (1770–1807). Novelist. Wrote five popular full-length works: *Claire d'Albe* (1799); *Amélie Mansfield* (1803); *Malvina* (1804); *Mathilde ou mémoires tirés de l'histoire des Croisades* (1805); *Elisabeth ou les exilés de Sibérie* (1806). She had a friendship with the historian Michaud.

Craven, Pauline (1808–91). Novelist; historical, religious and auto-biographical writer. Main autobiographical works: *Récit d'une sœur, souvenirs de famille* (1866); *Le Travail d'une âme, étude d'une conversion* (1877); *Réminiscences: souvenirs d'Angleterre et d'Italie* (1879); *Une année de méditations* (1881). Novels: *Anne Séverin* (1868); *Fleur-ange* (1871); *Le Mot de l'énigme* (1874); *Le Valbriant* (1886).

Dash, Comtesse [pseud. of Gabrielle-Anne Du Poilloüe de Saint-Mars] (1804–72). Novelist. After an unhappy marriage, turned to writing to support herself and her son. She was a journalist until 1839, but then produced a large number of novels, as well as the reactionary *Le Livre des femmes* (1860). Novels include: *L'Ecran* (1839); *La Marquise de Parabère* and *Les Bals masqués* (1842); *La Marquise sanglante* (1850); *La Comtesse de Bossut* (1855); *La Duchesse de Lauzun* (1858); *Un amour à la Bastille* (1862); *L'Arbre de la Vierge* (1872).

Daubié, Julie (1824–74). Working-class feminist writer. Won first place in an Académie de Lyon competition (1858) for her 450-page *La Femme pauvre au XIXe siècle* (published 1866). One of the judges was so impressed with this work that he encouraged her to sit for the *baccalauréat*, and in 1861 she became the first *bachelière* in France, subsequently obtaining a degree from the Sorbonne.

Daudet, Julia (1844–1940). Poet, essayist. Wife of Alphonse Daudet. Best-known works: *L'Enfance d'une Parisienne* (1883); *Fragments d'un livre inédit* (1884).

Démar, Claire (1800–33). Working-class feminist essayist: *Appel d'une femme au peuple sur l'affranchissement de la femme* (1833); *Ma loi d'avenir* (1834). Outspoken believer in free love and women's need for sexual pleasure. She committed suicide, leaving a note saying she thought she had been too daring.

Deraismes, Maria (1828–94). Feminist playwright, essayist and journalist. An educated and wealthy woman, and impressive public speaker, who helped to make feminism 'respectable' in France. Main works: *Théâtre chez soi* (1863); *Eve dans l'humanité* (1891), which includes some of her lectures.

Desbordes-Valmore, Marceline (1785–1859). The best-known French woman poet of the century. Daughter of an impoverished craftsman; after her mother's death, became an actress to earn her living. Verlaine regarded her as the only woman worthy of the title of *poète maudit*; she was also the only woman writer whose work was praised by Baudelaire. Collections: *Elégies et romances* (1819); *Elégies et poésies nouvelles* (1825); *Les Pleurs* (1833); *Pauvres Fleurs* (1839); *Bouquets et prières* (1843). She is published in the modern Gallimard *Poésies* series, with a preface by Yves Bonnefoy.

Descard, Maria (1847–1927). Novelist; Académie Française prize-winner. Daughter of a sea-captain, later wife of one; widely travelled, she put many of her experiences into her books. These include: *En Poitou* (1878); *Anne du Valmoët* (1880); *La Cousine Esther* (1889); *Annie* (1890).

Dieulafoy, Jane (1851–1916). Novelist and travel-writer. While travelling, she wore men's clothes, and continued to do so once back in Paris. Most famous travelogue: *La Perse, la Chaldée et la Susiane* (1886). Novels include *Parysatis* (1890), which won an Académie Française prize; *Volontaire: 1792–93* (1892); *Déchéance* (1897).

Dufrénoy, Adélaïde (1765–1825). Poet; Académie Française prize-winner. Main work: *Elégies* (1807); others include: *Etrennes à ma fille* (1815); *La Petite Ménagère* (1816); *Le Livre des femmes* (1823).

Duras, Claire de (1778–1828). Novelist and *salonnière*. She has recently been acquiring a reputation as the finest French woman novelist of the early century. Her only published works were *Ourika* (1824) and *Edouard* (1825); she also wrote and circulated privately *Olivier ou le secret*, whose plot inspired Stendhal's *Armance* (1827) but which was not published until 1971.

Estournelles, Louise d' (1792–1835). Novelist. Sister of Benjamin Constant. Works: *Alphonse et Mathilde* (1802); *Pascaline* (1821); *Deux femmes* (1836; posth.).

Gacon-Dufour, Marie (1753–1835). Novelist and discursive writer; writer of practical manuals and co-founder of the Bibliothèque Agronomique; defender of women's rights to education. Main nineteenth-century works: *Les Dangers d'un mariage forcé* and *La Femme-grenadier* (1801); *Mélicrète et Zirphile* (1802); *De la nécessité de l'instruction pour les femmes* (1805).

Gagneur, Louise Mignerot (1832–1902). Novelist and polemical writer; feminist and anti-clerical. Campaigner in favour of divorce law reform. Novels: *Le Calvaire des femmes* (1863); *La Croisade noire* (1866); *Les Réprouvées* (1867); *Les Forçats du mariage* (1870); *Les Crimes de l'amour* (1874); *Un Chevalier de sacristie* and *Le Roman d'un prêtre* (1881); *Le Crime de l'abbé Maufrac* (1882).

Gautier, Judith [briefly: Mendès] (1846–1917). Fiction-writer, poet, playwright, oriental scholar. Eldest daughter of Théophile Gautier; friend of Wagner. Works include: *Le Livre de Jade* (1867); *Le Dragon impérial* (1869); *La Sœur du soleil* (1875); *La Femme de Putiphar* (1884); *Isoline et la fleur serpent* (1882). Play: *La Marchande de sourires (pièce japonaise)* (1888). Opera libretto: *La Sonate du clair de lune* (1894).

Gay, Sophie (1776–1852). Novelist, playwright, *salonnière* renowned for her wit. Mother of Delphine de Girardin. Novels include: *Laure d'Estell* (1802); *Léonie de Montbreuse* (1813); *Anatole* (1815); *Théobald* (1828); *Un mariage sous l'Empire* (1832); *La Duchesse de Chateauroux* (1834); *La Comtesse d'Egmont* (1836); *Marie de Mancini* (1840). Play: *Le Marquis de Pomenars* (1820).

Genlis, Stéphanie-Félicité de (1746–1830). Educational writer, novelist, memoir-writer. Mistress of Duc d'Orléans and governess to his children; later, protected by Napoleon. With her experiences and her mix of progressive and highly reactionary views, she is an interesting figure (Hufton calls for a modern biography of her in *The Prospect Before Her*, 623). Published over eighty books. Main nineteenth-century works: *Mademoiselle de Clermont* (1802); *La Duchesse de La Vallière* (1804); *Mme de Maintenon* (1806); *De l'influence des femmes sur la littérature française comme protectrices des lettres et comme auteurs* (1811); *Mademoiselle de Lafayette* (1813); *Mémoires* (10 vols., 1825).

Girardin, Delphine de [pseud. Vicomte de Launay] (1804–55). Poet, dramatist, novelist, journalist, *salonnière*. Daughter of Sophie Gay, wife of press entrepreneur Emile de Girardin. She scored remarkable successes in all genres. Collected works: *Poésies complètes* (from early 1820s to mid-1830s); *Lettres parisiennes* (journalism, 1836–48). Fiction: *La Canne de Monsieur de Balzac* (1836). Drama: *L'Ecole des journalistes* (1839); *Judith* (1843); *Cléopâtre* (1847); *Lady Tartuffe* (1853).

Gréville, Henry [pseud. of Alice Durand-Gréville] (1842–1902). Novelist and journalist. Spent fifteen years in Russia, learned the language and wrote articles about Russian culture. Her popular novels also focused on Russia: *Les Koumiassine*; *Les Epreuves de Raïssa* (1877); *Un Violon russe* (1889); *Louk Loukitch* (1890). Also: *Instruction morale et civique des jeunes filles* (1881).

Guibert, Louise-Alexandrine (1758–1826). Novelist. Main nineteenth-century works: *Fedaretta* (1803); the pedagogical *Leçons sur la nature* (1806). Most renowned for editing *Lettres de Mlle de Lespinasse au comte de Guibert* [her husband], *1773–1776* (1809).

Guizot, Pauline (1773–1827). Novelist and literary journalist. Best-known work: *La Chapelle d'Ayton* (1800). Also: *Les Enfants: Contes à l'usage de la jeunesse* (1812); *L'Ecolier ou Raoul et Victor* (1821) (which won an Académie Française prize as a work 'useful to morals').

Gyp [pseud. of Gabrielle de Mirabeau] (1850–1932). Novelist. Anti-Semitic aristocrat descended from the Revolutionary politician Mirabeau. Wrote some hundred novels; a prime practitioner of the 'dialogue novel'. Witty; creates tomboyish or iconoclastic heroines. Novels include: *Petit Bob* (1882); *Autour du mariage* and *Ce que femme veut...?* (1883); *Elles et lui* (1885); *Autour du divorce* (1886); *Pas jalouse!* (1893).

Héricourt, Jenny d' (?–?). Middle-class feminist writer. Her *La Femme affranchie* (1860) is a critique or analysis of views on women expressed by Proudhon, Michelet and the Saint-Simonians.

Krüdener, Julie de [or Barbara Juliane von] (1764–1824). Writer in German and French; mystic. Main work: *Valérie* (1803), mod-elled on Goethe's *Werther* (1774) but perhaps more on Chateau-briand's *René* (1802).

Krysinska, Marie (1857–1908). Poet; also wrote a little fiction. Born in Warsaw, she moved to Paris at the age of sixteen. She frequented artistic and Bohemian circles, and acquired a wide range of literary friends and acquaintances. A talented musician, she performed as a song-writer/singer; she married the illustrator and lithographer Georges Bellenger. She published prose poems in periodicals and has a claim to be considered the first practitioner of free verse in France. She died apparently deserted by everyone: no one could be found to pay for a cemetery plot, and she was buried in a communal grave. Collected works include: *Rythmes pittoresques* (1890); *Joies errantes* (1894).

Lagrave, Comtesse de (eighteenth–nineteenth century). Novelist. Published some dozen novels; nineteenth-century ones are: *La Chaumière incendiée* and *M. Ménard ou l'homme comme il y en a peu* (1802); *Hector de Romagny ou l'erreur d'une bonne mère* and *Juliette Belfour ou les talents récompensés* (1803); *Paulina* (1804); *La Méprise du coche ou à quelque chose malheur est bon* (1805); *La Méprise de diligence* (1820).

La Tour du Pin, Henriette-Lucie de (1770–1853). Aristocratic memoir-writer who left to her sole surviving son a humane and well-written account of her childhood, her time at Court, her experiences during the Revolution and emigration, and life under Napoleon (*Journal d'une femme de cinquante ans*). Published in 1906, it has been popular ever since.

Léo, André [or Andrée; pseud. of Léodile Chamseix] (1824–1900). Feminist novelist and journalist; friend of Louise Michel. Main works: *Un mariage scandaleux* (1862); *Un divorce* (1866); *Les Femmes et les mœurs* (1869).

Lesueur, Daniel [pseud. of Jeanne Lapauze] (1860–1920). Novelist, poet, dramatist. Académie Française prize-winner for her verse. Poetry includes: *Poésies* (1896). Novels include: *Névrosée* (1890); *Justice de femme* (1893); *Haine d'amour* (1894). Also: *Théâtre féministe* (1899).

Mannoury d'Ectot, Mme de [used pseud. La Vicomtesse de Cœur-Brûlant] (nineteenth century). Erotic novelist. Little is known about her. She published two texts: *Les Cousines de la colonelle* (1880); *Le Roman de Violette* (early 1880s).

Marni, Jeanne [pseud. of Jeanne Marnière] (1854–1910). Precocious child author (a short story was published when she was eight); novelist, playwright, author of humorous journalistic pieces. Novels include: *La Femme de Silva* (1887); *L'Amour coupable* (1889).

Merard de Saint-Just, Anne-Jeanne-Félicité (1765–1830). Novelist. Her nineteenth-century novel *Six mois d'exil* (1805) is a testimony for the 'orphans of the Revolution'.

Mercœur, Elisa (1809–35); Mme Mercœur, her (unwed) mother (dates unknown). Elisa's *Œuvres complètes* were published posthumously in 1843 by her still grief-stricken mother, who included in them a long, intelligent and impassioned account of her daughter's brilliant childhood and unhappy life. Even allowing for exaggeration, Elisa was clearly a prodigy with an outstanding capacity for learning. She published poetry, for which she won prizes, and wrote a tragedy which was never performed.

Michel, Louise (1830–1905). Socialist activist and writer. Famous as the 'Red Virgin' of the Paris Commune. Exiled to New Caledonia after the Commune was crushed, she returned in 1880, but again had to leave France (for London) for political reasons. Main works: *Mémoires* (1886); *La Commune* (1898). Also: some novels and poetry (including the words of revolutionary songs).

Mogador, Céleste [later Chabrillan] (1824–1909). Autobiographer, novelist and playwright. A working-class woman, who had a wretched childhood and ran away from home after being raped at age fifteen by her mother's lover. After a series of adventures, she became a courtesan and dance-hostess (known by Baudelaire), and eventually married an aristocratic lover. She published her scandalous and best-selling memoirs in 1853–54 (*Adieux au monde*). Her fiction includes *Les Voleurs d'or* (1857) and *Sapho* (1858); her drama, a number of short plays.

Montanclos, Marie-Emilie de (1736–1812). Journalist and dramatist of enlightened views. Plays include *Alison et Sylvain* and *La Bonne Maîtresse* (publ. 1803).

Necker de Saussure, Albertine (1766–1841). Staël's cousin and biographer. Among her works are *L'Education progressive* (1828), which was awarded an Académie Française prize.

Niboyet, Eugénie (1804–83). Novelist and journalist. Socialist, feminist, pacifist. Novels include *Les Deux Frères* (1839); *Lucien* and *Quinze jours de vacances* (1841); *Catherine II et ses filles d'honneur* (1847). Founded the socialist journal *La Paix des deux mondes* in 1844 and the socialist feminist daily *La Voix des femmes* in 1848. Wrote *Le Vrai Livre des femmes* (1863) as a feminist counterblast to the Comtesse Dash's *Le Livre des femmes*.

Pert, Camille [pseud. of Louise Hortense Grillet or Rougeul] (1865–1952). Novelist. Anti-feminist; wrote only on the theme of love. Nineteenth-century works include *Amoureuses* (1895); *Amante* and *Le Frère* (1896); *Les Florifères* (1898).

Rachilde [pseud. of Marguerite Eymery] (1860–1953). Novelist and dramatist. Began a career in journalism and married Alfred de Vallette, editor of the *Mercure de France*. Published her first scandalous novel *Monsieur Vénus* in 1884, and continued with similar works that explore gender transpositions and sadism. She eventually (in 1928) declared herself not to be a feminist. She is increasingly considered to be one of the leading *fin-de-siècle* French writers. Nineteenth-century fiction includes: *La Marquise de Sade* (1887); *Mme Adonis* (1888); *Les Hors Nature* (1897); *L'Heure sexuelle* (1898); *La Tour d'Amour* (1899). She also wrote plays: *Théâtre* (1891).

Rattazzi, Maria (1830–1902). Novelist; historical, political and geographical writer. Lived in exile during the 1850s; on her return to France, worked as a journalist and editor. Among her many novels is an erotic one, which was banned: *Les Mariages de la Créole* (1866).

Rémusat, Claire de (1780–1821). Memoir-writer and educational writer. Lady-in-waiting to Josephine Bonaparte. Her memoirs were published posthumously by her grandson in 1880. Her *Essai sur l'éducation des femmes* was also published posthumously (1824).

Renneville, Sophie de [also de Senneterre] (1772–1822). Novelist. Highly educated; wrote prolifically, mainly for young people. Fiction includes *Lettres d'Octavie, une pensionnaire* (1806); *Contes à ma petite fille et à mon petit garçon* and *La Mère gouvernante* (1811); *Le Conteur moraliste* and *Les Secrets du cœur* (1816); *Zélie* (1820). Largely in charge of the (broadly) feminist journal *Athénée des dames*.

Reybaud, Henriette (1802–71). Prolific and popular novelist who was still publishing at age sixty-four. Works include *Clémentine* (1850) and *Les Deux Marguerites* (1866).

Robert, Louise-Félicité (1758–1821). Novelist, historian, political journalist, translator. In the late eighteenth century, she wrote fourteen volumes entitled *Collection des meilleurs ouvrages français composés par des femmes* (1786–88) and planned to continue with works by English and Italian women. Nineteenth-century works include *Les Crimes des reines de France* (1830, posth.); novels: *Amélia et Caroline ou l'amour et l'amitié* (1808); *Alphonse et Mathilde ou la famille espagnole* (1809); *Rose et Albert ou le tombeau d'Emma* (1810).

Sand, George [pseud. of Aurore Dupin Dudevant] (1804–76). The most famous nineteenth-century French woman writer; known better in the twentieth century for her life than for her works, but these have recently been undergoing a revival. She had liaisons with, amongst others, Musset and Chopin. Autobiography: *Histoire de ma vie* (1855). Novels include: *Indiana* (1832); *Lélia* (1833/1839); *Valentine* (1833); *Jacques* (1834); *Mauprat* (1837); *Spiridion* (1838); *Les Sept Cordes de la lyre* (1839); *Le Compagnon du tour de France* (1840); *Consuelo* and its sequel, *La Comtesse de Rudolstadt* (1842–44); *Jeanne* (1844); *Le Meunier d'Angibault* (1845); *La Mare au diable* (1846); *La Petite Fadette* (1849); *François le champi* (1850); *Les Maîtres Sonneurs* (1853). She was also a successful dramatist, adapting some of her fiction for the stage.

Savignac, Alida de (1790–1847). Novelist and educational writer. An unmarried woman who signed herself 'Mme' because her mother thought it more seemly. Main works: *La Comtessse de Meley* (1823); *Les Petits Proverbes dramatiques* (1826); *Les Vacances* (1828); *La Pauvre Cécile* (1829); *La Jeune Propriétaire ou l'art de vivre à la campagne* (1837).

Ségalas, Anaïs (1814–95). Poet, fiction-writer, dramatist. Known mainly for her poetry: *Les Algériennes* and *Poésies diverses* (1831); *Oiseaux de passage* (1836); *La Femme* (1847).

Ségur, Sophie de (1799–1874). Children's writer. A Russian émigrée who arrived in Paris in 1815. She had eight children and did not publish her first children's work until she was fifty-seven, in 1856 (*Nouveaux Contes de fées*). She then had a series of major successes, which have continued posthumously to this day: she was among the twenty most translated French authors in 1955, and in 1981 her first publisher Hachette boasted sales of her books of over twenty-eight million. Most famous work: *Les Malheurs de Sophie* (1859).

Séverine [pseud. of Caroline Rémy] (1855–1929). Known mainly for her journalism. Wrote for the newspaper of her lover, the revolutionary socialist Jules Vallès (*Le Cri du Peuple*), and took it over after his death in 1885. Collected writings include: *Pages rouges* (1893); *Notes d'une Frondeuse* (1894); *Pages mystiques* (1895); *En marche* (1896).

Souza, Adèle de (1761–1836). Novelist. Very popular at the turn of the nineteenth century; faded somewhat from view by the mid-century. Nineteenth-century novels: *Emilie et Alphonse* (1800); *Charles et Marie* (1802); *Eugène de Rothelin* (1808). Favourable to the idea that young lovers should be able to choose their own destiny.

Staël, Germaine de (1766–1817). One of the most remarkable of nineteenth-century European writers for the breadth of her interests, her bold feminism, her bravely upheld liberalism (which earned her Napoleon's wrath), and her intellectual originality (she can be credited at the least with the 'invention' of comparative literary criticism). She and Constant were lovers. Her writing was highly influential on both men and women. Main theoretical works: *De la littérature considérée dans ses rapports avec les institutions sociales* (1800); *De l'Allemagne* (1810). Novels: *Delphine* (1802); *Corinne ou l'Italie* (1807). Also: the autobiographical *Dix années d'exil* (1811); and *Considérations sur les principaux événements de la Révolution française* (1818, posth.).

Stern, Daniel [pseud. of Marie de Flavigny, later d'Agoult] (1805–76). Novelist, autobiographer, historical and political writer. In 1835 she eloped with Liszt, by whom she had two daughters; they separated in 1844. Fiction: *Nélida* (anagram of 'Daniel', 1846); *Valentia* (1883, posth.). Discursive works: *Essai sur la liberté* (1847); *Esquisses morales* (1849); *Histoire de la Révolution de 1848* (1850–53). Memoirs: *Mes souvenirs* (posth., 1877).

Tastu, Amable (1798–1885). Poet, educational writer, literary critic. Known mainly for her poetry, some of which memorably expresses the self-doubts of the woman writer. Main works: *Poésies* (1826); *Poésies nouvelles* (1835); *Tableau de la littérature italienne* (1843); *Tableau de la littérature allemande* (1844).

Tinayre, Marcelle (1877–1948). Novelist. Her works focus on love but have wider perspectives too, showing, for example, a clear understanding of the dilemmas faced by women in a still repressive society. Main nineteenth-century works: *Vive les vacances* (1885); *L'Enfant gaulois* (1887); *La Rançon* (1898); *Hellé* (1899).

Tristan, Flora (1803–44). Political writer and activist, auto-biographer, novelist. The illegitimate daughter of a French mother and a wealthy Peruvian father; Gauguin's grandmother. Her earliest well-known work is the story of her journey to Peru to reclaim her inheritance (she was unsuccessful): *Pérégrinations d'une paria* (1838). Her most influential political works were the powerful *Promenades dans Londres* (1840) and *Union ouvrière* (1843); this last shows a sophisticated understanding of the situation of the working class, aims to 'raise consciousness', and proposes a form of social security. Novel: *Méphis*, 1838.

Ulliac-Trémadeure, Sophie [briefly used pseud. Dudrezène] (1794–1862). Translator, journalist, novelist. Wrote mainly for 'young people', but some of her works have controversial and adult perspectives, particularly those in which she opposes women's creative talents to the humdrum tasks ('slavery') demanded of them: *Valérie ou la jeune artiste* (1836); *Emilie ou la jeune fille auteur* (1837). She received Academy prizes for some of her works, and edited the *Journal des jeunes personnes*. She continued publishing up to a year before her death: *Souvenirs d'une vieille femme* (1861).

Voilquin, Suzanne (1801–77). Journalist and autobiographer. A working-class feminist; eventually a professional midwife. A Saint-Simonienne who accompanied the group's expedition to Egypt. Edited *Tribune des femmes*, 1832–34. Autobiography: *Souvenirs d'une fille du peuple* (1866).

Witt, Henriette de (1829–1908). Protestant writer. Member of the Guizot family. Wrote a number of works of an educational, religious or biographical nature; also, notably, the very successful family chronicle *M. Guizot dans sa famille et avec ses amis, 1787–1874* (1880).

Notes

I PREJUDICE AND REASSESSMENT

1. For example, the *Cahiers staëliens* (1962–) predate 1970, as do occasional conferences on Staël, or editions of her correspondence. See S. Balayé, *Madame de Staël: lumières et liberté* (Paris: Klincksieck, 1979), 7–10, for a brief history of her reputation. A. Maurois published a biography of Sand in the early 1950s: *Lélia ou la vie de George Sand* (Paris: Hachette, 1952), while G. Lubin's multi-volumed edition of her correspondence began in 1964: *Correspondance de George Sand* (Paris: Garnier, 1964–91, 25 vols.). See too G. Cavalucci's critical bibliography of Desbordes-Valmore, published in the thirties and forties: *Bibliographie critique de Marceline Desbordes-Valmore d'après des documents inédits* (Naples: Pironti, 1935/1942).

2. For women writers' suppression from the canon of the nineteenth and other centuries, see the essays in J. DeJean and N. Miller (eds.), *Displacements: Women, Tradition, Literatures in French* (Baltimore: Johns Hopkins University Press, 1991).

3. M. Ambrière (ed.), *Précis de littérature française du XIXe siècle* (Paris: Presses Universitaires de France, 1990). Among reassessments of the major three writers are M. Gutwirth, *Madame de Staël, Novelist: The Emergence of the Artist as Woman* (Urbana: University of Illinois Press, 1978); J. Isbell, *The Birth of European Romanticism: Truth and Propaganda in Staël's De l'Allemagne* (Cambridge University Press, 1994); B. Johnson, 'Gender and poetry: Charles Baudelaire and Marceline Desbordes-Valmore', in DeJean and Miller (eds.), *Displacements*, 163–81; N. Schor, *George Sand and Idealism* (New York: Columbia University Press, 1993); B. Didier, *George Sand écrivain: 'Un grand fleuve d'Amérique'* (Paris: Presses Universitaires de France, 1998). Among works which include women writers in more general studies are J. Beizer, *Ventriloquized Bodies: Narratives of Hysteria in Nineteenth-Century France* (Ithaca and London: Cornell University Press, 1994); F. Miller Frank, *The Mechanical Song: Women, Voice, and the Artificial in Nineteenth-Century French Narrative* (Stanford University Press, 1995); R. Gordon, *Ornament, Fantasy and Desire in Nineteenth-Century French Literature* (Princeton University Press, 1992);

R. Lloyd, *The Land of Lost Content: Children and Childhood in Nineteenth-Century French Literature* (Oxford: Clarendon, 1992); M. Waller, *The Male Malady: Fictions of Impotence in the French Romantic Novel* (New Brunswick: Rutgers University Press, 1993). Major biobibliographies are C. Buck (ed.), *Bloomsbury Guide to Women's Literature* (London: Bloomsbury, 1992) (hereafter referred to as the *Bloomsbury Guide*); E. Martin Sartori and D. Wynne Zimmerman (eds.), *French Women Writers* (Lincoln: University of Nebraska Press, 1994).

4. For examples of studies which – valuable in themselves – cover only single genres or part of the century, see M. Cohen, 'Women and fiction in the nineteenth century', in T. Unwin (ed.), *The Cambridge Companion to the French Novel: From 1800 to the Present* (Cambridge University Press, 1997), 54–72; D. Holmes, *French Women's Writing 1848–1994* (London: Athlone, 1996).

5. Two such pieces are the humane and many-sided article by B. Slama, 'Femmes écrivains', in J.-P. Aron (ed.), *Misérable et glorieuse: la femme du XIXe siècle* (n.p.: Fayard, 1980), 213–48; and the very helpful summary given by J. Birkett and A. Hughes, 'Eighteenth- and nineteenth-century France', as part of their pioneering work in the *Bloomsbury Guide*, 54–60.

6. Slama, 'Femmes écrivains', 155; Birkett and Hughes, 'Eighteenth- and nineteenth-century France', 58. Estimates of numbers of published female authors vary (see, e.g., Holmes on this, *French Women's Writing*, 49), but whatever the estimates, they are high by comparison with previous centuries. J. Larnac cites a figure of 738 'femmes de lettres' in 1908 booksellers' catalogues (compared to 300 in the late eighteenth century) in his *Histoire de la littérature féminine en France* (Paris: Krâ, 1929), 155, 223. Birkett and Hughes ('Eighteenth- and nineteenth-century France', 57) give higher numbers: by the end of the century, there were, according to figures they draw from a late-century work, some 1200 female members of the Société des gens de lettres.

7. Figures and dates for new editions and reprintings, here and subsequently, normally come from the Bibliothèque Nationale *Catalogue des imprimés*. Full names and biographical details of women authors cited are in Appendix B, 'Biobibliographies'.

8. For reasons of space, full bibliographies for each writer cannot be provided; these, and names of other women writers I do not cover, can be found in the critical works cited in my bibliography.

9. Holmes puts this strongly when at the end of her book she remarks that in France 'Women's otherness has been celebrated, but the rhetoric of adoration has merely euphemized contempt' (*French Women's Writing*, 278).

10. The authors are Sophie Gay and Delphine de Girardin: see his *Portraits contemporains* (Paris: Charpentier, 1874), 22; *Portraits et souvenirs littéraires* (Paris: Michel Lévy, 1875), 96 (essays written in, respectively, 1852 and 1857).

11. Julie de Krüdener, *Valérie* (Paris: Quantin, 1878), 7–9, 36–7, 324. The preface is extracted from L.-G. Michaud's *Biographie universelle* (1843–61).

12. Baudelaire and one or two other male writers had already begun on this, but most of the onslaughts were posthumous. D. Dickenson gives details in *George Sand: A Brave Man – The Most Womanly Woman* (Oxford: Berg, 1988).

13. Women were just as inclined as men to gather the female writers of France together. Among those who do so to admire them are George Eliot (quoted in Sartori and Zimmerman, *French Women Writers*, xv) and Stéphanie de Genlis, *De l'influence des femmes sur la littérature française comme protectrices des lettres et comme auteurs* (Paris: Maradan, 1811). For others (and for eighteenth-century precedents), see Larnac, *Histoire de la littérature féminine*, 134–5, 166–7.

14. C.-A. Sainte-Beuve, *Portraits de femmes* (1844) (Paris: Didier, 1852), I. (The preface is 1845.) For Sainte-Beuve's 'muffling' of earlier women writers, see A. Jones and N. Vickers, 'Canon, rule, and the Restoration Renaissance', in DeJean and Miller (eds.), *Displacements*, 3–21.

15. 'Les femmes écrivent, écrivent avec une rapidité débordante; leur cœur bavarde à la rame . . . leur style traîne et ondoie comme leurs vêtements.' C. Baudelaire, 'Etudes sur Poe', in *Œuvres complètes* (Paris: Gallimard, 1975–6, 2 vols.), II 247–337 (282–3).

16. See Larnac, *Histoire de la littérature féminine*, 220–1, for this and similarly sexist late nineteenth-century works; also Cohen for comments on an early twentieth-century 'study' which simply pretended women's novels of the middle of the century did not exist: 'Women and fiction', 67.

17. Larnac, *Histoire de la littérature féminine*, 219.

18. Ibid., 197, 201, 208.

19. A. Lagarde et L. Michard, *XIXe Siècle: Les grands auteurs français du programme* (Paris: Bordas, 1963).

20. Although the literacy of both men and women of the lower classes increased during the nineteenth century, it rose more strikingly among women in the first half of the century. In 1801, 28 per cent of French women over the age of fourteen were literate; by the early 1850s, 52 per cent of women were. Men's literacy increased in the same period from 50 to 68 per cent. (The figures are higher for Paris: by 1848, 87 per cent of working-class Parisian men and 79 per cent of working-class Parisian women were literate.) By 1901, the national figures were 96 per cent (men), 94 per cent (women). See James Smith Allen, *Popular French Romanticism: Authors, Readers and Books in the Nineteenth Century* (Syracuse University Press, 1981), 155, 161; and his *In the Public Eye: A History of Reading in Modern France, 1800–1940* (Princeton University Press, 1991), table A7. See also D. Coward, 'Popular fiction in the nineteenth century', in Unwin (ed.), *Cambridge Companion*, 73–92.

21. It is for this reason that I mention male connections in Appendix B,

'Biobibliographies'. Critics such as Waller have begun to explore the interchanges; see also D. Kadish, *Politicizing Gender: Narrative Strategies in the Aftermath of the French Revolution* (New Brunswick: Rutgers University Press, 1991); D. Kelly, *Fictional Genders: Role and Representation in Nineteenth-Century French Narrative* (Lincoln: University of Nebraska Press, 1989).

22. C. Goldberg Moses, *French Feminism in the Nineteenth Century* (Albany: State University of New York Press, 1984), xii; Moses continues: 'feminists published newspapers, wrote letters, kept diaries, wrote memoirs, and often published book-length statements'. Here and elsewhere I use the inclusive term 'life-writing' to cover autobiography, memoirs, private diaries and biographies.

23. *Souvenirs d'une fille du peuple ou la Saint-simonienne en Egypte* (1866) (Paris: Maspero, 1978), 253.

24. Among the rare critics who briefly mention humour in these writers are Cohen (on Ségur's satire, 'Women and fiction', 67) and J.-L. Vissière, in his preface to D. de Girardin, *Chroniques parisiennes 1836–1848* (Paris: des femmes, 1986), 32, 34.

25. In his preface to Gay's *Laure d'Estell* (1802) (Paris: Michel Lévy, 1864), xxi.

26. *Léonie de Montbreuse* (1813) (Paris: Michel Lévy, 1871), 7.

27. Delphine de Girardin, *Œuvres complètes* (Paris: Plon, 1860–61, 6 vols.), VI 22.

28. *Pérégrinations d'une paria* (1838) (Paris: Maspero, 1979), 43.

29. 'Eve contre Dumas fils', in *Eve dans l'humanité* (a later collection of speeches and essays) (Paris: Sauvaitre, 1891), 116–48 (116).

30. *Journal de Marie Bashkirtseff* (1887) (Paris: Charpentier, 1890, 2 vols.), I 6.

31. *Voyage d'une femme au Spitzberg* (1854) (Paris: Félin, 1992), 119–20.

2 CONDITIONS FOR WOMEN WRITERS

1. O. Hufton, in her magisterial history of Western European women, devotes a chapter to women writers and the changing attitudes they encountered from 1500 to 1800: 'Corresponding Gentlewomen, Shameless Scribblers, Drudges of the Pen and the Emergence of the Critic', *The Prospect Before Her: A History of Women in Western Europe, 1500–1800* (London: HarperCollins, 1995), 419–57.

2. See H. Tassé, *Salons français du XIXe siècle* (Montreal: no publisher, 1952).

3. Hufton points out how socially diverse women writers had become by the end of the eighteenth century: *Prospect Before Her*, 442. See also the *Bloomsbury Guide*, 349. For Sand's social customs, see Sartori and Zimmerman, *French Women Writers*, xxi, and Dickenson, *George Sand*, 25.

4. *Les Salons de Paris, foyers éteints* (Paris: Tardieu, 1858). See also Sartori and Zimmerman, *French Women Writers*, for useful comments on the salons, xviii–xxi.

5. Moses, *French Feminism*, 4, 241 n.18; Hufton, *Prospect Before Her*, 428–33.
6. M. Perrot, 'Stepping out', in G. Fraisse and M. Perrot (eds.), *A History of Women in the West: Emerging Feminism from Revolution to World War* (Cambridge, MA: Belknap, 1993), 449–81 (481); Larnac, *Histoire de la littérature féminine*, 162. Recent histories have given us new information about the 'start–stop' progress of feminism in nineteenth-century France, as well as snapshot insights into the quality of women's lives during this politically changeable period. See particularly the important works by Moses and by Fraisse and Perrot (eds.); also M. Albistur and D. Armogathe, *Histoire du féminisme français* (Paris: des femmes, 1977), vol. II; Aron's preface in Aron (ed.), *Misérable et glorieuse*; J. Wallach Scott, *Gender and the Politics of History* (New York: Columbia University Press, 1988). A number of literary-critical works also give good summaries of the main political and legal problems facing French women during the nineteenth century: e.g. R. Bellet (ed.), *La Femme au XIXe siècle: Littérature et idéologie* (Presses Universitaires de Lyon, 1979), Part I; Birkett and Hughes, 'Eighteenth- and nineteenth-century France', 54–60; Holmes, *French Women's Writing*, ix, 3–25. (Holmes points out that the 'start–stop' character of French feminism continued into the twentieth century: ibid., 111.)
7. Moses, *French Feminism*, 18–19 (she reproduces the pertinent articles of the Code, 244–5); clear summaries of the new legal inequalities are also given in C. Goldberg Moses and L. Wahl Rabine, *Feminism, Socialism, and French Romanticism* (Bloomington: Indiana University Press, 1993), 12, 37.
8. Moses, *French Feminism*, 229.
9. I use the term 'French women writers' in this book to cover those publishing and living in France. (The very rare exceptions are such cases as the exiled Staël.) A few were of non-French birth, but moved to France at a young age and were thoroughly immersed in its society and culture (e.g. Ségur and Bashkirtseff, both from Russia).
10. David Perkins discusses the problems of historical and literary contextualization in *Is Literary History Possible?* (Baltimore: Johns Hopkins University Press, 1993); while Toril Moi points out that much feminist literary criticism has been beset by an overly biographical approach, or by 'naive realism' (*Textual/Sexual Politics*, London: Routledge, 1985, e.g. 42–5). See also Johnson's apt comments on 'biographical' feminist criticism in 'Gender and poetry', 176, 179 n.7.
11. Moses, *French Feminism*, 167.
12. Babois, *Œuvres* (n.p.: Nepveu, 1828), 138.
13. Larnac, *Histoire de la littérature féminine*, 195n.
14. See her mother's 'Mémoires et notices sur la vie d'Elisa Mercœur', in E. Mercœur, *Œuvres complètes* (Paris: Mme Veuve Mercœur, Pommeret et Guénot, 1843, 3 vols.), I i–clxxxviii (xxxix, lxxvii). Even if her mother is exaggerating, other evidence shows that Elisa was markedly in advance of her years: see her entry in the *Bloomsbury Guide*.

15. Voilquin, *Souvenirs*, 65; H. de La Tour du Pin, *Journal d'une femme de cinquante ans* (Paris: Chapelot, 1920, 2 vols.), II 132, 192.

16. Beizer gives names and details: *Ventriloquized Bodies*, 56; J. Matlock shows that reading for girls was sometimes blamed for, or identified with, hysteria, and describes the hostility often directed against 'reading women', in her *Scenes of Seduction: Prostitution, Hysteria, and Reading Difference in Nineteenth-Century France* (New York: Columbia University Press, 1994), e.g. 8–9, 199, 203, 254ff., 268, 354–5.

17. *Les Fauteuils illustres, ou Quarante études littéraires* (Paris: Ducrocq, 1860), 179, 231.

18. Holmes, *French Women's Writing*, 27.

19. Ibid., 14. 'Core' texts and authors such as the *Aeneid* or Homer figure, but on a much narrower scale than in men's writing.

20. Sartori and Zimmerman, *French Women Writers*, 123–4. For a full biography of Desbordes-Valmore, see F. Ambrière, *Le Siècle des Valmore* (Paris: Seuil, 1987, 2 vols.).

21. L. Ackermann, 'Ma vie', in *Œuvres* (Paris: Lemerre, 1885), i–xx (iii–iv).

22. *Bloomsbury Guide*, 459–60.

23. *Mémoires de Louise Michel, écrits par elle-même* (Paris: Maspero, 1976), 64–6, 92.

24. E.g. V. Ancelot, 'A ma fille, Madame Louise Lachaud', dedication in *Théâtre complet* (Paris: Beck, 1848, 4 vols.), I 3–7; Voilquin, *Souvenirs*, 51.

25. This letter is attached to the 1828 British Library copy of her *Œuvres*.

26. A. Soumet and G. Daltenheym (*sic*), *Le Gladiateur* (Paris: Tresse, 1846).

27. See Lloyd (*Land of Lost Content*, 48) and Sartori and Zimmerman (*French Women Writers*, 171) for rather contradictory views of this father–daughter relationship.

28. M.-C. Vallois, *Fictions féminines: Mme de Staël et les voix de la sibylle* (Saratoga: Anma Libri, 1987), 9.

29. This happened with Babois and, we may surmise, La Tour du Pin. See below, 40.

30. The Daubié who was educated by her brother combines feminist with other political concerns in her 450-page *La Femme pauvre au XIXe siècle*, which won first place in an 1858 competition organized by the Academy of Lyon and was published in 1866.

31. See the chapters on Cottin, Desbordes-Valmore and Sand in Sartori and Zimmerman, *French Women Writers*; also Slama, 'Femmes écrivains', 223, for the range of aims these authors had.

32. E. Blémont, 'Littérature étrangère: la poésie en Angleterre et aux Etats-Unis: poétesses anglaises', *La Renaissance littéraire et artistique*, I (1872), 146–7 (146).

33. For example, Desbordes-Valmore and Tastu received 'pensions' (Sartori and Zimmerman, *French Women Writers*, 129; Mercœur, *Œuvres complètes*, 293 n.). My Appendix B shows how many prize-winners there were. To pick out only two honours: in 1885 Daniel Lesueur (Jeanne

Lapauze) was given the 'Grand Prix de Poésie' of the Académie Française (*Poésies*, Paris: Lemerre, 1896), 87; while Henry Gréville (Alice Durand-Gréville) was the first woman to be awarded the Légion d'Honneur for literature, in 1899 (Cohen, 'Women and fiction', 68).

34. *Bloomsbury Guide*, 566.
35. Genlis appears in the thinnest of disguises in Gay's *Laure d'Estell* as the insufferable Mme de Gercourt; for Colet, see *Lui: roman contemporain* (Paris: Calmann-Lévy, 1880), vi; for Sand and Stern, see Sartori and Zimmerman, *French Women Writers*, 2, and P. Gsell (ed.), *Mémoires de Madame Judith* (Paris: Tallandier, 1911), 209–10; Bashkirtseff, *Journal*, 1 392; for Adam and d'Héricourt, see Moses, *French Feminism*, 269 n.43.
36. See Ancelot, *Salons*, 35–65.
37. Desbordes-Valmore, *Poésies* (Paris: Gallimard, 1983), 244.
38. Stern told Louise Ackermann that one of her characters was based on Lammenais: *Nélida* (Paris: Calmann-Lévy, 1987), 272 n.34; Ackermann in turn dedicated two poems to Stern: *Œuvres*, 49–51, 102.
39. See R. Little's edition of *Ourika* (University of Exeter Press, 1993), Annexes A, B.
40. 'A ma muse (Le jour de la fête de madame Dufrénoy): Sur la mort de madame Dufrénoy', *Poésies* (Paris, Didier, 1838), 154–6.
41. *Les Algériennes* and *Poésies diverses* (Paris: Charles Mary, 1831), 121. These words – the epigraph to the epilogue – are a quotation from Amable Tastu: thus the exhortation is itself a 'joint' one.
42. Moses and Rabine, *Feminism*, give extensive illustrations. For other examples of women's acknowledgement or support of each other, see Girardin, 'Napoline', in *Poésies complètes* (Paris: Michel Lévy, 1876), 121; and Marie Krysinska, who dedicated her poem 'Idylle' to Rachilde: *Joies errantes* (Paris: Lemerre, 1894), 55–6.
43. See Beizer, *Ventriloquized Bodies*, 78–9, 130, 158–61. A. Court brings out the inner contradictions with which Lamartine, for example, was apparently struggling: 'Lamartine et Mme Roland', in Bellet (ed.), *La Femme au XIXe siècle*, 55–82.
44. Holmes, *French Women Writers*, x. Moi stresses, in the context of feminist criticism, how untenable is the idea that we are mediated through and through by a uniform culture (*Textual/Sexual Politics*, e.g. 26–31).

3 OVERVIEW, 1800–1829

1. Dated *c*. 1799. See 'Eroticism and Pornography' in P. France (ed.), *The New Oxford Companion to Literature in French* (Oxford University Press, 1995).
2. *Les Dangers d'un mariage forcé* (Paris: Ouvrier, an IX).
3. J. DeJean, 'Classical reeducation: decanonizing the feminine', DeJean and Miller (eds.), *Displacements*, 22–36 (24–6).
4. Cohen, 'Women and fiction', 54–5; Waller, *Male Malady*, 24, 111, 115ff.
5. Larnac, *Histoire de la littérature féminine*, 173.

6. Hufton, *Prospect Before Her*, 451–2. For more names and works, see Appendices.
7. See, e.g., Kadish, *Politicizing Gender*, 101, on the 'empowerment' this could entail; and, for points of comparison with predecessors, J. Hinde Stewart, *Gynographs: French Novels by Women of the Late Eighteenth Century* (Lincoln: University of Nebraska Press, 1993).
8. Larnac, *Histoire de la littérature féminine*, 171.
9. Pixerécourt's play is discussed by Peter Brooks in *The Melodramatic Imagination: Balzac, Henry James, Melodrama, and the Mode of Excess* (New York: Columbia University Press, 1985), 24–8, 30. For Cottin, see below, 41–2.

4 'FOREMOTHERS' AND GERMAINE DE STAËL

1. For example, in Krüdener's *Valérie* the protagonist and his beloved read *Clarissa* together (203); this work also figures in Bawr's novel *Raoul, ou l'Enéide* (Paris: Fournier, 1832), 49.
2. S. Gilbert and S. Gubar remark that whereas a male writer looking back to predecessors may feel 'the anxiety of influence', in Bloom's well-known phrase, female ones are more likely to feel an 'anxiety of authorship' and to want predecessors to confirm the twin facts that women can write and have achievements: *The Madwoman in the Attic: The Woman Writer and the Nineteenth-Century Literary Imagination* (New Haven: Yale University Press, 1984), 45ff.
3. *Catherine II et ses filles d'honneur* (Paris: Dentu, 1847), iv.
4. L. Colet, *Poésies complètes* (Paris: Gosselin, 1844), 7; Ancelot, *Madame Roland*, in *Théâtre complet*, III 104.
5. Cited as a continuing inspiration by, e.g., Girardin in her 1825 poem 'La Vision', *Poésies*, 174–9; by Blanchecotte in 'Blanche', *Rêves et réalités* (1855) (Paris: Ledoyen, 1856), 6; by d'Altenheym in *Les Marguerites de France* (itself an account of France's illustrious women) (Paris: Vermot, 1858), 7; by Tastu ('Lyon en 1793'), 79; by Voilquin, *Souvenirs*, 124; and by Daniel Stern in *Nélida*, 219–20. Sand wrote a novel about an 'unknown Joan of Arc': *Jeanne* (1844).
6. See *Joan of Arc: The Image of Female Heroism* (London: Vintage, 1991), especially 255ff.; also R. Gildea, *The Past in French History* (New Haven: Yale University Press, 1994), 154–65, for more detail about the varied uses to which left and right have put Joan.
7. *Eve dans l'humanité*, 3. It is clear from the context that Deraismes includes, in 'spiritual', 'mind' as well as 'spirit'. Athene is also cited by Daniel Lesueur, who in 'Prière à Minerve' says the Parthenon is the most beautiful homage any people has presented to its god: 'Visions divines', in *Poésies*, 26. Other women from history and myth cited by these women writers are Lady Jane Grey (e.g. d'Altenheym) and Helen of Troy and Judith (Krysinska).

8. *Le Marquis de Pomenars* (Paris: Ladvocat, 1820), 47.
9. 'Dédicace', *Théâtre complet*, 1 5.
10. Genlis, in her *De l'influence des femmes* (1811), does devote a little space to Lafayette and Riccoboni; but she speaks with forked tongue about the former (vii, 114–34) and gives only three pages to the latter (278–81).
11. R. Winegarten, *Mme de Staël* (Leamington Spa: Berg, 1985), 105.
12. Isbell, *Birth of European Romanticism*, 7.
13. Deliberately so at moments, as Isbell shows: his sub-title is *Truth and Propaganda in Staël's De l'Allemagne*.
14. For details of their reception, see Winegarten, *Mme de Staël*, 58, 65.
15. II 141, 221. (At this time, Staël had influence through Constant.)
16. Sartori and Zimmerman, *French Women Writers*, 188.
17. *Emilie ou la jeune fille auteur: ouvrage dédié aux jeunes personnes* (Paris: Didier, 1854), 333–4. See too Tristan on Staël as one of our 'good authors', *Pérégrinations d'une paria*, 326.
18. *Poésies complètes*, 180–2.
19. 'La Servante', *Le Poème de la femme* (Paris: Perrotin, 1856).
20. *Chroniques parisiennes*, 316–17. See Slama, 'Femmes écrivains', 216, on Corinne as a model in France; for Corinne in England and the US see E. Moers, *Literary Women* (London: Allen, 1977), 172–210.
21. Bashkirtseff, *Journal*, 1 208; *Hellé* (Paris: Nelson and Calmann-Lévy, n.d.), 45.
22. They derive to some extent from late eighteenth-century women activists, but it is their recasting in *Delphine* that sets the literary pattern. See B. Didier, *Ecrire la Révolution: 1789–99* (Paris: Presses Universitaires de France, 1989), 57–72.
23. *Delphine* (Paris: des femmes, 1981, 2 vols.), II 101–2.
24. Comtesse Dash, *La Duchesse de Lauzun* (Paris: Michel Lévy, 1864), 6.
25. 'Napoline', *Poésies complètes*, 92–145.
26. Throughout this book, for the sake of convenience I make a perhaps artificial distinction between 'discursive' works (e.g. essays and works of argument) and 'imaginative' works or life-writing.
27. Vallois and Waller (e.g.) bring out her technical innovativeness in this.

5 WRITING ABOUT HISTORY: HENRIETTE DE LA TOUR DU PIN

1. A similar gap exists between composition and publication for many other women memoir-writers: e.g. Claire de Rémusat, who died in 1821 but whose memoirs were published only in 1880.
2. M. Crosland, in the introduction to the English translation *Memoirs of Madame de La Tour du Pin* by F. Harcourt (London: Century, 1985), 1, 5. Harcourt's translation, which I use, has helpful historical notes.
3. *L'Artémise française, ou les heureux effets de la Paix* (Paris: Fages, an IX [1801]).

4. *Parysatis* (Paris: Lemerre, 1890). Coward brings out well the central role of the popularizing historical novel throughout the century ('Popular fiction', e.g. 76, 79, 80, 82).

5. *Volontaire: 1792–93* (Paris: Colin, n.d.).

6. *Valérie*, 299.

7. Vallois argues, indeed, that the revolutionary situation is the 'point de départ' of the whole novel (*Fictions féminines*, 63). Other recent critics have emphasised the centrality of history in Staël's fictional and non-fictional works: e.g. Ambrière, *Précis de littérature française*, 40; Kadish, *Politicizing Gender*, 20, 22, 93ff.

8. In his 'Notice' to Claire de Duras, *Ourika* (Paris: Librairie des Biblio-philes, 1878), i.

9. 'In the Hôtel de la Mole', *Mimesis* (Princeton University Press, 1971), 454–92. R. Little stresses strongly that 'historical realism' is part of Duras's intentions, in the introduction and appendices to his edition of the work: viii, ix, 37, 41, 47. For the French debates about the slave trade that to some degree inspired Duras's work, see, e.g., the introduction by J. DeJean and M. Waller to J. DeJean (ed.), *Ourika* (New York: MLA, 1994), ix–xi.

10. Birkett and Hughes comment that 'Bridging the gap between history and fiction, autobiography provided a form in which women could write themselves into the historical record' ('Eighteenth- and nineteenth-century France', 59); see too E. Cantlie, 'Women's Memoirs in Early Nineteenth-Century France' (PhD thesis, University of Glasgow, 1999). Slama discusses women's contributions to the writing of history in the nineteenth century, the fact that they now wanted to 'bear witness' – and the misogynist Barbey d'Aurevilly's specific hostility to this activity ('Femmes écrivains', 218, 221, 222, 225). For a selection of other historical works by women of the period, see under 'Ideas', Appendix A; also L. Adler, 'Flora, Pauline et les autres', in Aron (ed.), *Misérable et glorieuse*, 191–209 (202).

11. See too, e.g., I 148–9, for La Tour du Pin's interest in the detail of clothes and furnishings; she also provides hard information about the family finances, down to actual figures (e.g. II 134–7). Cohen and Schor are often reluctant to read nineteenth-century French female novelists as 'realists' (see Cohen, 'Women and fiction', 56, 59–60, 64, 66); however, Holmes (among others) remarks that 'realism' is not an exclusively masculine domain (*French Women Writers*, 247); and, what-ever the arguments about the novel, the material I have surveyed suggests that in many spheres these writers can be interpreted as 'realists'.

12. E.g. I 29–31, II 369–70.

13. *Consuelo/La Comtesse de Rudolstadt* (Grenoble: Aurore, 1991, 3 vols.), I 207.

14. *Chroniques parisiennes*, 341.

15. In the preface to *Marie, ou trois époques*, in *Théâtre complet*, 1 12.
16. *Idées anti-proudhoniennes sur l'amour, la femme et le mariage* (Paris: Alphonse Taride, 1858), 87–8. See Holmes on the dubious benefits of the 'miraculée', after Pierre Bourdieu: *French Women Writers*, 28.
17. A full account is given in the preface by La Tour du Pin's great-grandson (1 5–32).

6 MAD MATRIARCHS AND OTHER FAMILY MEMBERS: SOPHIE COTTIN

1. 1 22, 34–8, 67–70.
2. A number of critics have discussed women's fictional and auto-biographical representation of family members, some with particular reference to French women's writing. Cohen outlines the clash between family loyalties and tyrannical parents' or relatives' wishes in early nineteenth-century fiction ('Women and fiction', 55, 57). Holmes talks of the creation, during both the nineteenth and the twentieth centuries, of 'good' mothers as well as those of a kind to make daughters fearful for their own future (*French Women Writers*, 251, 268; see also 228). Lloyd speaks of the 'visceral intensity' of the mother–daughter relationship in Desbordes-Valmore (*Land of Lost Content*, 93). Frank, drawing on recent theoretical work as well as on Klein, makes useful distinctions between 'good' and 'bad' mothers (*Mechanical Song*, e.g. 40–3). M. Maclean, in *The Name of the Mother: Writing Illegitimacy* (London: Routledge, 1994) discusses 'myth-making' focused on mothers; following M. Hirsch, she looks at the 'matricide in effigy common in the fiction of nineteenth- and early twentieth-century women writers who needed to achieve personal liberation from the law of the Father', and at 'the well-known problem of maternal reinforcement of that law' – co-existing, however, with devotion to one's own mother, a devotion evinced by many nineteenth-century French women writers (40–1). See Hirsch's *The Mother/Daughter Plot: Narrative, Psychoanalysis, Feminism* (Bloomington: Indiana University Press, 1989).
3. 'Mme Cottin était déclarée le premier écrivain de l'époque': *Les Misérables* (Paris: Gallimard, 1951), 123–4.
4. Sartori and Zimmerman, *French Women Writers*, 90. The last French edition of *Amélie Mansfield* was published in 1858; of *Elisabeth*, in 1896.
5. *Elisabeth ou les exilés de Sibérie* (Paris: Garnery, 1820).
6. *Amélie Mansfield* (Paris: Garnery, 1820, 3 vols.).
7. Many were intended especially for children and adolescents (for example, the moralizing tales of Pauline Guizot, which had titles like *Les Enfants: Contes à l'usage de la jeunesse* [1812] and were still being reissued into the mid-century), but the moral imperative was also there in such adults' works as Montanclos's turn-of-century play *La Bonne Maîtresse* (published 1803).

8. See, e.g., Vallois, *Fictions féminines*, 59–60.
9. *Eve*, 118; P. Craven, *Réminiscences: souvenirs d'Angleterre et d'Italie* (Paris: Didier, 1879), 31n. Voilquin also records the double influence of mother and father on her (e.g. 61, 74–5, 143–4); see Moses and Rabine on this (*Feminism*, e.g. 64, 69, 113, 125–38).
10. Niboyet, *Catherine II*, vi; T. Bentzon, *Yette: Histoire d'une jeune Créole* (Morne-Rouge, Martinique: Horizons Caraïbes, 1977), 383.
11. *Les Maîtres Sonneurs* (1853) (Paris: Gallimard, 1979), 327, 331. Adam expresses similar reservations (see Moses, *French Feminism*, 165).
12. Ibid., e.g. 134, 232.
13. For arranged marriage as a theme in eighteenth-century novels, see Stewart, *Gynographs*. Characters also point out with indignation the extreme youth of some of the brides (Duras, *Edouard*, 47; Krüdener, *Valérie*, 207).
14. Kadish discusses the presentation of both inimical and 'empowering' mothers in this novel: *Politicizing Gender*, 89–101.
15. I 17, 43, 67, 71–2; II 169; III 175, 199.
16. In 'Les Songes', *Poésies diverses*, 81–91.
17. Gréville, *Les Koumiassine* (Paris: Plon, 1878, 2 vols.).
18. In, e.g., Félicie de Choiseul-Meuse's *Julie ou j'ai sauvé ma rose* (Hamburg and Paris: chez les marchands de nouveautés, 1807, 2 vols.), I 13–25. Others later in the century occur in Colet's *Poème de la femme*, 7, and d'Aunet's *Jane Osborn* (London: Institute of Romance Studies, 1994), 15, 16.
19. *Amélie Mansfield*, III 155; *Elisabeth*, 161.
20. *L'Ecolier, ou Raoul et Victor* (Paris: Didier, 1845, 2 vols.), I 7.
21. In, respectively, d'Altenheym and Soumet's *Le Gladiateur*, 249; Colet's *Lui*, 123; Alida de Savignac's *La Jeune Propriétaire ou l'art de vivre à la campagne* (1837) (Paris: Martial Ardant, 1848); Stern's *Nélida*, 176; Sand's *Les Maîtres Sonneurs*, 253; and Bentzon's *Yette*, 282–3, 361.
22. *Pérégrinations d'une paria*, 302. Rabine, amongst others, points to the presentation in certain women writers of 'good fathers' and the desirability of reinstating the father as a model in feminist theory. She discusses both fathers and mothers in her 'Feminist texts and feminine subjects', and gives useful suggestions for further reading on this subject: Moses and Rabine, *Feminism*, 85–144 (especially 85–7, 143–4, 144 n.92).
23. See also her 'Tristesse' (87); 'Retour dans une église' (221).
24. Depictions of 'patriarchy' extend also to women's portrayal of powerful contemporary males. Here, it would be interesting to explore the title 'Father' given to the Saint-Simonian leader Prosper Enfantin, and the correspondence of his female followers, in which other family imagery follows in the wake of the main paternal one. (See the letters reproduced (in translation) in Moses and Rabine, *Feminism*, 218–81.) Napoleon was treated with still more fascination by women than by men

writers of the century, even into its last three decades. See, e.g., La Tour du Pin, II 247ff.; Belfort, *L'Artémise francaise*, 17, 29; Mercœur, *Œuvres complètes*, I 277–8; Girardin's 'Chant ossianique sur la mort de Napoléon', *Poésies complètes*, 346–7; Ancelot, *Marie, ou trois époques*, in *Théâtre complet*, I 20; Gyp, *Autour du Mariage* (Paris: Calmann-Levy, n.d.), 87.

25. See also Girardin's 1824 calque on *René*, 'La Confession d'Amélie', *Poésies complètes*, 71–3.

26. Pert, *Le Frère* (Paris: Simonis Empis, 1896).

27. See also Gay's 1802 *Laure d'Estell* (Paris: Michel Lévy, 1864), in which an otherwise feckless brother, Frédéric, is loyal to his sister Caroline depite the scandal she has occasioned by running off with an abbé.

28. Genlis, *Mademoiselle de Clermont* (Paris: Autrement, 1994), 42; author's ellipses. See too Genlis's educational works, in which, modifying Rousseau's stance in *Emile*, she argues for girls' education: Hufton, *Prospect Before Her*, 454; *Bloomsbury Guide*, 573. Kadish links the titillatory and the political when she writes: 'Sibling incest is the chief vehicle for bringing together and reconciling symbolically the familial and political oppositions between the patriarchical and monarchical, on the one hand, and the feminine and republican solutions on the other. Brothers and sisters . . . stand in a middle ground between patriarchy and revolution' (*Politicizing Gender*, 67).

7 RANK AND RACE: CLAIRE DE DURAS

1. *Amélie Mansfield*, I 9.

2. In, respectively, *Léonie de Montbreuse*; *Mademoiselle de Clermont*, 31, 49. Female dramatists of the period also base plots on the premiss that money is less important than love, or at least try to smooth away problems caused by unequal wealth: such are Marie-Emilie de Montanclos in her turn-of-the-century *Alison et Sylvain, ou les habitans de Vaucluse* (Paris: Barba, 1803), and Bawr in her 1811 *Le Double Stratagème* (Paris: Barba, 1813) and her 1813 *La Suite d'un bal masqué* (Paris: Vente, 1813).

3. In his 'Notice' to Gay's *Laure d'Estell* (xiii).

4. *Ourika*, for example, was re-edited no fewer than three times between 1993 and 1994 (by R. Little; D. Kadish and F. Massardier-Kenny; Joan DeJean: for details and reviews, see *French Studies* XLVIII [1994], 336–7; XLIX [1995], 460–1; L [1996], 206–7); and again a few years later by Little, in an amplified version and using a more authentic text (University of Exeter Press, 1998).

5. Succinct biographies are provided in Sartori and Zimmerman, *French Women Writers*, 153–60, and in the introduction to D. Virieux (ed.), *Olivier ou le secret* (the first proper establishment of the text itself) (Paris: Corti, 1971).

6. For the following facts, see S. Travers, *Catalogue of Nineteenth-Century French Theatrical Parodies* (New York: King's Crown, 1941), 105–6, 39.

7. See the 'Notice' to *Valérie*, and the essay on Krüdener in Sartori and Zimmerman, *French Women Writers*, for her bold self-publicity; Sainte-Beuve cites the parodic sequel to *Valérie* by the prince de Ligne (in which Gustave, dead of a broken heart, comes back to life) in *Portraits de femmes*, 389–90. Among other women authors parodied, according to Travers's list, were Ancelot, Sand, Girardin, Gautier and Gyp.

8. Information about her unpublished works can be found in J. DeJean (ed.), *Ourika*, xxiii; Little's 1993 edition, 34. Virieux, in her excellent edition of *Olivier*, gives full details of the reception of all three of Duras's novels, including hostile articles in the press (see particularly 34ff.).

9. Editions used are: *Ourika* (Paris: Librairie des Bibliophiles, 1878); *Edouard* (Paris: Mercure de France, 1983); *Olivier*, the 1971 Virieux edition.

10. In *Le Nègre romantique: personnage littéraire et obsession collective* (Paris: Payot, 1973), 224.

11. In agreement with such a proposition, either explicitly or implicitly, are C. Bertrand-Jennings (in 'Condition féminine et impuissance sociale: les romans de la duchesse de Duras', *Romantisme* 63 [1989], 39–50); Kadish (*Politicizing Gender*) and Kelly (*Fictional Genders*), who argue throughout their books that gender is an analogy and that woman 'equals' lower class; Slama, who writes that some women writers, at least, grasped the relationship between oppression of sex and class and the problem of power ('Femmes écrivains', 237); and D. Kadish and F. Massardier-Kenny (eds.), *Translating Slavery: Gender and Race in French Women's Writing, 1783–1823* (Kent State University Press, 1994), 2–5, 14, 35, 51. See below, 155–6, for predecessors and successors. Little voices serious doubts about such interpretations, but ends with the following quotation from John Fowles (the novelist, and a distinguished translator of *Ourika*): '[*Ourika*] goes just as well for any intelligent member of a despised minority in a jealous and blind majority culture' (1993 edition, 55, 59–62, 67).

12. Again, see Little's editions. He, and DeJean and Waller ('Introduction' to *Ourika*), point out how much more original and individualized is Duras's black character than those of previous French writers (precedents had been created by Olympe de Gouges [1755–93] and Staël).

13. Moses and Rabine remark that in the 1820s and early 30s, the meaning of 'class' was still very much in flux; thus 'low rank' could be a relatively all-embracing concept (*Feminism*, 71).

14. See Emma Wilson, *Sexuality and the Reading Encounter* (Oxford: Clarendon, 1996).

15. *Poésies*, 63–4.

16. The noun 'vers' can mean either 'worms' or 'line/s of poetry'.

17. Coward brings out the two sides well: 'Popular fiction', 77, 80–1, 85–6.

18. For the former, see, e.g., Sand's 1845 *Meunier d'Angibault*, Stern's 1846

Nélida; for the latter, Blanchecotte's narrative poems 'Jobbie' (1854) and 'Maria' (n.d.), in *Rêves et réalités*, 42–82.

19. See Hoffmann, *Nègre romantique*, for similarly ambivalent nineteenth-century male writers.

20. In Ségalas's 1831 *Les Algériennes*, the 'Africans' are, quite simply, the enemy: 66.

21. *Pérégrinations*, e.g. 29, 46, 268; Colet, 'La religieuse', in *Poème de la femme*, 114–15; Voilquin, *Souvenirs*, 233; Bentzon, *Yette*, e.g. 287–8, 295–7, 333.

22. See bibliography for details of publishers; Girardin, *Poésies complètes*, 54; various of Sand's letters, e.g. that quoted in the P. Reboul edition of *Lélia* (Paris: Garnier, 1960), 340, in which she remarks of someone that he's a Jew who doesn't give something for nothing. In *Un Hiver à Majorque*, she writes that the Jew as money-lender is inexorable but patient, pursuing his ends with a diabolical genius: *Œuvres autobiographiques* (Paris: Gallimard, 1970–1, 2 vols.), II 1158.

23. *Autour du divorce* (Paris: Calmann Lévy, 1893), 341–3. See W. Silverman, *The Notorious Life of Gyp: Right-Wing Anarchist in Fin-de-Siècle France* (Oxford University Press, 1995), for a discussion of Gyp's racism, which sinks to depths reached by no other woman writer of the century.

24. Krysinska, 'Contes', in *Rythmes pittoresques*, 69–74; for her Jewish ancestry, see Maria Szarama-Swolkieniowa, *Maria Krysińska: Poetka francuskiego symbolizmu* (Cracow: Nakładem Uniwersytetu Jagiellońskiego, 1972), 21 n.1.

25. Michel, *Mémoires*, 76–8.

26. Sand, *Un Hiver à Majorque*, in *Œuvres autobiographiques*, II 1103–5, and *Consuelo*, 46; Ségalas, *Les Algériennes*, 39; Voilquin, *Souvenirs*, 320–1; Tristan, *Pérégrinations*, 211, and *Union ouvrière* (Paris: des femmes, 1986), 164. (Even Tristan, however, is not always impeccable on this issue: see Adler, 'Flora', 195.)

27. For 'Ahasvérus', see *Poésies complètes*, 190.

28. See especially Hugo's *Préface de Cromwell*, 1827.

8 THE INVISIBLE WOMEN OF FRENCH THEATRE

1. V. Hallays-Dabot, *Histoire de la censure théâtrale en France* (Paris: Dentu, 1862), 199; F. Hemmings, *Theatre and State in France, 1760–1905* (Cambridge University Press, 1994), 162.

2. S. Bernhardt, *L'Art du théâtre: la voix, le geste, la prononciation* (Paris: Nilsson, 1923); Gsell (ed.), *Mémoires de Madame Judith*. See also F. Ambrière, *Mademoiselle Mars et Marie Dorval* (Paris: Seuil, 1992).

3. English Showalter Jr. gives a good account of eighteenth-century female playwrights and the difficulties (sometimes the obscenities) they faced: 'Writing off the stage: women authors and eighteenth-century theatre', in DeJean and Miller (eds.), *Displacements*, 144–62. See also P. Gethner (ed.), *Femmes dramaturges en France (1650–1750): pièces choisies*

(Paris: Papers on French Seventeenth-Century Literature, 1993). For Sand, see G. Manifold, *George Sand's Theatre Career* (Ann Arbor: UMI Research Press, 1985).

4. C. Beaumont Wicks, *The Parisian Stage: Alphabetical Indexes of Plays and Authors, 1800–1900* (University of Alabama Press, 1950–79, 5 vols. (vol. III with J. Schweitzer).

5. J. de Jomaron (ed.), *Le Théâtre en France*, vol. II: *De la Révolution à nos jours* (Paris: Colin, 1989).

6. Hemmings refers to Sand's theatrical productions, and does at least cite Girardin as 'one of the few distinguished women playwrights of the nineteenth century': *The Theatre Industry in Nineteenth-Century France* (Cambridge University Press: 1993), 251.

7. Hemmings, *Theatre Industry*, 37–8, 258–9, 177.

8. Hemmings, *Theatre and State*, 162; he describes the ruling as 'difficult to understand'. By the end of the century it was being ignored.

9. Hemmings, *Theatre Industry*, 258–9.

10. See, e.g., Ambrière, *Précis*, 367.

11. The 'precise' figure is 674, but because of the problem of anonymity, this and all following figures must be regarded as approximate; in addition, they refer only to productions in Paris – where, however, the vast majority of nineteenth-century French plays either started or finished. All figures are derived from Wicks. My thanks to Margaret Topping for her compilation of the statistics following in the rest of this chapter.

12. Total plays by, or contributed to by, women:
  1800–29 = 68
  1830–69 = 232
  1870–99 = 374.
Of these, single-author plays:
  1800–29 = 48 (70.5%)
  1830–69 = 169 (73%)
  1870–99 = 277 (74%).
I.e. women's plays written in collaboration:
  1800–29 = 20 (29.5%)
  1830–69 = 63 (27%)
  1870–99 = 97 (26%).

13. 'Women's' plays written with collaborators:
  1800–29: 1 collaborator = 19 plays (95% of all plays written collaboratively). 2 collaborators = 1 play (5%)
  1830–69: 1 collaborator = 55 plays (87.5%). 2 collaborators = 7 plays (11%). 3 collaborators = 1 play (1.5%)
  1870–99: 1 collaborator = 71 plays (73%). 2 collaborators = 26 plays (27%).
Proportion of co-authored plays in which the woman is named first of the collaborators:

1800–29: 45%
1830–69: 41%
1870–99: 20.5%.

14. *Theatre Industry*, 247–8.
15. Ibid., 248.
16. Single-author plays by women with only one act:
    1800–29 = 28 plays (58.5% of all single-author plays by women)
    1830–69 = 105 plays (62%)
    1870–99 = 211 plays (76%).
17. Hemmings, *Theatre Industry*, 233, 245–6.
18. I include in 'comedy' and 'vaudeville' the somewhat separate contemporary category 'comédie-vaudeville'.
19. Chabrillan was the married name of Céleste Mogador (see Appendix B). I have not been able to find biographical details for Bellier-Klecker.
20. Showalter, 'Writing off the stage', 161.
21. Proportions of all women's plays (whether single-author or written in collaboration) in the main 'popular' categories:
    1800–29: melodrama, 26.5%; comedy/comedy-vaudeville, 36.5%
    1830–69: comedy/comedy-vaudeville/vaudeville, 61.5%
    1870–99: comedy/vaudeville, 40%.
22. Proportion of women's plays (both single-author and collaborative) classified as 'drames':
    1800–29: 6%
    1830–69: 13%
    1870–99: 11.5%.
23. Hemmings, *Theatre Industry*, 252.
24. Ibid., 243–5, 249, 255.
25. Ibid., 135–48, 154–7, 171, 204.
26. A. de Bawr, *Mes souvenirs* (Paris: Passard, 1853), 138–9.
27. Bernhardt, *L'Art du théâtre*, 140–4; *Mémoires de Madame Judith*, 281–4. See M. Maclean, *Name of the Mother*, 53–7, for further details of life in the theatre, including the high incidence of illegitimate births and 'casting-couch' pregnancies.
28. Hemmings, *Theatre Industry*, e.g. 85, 88, 96–9, 259, 271–2.
29.
> L'Auteur d'un aussi faible Ouvrage,
> Tremble à présent pour le succès.
> Devrait-il manquer de courage,
> En chantant les braves Français?
> Ah! d'une critique sévère,
> Gardez-vous de lancer les traits:
> Ne lui déclarez pas la guerre,
> Au moment où il chante la paix.

I have not been able to find biographical details for Mme Belfort (no doubt a member of the acting family Belfort, which seems to have flourished in the late eighteenth and early nineteenth centuries).
30. Bawr, *Mes Souvenirs*, 250–1, 254–5.

31. *Chroniques parisiennes*, 198.
32. The following details are in her own and her mother's accounts: *Œuvres complètes*, I lxiv–lxxxv, clxxxi–ii, and 'Détails sur la lecture de ma tragédie au Théâtre-Français' (i.e. the Comédie Française), I 425–32.
33. This is *Catherine ou la belle fermière*, a highly successful three-act comedy first performed in 1797. It was written by Amélie Candeille, an actress/dramatist.
34. For Joanny, see Mercœur, *Œuvres complètes*, I 427; also Hemmings, *Theatre Industry*, 104–5.
35. *Théâtre complet*, I 6.
36. *Le Double Stratagème* (Paris: Barba, 1813).
37. *A bon chat bon rat* (Paris: Amyot, 1861), 24.
38. *Retour à ma femme* (Paris: Amyot, 1862).
39. Hemmings, *Theatre and State*, 162.
40. *L'Aveu* (Paris: Ollendorf, 1888).

9 OVERVIEW, 1830–1869

1. One of Girardin's dramatic characters remarks at a key moment that she is not what she seems to be, 'just as in melodrama' (*Lady Tartuffe*, in *Œuvres complètes*, VI 316); while a heroine of Deraismes's rejects 'sensibility' on the grounds that it is a means for men to exploit women – whom they label as always 'sensitive' ('sensibles': *Retour à ma femme*, 32).
2. *Dieu pardonne, ou les deux frères* (Paris: Rigaud, n.d.).
3. Thus Stern in *Nélida* (170–1) and Sand in the opening chapters of *Consuelo*.
4. *Clémentine* (Paris: Hachette, 1861), 1.
5. In *Valérie, ou la jeune artiste* (Brussels: Hauman and Cattoir, 1837), 103ff.
6. One such is Léonie d'Aunet; see her *Voyage d'une femme au Spitzberg*, e.g. 32, 130.
7. *Union ouvrière*, 263–4.
8. 'La Contradiction créatrice: quelques remarques sur la genèse d'*Un Cœur simple*', in *Imagination and Language: Collected Essays on Constant, Baudelaire, Nerval and Flaubert* (Cambridge University Press, 1981), 437–60.
9. See F. Steegmuller and B. Bray (trs. and ed.), *Flaubert–Sand: The Correspondence* (London: Harvill, 1993), xi–xii, for a brief discussion of this.
10. Dickenson, *George Sand*, 129.

10 GEORGE SAND, PRESIDING GENIUS

1. See Dickenson's chapter 'The extreme conventionality of the other sex' (*George Sand*, 142–76) for a clear synopsis of Sand's favourable recep-

tion. For full accounts of Sand's intellectual formation and life, see Didier, *George Sand écrivain*, and B. Jack, *George Sand: A Woman's Life Writ Large* (London: Chatto & Windus, 1999).

2. *Journal d'un voyageur pendant la guerre* and *Flamarande* respectively.

3. Edited by Lubin over a twenty-seven year period; reviewed with exemplary appreciativeness by L. J. Austin in *French Studies*.

4. Girardin, *Chroniques parisiennes*, 448; Voilquin, *Souvenirs*, 180, 188.

5. *Un divorce* (Paris: Hetzel, 1872), 325.

6. In her 1896 *Poésies*, 53–60.

7. M. Maclean expresses her reservations in similarly strong language: see *Name of the Mother*, e.g. 74, 78–80.

8. Ibid., 104–5.

9. Ibid., 78–9, and Slama, 'Femmes écrivains', 224.

10. Kadish and Massardier-Kenny define their own stance on 'ambivalent' writers through Raymond Williams's *Marxism and Literature* (1977), stressing with him that one should not overlook the importance of works and ideas which, 'while clearly affected by hegemonic limits and pressures, are at least in part significant breaks beyond them', and which in their 'most active elements' come through as independent and original (*Translating Slavery*, 91).

11. *Poésies complètes*, 216–17, 166–7.

12. *Voyage d'une femme au Spitzberg*, e.g. 53, 91, 109, 114. Tristan similarly, although humane about her pock-marked cousin and outraged by men's attitude to her (*Pérégrinations*, 132), is elsewhere ambivalent about women's looks.

13. *Corinne ou l'Italie* (Paris: des femmes, 1979, 2 vols.), I 43; *Consuelo*, I 77–9.

14. *La Petite Fadette* (Paris: Garnier Flammarion, 1967), 138, 140.

15. *Questions d'art et de littérature* (ed. D. Colwell) (Egham: Runnymede Books, 1992), v, 8–9.

16. *Laide* (Paris: Calmann Lévy, 1878), 26–7.

17. Sir Walter Scott had already initiated the 'regional novel' in Britain; it came rather later in France. See Coward, 'Popular Fiction', 80, 86, for an outline of its development during Sand's lifetime and after, a development in which Sand was central.

18. *François le champi* (Paris: Gallimard, 1973), 90; see also 119 for the rearrangement of narratives deemed unsuitable for the young. As is well known, Proust was to take this aspect of the *mise en abyme* even further in his own novel.

19. *Histoire de ma vie*, in *Œuvres autobiographiques*, I 127, 175.

20. *Indiana* (Paris: Gallimard, 1984), 49.

11 CONFIDENCE AND THE WOMAN WRITER: AMABLE TASTU AND SOPHIE ULLIAC-TREMADEURE

1. M. Michaud, 'Notice historique sur l'auteur', in *Elisabeth*, 5–10 (8).
2. F. Marotin, 'Le "Petit Journal" et la femme en 1865', in Bellet (ed.), *La Femme au XIXe siècle*, 97–112 (99).
3. Slama, 'Femmes écrivains', 220–2. Daumier's mid-century 'Bas-bleus' series amusingly but aggressively satirized women writers (Illustrations 1, 6). See Cohen on the controversies the woman writer aroused in this period, and the negative portrayals of her in novels by men ('Women and fiction', 60–1).
4. This is from the letter which accompanied the first edition of *Union ouvrière*, quoted by her in the 1844 preface to the second edition (114).
5. *Poésies complètes*, 92–136. Girardin writes elsewhere of talented girls being unfulfilled or disheartened, in poems of 1834 ('Désenchantement', 323–4) and 1835 ('Aux jeunes filles', 318–20).
6. *Poésies complètes*, 5–16, 143.
7. In *Poésies complètes*, 138; in *Lui*; and in the epigraph to *Le Poème de la femme*: 'Du verbe de la femme sortira son affranchissement' ('From the Word of woman will issue her liberation').
8. In 'Madame Tastu', *Causeries du lundi* (Paris: Garnier, 1852–62, 16 vols.), XVI 1–21.
9. As with La Tour du Pin, there is some chronological overlap between early and middle parts of the century.
10. *Poésies*, 15–21.
11. Ségalas, following Tastu and acknowledging her in an epigraph, also says in the last poem of her *Poésies diverses* that she is 'trying out' her steps near our (male) poets, who are able to breach conventional limits ('ceux-là, franchissant une ligne tracée'); they will have the laurels; all she hopes for in her ephemerality is a look, a smile; etc. (125).
12. *Emilie*, 276–8. Ulliac-Trémadeure makes plentiful use of ellipses and italics in *Emilie*; here and in following quotations, those used are her own.

12 SHAME, EMBARRASSMENT AND SOPHIE'S MISFORTUNES: THE COMTESSE DE SEGUR

1. *Emilie*, 57–62, 111, 118–19, 177–8.
2. Sartori and Zimmerman, *French Women Writers*, xv–xvi, xix–xx. Moses also brings out the ridicule that more generally greeted nineteenth-century women's attempts to break out of their roles: *French Feminism*, e.g. 146, 185, 195 (Sand herself joined in: ibid., 266 n.).
3. For the erection of 'les convenables' into an imperative rule in the nineteenth century, see Aron in *Misérable et glorieuse*, 18. Among other writers of this early period who criticize etiquette, gossips' malice, and

the blunt instrument that is ridicule, are Gay, in *Léonie de Montbreuse*, 189; Krüdener, in *Valérie*, 114.

4. *Chroniques parisiennes*, 255–6.
5. *Théâtre complet*, 1 4.
6. *Nélida*, 45, 52, 73, 158, 160, 169–70, 213, 244; see also Deraismes, *A bon chat bon rat*, 30–1.
7. *Questions d'art et de littérature*, 9–10.
8. *Poème de la femme*, 14–15, 121; *Poésies complètes*, 225–7, 273, 310.
9. *Rêves et réalités*, 139.
10. *Souvenirs*, 104, 109–10, 156, 172, 210–11.
11. Reprinted with one other story by Guizot at the end of Ulliac-Trémadeure's *Valérie*, 163–87.
12. Lloyd, *Land of Lost Content*, 21; see Sartori and Zimmerman, *French Women Writers*, 449. Details of other women who wrote for children are given in the *Bloomsbury Guide*, which however omits the extraordinary success story of Augustine Fouillée; see under G. Bruno, Appendix B.
13. *Les Malheurs de Sophie* (Paris: Gallimard, 1977), 9.
14. 'Embarrassé/e' – which I translate here as 'sheepish' – can mean 'nonplussed' as well as 'embarrassed', but the latter meaning is implicated in the former.
15. *Les Malheurs de Sophie*, 50, 81, 97, 102, 104, 114, 131.
16. Feminists, at least, sometimes identified their situation with that of children (not surprisingly, given women's status as 'minors' in the Code Civil), and were identified as such by misogynists like Barbey (who said that women should be put back in their place like a naughty child who deserves to be whipped): see Moses, *French Feminism*, 70; Slama, 'Femmes écrivains', 223.
17. For points of comparison with more moralizing children's writers, see, e.g., Coward, 'Popular fiction', 86–7, and Marotin ('Petit Journal', 105), who reproduces a highly sentimental newspaper depiction of a sweet little blonde girl adoring a doll like a miniature mother doting on her child.

13 ADVENTURE AND TRAVEL: FLORA TRISTAN AND
LÉONIE D'AUNET

1. Cantlie discusses both this fact, and the presentation of such tales, throughout her 'Women's Memoirs in Early Nineteenth-Century France'.
2. *Poésies*, 65–6. In Choiseul-Meuse's erotic novel *Julie*, the young heroine's freedom to run in the countryside unabashedly equals erotic freedom (1 32–5, 47).
3. *La Prise de Jéricho* (Paris: Garnery, 1820), 196.
4. A view discussed with nuance and a degree of scepticism by, e.g.,

Birkett and Hughes, 'Eighteenth- and nineteenth-century France', 56; Holmes, *French Women's Writing*, 9, 55; Moses, *French Feminism*, 36; Beizer, *Ventriloquized Bodies*, 57; Moses and Rabine, *Feminism*, 29. Also by Aron in *Misérable et glorieuse*, 17; A. Corbin, 'La prostituée', ibid., 41–58 (49); A. Martin-Fugier, 'La maîtresse de maison', ibid., 117–34 (117–20); and Slama, 'Femmes écrivains', 232, 236.

5. Blanchecotte, *Rêves et réalités*, 42–60; Stern, *Nélida*, 5.
6. *Poésies complètes*, 25.
7. In *What Katy Did*, published in the US in the second half of the nineteenth century.
8. See Voilquin's description of the especially unfortunate position of Egyptian women (*Souvenirs*, 315); Ségalas also stresses the relative freedom of French as opposed to Arab women: *Les Algériennes*, 16–22, 48–9.
9. Tristan wrote a novel, *Méphis* (1838), and d'Aunet wrote plays and novels.
10. See, e.g., L. Strumingher, *The Odyssey of Flora Tristan* (New York: Peter Lang, 1988). M. Maclean, amongst others, discusses Tristan's 'mythopoesis', coexisting with her 'remarkable capacity for verbal expression and persuasion' (*Name of the Mother*, 111; see her whole chapter 'The male/female Messiah: Flora Tristan', ibid., 106–25). There were, as I have shown, other sides to Tristan's character than self-aggrandizement.
11. *Union ouvrière*, 320 n.47.
12. W. Mercer gives fuller details in her introduction to the book.
13. *Chroniques parisiennes*, 230–3; see also 406.
14. See J. Charnley, 'La première femme à faire le tour du monde', *French Studies Bulletin* 68 (1998), 13–15.
15. See entry in Appendix B.
16. See also J. Robinson, *Unsuitable for Ladies: An Anthology of Women Travellers* (Oxford University Press, 1995), which shows the scarcity of the phenomenon.
17. Tristan describes the dress of Lima women as more liberating than that of Frenchwomen (*Pérégrinations*, 338, 340); Voilquin (claiming a reluctance which does not carry conviction) wears men's clothes when following a hospital clinic in Egypt (*Souvenirs*, 263); most famously, Sand wore men's clothes in 'normal' life, as did Jane Dieulafoy and the painter Rosa Bonheur (1822–99). Notionally, police permission had to be sought for this.

14 THE JOURNALIST: DELPHINE DE GIRARDIN

1. For futher details, and contemporaries' references, see Sartori and Zimmerman, *French Women Writers*, 188–97; also Ancelot, *Salons de Paris*, 64–5.
2. A little of her fiction has also been republished: see Sartori and Zimmerman, *French Women Writers*, 196.

3. See 'Press' in the *New Oxford Companion*. Allen gives rather lower figures (*In the Public Eye*, Table A3).

4. In her *Œuvres complètes*. The modern edition I use has changed the title to *Chroniques parisiennes* (Paris: des femmes, 1986).

5. Hufton, *Prospect Before Her*, 438–42; Marotin, 'Petit Journal', 100, 112 n.2.

6. Girardin herself had previously written for *La Mode* (*Chroniques parisiennes*, 23); later women wrote for, e.g., *La Renaissance littéraire et artistique*. E. Sullerot gives a full account of French women's journals from 1650 on in her *Histoire de la presse féminine en France, des origines à 1848*; see too her *La Presse féminine* (both Paris: Armand Colin, 1966).

7. Sand, for example, co-founded *La Revue indépendante* and the more local *L'Eclaireur de l'Indre et du Cher* to contribute to the education of the working class. For further information about women's journalism and the feminist press, see particularly Slama ('Femmes écrivains', 216–18, 225) and Moses (who, *inter alia*, points out that the feminist press expanded greatly in the mid-century: *French Feminism*, 37); also Birkett and Hughes, 'Eighteenth- and nineteenth-century France', 58; Ambrière, *Précis*, 278; Moses and Rabine, who quote substantial extracts from feminist newspapers, and describe the female Saint-Simonians' journal, which announced it would publish only articles by women, as 'likely the first consciously separatist women's movement in history' (*Feminism*, 7). Appendices A and B give further information about sporadic or more protracted contributions.

8. Vissière, preface to *Chroniques parisiennes*, 7–8. The earliest feminist newspapers predate Girardin's column, but their growth is certainly contemporaneous with it, or later than it.

9. The debt is obvious in, say, her repetition of the '-rama' joke of *Le Père Goriot* (1834) (*Chroniques parisiennes*, 103); in the 'artist versus press' aspects of her 1839 play *L'Ecole des journalistes*, written as *Illusions perdues* was appearing (1837–43); and in her novel *La Canne de M. de Balzac* (1836). Indeed, Cohen, in a rather extreme statement, singles out Girardin as the only novelist of the mid-century who did not 'steer clear of the polemic and conventions characterising realism' ('Women and fiction', 61).

10. All ellipses and italics are Girardin's, here and in the following quotation.

11. She wrote an almost equally insensitive poem on the same subject in 1837: 'Les Ouvriers de Lyon: aux économistes', *Poésies complètes*, 199–201.

15 FEELING AND POETIC TECHNIQUE: MARCELINE DESBORDES-VALMORE

1. Among authors of song-lyrics were Gay, Girardin, Tastu and later Michel – this last, of rousing political ones. See, for example, Girardin's 'Romance', *Poésies complètes*, 312–13; Tastu's imitations of Moore.

Wicks, *Parisian Stage*, gives the (many) names of those who wrote libretti or operetta scripts.

2. *Lui*, 363; see also *Poème de la femme*, where the 'forme' of an empty-headed orator hides his inanity, as opposed to the words of an inspired sibyl (ii).

3. See A.-M. Thiesse and H. Mathieu, 'The Decline of the Classical Age and the Birth of the Classics', in DeJean and Miller (eds.), *Displacements*, 74–96.

4. Here are the first four lines:

> Viens, c'est l'heure et j'attends; ma légère *nacelle*
> Jette au miroir du lac une image *fidèle*;
> Sur les flots, rafraîchis par les baisers du *soir*,
> On respire un parfum aussi doux que l'*espoir*.   (I 241)

(Come, 'tis the hour, I am waiting; my light boat throws out a faithful image to the mirror of the lake; on the waves, refreshed by the evening's kisses, wafts a scent as gentle as hope.)

5. Elsewhere too Blanchecotte is outstanding at interweaving alliterative patterns: to take one example of many, the first four verses of her 'Chants I' (*Rêves*, 208–9) have dominant sounds giving way to subsidiary ones which in their turn are built up, then give way to others.

6. *Bibliographie du roman érotique au XIXe siècle* (Paris: Fourdrinier, 1930, 2 vols.); see, e.g., I 65.

7. Duras as well as Stendhal may have used its impotent and suicidal Octave as a source.

8. For example, in *Elisabeth*, 39, and *La Prise de Jéricho* ('the wind, playing in the folds of her undulating dress, reveals new charms to Issachar, just behind her', 196).

9. See also Krüdener's *Valérie*, in which the heroine's passionate nature shows through in her singing voice, 'si mélancoliquement tendre!' ('so melancholic in its tenderness!', 205).

10. See especially Waller, *Male Malady*, e.g. 19, 139.

11. F. du Plessix Gray stresses this side of Colet in *Rage and Fire: A Life of Louise Colet: Pioneer Feminist, Literary Star, Flaubert's Muse* (New York: Simon and Schuster, 1994).

12. See also 1–2, 119, 201, 226, 272–3; *Poème de la femme*, 49–50, 121 (the sight of love-making with its 'rapid movements' arouses the nun), 126. Stern too broaches the subject of inhibition and desire in *Nélida* (10–11, 41, 49, 257).

13. *Lui*, 387.

14. Many scholars highlight the particular anxieties women of this period had in talking about female sexuality: it was too dangerous even for the Saint-Simoniennes. See Moses, *French Feminism*, 133, 231; Holmes, *French Women's Writing*, 41, 60; Slama, 'Femmes écrivains', 235; Kelly, *Fictional Genders*, 173; Birkett and Hughes, 'Eighteenth- and nineteenth-century France', 60; and for the pre-history, Hufton, *Prospect Before Her*, 425.

15. Traces remain in *Nélida*, 97, 100; *Consuelo*, 207; Blanchecotte, *Rêves*, 66.
16. *Théâtre complet*, I 317.
17. 'De sa pensée impure il [l'esprit] nous jette l'affront': in 'A ma mère', *Poésies complètes* (227).
18. C. Baudelaire, 'Marceline Desbordes-Valmore', in *Œuvres complètes*, II 145–9. The praise has sexist overtones none the less.
19. Larnac, *Histoire de la littérature féminine*, 200.
20. Among critics who discuss sacrifice and tragedy in women's writing of this century are Holmes, *French Women's Writing*, 269, and Vallois, *Fictions féminines*, 56–9.
21. For examples of 5-syllable lines, see 'La Sincère', 92–3; 7-syllable: 'Souvenir', 52, and 'La Mère qui pleure', 213–14; 11-syllable: 'Rêve intermittent d'une nuit triste', 206.
22. In her essay in DeJean and Miller (eds.), *Displacements*, 168, 170.
23. Not to be explained as simply a dream of death, as Bonnefoy seems to suggest. See his note to this poem, 'Le Mal du pays', in Desbordes-Valmore, *Poésies*, 89–91.
24. 'Son image' (37); 'Souvenir' (52). Johnson discusses the first of these in her essay.
25. See Bonnefoy's discussion in Desbordes-Valmore, *Poésies*, 20.
26. Ibid., 181. It is impossible to convey in a prose translation all the assonances and alliterations, or the force of the two enjambements.

16 WOMEN AND POLITICS

1. Desbordes-Valmore's 'Dans la rue: par un jour funèbre de Lyon' of 1834 was considered so radical that no journal would publish it in her lifetime. 'Le meurtre se fait roi. Le vainqueur siffle et passe. / Où va-t-il? Au Trésor, toucher le prix du sang' ('Murder makes itself king. The conqueror whistles and passes on. Where is he going? To the Treasury, to collect his blood-money') (143–4, 259–60 nn.). For the background, see R. Bezucha, *The Lyon Uprising of 1834: Social and Political Conflict in the Early July Monarchy* (Cambridge, MA: Harvard University Press, 1974).
2. The term *prolétaire* had been revived in the middle of the eighteenth century and used in 1789; but the more charged word *prolétariat*, signifying the condition of a class – an important concept, as we shall see, for many women of the period – appeared for the first time in 1832 (*Le Grand Robert*).
3. Moses and Rabine remind the reader that Engels was influenced by the feminist strand of Saint-Simonism (*Feminism*, 79), as was John Stuart Mill (Moses, *French Feminism*, 235).
4. Moses's account remains the most helpful; she emphasises the difficulties for feminism during these years, the intensity of the debates raging around it and the 'devastating' repression of 1850 – which did not, however, silence most feminists (ibid., e.g. 149, 158, 229); see also

Albistur and Armogathe, *Histoire du féminisme*; Bellet, *La Femme au XIXe siècle*; Aron, *Misérable et glorieuse*; Fraisse and Perrot, *History of Women in the West*; J. Scott, *Gender and the Politics of History.*

5. For histories of the 'woman question' in France (the various 'querelles des femmes'), see, e.g., G. Duby and M. Perrot (eds.), *A History of Women in the West* (Cambridge, MA: Belknap, 1992–3), vols. 1–3; I. Maclean, *Woman Triumphant: Feminism in French Literature 1610–1652* (Oxford: Clarendon, 1977); *Bloomsbury Guide*, 43–60. In the middle of the nineteenth century, there appeared not just isolated works on 'Woman' but outpourings in various media. Ancelot was already in 1848 alleging that she did not wish to add to 'all that has been written' on the destiny of women (Preface to *Marie ou trois époques*, in *Théâtre complet*, 1 12–13). To take only one short period, the two years 1858–60 saw the following: Proudhon's *De la justice dans la Révolution et dans l'Eglise* (1858), which attacks women and foreshadows his more virulent diatribe *La Pornocratie ou les femmes dans les temps modernes* (published posthumously in 1871); Michelet's *L'Amour* (1858) and *La Femme* (1860); Juliette Adam's *Idées anti-proudhoniennes sur l'amour, la femme et le mariage* (1858); Julie-Victoire Daubié's *La Femme pauvre au XIXe siècle*, which won the Academy of Lyon's competition in 1858; Jules Simon's *L'Ouvrière* (1860); and Jenny d'Héricourt's *La Femme affranchie* (1860). See Sartori and Zimmerman's 'Chronology' in *French Women Writers* for a brief but clear outline of the main political events and publications of the time.

6. *Histoire de la République de Florence: Première partie: Moyen-Age* (Paris: Montardier, 1837), v–vi.

7. *Politicizing Gender*, 20, 111–12; also 10, 22, 93ff., 96, 113–14, 133–8, 139. For women writers' heightened political interest in the middle period, see also, e.g., Slama, 'Femmes écrivains', 218, 227 (she goes so far as to speak of 'littérature engagée' after 1830: 236–7); Ambrière, *Précis*, 277–8; Cohen, 'Women and fiction', 62; Holmes, *French Women's Writing*, xvi; Lloyd, *Land of Lost Content*, 235; Birkett and Hughes, 'Eighteenth- and nineteenth-century France', 59.

8. *Le Mauvais Génie* (Paris: Gallimard, 1982).

9. Ibid., 166, 182, 185, 197–200, 203, 211.

10. See Colet's *Poésies complètes*, 294, and, e.g., *Les Maîtres Sonneurs*, 348 ('men have invented the death penalty, which God condemns').

11. *Indiana*, e.g. 68.

12. *Jane Osborn*, 28–9; *Spitzberg*, 202. Tastu too is aware of the realities of imperialism, writing about the liberation of Switzerland and Ireland (*Poésies*, 33ff., 85).

13. Slavery was finally made illegal in the colonies in 1848.

14. *Nélida*, 88, 197–224, 272 n.34.

15. It was republished in the 1980s (Paris: Balland, 1985); see Sartori and Zimmerman for a brief appreciation (*French Women Writers*, 6).

16. 'Préface II' in *La Petite Fadette*.

17. Marx lived in Paris from about 1843 to 1845.
18. *Union ouvrière*, e.g. 225ff., 235.
19. Ibid., e.g. 150 n.
20. Niboyet's *Le Vrai Livre des femmes* (Paris: Dentu, 1863) was a counter-blast to Dash's reactionary *Le Livre des femmes* (1860). For Sand, see *Questions d'art et de littérature* and *Questions politiques et sociales* (both 1879, posth.).
21. *Essai sur la religion intérieure*, unbound pamphlet (Paris: chez tous les libraires, 1864), 93.
22. A few early-century writers as well as Genlis (Gay, for example) had argued against Rousseau for proper education for girls. For 1830–69, see, e.g., Girardin, who in an 1831 prose version of 'Napoline', addressed to 'Delphine', stresses men's fear of reflective women (comparing it to an upper-class fear of servants who can read), and the problems of educated women choosing marriage partners (*Poésies complètes*, 140–5); also *Chroniques parisiennes*, 435; Sand, *Les Maîtres Sonneurs*, e.g. 171; Colet, *Poème de la femme*, 38ff., 61; Stern, *Nélida*, 21, 25, 128, 161. See also Deraismes's play *Retour à ma femme*, 20ff.
23. For the eighteenth century, see, e.g., Didier, 'Les femmes dans la lutte', in *Ecrire la Révolution*, 57–72.
24. *Union ouvrière*, 187–90, 249, 251, 205–6.
25. See above, 106, for Ulliac-Trémadeure's use of slave imagery for the breast-feeding Emilie; also, amongst others, Colet, who in her poetry observes more than once that modern woman is a 'left-over' from the slavery of the ancient world, and interweaves the exploitation of women, of workers, and of chained or captive beings (e.g. *Poésies complètes*, 70).
26. See Moses and Rabine, *Feminism*, e.g. 39, 282, 299, 304–5; also Moses, *French Feminism*, 45, 52, 63, 106, 214.
27. Girardin, 'Napoline', *Poésies*, 108, 116, and *Lady Tartuffe*, in *Œuvres*, VI 338; Ancelot, *Madame Roland*, in *Théâtre*, III 113; Stern, *Nélida*, 212.
28. For the first two cases, see, e.g., Ancelot, *Marie*, in *Théâtre*, I 57; Sand, *Les Maîtres Sonneurs*, 152.
29. Moses and Rabine, *Feminism*, 323 n.; Moses, *French Feminism*, 104.
30. The word 'correctif' is Voilquin's (*Souvenirs*, 101); see also ibid., 127–32, 185; Tristan, *Pérégrinations*, 62–3, 71–2, 74, 132; Stern, *Nélida*, 139; Niboyet, *Vrai Livre*, 170–1.
31. See Colet, *Poème de la femme*, v–vi, viii, 8, 20–1, 90, and *Lui*, 359–60, 365; Voilquin, *Souvenirs*, 57, 106ff. (Flaubert, and Voilquin's husband, had VD.)
32. Matlock writes extensively about the actual and symbolic role of the prostitute in her *Scenes of Seduction*. See also Corbin, 'La prostituée'.
33. Girardin writes a long poem about her over a five-year period (1822–7): 'Magdeleine', *Poésies*, 1–55; see also Cottin's *La Prise de Jéricho, ou la pécheresse convertie*.

34. Blanchecotte, *Rêves*, 101; Caro, *Le Péché de Madeleine* (Paris: Lévy, 1865); Girardin, *C'est la faute du mari* (a play of 1851), *Œuvres*, VI 248.

17 OVERVIEW, 1870–1899

1. Some were still doing so into the twentieth century: Slama, 'Femmes écrivains', 241.
2. Larnac refers to the adoption of deliberately sexless pseudonyms towards the end of the century (*Histoire de la littérature féminine*, 225).
3. J. Gautier, *Isoline et la fleur serpent* (Paris: Charavay, 1882); A. Fouillée (under the pseudonym G. Bruno), *Le Tour de la France par deux enfants* (Paris: Belin, 1877).
4. Slama suggests that this was a period when women more than ever sought financial independence and saw the popular novel as one of the permitted means to this ('Femmes écrivains', 223).
5. Moses, *French Feminism*, 173, 207, 222–3.
6. In 1880 the Camille Sée law provided secondary school education for girls; in 1881 primary education became free, lay and compulsory; in 1882 Blanche Edwards became the first woman to receive a medical degree in France and in 1884 Clémence Royer, a mathematician, the first to teach at the Sorbonne. See Larnac, *Histoire de la littérature féminine*, 221.
7. See Wicks's title-index for the period. The women's plays were by, respectively, Blanche Fromont and Mme E.-T. Paton.
8. *Œuvres*, e.g. 158, 159–65.
9. *Poésies*, 84, 87–92; see too Krysinska, e.g. *Rythmes pittoresques* (Paris: Lemerre, 1890), 120.
10. 'L'Ile de Chiloë', *La Renaissance littéraire et artistique*, 1 (1872), 46 (the June number). Verlaine's 'Il pleure' is given an October 1872 date by Jacques Borel (ed.), in Paul Verlaine, *Fêtes galantes, Romances sans paroles, Poèmes saturniens* (Paris: Gallimard, 1973), 176.
11. Daudet, 'Les Livres: impression d'enfance', *La Renaissance littéraire et artistique*, 2 (1873), 295–6. See too her *Fragments d'un livre inédit* (Paris: Charavay, 1884).
12. The young Proust's title for a subsection of *Les Plaisirs et les jours* (1896).

18 A NEW BOLDNESS: MARCELLE TINAYRE, LOUISE ACKERMANN AND GYP

1. Dieulafoy, *Volontaire*, 134–5.
2. Moses and Rabine (*Feminism*) bring this out strongly. See also above, 42–5, 86.
3. Respectively, *Léonie de Montbreuse* (76); *Le Mauvais Génie* (102).
4. *La Marchande de sourires* (Paris: Charpentier, 1888), 94.
5. Gagneur, in the preface to *Les Forçats du mariage* (Paris: Lacroix, Verboek-Loven, 1870); Michel, *Mémoires* (1886), 271; Deraismes, *Eve*

dans l'humanité (1891; published version of lectures given twenty years earlier), 22; Bashkirtseff, in diary entries of 1877 and 1883, I 389–90, II 1, 474; Ackermann – who says in 'Ma vie' (1874) that she is grateful to her mother for having stopped her becoming too literary ('*de lettres*', her italics), since women who write are, alas, naturally inclined to deplorable behaviour; nor did she ever tell her husband that she wrote before their marriage, since rhyming women are always more or less ridiculous ('Or, il ne faut pas se le dissimuler, la femme qui rime est toujours plus ou moins ridicule'): *Œuvres*, x, xii–xiii.

6. *Fragments*, 54–5.
7. Among critics who have commented on this are: Beizer, *Ventriloquized Bodies*, 256; D. Silverman, 'The "New Woman", feminism, and the decorative arts in fin-de-siècle France', in L. Hunt (ed.), *Eroticism and the Body Politic* (Baltimore: Johns Hopkins University Press, 1991), 144–63; J. Waelti-Walters, *Feminist Novelists of the Belle Epoque: Love as a Lifestyle* (Bloomington: Indiana University Press, 1990).
8. Holmes brings out well Tinayre's blend of conventionality and radicalism in her chapter 'Feminism, romance and the popular novel', in *French Women's Writing*, 47–62.
9. *Monsieur Vénus* (Paris: Flammarion, 1926), 34, 202.
10. *Joies errantes*, 86.
11. *Hellé*, 28, 130–2, 248; for Tinayre's references to Tolstoy, see 167–8.
12. *Le Frère*, 117, 145; *Monsieur Vénus*, 31–4, 37.
13. *Poésies*, 219–20; see also 195–6, 239–41 for moments when Lesueur makes her partner's response to her verse part of the subject of that verse.
14. For further alternations in Bashkirtseff between doubt and confidence, see *Journal*, I 12–13, 79, 390, 392; II 54, 105–6, 390, 396, 471, 535, 584.
15. E.g. Mme de Chabreul (pseudonym of Mlle Marguerite Du Parquet), *Jeux et exercices des jeunes filles* (Paris: Hachette, 1856), which was still being reissued in 1890; see also Matlock, *Scenes of Seduction*, 178.
16. J.-P. Peter, 'Les médecins et les femmes', and P. Perrot, 'Le jardin des modes', in Aron (ed.), *Misérable et glorieuse*, 81–100; 101–16.
17. N. Priollaud, in *La Femme au XIXe siècle* (Paris: Lévi/Messinger, 1983), reproduces other jolly advertisements for musical entertainments with such titles as *A bas la crinoline* ('Down with Crinolines'); as Frank remarks, this was the era of 'posters of ladies on bicycles' (*Mechanical Song*, 5).
18. Deraismes's italics; 'Eve contre Dumas fils', 117–19.
19. *Les Koumiassine*, II 46–9.
20. *Hellé*, 11, 14, 19, 46, 116, 213, 228, 251.
21. D'Aunet, *Spitzberg*, 109; Voilquin, *Souvenirs*, 321; Tristan, *Pérégrinations*, 138–9, 340.
22. *A bon chat*, 34.
23. Voilquin, *Souvenirs*, 253; Girardin, *Chroniques parisiennes*, 27–8.

24. D'Aunet, *Spitzberg*, 112; Ségur, *Le Mauvais Génie*, 116, 138; Voilquin, *Souvenirs*, 376.
25. *Autour du mariage* (Paris: Calmann-Lévy, n.d.), 149.
26. Rachilde, *Monsieur Vénus*, e.g. 25, 29, 97, 98, 100, 103, 106 (where Raoule forbids Jacques to smoke as a man might forbid a woman); Krysinska, *Rythmes pittoresques*, 56–8; *Joies errantes*, 73–4.
27. See *Hellé* for Tinayre's stress on education, and Holmes, who discusses such themes in this and other works by Tinayre (and in the very early twentieth-century writer Gabrielle Reval), in *French Women's Writing*, chapter 3.
28. As in, respectively, Gay's *Laure d'Estell* and Ulliac-Trémadeure's *Emilie*.
29. *La Marquise de Parabère* (Paris: Michel Lévy, 1859). Novels by Reybaud and d'Altenheym are similar.
30. See, e.g., d'Aunet, *Spitzberg*, 75–6; Tristan, *Union ouvrière*, 245; Sand, *Consuelo*, I 204–5, 210; and the exceptionally forthright Allart, *Essai sur la religion* (see above, 154–5).
31. Voilquin, *Souvenirs*, 215; Sand, e.g. *Consuelo*, I 289. See Baudelaire, *Œuvres complètes*, I 676–708 (686–7).
32. E.g. d'Altenheym, *Le Gladiateur*, 238; Tristan, *Union ouvrière*, 177; Stern, *Nélida*, 33–4.
33. E.g. Blanchecotte, *Rêves*, 140; Stern in *Nélida*; Tristan, *Pérégrinations*, 164, 167, 240ff.; Colet, 'La Religieuse', in *Poème de la femme*; Sand, *La Daniella* (1857).
34. E.g. *Rythmes pittoresques*, 36–7.
35. *Poésies*, 38–40, 66, 83, 84, 144–5.
36. E.g. *Eve*, 131.
37. *Mémoires*, 41, 83, 129–30, 149, 163, 209, 230.
38. *Bloomsbury Guide*, 611.
39. Following quotations are taken from *Autour du mariage* unless otherwise stated; all punctuation is Gyp's.
40. See Silverman, *The Notorious Life of Gyp*, 67–8, on Paulette's conventionality.
41. Gyp may not have been aware of how far she was going: she is reported as having expressed astonishment that Paulette, that 'pretty little poison' ('une jolie petite poison'), was 'liked, admired and taken as a model by young women of the time' (Silverman, *Notorious Life*, 271 n.73).

19 EXPERIMENT: NATURALISM, SYMBOLISM AND MARIE KRYSINSKA

1. As other dramatists had before them, of course. See Montanclos's *La Bonne Maîtresse*, 4, 8, 9, and her *Alison et Sylvain*.
2. Edouard sees how such clichés as 'ses formes étaient parfaites' ('he/she had perfect manners') bolster upper-class solidarity and usefully exclude genuine feeling (like his): *Edouard*, 51; see also 67, 73.

3. See, e.g., her 1850 foreword to *François le champi*, 51–3, and her 1853 dedication to *Les Maîtres Sonneurs*, 57–8.

4. *Chroniques parisiennes*, 323; *Le Mauvais Génie*, 75.

5. Isbell, *Birth of European Romanticism*, 67, 81, 85; especially 86–9.

6. *Lui*, 302; *Nélida*, 99, 268 n.13.

7. See, e.g., La Tour du Pin on Napoleon's 'tutoiement' of Josephine, *Journal*, II 253; Colet, *Lui*, 273, 302.

8. It is highlighted or commented on by, e.g., Bentzon, *Yette*, 281; Gréville, *Les Koumiassine*, II 324; Rachilde, *Monsieur Vénus*, 84; Gyp, *Autour du mariage*, 278, 342, and *Autour du divorce*, 411.

9. Cohen stresses that Gyp's novels are 'firmly within the parameters of realism' and that they 'employ socially nuanced diction' ('Women and fiction', 68).

10. Under her married name Mendès: *La Renaissance littéraire et artistique*, I (1872), 46, 94, 182.

11. *La Renaissance littéraire et artistique*, 2 (1873), 134.

12. M. Maclean additionally hails Michel's self-aware mix of genres and styles (including argot), and believes she was the first to 'inscribe' the speech of women prisoners (*Name of the Mother*, 136, 139).

13. *Vers libre* (Oxford: Clarendon, 1990). Scott gives the relevant references to other critics (e.g. S. Bernard in the 1950s and D. Grojnowski in the 1980s).

14. *Archives biographiques françaises* (second series) (Munich: Saur, 1993).

15. Szarama-Swolkieniowa, *Maria Krysińska*. My thanks to Peter Dylewski for translating this.

16. Biographical details are taken from Szarama-Swolkieniowa's work.

17. The poems were 'Chanson d'automne', 'Symphonie en gris', 'Ballade', 'Les Bijoux faux', 'Les Fenêtres', 'Le Hibou' and 'Le Démon de Racoczi', all subsequently reprinted in *Rythmes pittoresques* (1890).

18. In his chapter 'Origins and contexts', *Vers libre*, 54–119. For the facts and quotations in the rest of this paragraph, see ibid., 68–9.

19. Line-lengths are: alexandrine, octosyllable, 7-syllable, 11, 11, 6. Rhymes can occur inside a line ('tristement/mouvement') or, if they occur at the end, can turn into fleeting half-rhymes ('alourd*i*, gris*e*'); etc.

20. E.g. 'Ballade', *Rythmes pittoresques*, 75–8; 'Ronde de mai', *Joies errantes*, 95–7.

21. *Rythmes pittoresques*, 91–105.

22. *Joies errantes*, 81–3.

23. Even the two alexandrines (lines 2, 4) subvert the caesura. The first places it after the syllabic mute 'e' in 'espérantes' (permissible in the rare 'coupe lyrique', but this is not a 'coupe lyrique' proper); the second places it after the seventh, not the sixth, syllable ('que'). The situation is even more confusing if one decides not to give mute 'e' its full syllabic count.

20 CRUELTY TO HUMANS AND ANIMALS: LOUISE MICHEL

1. In the series *La Mémoire du peuple*. There was a conference on her in 1980: D. Armogathe (ed.), *Colloque Louise Michel 1980* (Marseille: Service des publications Marseille, 1982); a book in 1987: P. Durand, *Louise Michel: La passion* (Paris: Messidor, 1987); and a chapter in Marie Maclean's 1994 book *The Name of the Mother* ('My mother the Revolution: Louise Michel', 126–41). Maclean and Moses (*French Feminism*, 273) provide references to other critics. See also G. Gullickson, *Unruly Women of Paris: Images of the Commune* (Ithaca: Cornell University Press, 1996).
2. *Réminiscences*, e.g. 19–26, 28–9.
3. Gyp, *Autour du divorce*, 125–6; Tinayre, *Hellé*, 101, 145; Bashkirtseff, *Journal*, II 7, 61, 231, 235–6, 323–4.
4. Lesueur, *Poésies*, 87–97; see also her 'Le Progrès et les dieux', 16–18, for comments on the slavery of the modern urban working class. Others who wrote about a range of political issues – Prussia, the plight of the poor, the reputation of Gambetta, etc. – are Dieulafoy, *Volontaire* (e.g. 5–6); Daudet, *Fragments*, 10, 33, 35–6. The Dreyfus Affair, which reached its high point from late 1897, was to intensify divisions even further for those who wrote on into the twentieth century.
5. The young Desbordes-Valmore wrote other fables besides 'Le Ver luisant' (see Bonnefoy's note to this, *Poésies*, 255).
6. Tastu, *Poésies*, 127–35.
7. Priollaud, *La Femme au XIXe siècle*, 237, 240; see also Kelly, amongst others, for the equation of women with images of beasts: *Fictional Genders*, 96.
8. *Souvenirs*, 64, 183; see also 358. Suzanne's mother's words are a slight variation on a French proverb whose nearest English equivalent would be: 'one must make the best of things'.
9. La Tour du Pin, *Journal*, II 111–12; *Chroniques parisiennes*, 86–7.
10. Lloyd refers to an 'unconscious and unspoken unease' in Ségur about the relationship between man and animal: *Land of Lost Content*, 205–6.
11. *Pérégrinations*, 117, 327.
12. 'Ma vie', in *Œuvres*, ii.
13. *Yette*, chap. 5.
14. *Yette*, 303–8. See too Bashkirtseff, who like Tristan describes the horrors of bull-fighting, this time in Madrid (*Journal*, II 302).
15. See M. Maclean, *Name of the Mother*, for the attitudes of a number of French women writers, including Michel, to their own illegitimacy.
16. See Gullickson on her sexuality: *Unruly Women*, 211.
17. Ibid., 210; Moses, *French Feminism*, 191–2.
18. P.-V. Stock, memorandum of 1935 added to the 1971 re-edition of Michel's *La Commune* (Paris: Stock, 1971), 493–4. (Michel relates that

her own mother's funeral, which took place while she was in prison, was very well attended, out of solidarity with Michel herself: *Mémoires*, 299–300.)

19. Reproduced in the foreword to *La Commune*, 9.
20. *Name of the Mother*, 127.
21. J. Scott, *Gender and the Politics of History*, 93–163; for the conditions of Lille workers, see P. Hilden, *Working Women and Socialist Politics in France, 1880–1914: A Regional Study* (Oxford: Clarendon, 1986).
22. *Commune*, 10–11; *Mémoires*, 158–9.
23. Huysmans, *A Rebours* (1884).

21 RACHILDE AND THE HORROR OF GENDER CONFUSION

1. For example, L. Porter, 'Decadence and the *fin-de-siècle* novel', in Unwin (ed.), *Cambridge Companion to the French Novel*, 93–110 (105).
2. E.g. J. Birkett in *The Sins of the Fathers: Decadence in France 1870–1914* (London: Quartet, 1986); Gordon, *Ornament, Fantasy and Desire*; Frank, *The Mechanical Song*. See also E. Apter, *Feminizing the Fetish: Psychoanalysis and Narrative Obsession in Turn-of-the-Century France* (Ithaca: Cornell University Press, 1991).
3. For example, Gordon, *Ornament*, 227; Kelly, *Fictional Genders*, 150 (despite a generally sympathetic account); Birkett, *Sins of the Fathers*.
4. Beizer sees this side well, arguing that Rachilde is 'full of' ironizing citation and reversal of nineteenth-century commonplaces (*Ventriloquized Bodies*, 11 n.18; 236ff.).
5. Barrès wrote a later preface to *Monsieur Vénus* claiming not to be shocked, but his attempts to condescend to the work and explain how a 'girl' could have written it belie the claim (1926 edition, xi–xiii).
6. *Le Mauvais Génie*, 26.
7. Waelti-Walters stresses this (*Feminist Novelists*, e.g. 161), while Kelly brings out the complication of the cross-identifications, remarking that finally 'one loses one's bearings and after a while notices only . . . the artificial nature of gender identity itself' (*Fictional Genders*, 152).
8. See Frank's discussion of the nineteenth-century 'artificial woman' (*Mechanical Song*, e.g. 119, 137, 140).
9. For Allart, see above, 151; Colet, *Lui*, 355; Ulliac-Trémadeure, *Emilie*, 3, 127.
10. Choiseul-Meuse, *Julie*, 1 94ff., 236–8; 11 216ff.; Blanchecotte, *Rêves*, 158, 176–7; Stern, *Nélida*, 9–17; Tastu, *Poésies*, 155; see also Sand's *Lélia*.
11. Tastu wrote a 'Chant de Sapho au bûcher d'Erinne' (*Poésies*, 221–5). The following also refer to Sappho: Voilquin, *Souvenirs*, 77 (she elsewhere mentions homosexual prostitution, 319); Ackermann, *Œuvres*, 35–6; Gautier, *Livre de Jade*, 7; Tinayre, *Hellé*, 189, 196.

12. See above, 89–90, and especially *Petite Fadette*, 241: he 'could not feel any taste for marriage'.
13. *Eve*, 119, 130.
14. *Journal*, II 26; see also II 543.
15. See, e.g., Holmes, *French Women's Writing*, 83ff.; Waelti-Walters, *Feminist Novelists*, 19ff.
16. *Le Mauvais Génie*, e.g. 128; *Consuelo*, I 103; Bashkirtseff, *Journal*, II 6.
17. Rachilde's italics; 106. The translation of 'jaloux' is Beizer's (*Ventriloquized Bodies*, 233).
18. Other critics have brought out the significance of this opening: Beizer talks of the *threshold* Raoule literally crosses as she goes into the apartment (229); Kelly suggests the *apples* represent sexuality (146).
19. *La Tour d'amour* (Paris: Crès, 1916).
20. Holmes stresses this: *French Women's Writing*, 76–7.
21. The vertigo especially is emphasized again: *Tour d'amour*, 61, 79.
22. Ibid., 168, 112, 160.
23. Ibid., 99, 162, 169, 89.
24. The devil, and hell, are among images for Barnabas and the lighthouse: ibid., e.g. 175, 190.
25. See Cottin's and Duras's Amélie and Louise; and Blanchecotte for the madness ('démence') caused by unhappiness ('N'aimons jamais', *Rêves*, 218–19). Colet can present madness as to some degree visionary: in this she approaches the less fatalistic view of many nineteenth-century male writers (*Poème de la femme*, v). Sand, still more originally, broaches 'therapies' for neurosis and madness: *La Petite Fadette* (97, 236–9), *Consuelo* (e.g. I 211, 254, 287, 331–2). See also Voilquin on this 'frightful mystery' (*Souvenirs*, 167–8), and Stern, *Nélida* (159, 215–16: the Mme Roland figure is held to be mad because she is a socialist).

22 POSTSCRIPT: ENGLAND

1. 'La France et l'industrie', *Poésies*, 48. For Babois, see *Œuvres* (viii and 'Elégies nationales'); in *Corinne*, Staël presents England as the embodiment of patriarchy. For her blend of Anglophobia/philia, see, e.g., Waller, *Male Malady*, 20, 77; Kadish, *Politicizing Gender*, 22; Kadish and Massardier-Kenny, *Translating Slavery*, 160.
2. See Adler, 'Flora', 193 and n.4.
3. See, e.g., La Tour du Pin for a citation of the English as 'all more or less eccentric' (*Journal*, II 34). Many women writers of imaginative works give their English characters somewhat off-key or misspelled names, either mistakenly or else tailored to what they think a French audience will accept as 'English': again these probably convey an air of eccentricity even to French readers, as with Staël's Oswald Nelvil or Ségur's M. Georgey.

4. See Little's edition of *Ourika*, 37, for Duras's Anglophilia. Gay – like Staël and others – also urges tolerance of Protestantism, which as we have seen may be preferred by some of these writers to Catholicism: another indirect 'promotion' of England (*Laure d'Estell*, 7, 73, 78). Staël and Cottin were themselves Protestant.

5. *Poésies complètes*, 109, 140–1.

6. *Chroniques parisiennes*, 81, 237–8.

7. Daudet, *Fragments*, 27–9.

8. Craven, *Réminiscences*, 48–50, 60, 100–1, 103–4, 111.

9. *Les Forçats du mariage*, 6–7.

10. *Mémoires*, 174, 260–2, 273.

11. Anarchism had an important presence in British socialist thought of the 1880s, but there is no suggestion in the leading book on the subject that it had penetrated the House of Commons: G. Woodcock, *Anarchism: A History of Libertarian Ideas and Movements* (Harmondsworth: Penguin, 1975), 370ff.

12. See Richard Bolster's introduction to his edition of *Histoire d'Eléonore de Parme* (University of Exeter Press, 1997), vii–xxxv.

13. For these and following facts, see Fraisse and Perrot (eds.), *A History of Women*, which provides numerous comparative accounts: in, e.g., N. Arnaud-Duc, 'The law's contradictions', 80–113; M. de Giorgio, 'The Catholic model', 166–97; J. Baubérot, 'The Protestant woman', 198–212; F. Mayeur, 'The secular model of girls' education', 228–45; A. Higonnet, 'Images – appearances, leisure, and subsistence', 246–61, and 'Representations of women', 306–18; Y. Knibiehler, 'Bodies and hearts', 325–68; M. Perrot, 'Stepping out', 460–81. See also J. Scott, 'Gender in history', in *Gender and the Politics of History*, 93–163; Moses, *French Feminism*, x, 23–4, and Bellet, *La Femme au XIXe siècle*, 5 (for comparisons between French feminism and the more steadily growing British and American feminism); Aron, *Misérable et glorieuse*, 20; F. Mayeur, *L'Education des filles en France au XIXe siècle* (Paris: Hachette, 1979); R. Gildea, *Education in Provincial France, 1800–1914: A Study of Three Departments* (Oxford: Clarendon, 1983).

14. 'Women as creatures and creators', in *A History of Women*, 117–20 (118). See also de Giorgio, 'The Catholic model'. Larnac says of Staël that as a foreigner and Calvinist she did not have to undergo 'the constraint that French Catholics bring to bear upon women' ('la contrainte que les Français catholiques font peser sur la femme', *Histoire de la littérature féminine*, 175).

15. See Holmes for this and other repressive aspects of twentieth-century France, e.g. chapters 6 and 10: 'Women in French society 1914–58/1958–94'.

16. See above, 29.

17. Hufton, *Prospect Before Her*, 432–3; see also Slama, 'Femmes écrivains', 215.

18. *Les Malheurs de Sophie*, iv (others by Ségur in this series carry the same 'warning').
19. Yourcenar was the first woman to be elected to the French Academy (at age seventy-seven, in 1980).
20. E. Fallaize, *French Women's Writing: Recent Fiction* (London: Macmillan, 1993), 20–1. Contributors to DeJean and Miller (eds.), *Displacements*, have also briefly mentioned divergences in development and attitude between French and Anglo-American women's writing (e.g. vii–viii, 194, 200–1). Holmes, among others, points out that 'women's studies' and female intellectuals still have a very low profile in France: *French Women's Writing*, 214–15.

23 LEGACIES

1. Gagneur candidly admits at the end of the preface to her pro-divorce *Les Forçats du mariage* that she has sacrificed the aesthetic to the 'message': 'In aid of the goal, the reader will excuse the forced realism of certain characters and tableaux' (13).
2. Larnac himself links early twentieth-century women writers' intense descriptions of nature with a more general 'liberation of the senses' (*Histoire de la littérature féminine*, 234).
3. Moses, among others, reproduces cartoons of the period in her *French Feminism*; see Moses and Rabine, *Feminism*, for 'equality' versus 'difference' in nineteenth-century feminist debates.
4. See Frank, *Mechanical Song*, 106ff.; compare also the 'gender-crossing' in Gautier's *Mademoiselle de Maupin*.
5. Johnson, 'Gender and poetry', 178.
6. 'Avant-propos' to the *Comédie humaine* (Paris: Gallimard, 1976), I 7–20 (8–9).
7. *Le Deuxième Sexe* (Paris: Gallimard, 1976, 2 vols.), I 12; II 227.

Bibliography

PRIMARY TEXTS

Ackermann, L., *Œuvres*, Paris: Lemerre, 1885.

Adam, J., *Idées anti-proudhoniennes sur l'amour, la femme et le mariage*, Paris: Alphonse Taride, 1858.

Laide, Paris: Calmann Lévy, 1878.

Allart, H., *Essai sur la religion intérieure* [unbound pamphlet], Paris: chez tous les libraires, 1864.

Histoire de la République de Florence: Première partie: Moyen-Age, Paris: Montardier, 1837.

Altenheym, G. d', *Dieu pardonne, ou les deux frères*, Paris: Rigaud, n.d.

Les Fauteuils illustres, ou Quarante études littéraires, Paris: Ducrocq, 1860.

Les Marguerites de France, Paris: Vermot, 1858.

Altenheym, G. d', and Soumet, A., *Le Gladiateur*, Paris: Tresse, 1846.

Ancelot, V., *Théâtre complet*, Paris: Beck, 1848, 4 vols.

Les Salons de Paris, foyers éteints, Paris: Tardieu, 1858.

Aunet, L. d', *Jane Osborn* (ed. W. Mercer), London: Institute of Romance Studies, 1994.

Voyage d'une femme au Spitzberg (ed. W. Mercer), Paris: Félin, 1992.

Babois, V., *Œuvres*, n.p.: Nepveu, 1828.

Bashkirtseff, M., *Journal de Marie Bashkirtseff*, Paris: A. de Charpentier, 1890, 2 vols.

Bawr, A. de, *Le Double Stratagème*, Paris: Barba, 1813.

Mes souvenirs, Paris: Passard, 1853.

Raoul, ou l'Enéide, Paris: Fournier, 1832.

La Suite d'un bal masqué, Paris: Vente, 1813.

Belfort, Mme, *L'Artémise française, ou les heureux effets de la Paix*, Paris: Fages, an ix [1801].

Bentzon, T., *Un divorce*, Paris: Hetzel, 1872.

Yette: Histoire d'une jeune Créole, Morne-Rouge, Martinique: Horizons Caraïbes, 1977.

Bernhardt, S., *L'Art du théâtre: la voix, le geste, la prononciation*, Paris: Nilsson, 1923.

L'Aveu, Paris: Ollendorf, 1888.

Blanchecotte, A., 'Impression', *La Renaissance littéraire et artistique*, 2 (1873), 134.

Rêves et réalités, Paris: Ledoyen, 1856.

Bruno, G., *Le Tour de la France par deux enfants*, Paris: Belin, 1877.

Caro, P., *Idylle nuptiale*, Paris: Calmann Lévy, 1896.

Le Péché de Madeleine, Paris: Lévy, 1865.

Chabreul, Mme de [pseud. of Du Parquet, M.], *Jeux et exercices des jeunes filles*, Paris: Hachette, 1856.

Choiseul-Meuse, F. de, *Julie ou j'ai sauvé ma rose*, Hamburg and Paris: chez les marchands de nouveautés, 1807, 2 vols.

Colet, L., *Lui: roman contemporain*, Paris: Calmann Lévy, 1880.

Le Poème de la femme, Paris: Perrotin, 1856.

Poésies complètes, Paris: Gosselin, 1844.

Cottin, S., *Amélie Mansfield*, Paris: Garnery, 1820, 3 vols.

Elisabeth, ou les exilés de Sibérie, Paris: Garnery, 1820.

La Prise de Jéricho, ou la pécheresse convertie, Paris: Garnery, 1820.

Craven, P., *Réminiscences: souvenirs d'Angleterre et d'Italie*, Paris: Didier, 1879.

Dash, Comtesse, *La Duchesse de Lauzun*, Paris: Michel Lévy, 1864.

La Marquise de Parabère, Paris: Lévy, 1859.

Daudet, J., *Fragments d'un livre inédit*, Paris: Charavay, 1884.

'Les Livres: impression d'enfance', *La Renaissance littéraire et artistique*, 2 (1873), 295–6.

Deraismes, M., *A bon chat bon rat*, Paris: Amyot, 1861.

Eve dans l'humanité, Paris: Sauvaitre, 1891.

'Eve contre Dumas fils', in *Eve dans l'humanité*, 116–48.

Retour à ma femme, Paris: Amyot, 1862.

Desbordes-Valmore, M., *Poésies*, Paris: Gallimard, 1983.

Dieulafoy, J., *Parysatis*, Paris: Lemerre, 1890.

Volontaire: 1792–93, Paris: Colin, n.d.

Duras, C. de, *Edouard*, Paris: Mercure de France, 1983.

Olivier ou le secret (ed. D. Virieux), Paris: Corti, 1971.

Ourika, Paris: Librairie des Bibliophiles, 1878.

Ourika (ed. J. DeJean), New York: MLA, 1994.

Ourika (ed. R. Little), University of Exeter Press, 1993.

Ourika (ed. R. Little), University of Exeter Press, 1998.

Gacon-Dufour, M., *Les Dangers d'un mariage forcé*, Paris: Ouvrier, an IX [1801].

Gagneur, L., *Les Forçats du mariage*, Paris: Lacroix, Verboeck-Loven, 1870.

Gautier, J., 'L'île de Chiloë', *La Renaissance littéraire et artistique*, 1 (1872), 46 [under her married name Mendès].

Isoline et la fleur serpent, Paris: Charavay, 1882.

Le Livre de Jade, Paris: Tallandier, 1928.

La Marchande de sourires: pièce japonaise, Paris: Charpentier, 1888.

Gay, S., *Laure d'Estell*, Paris: Michel Lévy, 1864.

Léonie de Montbreuse, Paris: Michel Lévy, 1871.

Le Marquis de Pomenars, Paris: Ladvocat, 1820.

Genlis, S. de, *De l'influence des femmes sur la littérature française comme protectrices des lettres et comme auteurs*, Paris: Maradan, 1811.

Mademoiselle de Clermont, Paris: Autrement, 1994.

Girardin, D. de, *Chroniques parisiennes 1836–1848*, Paris: des femmes, 1986.

Lettres parisiennes: see *Chroniques parisiennes*.

Œuvres complètes, Paris: Plon, 1860–1, 6 vols.

Poésies complètes, Paris: Michel Lévy, 1876.

Gréville, H., *Les Koumiassine*, Paris: Plon, 1878, 2 vols.

Gsell, P. (ed.), *Mémoires de Madame Judith*, Paris: Tallandier, 1911.

Guizot, P., *L'Ecolier, ou Raoul et Victor*, Paris: Didier, 1845, 2 vols.

Les Enfants: Contes à l'usage de la jeunesse, Paris: Didier, 1852.

Le Chapeau, publ. at end of Ulliac-Trémadeure, *Valérie, ou la jeune artiste*.

Gyp, *Autour du divorce*, Paris: Calmann-Lévy, 1893.

Autour du mariage, Paris: Calmann-Lévy, n.d.

Judith: *see* Gsell, P.

Krüdener, J. de, *Valérie*, Paris: Quantin, 1878.

Krysinska, M., *Joies errantes: nouveaux rythmes pittoresques*, Paris: Lemerre, 1894.

Rythmes pittoresques, Paris: Lemerre, 1890.

La Tour du Pin, H. de, *Journal d'une femme de cinquante ans, 1778–1815*, Paris: Chapelot, 1920, 2 vols.

Memoirs of Madame de La Tour du Pin (ed. and trs. F. Harcourt), London: Century, 1985.

Lesueur, D., *Poésies*, Paris: Lemerre, 1896.

Mercœur, E. [and Mme Mercœur], *Œuvres complètes*, Paris: Mme Veuve Mercœur, Pommeret et Guénot, 1843, 3 vols.

Michel, M., *La Commune*, Paris: Stock, 1971.

Mémoires de Louise Michel, écrits par elle-même, Paris: Maspero, 1976.

Montanclos, M. de, *Alison et Sylvain, ou les habitans de Vaucluse*, Paris: Barba, 1803.

La Bonne Maîtresse, Paris: Hugelet, 1803.

Niboyet, E., *Catherine II et ses filles d'honneur*, Paris: Dentu, 1847.

Le Vrai Livre des femmes, Paris: Dentu, 1863.

Pert, C., *Le Frère*, Paris: Simonis Empis, 1896.

Rachilde, *Monsieur Vénus*, Paris: Flammarion, 1926.

La Tour d'amour, Paris: Crès, 1916.

Reybaud, H., *Clémentine*, Paris: Hachette, 1861.

Sand, G., *Consuelo/La Comtesse de Rudolstadt*, Grenoble: Aurore, 1991, 3 vols.

Correspondance (ed. G. Lubin), Paris: Garnier, 1964–91, 25 vols.

François le champi, Paris: Gallimard, 1973.

Histoire de ma vie, in *Œuvres autobiographiques*.

Indiana, Paris: Gallimard, 1984.

Lélia (ed. P. Reboul), Paris: Garnier, 1960.

Les Maîtres Sonneurs, Paris: Gallimard, 1979.

La Mare au diable, Paris: Gallimard, 1973.

Mauprat, Paris: Gallimard, 1981.

Œuvres autobiographiques, Paris: Gallimard, 1970–1, 2 vols.

La Petite Fadette, Paris: Garnier Flammarion, 1967.

Questions d'art et de littérature (ed. D. Colwell), Egham: Runnymede Books, 1992.

Questions politiques et sociales, Paris: Calmann Lévy, 1879.

Savignac, A. de, *La Jeune Propriétaire ou l'art de vivre à la campagne*, Paris: Martial Ardant, 1848.

Ségalas, A., *Les Algériennes* and *Poésies diverses*, Paris: Charles Mary, 1831.

Ségur, S. de, *Les Malheurs de Sophie*, Paris: Gallimard, 1977.

Le Mauvais Génie, Paris: Gallimard, 1982.

Staël, G. de, *Corinne ou l'Italie*, Paris: des femmes, 1979, 2 vols.

Delphine, Paris: des femmes, 1981, 2 vols.

Stern, D., *Histoire de la Révolution de 1848*, Paris: Balland, 1985.

Nélida, Paris: Calmann-Lévy, 1987.

Tastu, A., *Poésies*, Paris, Didier, 1838.

Tinayre, M., *Hellé*, Paris: Nelson and Calmann-Levy, n.d.

Tristan, F., *Pérégrinations d'une paria*, Paris: Maspero, 1979.

Union ouvrière, Paris: des femmes, 1986.

Ulliac-Trémadeure, S., *Emilie ou la jeune fille auteur: ouvrage dédié aux jeunes personnes*, Paris: Didier, 1854.

Valérie, ou la jeune artiste, Brussels: Hauman and Cattoir, 1837.

Voilquin, S., *Souvenirs d'une fille du peuple ou la Saint-simonienne en Egypte*, Paris: Maspero, 1978.

OTHER WORKS

Adler, L., 'Flora, Pauline et les autres', in Aron (ed.), *Misérable et glorieuse*, 191–209.

Albistur, M., and Armogathe, D., *Histoire du féminisme français*, Paris: des femmes, 1977, vol. II.

Allen, J. Smith, *Popular French Romanticism: Authors, Readers and Books in the Nineteenth Century*, Syracuse University Press, 1981.

In the Public Eye: A History of Reading in Modern France, 1800–1940, Princeton University Press, 1991.

Ambrière, F., *Mademoiselle Mars et Marie Dorval*, Paris: Seuil, 1992.

Le Siècle des Valmore, Paris: Seuil, 1987, 2 vols.

Ambrière, M. (ed.), *Précis de littérature française du XIXe siècle*, Paris: Presses Universitaires de France, 1990.

Apter, E., *Feminizing the Fetish: Psychoanalysis and Narrative Obsession in Turn-of-the-Century France*, Ithaca: Cornell University Press, 1991.

Archives biographiques françaises [microfiches], first series, London: Saur, 1988–90; second series, Munich: Saur, 1993.

Armogathe, D. (ed.), *Colloque Louise Michel 1980*, Marseille: Service des publications Marseille, 1982.

Arnaud-Duc, N., 'The law's contradictions', in Fraisse and Perrot (eds.), *A History of Women in the West*, 80–113.

Aron, J.-P. (ed.), *Misérable et glorieuse: la femme du XIXe siècle*, n.p.: Fayard, 1980.

'Préface', in Aron (ed.), *Misérable et glorieuse*, 7–24.

Auerbach, E., *Mimesis*, Princeton University Press, 1971.

Balayé, S., *Madame de Staël: lumières et liberté*, Paris: Klincksieck, 1979.

Balteau, J., Barroux, M., Prévost, M. (eds.), *Dictionnaire de biographie française*, Paris: Letouzey et Ané, 1933– .

Balzac, H. de, 'Avant-propos', *La Comédie humaine*, Paris, Gallimard, 1976, 1 7–20.

Barrès, M., 'Complications d'amour', preface to Rachilde, *Monsieur Vénus*, Paris: Flammarion, 1926.

Baubérot, J., 'The Protestant woman', in Fraisse and Perrot (eds.), *A History of Women in the West*, 198–212.

Baudelaire, C., *Œuvres complètes*, Paris: Gallimard, 1975–6, 2 vols.

Beauvoir, S. de, *Le Deuxième Sexe*, Paris: Gallimard, 1976, 2 vols.

Beizer, J., *Ventriloquized Bodies: Narratives of Hysteria in Nineteenth-Century France*, Ithaca and London: Cornell University Press, 1994.

Bellet, R. (ed.), *La Femme au XIXe siècle: Littérature et idéologie*, Presses Universitaires de Lyon, 1979.

Bertrand-Jennings, C., 'Condition féminine et impuissance sociale: les romans de la duchesse de Duras', *Romantisme*, 63 (1989), 39–50.

Bezucha, R., *The Lyon Uprising of 1834: Social and Political Conflict in the Early July Monarchy*, Cambridge, MA: Harvard University Press, 1974.

Birkett, J., *The Sins of the Fathers: Decadence in France 1870–1914*, London: Quartet, 1986.

Birkett, J., and Hughes, A., 'Eighteenth- and nineteenth-century France', in the *Bloomsbury Guide*, 54–60.

Blémont, E., 'Littérature étrangère: la poésie en Angleterre et aux Etats-Unis: poétesses anglaises', *La Renaissance littéraire et artistique*, 1 (1872), 146–7.

Bloomsbury Guide: see Buck, C. (ed.).

Bolster, R. (ed.), *Histoire d'Eléonore de Parme*, University of Exeter Press, 1997.

Bonnefoy, Y., 'Préface', in Desbordes-Valmore, *Poésies*.

Borel, J. (ed.), Paul Verlaine, *Fêtes galantes, Romances sans paroles, Poèmes saturniens*, Paris: Gallimard, 1973.

Brooks, P., *The Melodramatic Imagination: Balzac, Henry James, Melodrama, and the Mode of Excess*, New York: Columbia University Press, 1985.

Buck, C. (ed.), *Bloomsbury Guide to Women's Literature*, London: Bloomsbury, 1992.

Cantlie, E., 'Women's Memoirs in Early Nineteenth-Century France', PhD thesis, University of Glasgow, 1999.

Cavalucci, G., *Bibliographie critique de Marceline Desbordes-Valmore d'après des documents inédits*, Naples: Pironti, 1935/1942.

Charnley, J., 'La première femme à faire le tour du monde', *French Studies Bulletin*, 68 (1998), 13–15.

Cohen, M., 'Women and fiction in the nineteenth century', in Unwin (ed.), *Cambridge Companion to the French Novel*, 54–72.

Corbin, A., 'La prostituée', in Aron (ed.), *Misérable et glorieuse*, 41–58.

Court, A., 'Lamartine et Mme Roland', in Bellet (ed.), *La Femme au XIXe siècle*, 55–82.

Coward, D., 'Popular fiction in the nineteenth century', in Unwin (ed.), *Cambridge Companion to the French Novel*, 73–92.

DeJean, J., 'Classical reeducation: decanonizing the feminine', in DeJean and Miller (eds.), *Displacements*, 22–36.

DeJean, J., and Miller, N. (eds.), *Displacements: Women, Tradition, Literatures in French*, Baltimore: Johns Hopkins University Press, 1991.

DeJean, J., and Waller, M., 'Introduction', in J. DeJean (ed.), *Ourika*, New York: MLA, 1994.

Dickenson, D., *George Sand: A Brave Man – The Most Womanly Woman*, Oxford: Berg, 1988.

Dictionnaire de biographie française: see Balteau, J., *et al.* (eds.).

Didier, B., *Ecrire la Révolution: 1789–99*, Paris: Presses Universitaires de France, 1989.

  George Sand écrivain: 'Un grand fleuve d'Amérique', Paris: Presses Universitaires de France, 1998.

Duby, G., and Perrot, M. (eds.), *A History of Women in the West*, Cambridge, MA: Belknap, 1992–3, vols. 1–3.

Du Plessix Gray, F., *Rage and Fire: A Life of Louise Colet: Pioneer Feminist, Literary Star, Flaubert's Muse*, New York: Simon and Schuster, 1994.

Durand, P., *Louise Michel: la passion*, Paris: Messidor, 1987.

Fairlie, A., 'La Contradiction créatrice: quelques remarques sur la genèse d'*Un Cœur simple*', in *Imagination and Language: Collected Essays on Constant, Baudelaire, Nerval and Flaubert*, Cambridge University Press, 1981, 437–60.

Fallaize, E., *French Women's Writing: Recent Fiction*, London: Macmillan, 1993.

Fraisse, G., and Perrot, M. (eds.), *A History of Women in the West: Emerging Feminism from Revolution to World War*, Cambridge, MA: Belknap, 1993, vol. IV.

Fraisse, G., and Perrot, M., 'Women as creatures and creators', in Fraisse and Perrot (eds.), *A History of Women in the West*, 117–20.

France, P. (ed.), *The New Oxford Companion to Literature in French*, Oxford University Press, 1995.

Frank, F. Miller, *The Mechanical Song: Women, Voice, and the Artificial in Nineteenth-Century French Narrative*, Stanford University Press, 1995.

Gautier, T., *Portraits contemporains*, Paris: Charpentier, 1874.

  Portraits et souvenirs littéraires, Paris: Michel Lévy, 1875.

Gethner, P. (ed.), *Femmes dramaturges en France (1650–1750): pièces choisies* (Paris: Papers on French Seventeenth-Century Literature, 1993).

Gilbert, S., and Gubar, S., *The Madwoman in the Attic: The Woman Writer and the Nineteenth-Century Literary Imagination*, New Haven: Yale University Press, 1984.

Gildea, R., *Education in Provincial France, 1800–1914: A Study of Three Depart-ments*, Oxford: Clarendon, 1983.

The Past in French History, New Haven: Yale University Press, 1994.

Giorgio, M. de, 'The Catholic model', in Fraisse and Perrot (eds.), *A History of Women in the West*, 166–97.

Gordon, R., *Ornament, Fantasy and Desire in Nineteenth-Century French Literature*, Princeton University Press, 1992.

Grand Dictionnaire universel du XIXe siècle: see Larousse, P. (ed.).

Gullickson, G., *Unruly Women of Paris: Images of the Commune*, Ithaca: Cornell University Press, 1996.

Gutwirth, M., *Madame de Staël, Novelist: The Emergence of the Artist as Woman*, Urbana: University of Illinois Press, 1978.

Hallays-Dabot, V., *Histoire de la censure théâtrale en France*, Paris: Dentu, 1862.

Hemmings, F., *The Theatre Industry in Nineteenth-Century France*, Cambridge University Press, 1993.

Theatre and State in France, 1760–1905, Cambridge University Press, 1994.

Higonnet, A., 'Images – appearances, leisure, and subsistence', in Fraisse and Perrot (eds.), *A History of Women in the West*, 246–61.

'Representations of women', in Fraisse and Perrot (eds.), *A History of Women in the West*, 306–18.

Hilden, P., *Working Women and Socialist Politics in France, 1880–1914: A Regional Study*, Oxford: Clarendon, 1986.

Hirsch, M., *The Mother/Daughter Plot: Narrative, Psychoanalysis, Feminism*, Bloomington: Indiana University Press, 1989.

Hoffmann, L.-F., *Le Nègre romantique: personnage littéraire et obsession collective*, Paris: Payot, 1973.

Holmes, D., *French Women's Writing 1848–1994*, London: Athlone, 1996.

Hufton, O., *The Prospect Before Her: A History of Women in Western Europe, 1500–1800*, London: HarperCollins, 1995.

Hugo, V., *Les Misérables*, Paris: Gallimard, 1951.

Isbell, J., *The Birth of European Romanticism: Truth and Propaganda in Staël's De l'Allemagne*, Cambridge University Press, 1994.

Jack, B., *George Sand: A Woman's Life Writ Large*, London: Chatto & Windus, 1999.

Johnson, B., 'Gender and poetry: Charles Baudelaire and Marceline Desbordes-Valmore', in DeJean and Miller (eds.), *Displacements*, 163–81.

Jomaron, J. de (ed.), *Le Théâtre en France: de la Révolution à nos jours*, Paris: Colin, 1989, vol. II.

Jones, A., and Vickers, N., 'Canon, rule, and the Restoration Renaissance', in DeJean and Miller (eds.), *Displacements*, 3–21.

Kadish, D., *Politicizing Gender: Narrative Strategies in the Aftermath of the French Revolution*, New Brunswick: Rutgers University Press, 1991.

Kadish, D., and Massardier-Kenny, F. (eds.), *Translating Slavery: Gender and Race in French Women's Writing, 1783–1823*, Kent State University Press, 1994.

Kelly, D., *Fictional Genders: Role and Representation in Nineteenth-Century French Narrative*, Lincoln: University of Nebraska Press, 1989.

Knibiehler, Y., 'Bodies and hearts', in Fraisse and Perrot (eds.), *A History of Women in the West*, 325–68.

Lagarde, A., et Michard, L., *XIXe Siècle: Les grands auteurs français du programme*, Paris: Bordas, 1963.

Larnac, J., *Histoire de la littérature féminine en France*, Paris: Krâ, 1929.

Larousse, P. (ed.), *Grand Dictionnaire universel du XIXe siècle*, Paris: Larousse, 1866–79, 17 vols. (Reprinted: Geneva: Slatkine, 1982.)

Lloyd, R., *The Land of Lost Content: Children and Childhood in Nineteenth-Century French Literature*, Oxford: Clarendon, 1992.

Maclean, I., *Woman Triumphant: Feminism in French Literature 1610–1652*, Oxford: Clarendon, 1977.

Maclean, M., *The Name of the Mother: Writing Illegitimacy*, London: Routledge, 1994.

Manifold, G., *George Sand's Theatre Career*, Ann Arbor: UMI Research Press, 1985.

Marotin, F., 'Le "Petit Journal" et la femme en 1865', in Bellet (ed.), *La Femme au XIXe siècle*, 97–112.

Martin-Fugier, A., 'La maîtresse de maison', in Aron (ed.), *Misérable et glorieuse*, 117–34.

Matlock, J., *Scenes of Seduction: Prostitution, Hysteria, and Reading Difference in Nineteenth-Century France*, New York: Columbia University Press, 1994.

Maurois, A., *Lélia ou la vie de George Sand*, Paris: Hachette, 1952.

Mayeur, F., *L'Education des filles en France au XIXe siècle*, Paris: Hachette, 1979.
'The secular model of girls' education', in Fraisse and Perrot (eds.), *A History of Women in the West*, 228–45.

Moers, E., *Literary Women*, London: Allen, 1977.

Moi, T., *Textual/Sexual Politics*, London: Routledge, 1985.

Moses, C. Goldberg, *French Feminism in the Nineteenth Century*, Albany: State University of New York Press, 1984.

Moses, C. Goldberg, and Rabine, L. Wahl, *Feminism, Socialism and French Romanticism*, Bloomington: Indiana University Press, 1993.

New Oxford Companion to Literature in French, The: see France, P. (ed.).

Perceau, L., *Bibliographie du roman érotique au XIXe siècle*, Paris: Fourdrinier, 1930, 2 vols.

Perkins, D., *Is Literary History Possible?*, Baltimore: Johns Hopkins University Press, 1993.

Perrot, M., 'Stepping out', in Fraisse and Perrot (eds.), *A History of Women in the West*, 449–81.

Perrot, P., 'Le jardin des modes', in Aron (ed.), *Misérable et glorieuse*, 101–16.

Peter, J.-P., 'Les médecins et les femmes', in Aron (ed.), *Misérable et glorieuse*, 81–100.

Porter, L., 'Decadence and the *fin-de-siècle* novel', in Unwin (ed.), *Cambridge Companion to the French Novel*, 93–110.

Priollaud, N., *La Femme au XIXe siècle*, Paris: Lévi/Messinger, 1983.

Robinson, J., *Unsuitable for Ladies: An Anthology of Women Travellers*, Oxford University Press, 1995.

Sainte-Beuve, C.-A., *Causeries du lundi*, Paris: Garnier, 1852–62, 16 vols.
Portraits de femmes, Paris: Didier, 1852.
Preface to Gay, *Laure d'Estell*.

Sartori, E. Martin, and Zimmerman, D. Wynne (eds.), *French Women Writers*, Lincoln: University of Nebraska Press, 1994.

Schor, N., *George Sand and Idealism*, New York: Columbia University Press, 1993.

Scott, C., *Vers libre*, Oxford: Clarendon, 1990.

Scott, J. Wallach, *Gender and the Politics of History*, New York: Columbia University Press, 1988.

Showalter, English Jr., 'Writing off the stage: women authors and eighteenth-century theatre', in DeJean and Miller (eds.), 144–62.

Silverman, D., 'The "New Woman", feminism, and the decorative arts in fin-de-siècle France', in L. Hunt (ed.), *Eroticism and the Body Politic*, Baltimore: Johns Hopkins University Press, 1991, 144–63.

Silverman, W., *The Notorious Life of Gyp: Right-Wing Anarchist in Fin-de-Siècle France*, Oxford University Press, 1995.

Slama, B., 'Femmes écrivains', in Aron (ed.), *Misérable et glorieuse*, 213–48.

Steegmuller, F., and Bray, B. (trs. and eds.), *Flaubert–Sand: The Correspondence*, London: Harvill, 1993.

Stewart, J. Hinde, *Gynographs: French Novels by Women of the Late Eighteenth Century*, Lincoln: University of Nebraska Press, 1993.

Strumingher, L., *The Odyssey of Flora Tristan*, New York: Peter Lang, 1988.

Sullerot, E., *Histoire de la presse féminine en France, des origines à 1848*, Paris: Armand Colin, 1966.
La Presse féminine, Paris: Armand Colin, 1966.

Szarama-Swolkieniowa, M., *Maria Krysińska: Poetka francuskiego symbolizmu*, Cracow: Nakładem Uniwersytetu Jagiellońskiego, 1972.

Tassé, H., *Salons français du XIXe siècle*, Montreal: no publisher, 1952.

Thiesse, A.-M., and Mathieu, H., 'The decline of the classical age and the birth of the classics', in DeJean and Miller (eds.), *Displacements*, 74–96.

Travers, S., *Catalogue of Nineteenth-Century French Theatrical Parodies*, New York: King's Crown, 1941.

Unwin, T. (ed.), *The Cambridge Companion to the French Novel: From 1800 to the Present*, Cambridge University Press, 1997.

Vallois, M.-C., *Fictions féminines: Mme de Staël et les voix de la sibylle*, Saratoga: Anma Libri, 1987.

Vissière, J.-L., preface to D. de Girardin, *Chroniques parisiennes 1836–1848*, Paris: des femmes, 1986.

Waelti-Walters, J., *Feminist Novelists of the Belle Epoque: Love as a Lifestyle*, Bloomington: Indiana University Press, 1990.

Waller, M., *The Male Malady: Fictions of Impotence in the French Romantic Novel*, New Brunswick: Rutgers University Press, 1993.

Warner, M., *Joan of Arc: The Image of Female Heroism*, London: Vintage, 1991.

Wicks, C. Beaumont, *The Parisian Stage: Alphabetical Indexes of Plays and Authors, 1800–1900*, University of Alabama Press, 1950–79, 5 vols. (vol. III with J. Schweitzer).

Wilson, E., *Sexuality and the Reading Encounter*, Oxford: Clarendon, 1996.

Winegarten, R., *Mme de Staël*, Leamington Spa: Berg, 1985.

Woodcock, G., *Anarchism: A History of Libertarian Ideas and Movements*, Harmondsworth: Penguin, 1975.

Index

CAMBRIDGE STUDIES IN FRENCH